DiRōNA Fine Dining Guide

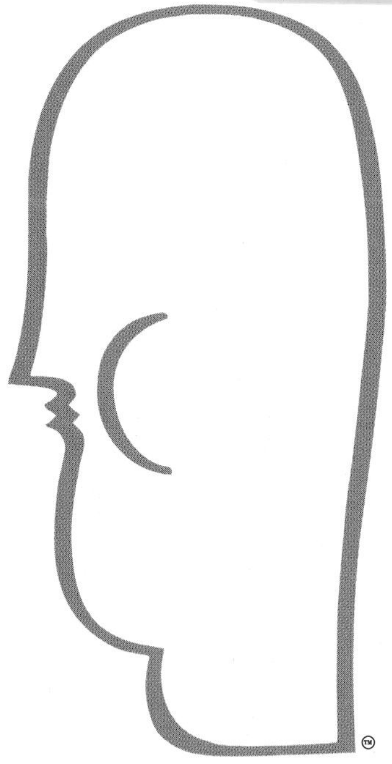

2001 Guide to DiRōNA® Award Restaurants

LEBHAR-FRIEDMAN BOOKS
NEW YORK • CHICAGO • LOS ANGELES • LONDON • PARIS • TOKYO

Lebhar-Friedman Books
425 Park Avenue
New York, NY 10022

Published by Lebhar-Friedman Books
Lebhar-Friedman Books is a company of Lebhar-Friedman, Inc.

Printed in the United States of America

ISBN: 0-86730-808-7

Library of Congress Cataloging in Publication Data on file at the Library of Congress.

Editors: Jay Levin, Lisa Lindsay, Martin Everett
Contributing Editor: Shelley Wolson
Project Manager: Paula Kaye Scheiber
Production Assistants: Karalee Harrigan, Robin Zane, Gwen Jagde, Jill Rembar, Dan Zanier, Sheri Leonard

Book Design: Nancy Koch, NK Design
Associate Designers: Michael Dumcyz, LaDue Design, Julia Unger

An SCI production

Visit our Web site at lfbooks.com

A complete list of DiRōNA Award winning restaurants is available at www.dirona.com.

Contents

Introduction	v
About DiRōNA	vii
Inspection Program	viii
How to Use This Guide	ix
DiRōNA Officers and Directors	x
The DiRōNA Guarantee	xii

THE UNITED STATES OF AMERICA

Alaska	1
Arizona	3
California	
Northern California	8
Southern California	28
Colorado	53
Connecticut	66
Delaware	67
District of Columbia	68
Florida	79
Georgia	116
Hawaii	128
Idaho	131
Illinois	132
Indiana	142
Kentucky	144
Louisiana	146
Maine	156
Maryland	158
Massachusetts	164
Michigan	177
Minnesota	184
Mississippi	188

Missouri 189
Nevada 198
New Hampshire 206
New Jersey 207
New Mexico 217
New York 221
North Carolina 255
Ohio 256
Oregon 262
Pennsylvania 265
Rhode Island 278
South Carolina 280
Tennessee 284
Texas 293
Utah 305
Vermont 307
Virginia 309
Washington State 317
Wisconsin 319
Wyoming 323

CANADA

Alberta 324
British Columbia 327
Manitoba 331
Nova Scotia 332
Ontario 333
Quebec 342

MEXICO 353

INDEX OF RECIPIENTS (ALPHABETICAL) 359
INDEX OF RECIPIENTS (BY CUISINE) 364

Introduction

Dear Distinguished Diner,

John Folse

Welcome to the DiRōNA Award Guide! The DiRōNA Award is the only award that results from an independent and anonymous restaurant inspection. Created by Distinguished Restaurants of North America, this guide is representative of the greatest dining opportunities in Canada, Mexico, and the United States of America. The restaurants are listed in alphabetical order by country, state, and city.

The DiRōNA Award is recognized by *Wine Spectator* as being The Guide to distinguished restaurants. *Wine Spectator* publishes this list twice annually. The National Restaurant Association recommends DiRōNA Award restaurants and The Guide as the most reliable source to explore the greatest dining experiences in North America.

To qualify for the DiRōNA Award, a restaurant must be in business under the same ownership for at least three years and pass a rigorous evaluation conducted anonymously by specially trained, independent inspectors. The inspection emphasizes the quality of food, service, atmosphere, safety, and sanitation. The process examines the total dining experience from reservations to dessert.

The Award itself is a whimsical figure of a happy diner. Enjoy the guide to the best "distinguished" dining experiences throughout North America.

Happy Distinguished Dining!

CHEF JOHN FOLSE, CEC, AAC
Chairman of the Board, 1999-2001

About the Endpaper Art

Guy Buffet is famous for his whimsical fantasies. He has a remarkable ability to capture the essence of the moment and to visually articulate a sense of character and place. He is a recognized master of such subjects as chefs, sommeliers, and wine makers. He is also widely respected for his paintings of historical events. Corporations, private collectors, museums, and special-events committees from around the world continue to commission his work.

About DiRōNA

Distinguished Restaurants of North America is a nonprofit organization which, by recognizing excellence, seeks to raise dining standards and promote distinguished dining throughout the United States, Canada, and Mexico. The organization was founded in 1990 and is governed by an independent board of directors.

In 1992, the DiRōNA Award Program was launched, recognizing restaurants that exemplify the highest quality standards in all aspects of the dining experience – thus, "The Award of Excellence." The founding members were the recipients of the Travel Holiday Award in 1989, which was the last year that award was presented. Founding sponsors of the DiRōNA Award Program are American Express and Allied Domecq Spirits, U.S.A.

The DiRōNA Award Inspection Program is the ONLY independent and anonymous restaurant inspection program in North America. The DiRōNA Award recipients are selected through a rigorous inspection process. To qualify, a restaurant must be in business under the same ownership and concept for at least three years and pass a 75-point evaluation conducted anonymously by a specially trained, independent panel of qualified professionals and consumers of distinguished dining. The inspection process examines the total dining experience and is supervised by the DiRōNA Council of Inspection, Evaluation, and Criteria. The Council also conducts an annual review of the process and requalifies the professional inspectors.

The DiRōNA designation remains in effect for three years, at which point the inspection process begins anew and the establishment is evaluated again, using the exact same criteria. If a restaurant undergoes a change of ownership or concept during the three years the Award is in effect, it forfeits the DiRōNA Award until such time as it has fulfilled the "three years in business" requirement and passes inspection.

The mission of Distinguished Restaurants of North America is to preserve and promote the ultimate in distinguished dining.

www.dirona.com

Inspection Program

The DiRōNA Award results from an independent and anonymous restaurant inspection, administered by Harold Stayman, Director of Inspections. Mr. Stayman heads a team of 40 inspectors who are requalified and audited for Distinguished Restaurants of North America annually by Dr. Morris Gaebe, Chancellor of Johnson and Wales University. The inspectors are thoroughly oriented with the 75-point criteria, developed by Cornell University, which is the basis for all inspections. They have impeccable credentials and are experienced in fine dining.

Inspectors visit restaurants throughout North America at the direction of the Director of Inspections, who monitors thousands of restaurants each year. Candidates for inspections are identified through a multitude of resources, including requests for inspections that are submitted to DiRōNA headquarters by operators hoping to become DiRōNA members. With the exception of the Director of Inspections, the team of inspectors is unknown to the Board and the DiRōNA Award Restaurants. Dr. Gaebe provides an annual report, verifying for the Board that he personally evaluates the Director of Inspections Annual Workshop for inspectors and each participating inspector.

A restaurant must be in business for three years before it is eligible for inspection, and once a restaurant earns the DiRōNA Award, it must be reinspected within three years in order to maintain the membership.

A 75-point list of criteria is used to evaluate the restaurant on quality of overall environment, cuisine, beverages, and service. The physical property and the decor are evaluated, with comfort, cleanliness, room temperature, and light levels observed.

Cuisine quality is the most important criterion in the decision to confer the DiRōNA Award to a restaurant. The menu is examined for accuracy, variety of items, cooking techniques, creativity, and originality, as well as for health and nutrition-oriented items. The food is evaluated on temperature, appearance, and quality of ingredients. Beverages offered by restaurants are evaluated on the basis of variety, availability, value, and food affinity.

The service criteria evaluate guest interaction with the service staff, starting from the reservation process, greeting and seating, service throughout the meal, and assistance with departure. The staff's knowledge of the menu is tested and their friendliness, attentiveness, cleanliness, and attire are appraised. Finally, the restaurant's procedures for handling the check are evaluated by verifying that the check is a consolidated bill which is accurate, legible, and professionally presented.

DiRōNA

How to Use This Guide

We made the Guide to Distinguished Restaurants of North America as user-friendly as possible. U.S. restaurants are listed alphabetically, by state and then by city. Canadian restaurants follow, listed alphabetically by province and then by city. Restaurants in Mexico, alphabetized by city, follow the Canada listings.

For each restaurant, the following information is provided:

- **A locator map**
- **Address**
- **Phone and fax numbers**
- **Web site address** (where applicable)
- **The owner or owners**
- **Type of cuisine**
- **Days open**
- **Pricing** a range for dinner for one, without tax, tip, or drinks
- **Dress code**
- **Reservations policy**
- **Parking availability**
- **Distinctive features**
- **Credit cards accepted**

AE = American Express
VC = Visa
MC = MasterCard
CB = Carte Blanche
DC= Diners Club
ER = En Route
JCB
DS = Discover

Smoking area available

No smoking

Wine Spectator Awards

Distinguished Restaurants of North America is proud to include among its sponsors *Wine Spectator,* which each year recognizes those DiRōNA Award recipients who have won *Wine Spectator* wine list awards. Since 1981, *Wine Spectator*'s Restaurant Awards Program has encouraged restaurants to strive for better quality wine programs. This program currently recognizes over 2000 restaurants worldwide for their wine lists.

Wine lists are judged for one of three awards: *Award of Excellence,* the *Best of Award of Excellence,* and the coveted *Grand Award.* New award winners are announced in the September 30th issue of *Wine Spectator.*

For complete information on entering the 2001 *Wine Spectator* Restaurant Awards Program, call *Wine Spectator* at (212) 684-4224, extension 781, or email to restaurantawards@mshanken.com.

Wine Spectator award winners are indicated in this guide by the wineglass symbol:

- *Award of Excellence* (one glass)
- *Best of Award of Excellence* (two glasses)
- *Grand Award* (three glasses)

Distinguished Restaurants of North America

BOARD OF DIRECTORS

EXECUTIVE OFFICERS

CHAIRMAN
John Folse
Lafitte's Landing
2517 S. Philippe Avenue
Gonzales, LA 70737
Tel: 225-644-6000
Fax: 225-647-0316
* Chairman 1999-2000
folse@jfolse.com

VICE CHAIRMAN
Kurt Knowles
The Manor
111 Prospect Avenue
West Orange, NJ 07052
Tel: 973-731-2360
Fax: 973-731-5168

PRESIDENT
John Arena
130 Kingscross Drive
King City, L7B1E6
Ontario, Canada
Tel: 905-833-8388
Fax: 905-833-7422
* Chairman 1990-1991

SECRETARY
Rick Powers
Beverly's
2nd & Front Street
Coeur d'Alene, ID 83814
Tel: 208-765-4000
Fax: 208-667-2707
rpowers@cdaresort.com

TREASURER
Alon Yu
Tommy Toy's Cuisine Chinoise
655 Montgomery Street
San Francisco, CA 94111
Tel: 415-397-4888
Fax: 415-397-0469

PAST CHAIRMAN
Paul Athanas
Anthony's Pier 4
299 Salem Street
Swampscott, MA 01907
Tel: 781-599-0240
Fax: 781-598-9321
* Chairman 1998-1999
pathanas@pier4.com

DIRECTORS

Richard Alberini
Alberini's
1201 Youngstown Warren Rd.
Rte. 422
Niles, OH 44446
Tel: 330-652-5895
Fax: 330-652-7041
Alberinis@aol.com

Ted J. Balestreri
Sardine Factory
765 Wave Street
Monterey, CA 93940
Tel: 831-649-6690
Fax: 831-649-1864
*Chairman 1992-1994
Tbalestreri@canneryrow.com

Reinhard Barthel
Cafe 36
36 S. La Grange Road
La Grange, IL 60046
Tel: 708-354-5722
Fax: 708-354-5042
NEPoremba@cs.com

James Blandi, Jr.
100 Lakeland Drive
Mars, PA 16046
Tel: 724-934-5451
Fax: 412-488-0646
jblandi@sgi.net

Vincent Bommarito
Tony's
410 Market Street
St. Louis, MO 63102
Tel: 314-231-7007
Fax: 314-231-4740

Michael Carlevale
Prego Della Piazza
150 Bloor Street
West Toronto, M5S 2X9
Ontario, Canada
Tel: 416-920-9900
Fax: 416-920-9949

Alfred Caron
360 Restaurant at the Tower
301 Front Street
West Toronto, Ontario,
Canada M5V2T6
Tel: 416-360-8500
Fax: 416-601-4713
acaron@cntower.ca

Vincent J. Catania
The Dan'l Webster Inn
141 Falmouth Road (Rte. 28)
Hyannis, MA 02601
Tel: 508-771-0040
Fax: 508-771-0883
v.j.catania@aol.com

Priscilla Cretier
Le Vichyssois
220 W. Rte. 120
Lakemoor, IL 60050
Tel: 815-385-8221
Fax: 815-385-8223
Levichys@imaxx.net

Bert Cutino
Sardine Factory
765 Wave Street
Monterey, CA 93940
Tel: 831-649-6690
Fax: 831-649-1963
* Chairman 1996-1997
Bcutino@canneryrow.com

Jack Czarnecki
Joel Palmer House
600 Ferry Street, P.O. Box #594
Dayton, OR 97114
Tel: 503-864-2995
Fax: 503-864-3246
JoelPalmerhouse@onlinemac.com

Remo d'Agliano
Raffaello
P. O. Box 4419
Carmel, CA 93921
Tel: 831-624-1541
Fax: 831-624-9411
Dedona@earthlink.com

Jordi Escofet
La Cava
S. A. de C.V. Insurgentes
Sur 2465
Mexico, D.F. 01000
Tel: 011-525-616-1376
Fax: 011-525-550-3801
Lacava@prodigy.net.mx

Ralph Evans
8340 Greensboro Drive #801
McLean, VA 22102
Tel: 703-821-8565
Fax: 703-356-3708
ralphbevans@earthlink.net

Mario Ferrari
Mario's
2005 Broadway
Nashville, TN 32703
Tel: 615-327-3232
Fax: 615-321-2675

Dominic Galati
Dominic's
5101 Wilson Avenue
St. Louis, MO 63110
Tel: 314-771-1632
Fax: 314-771-1695

Norbert Goldner
Cafe L'Europe
331 South County Road
Palm Beach, FL 33480
Tel: 561-655-4020
Fax: 561-659-6619

Rita Jammet
La Caravelle
33 West 55th Street
New York, NY 10019
Tel: 212-586-4252
Fax: 212-956-8269
lacaravelle@msn.com

Wade Knowles
The Manor
111 Prospect Avenue
West Orange, NJ 07052
Tel: 973-731-2360
Fax: 973-731-5168
themanor@erols.com

Joe Mannke
Rotisserie for Beef & Bird
2200 Wilcrest Street
Houston, Texas 77042
Tel: 713-977-9524
Fax: 713-977-9568

Tony May
San Domenico
240 Central Park South
New York, NY 10019
Tel: 212-459-9016
Fax: 212-397-0844
Sandomny@aol.com

Michael McCarty
Michael's
1147 3rd Street
Santa Monica, CA 90403
Tel: 310-451-0843
Fax: 310-394-1830

Leonard Mirabile
Jasper's
1201 W. 103rd Street
Kansas City, MO 64114
Tel: 816-941-6600
Fax: 816-941-4346
jmirab2900@aol.com

Julian Niccolini
The Four Seasons Restaurant
99 E. 52nd Street
New York, NY 10022
Tel: 212-754-9494
Fax: 212-754-1077

Gunter Preuss
Broussard's
819 Rue Conti, Vieux Carré
New Orleans, LA 70122
Tel: 504-581-3866
Fax: 504-581-3873
broussrd@bellsouth.net

Christianne Ricchi
i Ricchi
1220 19th Street NW
Washington, D.C. 20036
Tel: 202-835-2021
Fax: 202-872-1220
* Chairman 1997-1998
Crricchi@aol.com

Piero Selvaggio
Valentino
3115 Pico Boulevard
Santa Monica, CA 90405
Tel: 310-829-4313
Fax: 310-315-2791

David Stockman
Lawry's Restaurant, Inc.
234 E. Colorado Blvd.
Ste. #500
Pasadena, CA 91101
Tel: 626-440-5234
Fax: 626-440-5232
Dstockman@Lawrysonline.com

Larry Work
Sam & Harry's
8240 Leesburg Pike
Vienna, VA 22182
Tel: 703-448-2464
Fax: 703-448-0104
Larry@samandharrys.com

Ernest Zingg
The Cellar
305 N. Harbor Boulevard
Fullerton, CA 92632
Tel: 714-525-5682
Fax: 714-525-3853
TheCellar@msn.com

Directors Emeritus

Jerry Berns
The 21 Club
14 East 75th Street
New York, NY 10021-2657
Tel: 212-988-1121

Ella Brennan
Commander's Palace
1403 Washington Avenue
New Orleans, LA 70130
Tel: 504-899-8231
Fax: 504-891-3242

Victor Gotti
Ernie's
3010 Pacific Avenue
San Francisco, CA 94115
Tel: 415-346-0629
Fax: 415-346-0602

Warren Leruth
939 East Scenic Drive
Pass Christian, MS 39571
Tel: 228-452-2977
Fax: 228-452-3907

Tom Margittai
The Four Seasons
31 San Juan Ranch Road
Sante Fe, NM 87501
Tel: 505-986-1000
Fax: 505-986-1276
* Chairman 1991-1992

Richard Marriott
Host Marriott Corporation
10400 Fernwood Road
Bethesda, MD 20817-1109
Tel: 301-380-1420
Fax: 301-380-6993

DiRōNA Headquarters

456 Washington Street
Monterey, CA 93940
Tel: 831-649-6542
Fax: 831-372-4142
dirona@armanasco.com
David Armanasco
Administrative Director

Jonitha MacKenzie
Administrative Manager

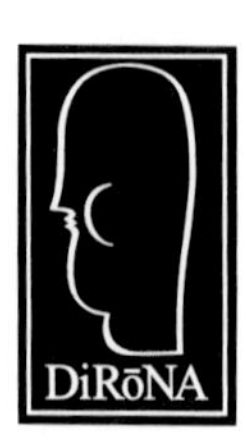

The Award of Excellence from Distinguished Restaurants of North America

The DiRōNA Fine Dining Guarantee

Congratulations! You hold in your hands a guide to one of the most exclusive collections of fine dining establishments in the world. The Distinguished Restaurants of North America organization stands behind its award qualifications and inspection process. DiRōNA guarantees diners will have an exceptional dining experience at restaurants included in this Guide.

Diners who have completed the following steps may request a reimbursement of their dining bill, up to $200, if they have experienced an unsatisfactory dining experience that is not remedied to their satisfaction at a DiRōNA Award restaurant featured in this Guide.

1. Register your name and where you purchased the Guide by February 1, 2001, with DiRōNA headquarters by sending your name, address, and proof of Guide purchase (original receipt or photocopy) to: DiRōNA Fine Dining Guarantee Registration, 456 Washington Street, Monterey, CA 93940. Or fax: to (831) 372-4142. Only readers and diners who have registered their names and Guide purchase with DiRōNA by the above date are eligible for the guarantee reimbursement.

2. The DiRōNA Fine Dining Guarantee is eligible for parties up to four dining at a Guide restaurant.

3. Before applying for a reimbursement from DiRōNA, diners must express in writing their reason for dissatisfaction to the responsible restaurant owner and/or manager. Diners must provide the restaurant with every opportunity to remedy their complaint in a timely manner.

4. If still unsatisfied, diners must provide a copy of the complaint, a copy of the dining receipt, and the restaurant's reply in writing to DiRōNA Award headquarters at 456 Washington Street, Monterey, CA 93940. Upon submission of these materials, DiRōNA will respond within 90 days with either a reimbursement check or an equivalent-value offer of dining at another DiRōNA Award restaurant.

About the Publisher

Lebhar-Friedman Books is one of America's newest and most dynamic publishers of quality hardcover and paperback books. Its growing list of publishing partners includes the American Academy of Chefs, the Culinary Institute of America, *The New York Times* and the History Channel. A sister company of *Nation's Restaurant News,* Lebhar-Friedman Books is also the publisher of luminaries in the food world including John Mariani, Fred Ferretti, and Jane and Michael Stern.

Since 1967, *Nation's Restaurant News* has been the leading voice for the country's restaurant and foodservice industries. The weekly trade magazine is the ultimate resource that provides readers with the news, trends, and information they need to stay ahead of the competition. *Nation's Restaurant News* has evolved significantly over the years, adding new sections and specialists to serve the informational needs of its widely varied readership. To subscribe to *Nation's Restaurant News,* call 800-944-4676.

DiRōNA Scholarship Program

The DiRōNA Award Scholarship Fund, initiated in 1989, has helped many young students achieve their goals in the culinary world. Ted Balestreri, Scholarship Committee Chairman and past DiRōNA Chairman, states that "education is the best gift we can give to our youth." Distinguished Restaurants of North America is proud to help promote distinguished dining through the education of tomorrow's leaders.

DiRōNA Award Scholarships are presented to deserving individuals pursuing careers in the restaurant and hospitality industry. Recipients are selected through a review of applications from students throughout North America who exhibit a genuine interest in seeking an education in preparation for a professional foodservice career.

Fifteen scholarships are given each year through the National Restaurant Association Education Foundation. Three scholarships are given in the name of *Wine Spectator* magazine, one in the name of *Foodservice and Hospitality* magazine, and 11 in the name of past DiRōNA Chairmen.

The DiRōNA Award Scholarship Fund is managed and administered for Distinguished Restaurants of North America by the National Restaurant Association Educational Foundation. Applicants should contact Emilee Rogan, Director, Scholarships Initiative, at:

National Restaurant Association
Education Foundation
250 South Wacker Drive
Suite 1400
Chicago, Ill. 60606-5834

Additional information can be obtained from the DiRōNA Headquarters in Monterey, CA: telephone (831) 649-6542; e-mail dirona@armanasco.com.

The Crow's Nest

Hotel Captain Cook

An evening at the Crow's Nest is more than dining—it is an experience. Offering stunning views of Cook Inlet and the Alaska Range from atop the Hotel Captain Cook, The Crow's Nest has been a landmark in the Great North for more than 20 years. Chef de Cuisine Loren Gahala's innovative cuisine uses only the freshest, seasonally available ingredients, including Alaska seafood. The award-winning wine list offers more than 1,200 selections.

Lamb chops

Intimate dining

Stunning views from lounge

AWARD WINNER
SINCE 1992

Directions

In downtown, 10 min. from Anchorage International Airport

Hotel Captain Cook
4th and K Streets
Anchorage, AK 99501
PH: (907) 276-6000
FAX: (907) 343-2221
www.captaincook.com

Owners
Walter Hickel Jr.

Cuisine
New American with French flair

Days Open
Open Tues.-Sat. for dinner, Sun for brunch

Pricing
Dinner for one, without tax, tip, or drinks: $40-$60

Dress Code
Casual

Reservations
Recommended

Parking
Valet, garage nearby

Features
Private room

Credit Cards
AE, VC, MC, CB, DC, DS

The Pump House

Directions

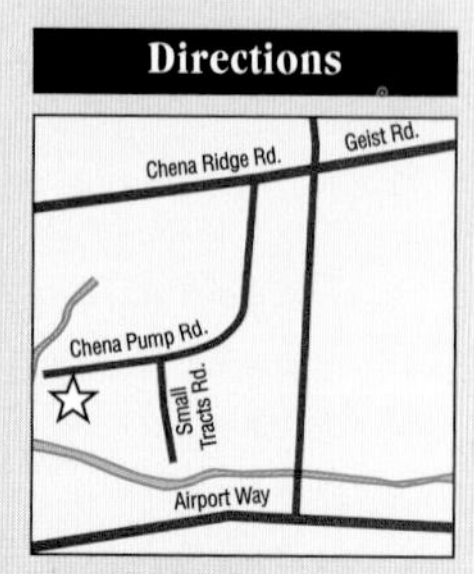

Off Parks Highway, 7 min. from University of Alaska-Fairbanks and 5 min. from Fairbanks International Airport

796 Chena Pump Road
Fairbanks, AK 99709
PH: (907) 479-8452
FAX: (907) 479-8432
www.pumphouse.com

Owners
Vivian Bubbel

Cuisine
American, emphasizing Alaskan seafood

Days Open
Open daily for lunch (May through September) and dinner (year-round); Sunday brunch year-round

Pricing
Dinner for one, without tax, tip, or drinks: $20-$40

Dress Code
Casual

Reservations
Recommended

Parking
Free on site

Features
Private room/parties, outdoor dining, entertainment, cigar/cognac events

Credit Cards
AE, VC, MC, DS

Patio dining overlooking Chena River

The most unique restaurant in Alaska has been serving up Fairbanks hospitality since 1977. Relics from the town's Gold Rush past fill this National Historic Site on the banks of the Chena River. The menu features fresh Alaskan seafood — salmon is delivered to the restaurant's dock by float plane — as well as wild game and alder-smoked specialties. The Senator's Saloon is home to "The World's Most Northern Oyster Bar," and the wine list features the best of the Pacific Northwest.

AWARD WINNER
SINCE 1997

The Chaparral

Main dining room

The Chaparral at Marriott's Camelback Inn specializes in fresh seafood selections, certified Black Angus steaks, inn-baked soufflés, and an award-winning wine list that features more than 12,000 bottles and over 40 wines by the glass. The adobe-style setting is comfortable and cozy, and unique iron and bronze sculptures highlight the contemporary decor. Service is impeccable, hospitable, and caring, and the spectacular sunset views of Camelback Mountain complement the fine dining.

Wellington Petite and other tempting dishes

Award-winning wines complement the menu

Desserts galore

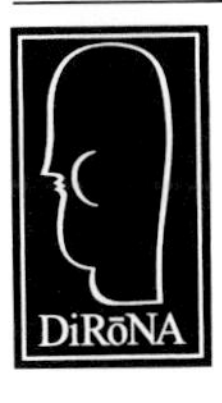

AWARD WINNER
SINCE 1993

Directions

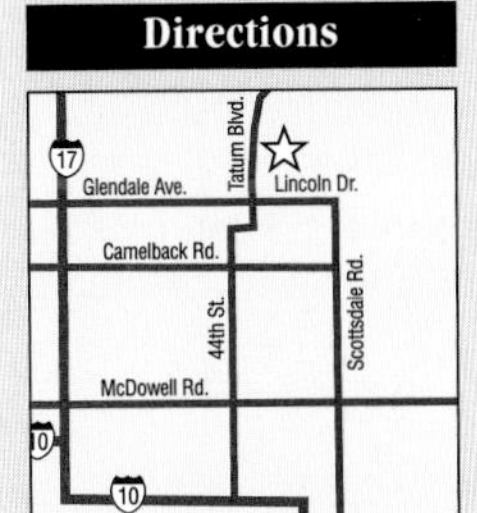

On E. Lincoln Drive near Scottsdale Road, 20 min. from Phoenix Sky Harbor International Airport

Marriott's Camelback Inn
5402 E. Lincoln Drive
Scottsdale, AZ 85253
PH: (480) 948-1700
FAX: (480) 951-8469
www.camelbackinn.com

Owners
Marriott International

Cuisine
American

Days Open
Open daily for dinner

Pricing
Dinner for one,
without tax, tip, or drinks:
$20-$40

Dress Code
Business casual

Reservations
Required

Parking
Free on site, valet

Features
Private parties

Credit Cards
AE, VC, MC, CB, DC,
ER, JCB, DS

Marquesa

Directions

Princess Dr.
Hayden
Bell
Bell Rd.
Pima Rd.
Camelback Rd.
Scottsdale Rd.
McDowell Rd.
Squaw Peak
Van Buren
Hohokam Expwy.
Sky Harbor Airport
Sky Harbor Blvd.

At The Fairmont Scottsdale Princess in north Scottsdale, near Bell and Scottsdale roads and 40 min. from Phoenix Sky Harbor International Airport

7575 E. Princess Drive
Scottsdale, AZ 85255
PH: (480) 585-4848
FAX: (480) 585-0086
www.fairmont.com

Owners
The Fairmont Scottsdale Princess

Cuisine
Mediterranean

Days Open
Open Tues.-Sat. for dinner and Sun. for brunch

Pricing
Dinner for one, without tax, tip, or drinks: $60-$80

Dress Code
Business casual

Reservations
Recommended

Parking
Free on site, valet

Features
Private room/parties, outdoor dining, entertainment

Credit Cards
AE, VC, MC, DC, DS

Exquisite dining

The AAA Five-Diamond Marquesa, at The Fairmont Scottsdale Princess, features award-winning Mediterranean cuisine with a unique blend of Catalan, Italian, and French influences. Executive Chef Reed Groban's menu presents exquisite Mediterranean delicacies radiantly seasoned with fresh herbs, fruity olive oil, roasted garlic, and sun-ripened fruits and vegetables. In addition to the main dining room, there is a private dining room with a fireplace, a separate lounge, and an intimate courtyard.

Marquesa dining room

Marinated rack of lamb

Chocolate ganache Dali

AWARD WINNER
SINCE 1993

L'Auberge de Sedona

Terrace on the creek

Overlooking the quiet beauty of Oak Creek, the charming L'Auberge de Sedona has an enchanting air. The glow of candlelight and fragrance of flowers enhances the mood while considerate service attends to every need. A sumptuous lunch and dinner menu, presenting a superb and varied repertoire of French delights, is created weekly from only the freshest of ingredients. Specialties include foie gras with Parma ham and caramelized melon, and lobster with squash, spinach, and mussel-saffron vinaigrette.

Exquisite Sunday brunch

Cuisine extraordinaire

French country dining

AWARD WINNER
SINCE 1993

Directions

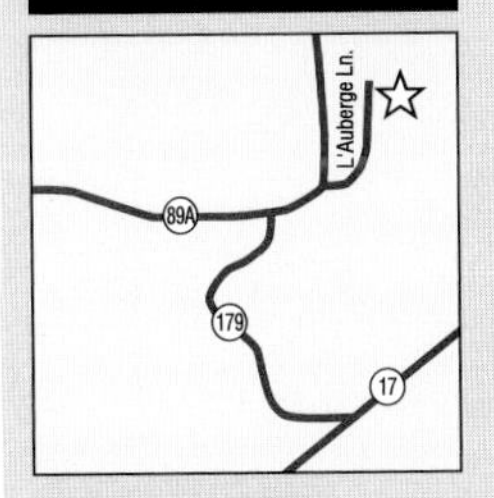

Off Highway 89A in Sedona, 2 hr. north of Phoenix Sky Harbor International Airport

301 L'Auberge Lane
Sedona, AZ 86336
PH: (520) 282-1661
FAX: (520) 282-1064
www.lauberge.com

Owners
Charles Sweeney

Cuisine
Contemporary French

Days Open
Open daily for breakfast, lunch, and dinner

Pricing
Dinner for one, without tax, tip, or drinks: $60-$80

Dress Code
Jacket required, tie optional

Reservations
Recommended

Parking
Free on site

Features
Private room/parties, outdoor dining

Credit Cards
AE, VC, MC, DC, DS

Anthony's in the Catalinas

Directions

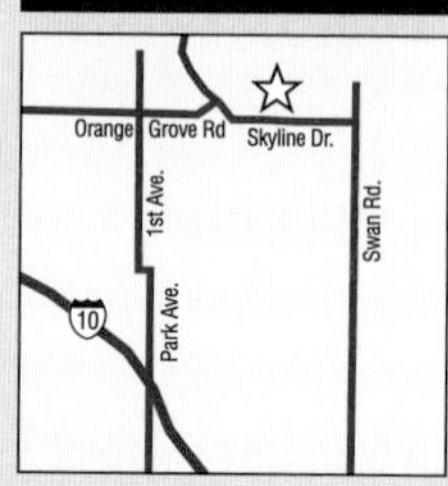

At the foot of the Catalina Mountains, a half-block north of Sunrise Road, 30 min. from Tucson International Airport

6440 N. Campbell Avenue
Tucson, AZ 85718
PH: (520) 299-1771
FAX: (520) 299-6635

Owners
Anthony and Brooke Martino

Cuisine
Continental

Days Open
Open Mon.-Fri. for lunch, daily for dinner

Pricing
Dinner for one, without tax, tip or drinks: $40-$60

Dress Code
Business casual

Reservations Policy
Recommended

Parking
Free on site, valet

Features
Prviate rooms, parties, entertainment, cigar/cognac events

Credit Cards
AE, VC, MC, CB, DC

A beautiful Southwestern setting

With breathtaking views of the Santa Catalina Mountains, Anthony's offers a unique dining experience. Elegant tables, set with light pink linens, fresh flowers, and Villeroy and Boch china, combine to provide an intimate setting to foster romances or friendships. The impeccable service and outstanding food is sure to impress friends as well as business associates. The award-winning wine list ensures a great selection of vintages, housed in an underground cellar.

Wine cellar

Sumptuous dining

Elegant dining in the main room

AWARD WINNER SINCE 1994

Ventana Room

A view of city lights

Savor the panoramic views of Tucson or the canyon waterfall while enjoying an exquisite meal at the Ventana Room. Ranked tops in the Southwest by *Condé Nast Traveler* and the 2000 *Zagat Survey*, the restaurant is renowned for its innovative new American cuisine, attentive service, and extensive wine list. Representative of the menu are grilled buffalo tenderloin with potato pancake and spaghetti squash; and rack of wild boar with brandy poached apple, pumpkin spaetzle, and cider jus.

Chef Jeffrey Russell

Elegant dining

AWARD WINNER
SINCE 1994

Directions

At the Loews Ventana Canyon Resort, 30 min. from Tucson International Airport

7000 N. Resort Drive
Tucson, AZ 85750
PH: (520) 299-2020
FAX: (520) 299-4151
www.ventanaroom.com

Owners
Loews Ventana Canyon Resort

Cuisine
New American

Days Open
Open daily for dinner

Pricing
Dinner for one, without tax, tip, or drinks: $40-$60

Dress Code
Jacket requested

Reservations
Recommended

Parking
Free on site, valet

Features
Private room/parties, entertainment

Credit Cards
AE, VC, MC, CB, DC, DS

Directions

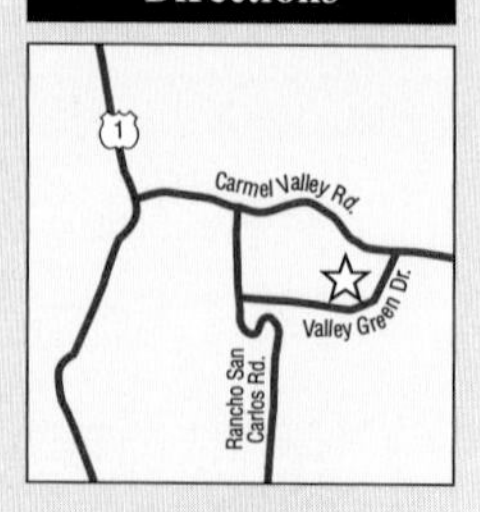

At the Quail Lodge Resort, 20 min. from Monterey Peninsula Airport

8205 Valley Greens Drive
Carmel, CA 93923
PH: (831) 624-2888
FAX: (831) 624-3726
www.quail-lodge-resort.com

Owners
Hong Kong Shanghai Hotels Ltd.

Cuisine
Wine Country

Days Open
Open daily for breakfast, lunch, and dinner

Pricing
Dinner for one, without tax, tip, or drinks: $20-$40

Dress Code
Business casual

Reservations Policy
Recommended

Parking
Free on site

Features
Private room/parties, outdoor dining

Credit Cards
AE, VC, MC, CB, DC, JCB

The Covey

Outdoor dining

The Covey, at the Quail Lodge Resort, offers inventive Wine Country cuisine using the freshest local ingredients, complemented by an award-winning wine list highlighting the best of Monterey County. Roast rack of lamb and crab-crusted halibut are among the specialties. Enjoy The Covey's casual ambience while overlooking a sparkling lake, flourishing gardens, and the rolling hills of Carmel.

Casual ambience

View of the lake

AWARD WINNER SINCE 1992

Raffaello

The dining room

Remo d'Agliano imports a hint of Florentine art and ambience to picturesque Carmel at Raffaello. Beveled glass etched with fleurs-de-lis highlights the decor, which along with the menu reflect d'Agliano's youth and apprenticeship at his family's restaurant in Florence. Formal training at the Culinary Academy in Paris broadened his style, adding a touch of French flair to his Italian repertoire. You'll find a host of appealing specialties as well as homemade pastas.

Owner/Chef Remo d'Agliano

Old world ambience

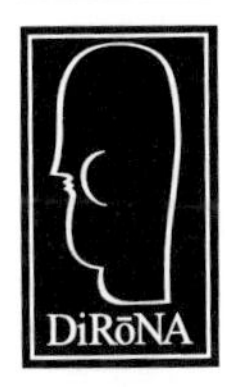

AWARD WINNER SINCE 1992

Directions

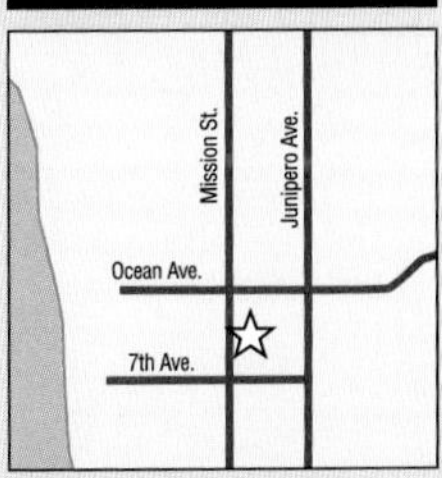

On Mission Street, between Ocean and 7th avenues in Carmel, 15 min. from Monterey Peninsula Airport

Mission Street
Carmel, CA 93921
PH: (831) 624-1541
FAX: (831) 624-9411

Owners
Remo d'Agliano

Cuisine
Italian

Days Open
Open Wed.-Mon. for dinner

Pricing
Dinner for one,
without tax, tip, or drinks:
$20-$40

Dress Code
Business casual

Reservations
Recommended

Parking
Free on site

Features
Private parties

Credit Cards
AE, VC, MC, CB, DC

Trader Vic's

Directions

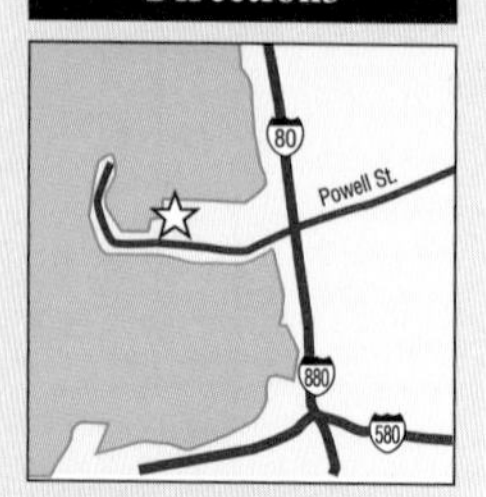

Off Interstate 80's Powell Street exit, 20 min. from Oakland International Airport

9 Anchor Drive
Emeryville, CA 94608
PH: (510) 653-3400
FAX: (510) 653-9384

Owners
The Bergeron family

Cuisine
Island

Days Open
Open Mon.-Fri. for lunch, daily for dinner

Pricing
Dinner for one, without tax, tip, or drinks: $40-$60

Dress Code
Business casual

Reservations
Recommended

Parking
Valet

Features
Private room/parties, outdoor dining, entertainment

Credit Cards
VC, MC

The flavor of the islands

Overlooking the Emeryville Marina on San Francisco Bay, Trader Vic's has been a Bay Area institution since 1934, famous for its tropical decor and island-style cuisine and drinks. Home of the original mai tai, Trader Vic's offers prime meats and fowl and daily seasonal fish specials cooked to order — steamed, grilled, or barbecued. Be sure to visit Trader Vic's other locations around the world, in such cities as Tokyo, Atlanta, Beverly Hills, and Hamburg.

AWARD WINNER
SINCE 1996

The Lark Creek Inn

Entrance to the Lark Creek Inn

Ensconced in the redwoods with a creek-side dining patio, the Lark Creek Inn is only 15 minutes north of the Golden Gate Bridge. Executive Chef Bradley Ogden's daily changing menu offers farm-fresh American fare using local bounty, delivered daily. The updated, lightened conceptions are served with pride and skill. Among the specialties are applewood smoked pork loin chop with plum compote, and grilled king salmon filet with corn and Miami onions. The carefully composed wine list has more than 200 selections.

Dining patio

Crab and onion pancake

Sun room

AWARD WINNER
SINCE 1993

Directions

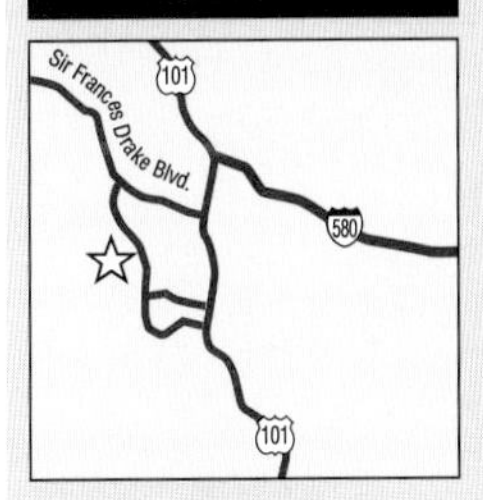

A short distance off Highway 101's Tamalpais Drive/ Paradise Drive exit, 1 hr. from San Francisco International Airport

234 Magnolia Avenue
Larkspur, CA 94939
PH: (415) 924-7766
FAX: (415) 924-7117

Owners
Bradley Ogden and Michael Dellar

Cuisine
American

Days Open
Open daily for lunch and dinner, brunch on Sun.

Pricing
Dinner for one, without tax, tip, or drinks: $40-$60

Dress Code
Any style of dress - casual, business casual, jacket and tie - is appropriate

Reservations
Recommended

Parking
Valet

Features
Private room/parties, outdoor dining

Credit Cards
AE, VC, MC, DC

Wente Vineyards Restaurant

Directions

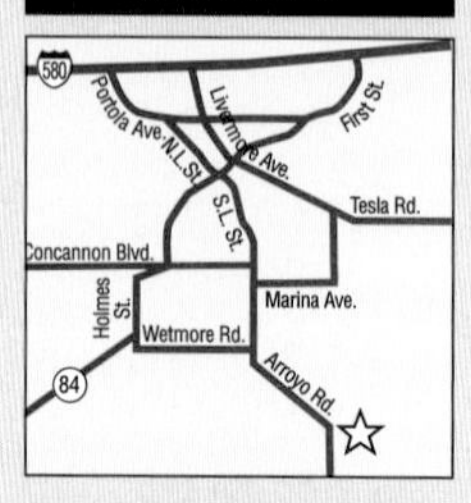

Off Highway 580 in Livermore, 30 min. from Oakland International Airport

5050 Arroyo Road
Livermore, CA 94550
PH: (925) 456-2460
FAX: (925) 456-2401
www.wentevineyards.com

Owners
The Wente family

Cuisine
Wine Country

Days Open
Open daily for lunch and dinner

Pricing
Dinner for one,
without tax, tip, or drinks:
$20-$40

Dress Code
Business casual

Reservations
Recommended

Parking
Free on site

Features
Private room/parties, outdoor dining, summer concerts

Credit Cards
AE, VC, MC, DC, DS

Wente Vineyards is a truly unique dining destination. Where else can a discriminating diner savor superlative wines and food, play on a Greg Norman-designed championship golf course, and enjoy a summer night's entertainment by world-renowned performers? Executive Chef Kimball Jones' menu, which changes daily, features wine country dishes prepared with fresh seasonal ingredients. Full-service catering is available.

Creative cuisine

Executive Chef Kimball Jones

Excellent service

AWARD WINNER
SINCE 1993

Dal Baffo

Main dining room

Dal Baffo offers a culinary experience characterized by sophistication, elegance, and charm. The establishment features a relaxed lounge, a refined dining area, and a private banquet room. Boasting over 1,200 selections, the wine list has made *Wine Spectator*'s top 100 wine list since 1986. Chef/Owner Vincenzo Lo Grasso frequently creates new dishes and design concepts to ensure that Dal Baffo always offers a fresh approach, staying ahead of food and restaurant trends.

Chef/Owner Vincenzo Lo Grasso

Innovative cuisine

The Siena Room

AWARD WINNER
SINCE 1992

Directions

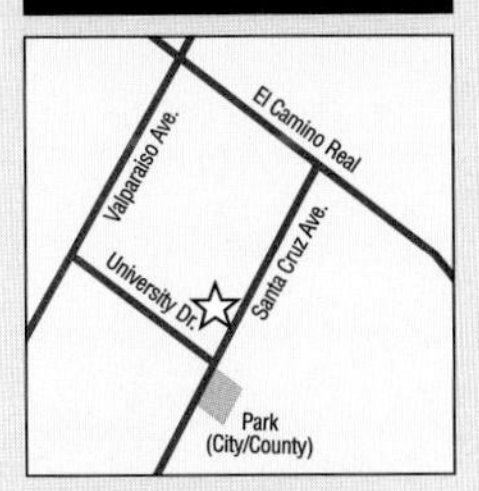

Near Stanford Shopping Center, 30 min. from both San Francisco International and San Jose International airports

878 Santa Cruz Avenue
Menlo Park, CA 94025
PH: (650) 325-1588
FAX: (650) 326-2780
www.dalbaffo.com

Owners
Vincenzo Lo Grasso

Cuisine
Continental/Italian

Days Open
Open Mon.-Fri. for lunch and Mon.-Sat. for dinner

Pricing
Dinner for one,
without tax, tip or drinks:
$40-$60

Dress Code
Business casual

Reservations
Recommended

Parking
Free on site

Features
Private room/parties

Credit Cards
AE, VC, MC, CB, DC, JCB, DS

Fresh Cream Restaurant

Directions

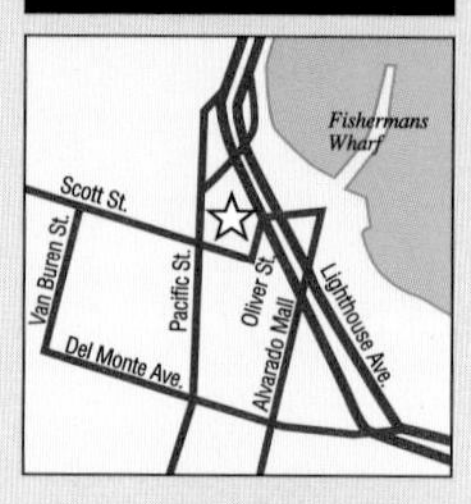

On Pacific Street near Fisherman's Wharf, 15 min. from Monterey Peninsula Airport and 2 hrs. from San Francisco International

99 Pacific Street
Monterey, CA 93940
PH: (831) 375-9798
FAX: (831) 375-2283
www.freshcream.com

Owners
Steven R. Chesney

Cuisine
French nouvelle

Days Open
Open daily for dinner

Pricing
Dinner for one,
without tax, tip, or drinks:
$40-$60

Dress Code
Business casual

Reservations
Recommended

Parking
Garage nearby

Features
Private room/parties

Credit Cards
AE, VC, MC, CB, DC, DS

Monterey sunset

Fresh Cream has been receiving critical praise for award-winning cuisine for more than 20 years. Stunning views, elegant decor, and impeccable service set the mood for imaginatively conceived and artfully presented dishes. Among the celebrated house specialties are rack of lamb Dijonnaise, roast boned duck in black currants, Holland dover sole, and delectable vegetarian creations. A diversified wine list and full bar service enhance the dining experience.

Grilled prawn appetizer

Julie and Steven R. Chesney

Harbor View Room

AWARD WINNER
SINCE 1994

The Sardine Factory

The Conservatory

The Sardine Factory continues to reflect the excellence which made it world-famous over 30 years ago. The creatively composed entrees of the freshest seafood and prime meats, gracious service, unique dining areas, and the award-winning wine list offer the perfect combination for people who truly love an extraordinary dining experience. Whet your appetite with such delectable favorites as seared Monterey Bay prawns, Cannery Row cioppino, and prime meat. Join the impressive guest list of those who have dined at this Monterey icon and create your own memories.

The Wine Cellar

Creative entrees

Owners Bert Cutino and Ted Balestreri

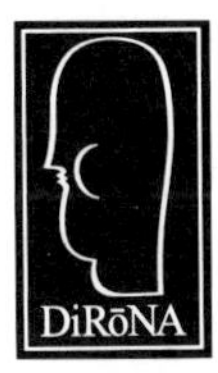

AWARD WINNER
SINCE 1996

Directions

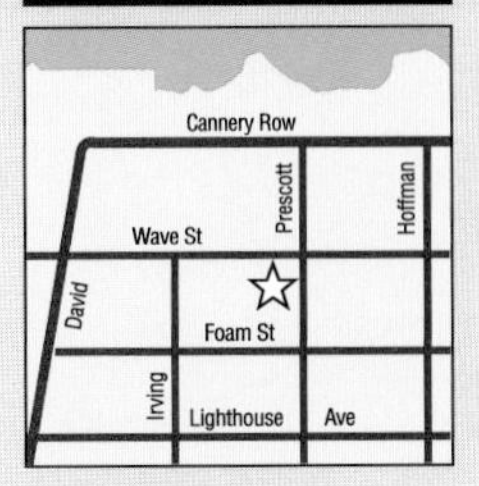

Corner of Wave and Prescott, 15 min. from Monterey Airport, 2 hrs. from San Francisco Int'l Airport

701 Wave Street
Monterey, CA 93940
PH: (831) 373-3775
FAX: (831) 373-4241
www.sardinefactory.com

Owners
Ted Balestreri and
Bert Cutino

Cuisine
Seafood and prime meat

Days Open
Open daily for dinner

Pricing
Dinner for one,
without tax, tip, or drinks:
$20-$40

Dress Code
Upscale casual

Reservations
Recommended

Parking
Free on site, valet

Features
Private room/parties

Credit Cards
AE, VC, MC, CB, DC, DS

Biba

Directions

Corner of Capitol Avenue and 28th Street, 20 min. from Sacramento International Airport

2801 Capitol Avenue
Sacramento, CA 95816
PH: (916) 455-2422
FAX: (916) 455-0542
www.biba-restaurant.com

Owners
Biba Caggiano

Cuisine
Italian

Days Open
Open Mon.-Fri. for lunch, Mon.-Sat. for dinner

Pricing
Dinner for one, without tax, tip, or drinks: $20-$40

Dress Code
Business casual

Reservations
Recommended

Parking
Garage nearby

Features
Private room/parties, outdoor dining, entertainment

Credit Cards
AE, VC, MC, DC

A citadel of Italian cuisine

Owned and operated by Biba Caggiano, the acclaimed cookbook author and host of "Biba's Italian Kitchen" on The Learning Channel, Biba serves exceptional classic Italian cuisine. Pastas, gnocchi, risotto, braised rabbit and duck are just a few of the marvelous specialties. The service is refined but friendly, ensuring a smooth and pleasurable dining experience.

Creative entrees

Owner Biba Caggiano

Dining room

AWARD WINNER
SINCE 1992

The Restaurant at Meadowood

Croquet at Meadowood

Located at the beautiful Meadowood Napa Valley, a Relais & Chateaux hotel, private club, and home of the annual Napa Valley Wine Auction, this establishment overlooks the fairways, croquet lawns, and surrounding wooded hillsides. The restaurant offers a menu that reflects local bounty and the changing of the seasons. The ever-changing, prix-fixe Vintners Menu, featuring dishes paired with local wines, celebrates the restaurant's close association with the local wine-making community.

Chef Pilar Sanchez

Elegant dining

Wine country chic

AWARD WINNER
SINCE 1992

Directions

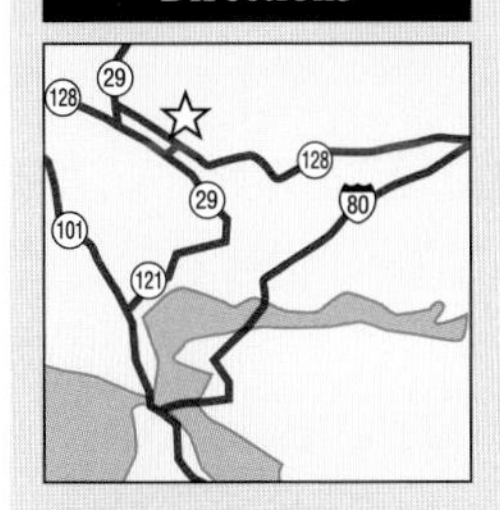

At Meadowood Napa Valley Hotel, 90 min. from San Francisco International Airport

900 Meadowood Lane
St. Helena, CA 94574
PH: (707) 963-3646
FAX: (707) 963-3532
www.meadowood.com

Owners
H. William Harlan

Cuisine
California wine country

Days Open
Open daily for dinner, brunch on Sun.

Pricing
Dinner for one, without tax, tip, or drinks: $40-$60

Dress Code
Country elegant

Reservations
Recommended

Parking
Free on site

Features
Outdoor dining

Credit Cards
AE, VC, MC, CB, DC, DS

Fior d'Italia

Beloved by it's loyal clientele

An important part of San Francisco's grand and glorious history for 114 years, this venerable Italian restaurant has been a leader in building the great tradition of excellent cuisine for which the city is so famous. The extensive menu boasts almost 90 items, and the Fior's loyal clientele highly rate its calamari, gnocchi, osso buco, and Caesar salad, as well as its veal and pasta dishes, all freshly prepared.

Chef Gianni Audieri and owner Bob Larive

A North Beach landmark since 1886

Trattoria looks out on Washington Square

AWARD WINNER
SINCE 2001

Directions

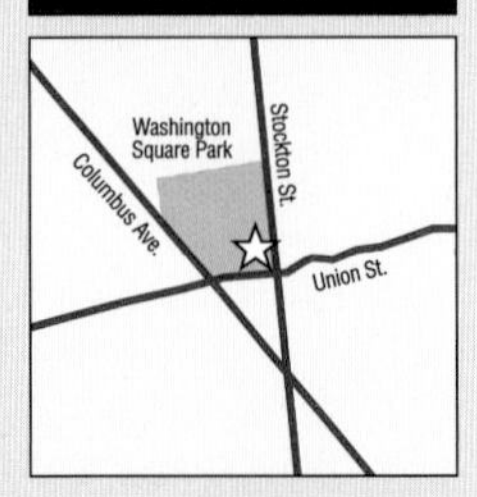

In the heart of North Beach, 30 min. from San Francisco International Airport

601 Union Street
San Francisco, CA 94133
PH: (415) 986-1886
FAX: (415) 986-7031
www.fior.com

Owners
Bob Larive

Cuisine
Italian

Days Open
Open daily for lunch and dinner

Pricing
Dinner for one, without tax, tip or drinks: $20-$40

Dress Code
Business casual

Reservations
Recommended

Parking
Valet

Features
Private room/parties, outdoor dining

Credit Cards
AE, MC, CB, DC, JCB, DS

Fournou's Ovens

European roasting ovens

Fournou's Ovens, one of San Francisco's finest restaurants, is located in the Renaissance Stanford Court Hotel atop historic Nob Hill. Enjoy a Mediterranean-themed setting and a menu that emphasizes seasonal specialties. Fournou's Ovens is named for its visual focal point, the massive, 54-square-foot European-style roasting ovens. For ten consecutive years, the wine list has been chosen as an award winner by *Wine Spectator* magazine. Champagne brunch is served on Saturday and Sunday.

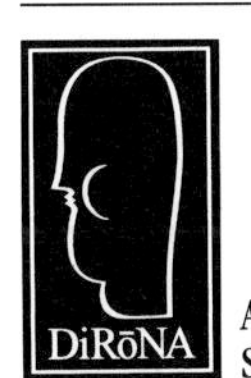

AWARD WINNER
SINCE 1993

Directions

Corner of California and Powell streets, near Union Square and 25 min. from San Francisco International Airport

905 California Street
San Francisco, CA 94108
PH: (415) 989-1910
FAX: (415) 732-4017
www.renaissancehotels.com

Owners
Renaissance Stanford Court Hotel

Cuisine
American, with a Mediterranean flair

Days Open
Open daily for breakfast, lunch, and dinner

Pricing
Dinner for one, without tax, tip, or drinks: $40-$60

Dress Code
Business casual

Reservations
Recommended

Parking
Valet

Features
Private room/parties, near theater

Credit Cards
AE, VC, MC, CB, DC, JCB, DS

Harris' Restaurant

Directions

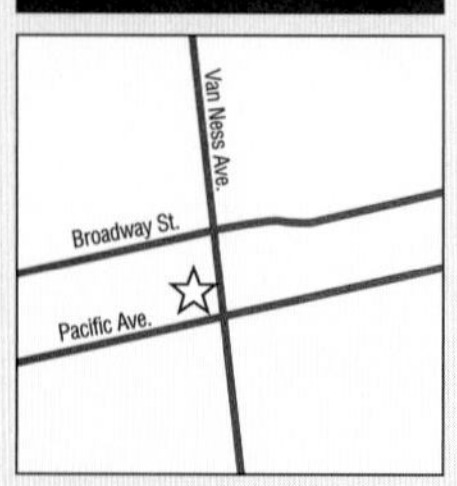

At Van Ness and Pacific avenues, 30 min. from San Francisco International Airport

2100 Van Ness Avenue
San Francisco, CA 94109
PH: (415) 673-1888
FAX: (415) 673-8817
www.harrisrestaurant.com

Owners
Ann Lee Harris, Goetz Boje

Cuisine
Steak and seafood

Days Open
Open daily for dinner

Pricing
Dinner for one,
without tax, tip, or drinks:
$40-$60

Dress Code
Business casual

Reservations
Recommended

Parking
Valet

Features
Private room/parties, entertainment

Credit Cards
AE, VC, MC, CB, DC, JCB, DS

Ask any San Franciscan about the City by the Bay's best steak, and they're certain to tell you about Harris', which uses a 21-day dry-aging process for its beef. The result is tender and succulent steaks that are sliced on the premises. The richly appointed dining rooms feature over-stuffed leather booths, mahogany-paneled walls, and warm murals painted by local artists. Choose a vintage from the extensive wine list, or try a famous Harris' martini.

Main dining room

Pacific Room

Board room

AWARD WINNER
SINCE 1996

La Folie

Russian Hill Jewel

Recently renovated, this intimate, 75-seat jewel has been transformed into an elegant, theatrical establishment, with dark burgundy stage curtains and guignols (authentic French puppets) dotting the ceiling and walls. This dramatic decor is a perfect showcase for Roland Passot's artistic food presentations that combine his culinary creativity and local ingredients. Brother Georges Passot, general manager and sommelier, directs the gracious staff while happily assisting guests in their wine selections from the restaurant's extensive list.

Main dining room

Egg surprise

Roti of quail and squab

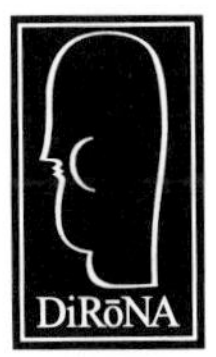

AWARD WINNER
SINCE 1992

Directions

On Polk Street between Union and Green streets in Russian Hill, 40 min. from San Francisco International Airport

2316 Polk Street
San Francisco, CA 94109
PH: (415) 776-5577
FAX: (415) 776-3431
www.lafolie.com

Owners
Roland and Jamie Passot

Cuisine
French

Days Open
Open Mon.-Sat. for dinner

Pricing
Dinner for one,
without tax, tip, or drinks:
$60-$80

Dress Code
Business casual

Reservations
Recommended

Parking
Valet

Features
Private room/parties, near theater

Credit Cards
AE, VC, MC, CB, DC

Le Central Bistro

Directions

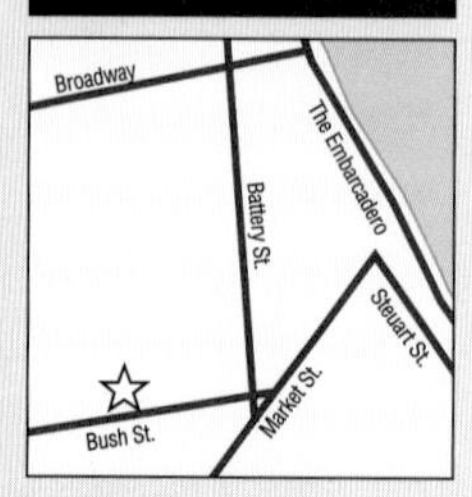

On Bush street at Grant, 30 min. from San Francisco International Airport

453 Bush Street
San Francisco, CA 94108
PH: (415) 391-2233
FAX: (415) 391-3615
www.citysearch.com

Owners
Paul Tanphanich, Johnny Tanphanich, Michel Bonnet

Cuisine
French

Days Open
Open Mon.-Sat. for lunch and dinner

Pricing
Dinner for one,
without tax, tip, or drinks:
$40-$60

Dress Code
Business casual

Reservations
Recommended

Parking
Garage nearby

Features
Private parties, near theater

Credit Cards
AE, VC, MC, CB, JCB

Le Central Bistro

Since opening in 1974, this lively yet intimate establishment has become a classic San Francisco dining spot. Le Central offers French bistro cuisine expertly prepared by John and Paul Tanphanich, in an authentic French brasserie setting. Specialties of the house include the cassoulet, choucroute a l'Alsacienne, boudin noir aux pommes, steak tartare, and roasted chicken. To finish, choose from a carefully selected wine list of French and California vintages and tempting desserts.

The cassoulet

Owner Michel Bonnet

Owner Paul Tanphanich

AWARD WINNER
SINCE 1993

Silks

Main dining room

Chef de Cuisine Dante Boccuzzi looks forward to pleasing your palate with his repertoire of innovative appetizers and entrees, including his signature dish, French foie gras terrine. Silks' newly renovated dining room is awash in rich colors, fabrics, and textures that evoke the odyssey of Marco Polo's discovery of silk. Located in the heart of the city, Silks is an ideal place for any meal.

Ahi and hamachi sashimi

Elegant place settings

Chef de Cuisine Dante Boccuzzi

AWARD WINNER
SINCE 1998

Directions

California
Pine
Sansome
Battery
Market St.
1st St.
80

On Sansome between California and Pine, near Chinatown and the Embarcadero Center, 30 min. from San Francisco International Airport

Mandarin Oriental, SF
222 Sansome Street
San Francisco, CA 94104
PH: (415) 986-2020
FAX: (415) 433-0289
www.mandarinoriental.com

Owners
Mandarin Oriental, San Francisco

Cuisine
California with Asian accents

Days Open
Open daily for breakfast and dinner, Mon.-Fri. for lunch

Pricing
Dinner for one,
without tax, tip, or drinks:
$20-$40

Dress Code
Business casual

Reservations
Recommended

Parking
Valet

Features
Private room/parties

Credit Cards
AE, VC, MC, DC

Tommy Toy's Cuisine Chinoise

Directions

Across from the Transamerica Pyramid in the Financial District, 45 min. from San Francisco International Airport

655 Montgomery Street
San Francisco, CA 94111
PH: (415) 397-4888
FAX: (415) 397-0469
www.tommytoys.com

Owners
Tommy Toy

Cuisine
Chinese-French

Days Open
Open Mon.-Fri. for lunch, daily for dinner

Pricing
Dinner for one, without tax, tip, or drinks: $40-$60

Dress Code
Jacket and tie requested

Reservations
Recommended

Parking
Valet, garage nearby

Features
Private room/parties

Credit Cards
AE, VC, MC, CB, DC, JCB, DS

Main dining room

This elegant and refined restaurant is renowned for its combination of Chinese cookery and French service. Specialties include whole Maine lobster in peppercorn sauce and Peking duck carved tableside. Tommy Toy's has received many accolades, including Mobil's Four Star Award for Excellence and induction into *Nation's Restaurant News*' Hall of Fame.

Tommy Toy, right, with chef

Romantic dining

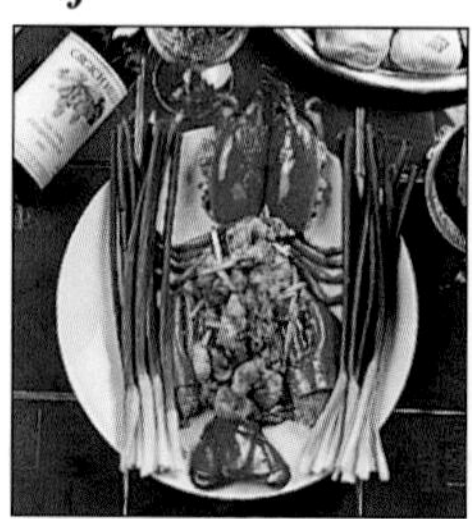

Lobster and Peking duck

AWARD WINNER
SINCE 1992

Paolo's Restaurant

The dining room

Paolo's has long been a favorite of Silicon Valley locals and visitors alike. Second-generation owner Carolyn Allen maintains her family's commitment to their heritage through the unique art and traditions of regional Italian cuisine, acquiring the finest local and imported ingredients. The maitre d', Jalil Samavarchian, directs a knowledgeable and professional staff in a dramatic setting overlooking Guadalupe River Park, all the while maintaining a wine list of exceptional breadth and depth and developing a uniquely personal rapport with the clientele. Paolo's style is as fashionable and contemporary today as it was when it opened more than 40 years ago.

Unmistakably Italian entrees

Private dining

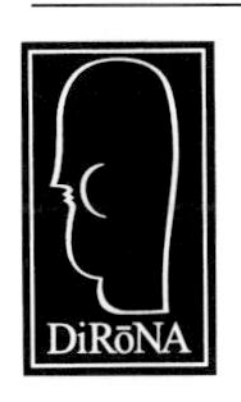

AWARD WINNER
SINCE 1993

Directions

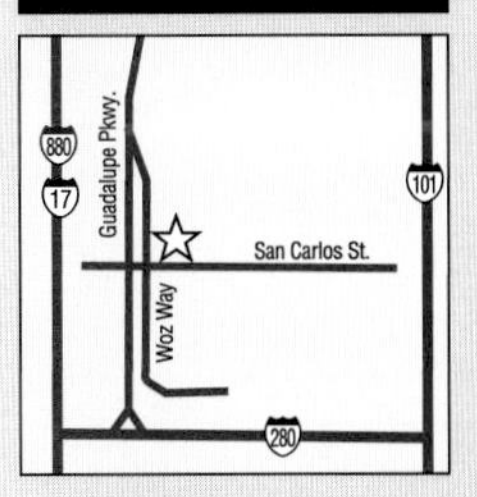

One block from the convention center in downtown San Jose, 10 min. from San Jose International Airport

333 W. San Carlos Street
#150
San Jose, CA 95110
PH: (408) 294-2558
FAX: (408) 294-2595
www.paolosrestaurant.com

Owners
Carolyn Allen

Cuisine
Modern regional Italian

Days Open
Open Mon.-Fri. for lunch, Mon.-Sat. for dinner

Pricing
Dinner for one, without tax, tip, or drinks: $20-$40

Dress Code
Business casual

Reservations
Recommended

Parking
Free on site

Features
Private room/parties, outdoor dining, entertainment, near theater, cigar/cognac events

Credit Cards
AE, VC, MC, CB, DC, DS

Le Mouton Noir

Directions

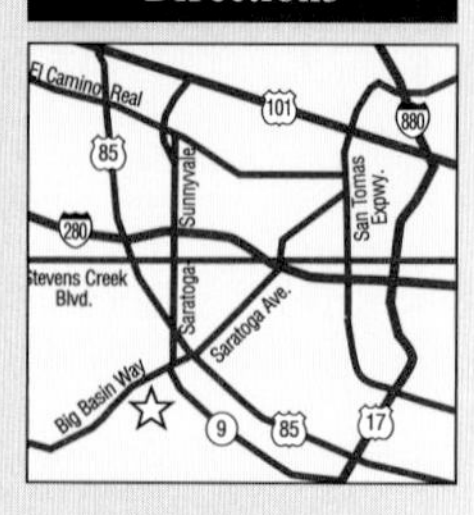

On Highway 9 between 4th and 5th streets, 20 min. from San Jose Airport

14560 Big Basin Way
Saratoga, CA 95070
PH: (408) 867-7017
FAX: (408) 867-5048
www.lemoutonnoir.citysearch.com

Owners
Jeffrey and Karen Breslow

Cuisine
French-inspired California cuisine

Days Open
Open Fri.-Sat. for lunch, daily for dinner

Pricing
Dinner for one, without tax, tip, or drinks: $40-$60

Dress Code
Business casual

Reservations
Recommended

Parking
Free on site, valet

Features
Private room/parties, outdoor dining, cognac events, wine tasting

Credit Cards
AE, VC, MC, CB, DC, DS

Grilled quail salad with poached quail eggs

Le Mouton Noir's fine food and enchanting atmosphere have made it a four-star institution for nearly 25 years. Housed in a renovated 145-year-old Victorian, the restaurant offers tantalizing, eclectic, French-inspired California cuisine, incorporating locally grown organic produce with prime meats, seafood, and exotic game. For adventurous palates, the seasonal tasting menu is ideal. The extensive wine list, the highly attentive wait staff, and sensational desserts cap off the experience.

Valrhona warm chocolate cake

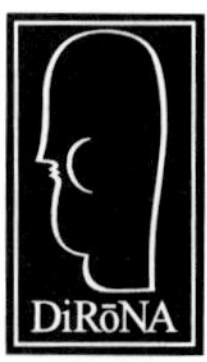

AWARD WINNER
SINCE 1992

The Plumed Horse

The Green Room

Situated in the quiet village of Saratoga, The Plumed Horse offers guests a welcome retreat and panoramic views of redwoods and the Santa Cruz Mountains. Proximity to Silicon Valley, the San Jose Convention Center, and San Jose International Airport makes The Plumed Horse a convenient meeting place for those on tight schedules. The seasonal menu changes daily, and the wine list is a winner of *Wine Spectator*'s Grand Award.

The inviting Crazy Horse Lounge

The Pache family

Rack of lamb, the house specialty

AWARD WINNER
SINCE 1992

Directions

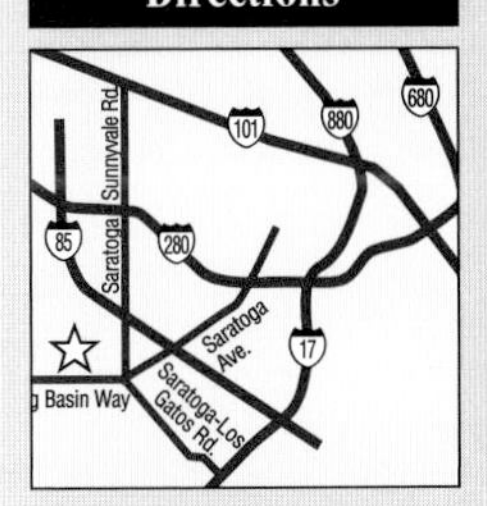

In Saratoga, 20 min. from San Jose International Airport and 45 min. from San Francisco International Airport

14555 Big Basin Way
Saratoga, CA 95070
PH: (408) 867-4711
FAX: (408) 867-6919
www.plumedhorse.com

Owners
The Pache family

Cuisine
Seasonal French country

Days Open
Open Mon.-Sat. for dinner

Pricing
Dinner for one,
without tax, tip, or drinks:
$20-$40

Dress Code
Business casual

Reservations
Recommended

Parking
Valet

Features
Private room/parties, entertainment

Credit Cards
AE, VC, MC, CB, DC

Anaheim White House

Directions

2 miles northeast of Anaheim Convention Center, 20 min. from Orange County's John Wayne Airport

887 S. Anaheim Boulevard
Anaheim, CA 92805
PH: (714) 772-1381
FAX: (714) 772-7062
www.anaheimwhitehouse.com

Owners
Bruno Serato

Cuisine
Northern Italian

Days Open
Open Mon.-Fri. for lunch, daily for dinner

Pricing
Dinner for one, without tax, tip, or drinks: $20-$40

Dress Code
Business casual

Reservations
Recommended

Parking
Valet

Features
Private room/parties, outdoor dining, entertainment

Credit Cards
AE, VC, MC

Stately elegance

Occupying a lovely home built in 1909, Anaheim White House serves award-winning Northern Italian fare — chicken breast baked in parchment with a julienne of leeks, shiitake, and broken garlic is one specialty — in eight romantic dining areas. The wine list offers nearly 200 selections. Anaheim White House is ideal for groups of all sizes, and is convenient to the Anaheim Convention Center, Arrowhead Pond, Edison Field, and major hotels.

Assortimento di Dolce

Intimate dining

AWARD WINNER
SINCE 1998

JW's Steakhouse

Even in these health-conscious times, the lure of the perfectly done steak proves irresistible and there's no better place to indulge your passion for this most simple and glorious of foods than at JW's Steakhouse, located in the Anaheim Marriott. JW's specializes in fine Angus beef, grilled to perfection. The freshest seafood is imaginatively prepared, the salads and side dishes are robust, and the wine list is first-rate. All this, in an intimate, Old World setting.

Directions

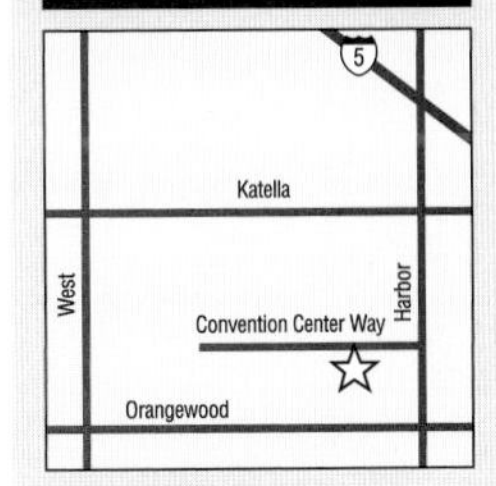

Next to the Anaheim Convention Center, 20 min. from Orange County's John Wayne Airport

700 W. Convention Way
Anaheim, CA 92802
PH: (714) 703-3187
FAX: (714) 750-9100

Owners
Marriott International

Cuisine
Traditional steakhouse

Days Open
Open Tues.-Sat. for dinner

Pricing
Dinner for one,
without tax, tip, or drinks:
$20-$40

Dress Code
Business casual

Reservations
Recommended

Parking
Valet

Features
Private room

Credit Cards
AE, VC, MC, CB, DC, ER, JCB, DS

AWARD WINNER
SINCE 1992

Hasting's Grill

Directions

91
Riverside Fwy.
5
Santa Ana Fwy.
West St.
Disneyland® Park
Katella Ave.
Anaheim Conv. Center
Harbor Blvd.
Convention Way
Chapman Ave.
Garden Grove Fwy.
22

At Hilton Anaheim, next to the Anaheim Convention Center and 20 min. from Orange County's John Wayne Airport

777 Convention Way
Anaheim, CA 92802
PH: (714) 740-4422
FAX: (714) 740-4702
www.anaheim.hilton.com

Owners
Hilton Anaheim

Cuisine
California

Days Open
Open daily for dinner

Pricing
Dinner for one,
without tax, tip, or drinks:
$20-$40

Dress Code
Business casual

Reservations
Recommended

Parking
Free on site, valet

Features
Private parties

Credit Cards
AE, VC, MC, CB, DC, ER, JCB, DS

Main dining room

Located in the Hilton Anaheim in the convention district, the critically acclaimed Hasting's Grill is renowned for an innovative menu that draws on the best influence of California and Pacific Rim cuisines. Polished brass, mahogany paneling, and etched glass create an elegant yet informal club-like setting. Attentive, personal service and an extensive wine list enhance the dining experience. Specialties include lobster tail and Japanese white noodles, and grilled marinated lamb brochette.

Dramatic entryway

Food and beverage team

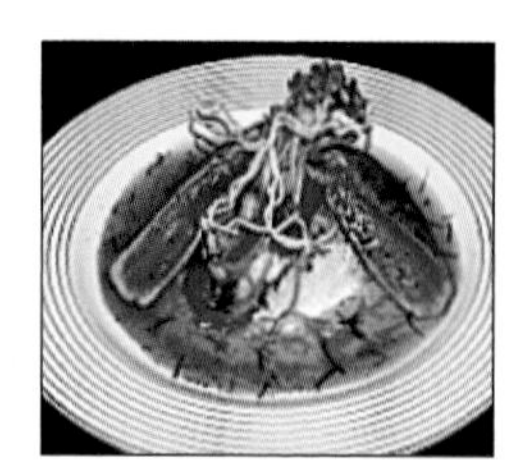

Innovative Pacific Rim creations

AWARD WINNER
SINCE 1998

Mr. Stox

Convenient to the Anaheim Convention Center, Mr. Stox has been operated by the Marshall family since 1977. The early Mission-style exterior belies the elegant dining rooms and cozy fireplace inside. The menu features Colorado lamb, veal, prime steaks, and a wide variety of fresh fish. Mr. Stox is noted for its home-baked breads and pastries, fresh pastas, and exquisite desserts. The award-winning wine cellar has a staggering 24,000 bottles.

Brothers Ron (sitting) and Chick Marshall and Ron's wife, Debbie

AWARD WINNER
SINCE 1998

Directions

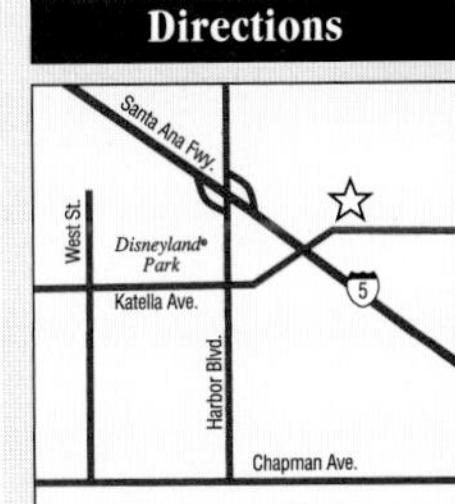

At E. Katella Avenue and State College Boulevard, near Anaheim Convention Center and 20 min. from Orange County's John Wayne Airport

1105 E. Katella Avenue
Anaheim, CA 92805
PH: (714) 634-2994
FAX: (714) 634-0561
www.mrstox.com

Owners
Chick Marshall and Ron and Debbie Marshall

Cuisine
Contemporary Continental

Days Open
Open Mon.-Fri. for lunch, daily for dinner

Pricing
Dinner for one, without tax, tip, or drinks: $40-$60

Dress Code
Business casual

Reservations
Recommended

Parking
Valet

Features
Private room/parties, entertainment

Credit Cards
AE, VC, MC, CB, DC, DS

The Grill on the Alley

The place for power lunches

Directions

Burton Way
Santa Monica Blvd.
Dayton Way
Wilshire Blvd.
Camden Dr.

At Dayton Way and Wilshire Boulevard in the heart of Beverly Hills, 20 min. from Los Angeles International Airport

9560 Dayton Way
Beverly Hills, CA 90212
PH: (310) 276-0615
FAX: (310) 276-0284
www.thegrill.com

Owners
Grill Concepts Inc.

Cuisine
American

Days Open
Open Mon.-Sat. for lunch, daily for dinner

Pricing
Dinner for one, without tax, tip, or drinks: $40-$60

Dress Code
Business casual

Reservations
Recommended

Parking
Valet

Features
Private parties

Credit Cards
AE, VC, MC, DC

When Angelenos are in search of exceptionally fresh grill fare in a truly American setting, they head for this popular Beverly Hills restaurant, a power lunch spot where talent agents and stars frequently talk business over steaks and martinis. The Grill's founders, Dick Shapiro, Bob Spivak, and Mike Weinstock, along with Executive Chef John Sola, have continued the legend of the great grill restaurants found in New York and San Francisco, and built a comfortable, inviting restaurant with a sophisticated big-city spirit.

The bar

AWARD WINNER
SINCE 1997

La Vie en Rose

Main dining room

La Vie en Rose is a charming reproduction of a Normandy farmhouse in the heart of Orange County. Proprietor Louis Laulhere came to America with family recipes from Gascony and Provence. La Vie en Rose means "life is rosy," and that is how an evening here will make you feel. An extensive wine list complements such specialties as roasted rack of lamb and sauteed duck breast.

Lavender Room

Summer Room

Wine Room

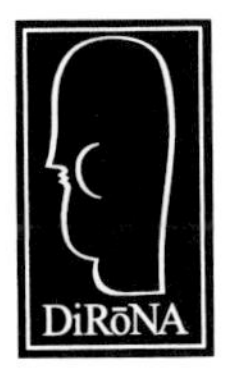

AWARD WINNER
SINCE 1993

Directions

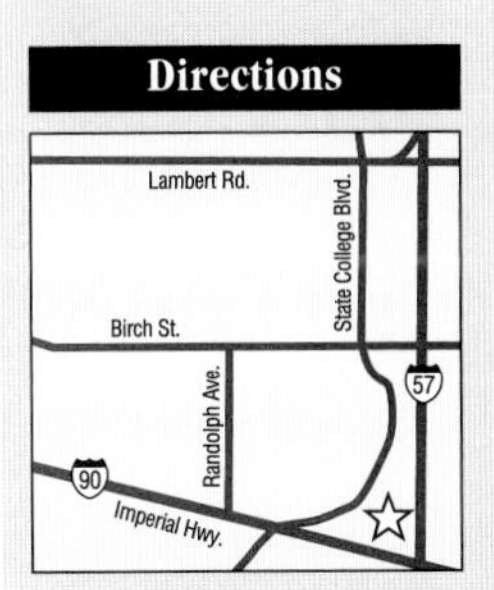

On State College Boulevard, 15 min. from John Wayne/ Orange County Airport

240 S. State College Boulevard
Brea, CA 92821
PH: (714) 529-8333
FAX: (714) 529-2751
www.lavnrose.com

Owners
Louis Laulhere

Cuisine
French Country

Days Open
Open Mon.-Fri. for lunch, Mon.-Sat. for dinner

Pricing
Dinner for one, without tax, tip, or drinks: $20-$40

Dress Code
Dressy casual

Reservations
Recommended

Parking
Free on site

Features
Private rooms/parties, outdoor dining, cognac events and other special events, near theater

Credit Cards
AE, VC, MC

Five Crowns

Directions

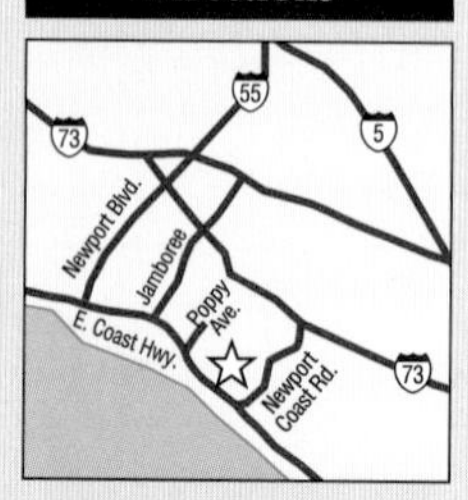

A mile south of MacArthur Boulevard, 15 min. from Orange County's John Wayne Airport

3801 East Coast Highway
Corona del Mar, CA 92625
PH: (949) 760-0331
FAX: (949) 760-3987
www.lawrysonline.com

Owners
Lawry's Restaurants, Inc.

Cuisine
Continental

Days Open
Open daily for dinner, Sun. brunch

Pricing
Dinner for one,
without tax, tip or drinks:
$20-$40

Dress Code
Business casual

Reservations
Recommended

Parking
Valet

Features
Private room/parties, outdoor dining, wine dinners, weddings

Credit Cards
AE, VC, MC, DC, DS, JCB

A 35-year tradition

A beautiful replica of one of England's oldest country inns, Five Crowns is a place of candlelight and cozy fireplaces, where good cheer and warm hospitality invite guests to leave their cares at the door. There is something to delight the eye at every turn, with many antiques and rare paintings. Visitors also find award-winning food, exceptional service and unmistakable style that have made this establishment a dining legend since 1965.

An elegant dining room

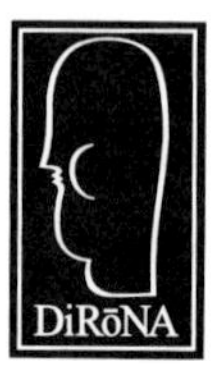

AWARD WINNER
SINCE 1999

The Cellar

Main dining room

Discriminating diners expect nothing less than the best — divine cuisine, impeccable service, award-winning wine selection, and a beautiful setting — and The Cellar delivers. Chef de Cuisine David Kesler has created a menu full of such memorable dishes as grilled veal chop with apples, walnuts, Calvados, and saffron parsleyed risotto, not to mention roasted breast of Muscovy duck with poached sour cherries, cherry brandy, and The Cellar's own duck stock reduction. Year after year, The Cellar maintains a tradition of gracious European cuisine and service.

Convivial bar

Rack of lamb

Trudy and Ernest Zingg

AWARD WINNER
SINCE 1995

Directions

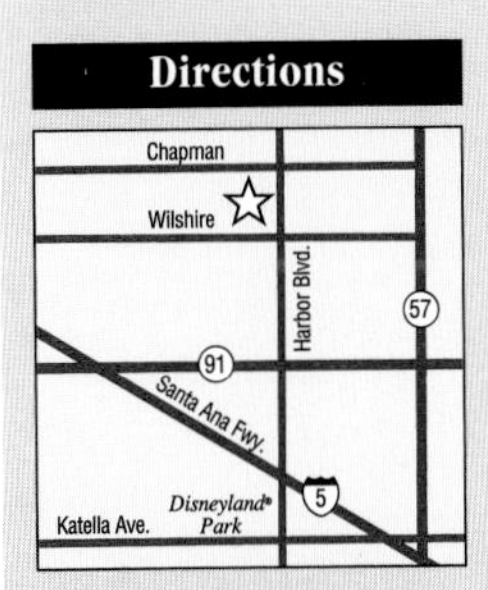

On North Harbor Boulevard, 20 min. from Orange County's John Wayne Airport and 35 min. from Los Angeles International

305 N. Harbor Boulevard
Fullerton, CA 92832
PH: (714) 525-5682
FAX: (714) 525-3853
www.imenu.com/thecellar

Owners
Ernest and Trudy Zingg

Cuisine
Classic French

Days Open
Open Tues.-Sat. for dinner

Pricing
Dinner for one,
without tax, tip, or drinks:
$20-$40

Dress Code
Business casual

Reservations
Recommended

Parking
Free on site, complimentary valet, garage nearby

Features
Private room/parties, near theater

Credit Cards
AE, VC, MC, CB, DC, JCB, DS

Gennaro's Ristorante

Directions

Kenneth Rd.
Mountain St.
Central Ave.
Brand Blvd.
Stocker St.
Glenoaks Blvd.

2 blocks north of the 134 Freeway, 15 min. from Burbank-Glendale-Pasadena Airport

1109 N. Brand Boulevard
Glendale, CA 91202
PH: (818) 243-6231
FAX: (818) 243-8628

Owners
Gennaro Rosato

Cuisine
Italian

Days Open
Open Mon.-Fri. for lunch, Mon.-Sat. for dinner

Pricing
Dinner for one, without tax, tip or drinks: $20-$40

Dress Code
Business casual

Reservations
Recommended

Parking
Valet

Features
Private parties

Credit Cards
AE, VC, MC, CB, DC

A Glendale landmark

This intimate, elegant restaurant delights both loyal patrons and newcomers, who often come to celebrate special occasions. Service is warm and attentive, and the Northern Italian fare is delicious and inviting. Feast on roast pheasant with pearl onions and Marsala wine sauce, or Muscovy duck breast sauteed in port and garnished with fresh melon. "A restaurant for wine lovers," according to *Wine Spectator*; the wine list features over 150 Italian, French, and California selections.

Cozy fireplace

The bar

The dining room

AWARD WINNER
SINCE 1995

George's at the Cove

Chef Trey Foshee and owners George Hauer and Mark Oliver at La Jolla Cove

This acclaimed restaurant offers three levels of dining overlooking picturesque La Jolla Cove, the atmosphere ranging from elegant in the first-level Ocean View Room to very casual on the rooftop Ocean Terrace. Executive Chef Trey Foshee's menu includes such innovative fare as seared rare ahi tuna with olive smashed potatoes, shaved raw artichoke salad, and saffron aioli; and grilled rack of lamb with green lentil, apple, and celery root ragout, baby spinach, fresh yogurt, and curried lamb jus. Little surprise that George's was again voted San Diego's most popular restaurant in the 1999 *Zagat Survey*.

AWARD WINNER
SINCE 1992

Directions

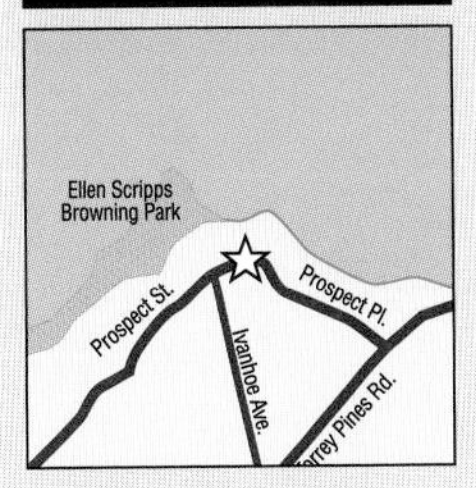

On Prospect Street in heart of La Jolla, 20 min. from San Diego International Airport

1250 Prospect Street
La Jolla, CA 92037
PH: (858) 454-4244
FAX: (858) 454-5458
www.georgesatthecove.com

Owners
George Hauer and Mark Oliver

Cuisine
Creative regional

Days Open
Open daily for lunch and dinner

Pricing
Dinner for one,
without tax, tip, or drinks:
$40-$60

Dress Code
Business casual

Reservations
Recommended

Parking
Valet

Features
Private room/parties, outdoor dining

Credit Cards
AE, VC, MC, CB, DC, DS

The Marine Room

Directions

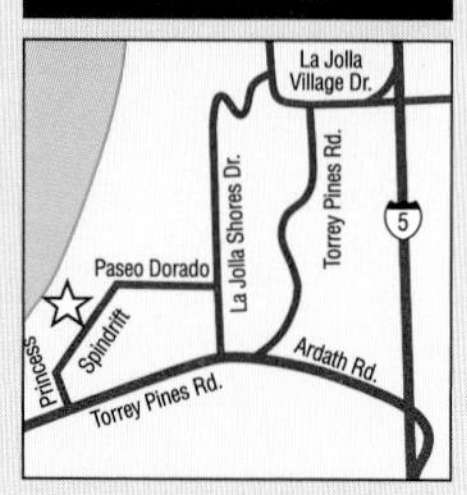

Off Torrey Pines Road in La Jolla Shores, 25 min. from San Diego International Airport

2000 Sprindrift Drive
La Jolla, CA 92037
PH: (858) 459-7222
FAX: (858) 551-4673
www.marineroom.com

Owners
La Jolla Beach & Tennis Club, Inc.

Cuisine
Continental with French flair

Days Open
Open daily for lunch and dinner

Pricing
Dinner for one,
without tax, tip, or drinks:
$40-$60

Dress Code
Business casual

Reservations
Strongly recommended

Parking
Free on site, valet

Features
Private parties, entertainment

Credit Cards
AE, VC, MC, CB, DC, ER, JCB, DS

Elegance by the sea

The Marine Room, at the La Jolla Beach & Tennis Club, has been a citadel of sophisticated dining for more than half a century. Graceful service and soft music complement a superb wine list and the Continental cuisine orchestrated by award-winning Executive Chef Bernard Guillas, a James Beard House invitee in 2000. The atmosphere is warm and inviting, with exhilarating ocean vistas, and there is live entertainment and dancing nightly.

Creative entrees

Executive Chef Bernard Guillas

The Marine Room, circa 1949

AWARD WINNER
SINCE 1996

Cafe Del Rey

Main dining room

Overlooking the Marina del Rey yacht harbor, this casually elegant restaurant is proof that you can have your view and eat well too. Nationally acclaimed Executive Chef Katsuo Nagasawa directs a kitchen that turns out a blend of classic French, Italian, and Pacific Rim cuisine. An impressive collection of California and imported wines adds to the dining experience. Cafe Del Rey has a patio for al fresco dining and an inviting bar area with adjacent lounge and fireplace for conversation and relaxation.

Oven roasted seafood tower

Executive Chef Katsuo Nagasawa

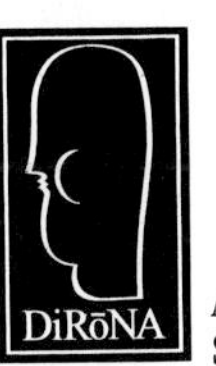

AWARD WINNER
SINCE 1996

Directions

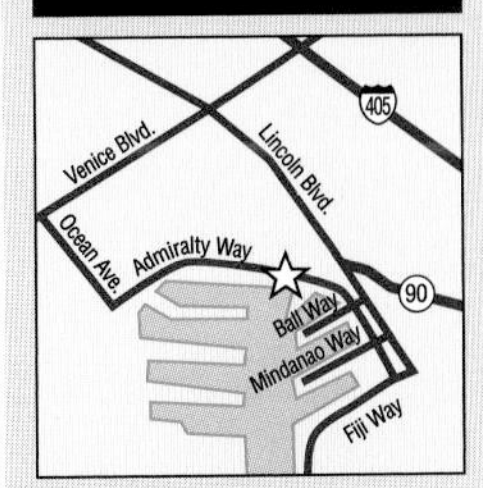

On yacht harbor in Marina del Rey, near 90 Freeway and 15 min. from Los Angeles International Airport

4451 Admiralty Way
Marina del Rey, CA 90292
PH: (310) 823-6395
FAX: (310) 821-3734
www.calcafe.com

Owners
Constellation Concepts Inc.

Cuisine
Blend of classic French, Italian, and Pacific Rim

Days Open
Open daily for lunch and dinner

Pricing
Dinner for one, without tax, tip, or drinks: $40-$60

Dress Code
Business casual

Reservations
Recommended

Parking
Free on site, valet

Features
Private room/parties, outdoor dining, entertainment

Credit Cards
AE, VC, MC, CB, DC, DS

Pavilion

Directions

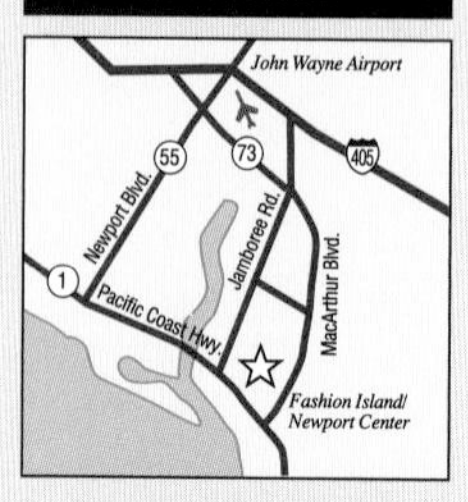

On Newport Center Drive, 15 min. from Orange County's John Wayne Airport

690 Newport Center Drive
Newport Beach, CA 92660
PH: (949) 760-4920
FAX: (949) 760-8073
www.fourseasons.com

Owners
Four Seasons Hotel Newport Beach

Cuisine
California, with Mediterranean influences

Days Open
Open daily for breakfast, lunch, and dinner

Pricing
Dinner for one, without tax, tip, or drinks: $40-$60

Dress Code
Business casual

Reservations
Recommended

Parking
Complimentary valet

Features
Private room, outdoor dining

Credit Cards
AE, VC, MC, CB, DC, JCB, DS

An elegant dining experience

In a community renowned for its casual grace, Four Seasons Hotel Newport Beach is the preeminent example of gracious hospitality. Enjoy Newport Beach's finest dining experience at Pavilion, where the specialties include Pacific sea bass broiled under fresh herb crust; pepper-crusted lamb with port wine reduction; and Grand Marnier soufflé with orange Anglaise. The chef's daily prix fixe menu is the best value in town.

Gardens Lounge

Petit Pavilion

Four Seasons Hotel Newport Beach

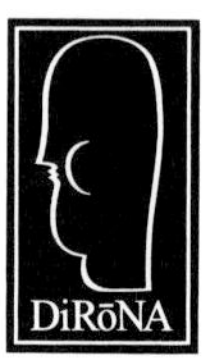

AWARD WINNER SINCE 1992

The Ritz Restaurant & Garden

Escoffier Room

With service that *Condé Nast Traveler* has called the "Best in America," The Ritz Restaurant & Garden offers an experience to remember. The formal Escoffier Room, causal outdoor Garden, and clubby bar all offer a full menu of contemporary dishes, fresh seasonal fare, unique desserts, and an award-winning wine list. Locals have voted this their "most popular" gathering place, but it also appeals to visiting dignitaries. There is live piano music nightly.

Epicurean wine cellar

AWARD WINNER
SINCE 1992

Directions

On Newport Center Drive, 15 min. from Orange County's John Wayne Airport

880 Newport Center Drive
Newport Beach, CA 92660
PH: (949) 720-1800
FAX: (949) 720-3973
www.theritzrestaurant.com

Owners
Hans and Charlene Prager

Cuisine
Classic Continental with contemporary California influence

Days Open
Mon.-Fri. for lunch, daily for dinner

Pricing
Dinner for one,
without tax, tip, or drinks:
$40-$60

Dress Code
Business casual

Reservations
Recommended

Parking
Valet

Features
Private room/parties, outdoor dining, entertainment, near theater, cigar/cognac events

Credit Cards
AE, VC, MC, DC

Le Petit Chateau

San Fernando Valley landmark

Directions

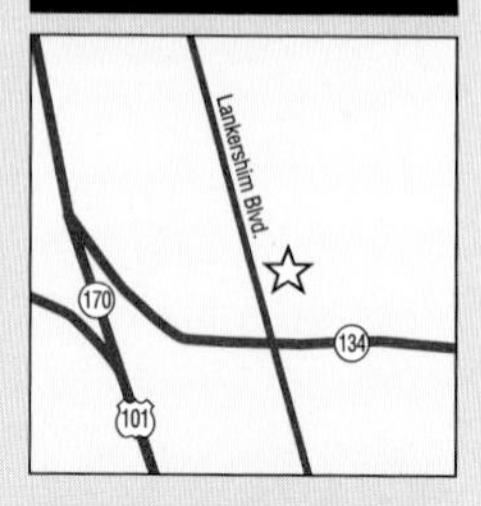

On Lankershim Boulevard just north of Riverside Drive in the San Fernando Valley, 10 min. from Burbank Airport and 30 min. from Los Angeles International

4615 Lankershim Boulevard
North Hollywood, CA 91602
PH: (818) 769-1812
FAX: (818) 769-3431

Owners
Andrew and Christiane Higgs

Cuisine
French

Days Open
Open Mon.-Fri. for lunch, daily for dinner

Pricing
Dinner for one, without tax, tip, or drinks: $20-$40

Dress Code
Business casual

Reservations
Recommended

Parking
Valet

Features
Private parties, near theater

Credit Cards
AE, VC, MC, CB, DC, DS

Trendy restaurants come and go, but few stand the test of time. Le Petit Chateau, a true San Fernando Valley landmark, is one of those few. It has been serving classic French country cooking for 35 years. From tender veal specialties to steaks and seafood, the menu has all your favorites (don't miss the roast duck). Le Petit Chateau is easily reached by all major freeways and is a mile from Universal Studios.

Dining room

Owners Christiane and Andrew Higgs

AWARD WINNER
SINCE 1996

The Hobbit

An Orange landmark since 1972

The Hobbit has offered a truly elegant dining experience since 1972, winning numerous awards in the process. The menu changes weekly. A seven-course prix fixe meal begins with champagne and hors d'ouevres in the award-winning wine cellar, which boasts more than 1,000 selections. Once seated, diners enjoy an appetizer, a fish or fowl course, and salad. Then comes a brief intermission to meet the chef-proprietor, Michael Philippi, or linger on the patio before settling in for the main course and dessert.

Owners Debra and Michael Philippi

Michael Philippi in the wine cellar

AWARD WINNER
SINCE 1999

Directions

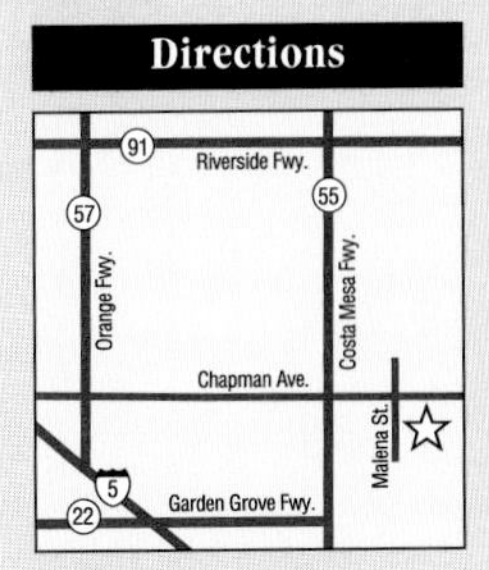

Less than a mile from Costa Mesa Freeway, 15 min. from Orange County's John Wayne Airport

2932 E. Chapman Avenue
Orange, CA 92869
PH: (714) 997-1972
FAX: (714) 997-3181

Owners
Michael and Debra Philippi

Cuisine
Contemporary Continental

Days Open
Open Tues.-Sun. for dinner

Pricing
Dinner for one,
without tax, tip, or drinks:
$40-$60

Dress Code
Business casual

Reservations
Required

Parking
Free on site

Features
Private room/parties

Credit Cards
VC, MC

LG's Prime Steakhouse

Directions

Monterey Ave.
Portola Ave.
Deep Canyon Rd.
111
74
Shadow Mountain Dr.

On Highway 111 near the Hyatt Regency Grand Champions, 30 min. from Palm Springs Regional Airport

74-225 Highway 111
Palm Desert, CA 92260
PH: (760) 779-9799
FAX: (760) 779-1979
www.lgsprimesteakhouse.com

Owners
Leon and Gail Greenberg

Cuisine
USDA Prime steak

Days Open
Open daily for dinner

Pricing
Dinner for one,
without tax, tip, or drinks:
$40-$60

Dress Code
Casual

Reservations
Recommended

Parking
Free on site, valet

Features
Private parties

Credit Cards
AE, VC, MC, DC, DS

The place for great steaks

Housed in a historic adobe building, award-winning LG's features eight different USDA Prime sizzling steaks and has an 'on-premises' dry-age facility for its "Jewel in the Crown," a 20-ounce porterhouse for one, and the even bigger 30-ounce porterhouse dubbed "The Gold Strike 49er." The menu also features rack of lamb, prime rib, and fresh fish and seafood. The LG's at 255 South Palm Canyon in Palm Springs serves the same great menu.

Owners Gail and Leon Greenberg

Sizzled to perfection

Service by the armful

AWARD WINNER
SINCE 1998

Melvyn's Restaurant

Main dining room

With intimate ambience, gracious service, and elegant decor, magical Melvyn's, located at the Ingleside Inn, provides the perfect setting for cozy Continental dining. This restaurant was the 1999 winner of four prestigious awards from the *Desert Sun*, including Best Fine Dining and Most Romantic Restaurant. Guests delight in oysters Rockefeller, baked with a special Pernod-spinach topping glazed with Hollandaise, and chateaubriand bouquetiere for two, carved tableside and served with Bordelaise sauce and fresh vegetables.

Casablanca Lounge

Owner Mel Haber

Al fresco dining on patio

AWARD WINNER
SINCE 1999

Directions

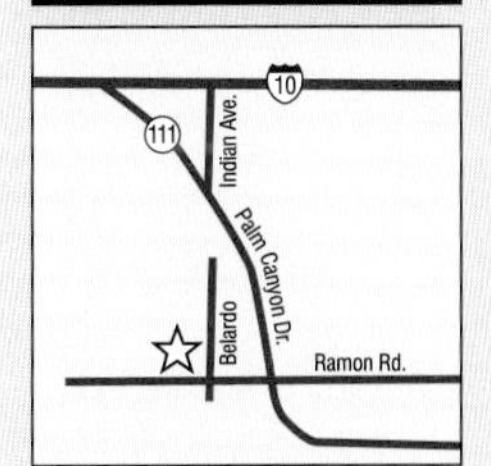

On West Ramon Road, 7 min. from Palm Springs Regional Airport

200 W. Ramon Road
Palm Springs, CA 92264
PH: (760) 325-2323
FAX: (760) 325-0710
www.inglesideinn.com

Owners
Mel Haber

Cuisine
Continental

Days Open
Open daily for lunch and dinner, Sat.-Sun. for brunch

Pricing
Dinner for one, without tax, tip, or drinks: $20-$40

Dress Code
Business casual

Reservations
Recommended

Parking
Valet

Features
Private room/parties, outdoor dining, entertainment, near theater

Credit Cards
AE, VC, MC, CB, DC

Wally's Desert Turtle

Directions

On Highway 111, 25 min. from Palm Springs Regional Airport

71-775 Highway 111
Rancho Mirage, CA 92270
PH: (760) 568-9321
FAX: (760) 568-9713
www.wallys-desert-turtle.com

Owners
Michael Botello

Cuisine
French Continental

Days Open
Open daily for dinner (closed June through Sept.)

Pricing
Dinner for one, without tax, tip, or drinks: $40-$60

Dress Code
Business casual

Reservations
Required

Parking
Valet

Features
Private room/parties, entertainment

Credit Cards
AE, VC, MC, DC

Semi-private dining room

A culinary oasis in the desert, Wally's Desert Turtle serves unforgettable Continental cuisine amid the elegance of beveled, mirrored ceilings, Peruvian artifacts, and hand-painted murals. Don't miss the fresh foie gras with apricot, pistachio, organic greens, and sweet Marsala or the imported Dover sole almandine. More than 200 selections of imported and California wines complement the menu. Catering is available, and large groups can "buy out" the entire restaurant.

Exquisite cuisine

Garden patio

Rack of lamb and other delicacies

AWARD WINNER
SINCE 1994

Mille Fleurs

Hearthside dining

Located in the heart of a historic village, this nationally acclaimed restaurant offers haute cuisine in gracious surroundings. Chef Martin Woesle creates new menus daily, using seasonal ingredients that inspire his artistry. Owner Bertrand Hug lends his charismatic charm to the dining room, a collection of intimate dining areas with two fireplaces. An award-winning wine lists adds to this delightful culinary experience.

The Terrace Room

AWARD WINNER
SINCE 1992

Directions

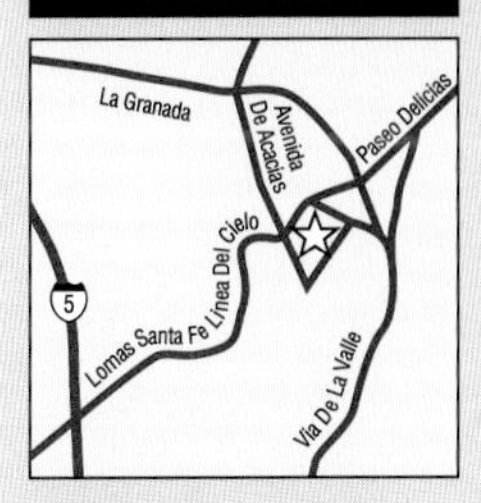

In Rancho Santa Fe, 35 min. from San Diego International Airport

6009 Paseo Delicias
P.O. Box 2548
Rancho Santa Fe, CA
92067
PH: (858) 756-3085
FAX: (858) 756-9945
www.millefleurs.com

Owners
Bertrand

Cuisine
French

Days Open
Open Mon.-Fri. for lunch, daily for dinner

Pricing
Dinner for one, without tax, tip, or drinks: $60-$80

Dress Code
Business casual

Reservations
Recommended

Parking
Free on site

Features
Private room/parties, outdoor dining, entertainment

Credit Cards
AE, VC, MC, DC

Anthony's Star of the Sea

Directions

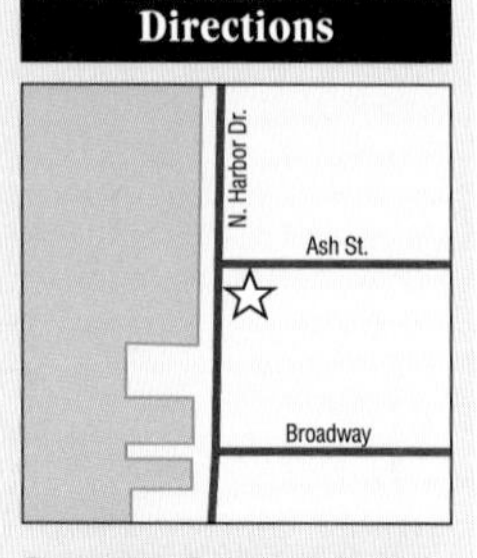

On Harbor Drive just north of Broadway in downtown, 5 min. from San Diego International Airport

Anthony's Star of the Sea
1360 Harbor Drive
San Diego, CA 92101
PH: (619) 232-7408
FAX: (619) 232-1877
www.starofthesea.com

Owners
Ghio and Mascari families

Cuisine
Seafood fine dining

Days Open
Open daily for dinner

Pricing
Dinner for one,
without tax, tip, or drinks:
$40-$60

Dress Code
Business casual

Reservations
Recommended

Parking
Valet

Features
Jazz on Thursday and Friday nights

Credit Cards
AE, VC, MC, CB, DC, DS

Main dining room

Anthony's Star of the Sea, on San Diego's bustling bay front, creates magical moments with innovative, uncompromising coastal cuisine and caring, stylish service. The beautiful water views provide fresh sunsets, served nightly. By using only the day's freshest seafood and ingredients, Chef Brian Johnston embraces the French concept of *cuisine actuelle*. The result is coastal cuisine, unique to San Diego.

On the bay

Chef Brian Johnston

AWARD WINNER
SINCE 1993

El Bizcocho

Main dining room

El Bizcocho, the top-rated San Diego restaurant in the *Zagat Survey,* serves classical French cuisine and seasonal specialties with unparalleled service and style. Located at the Rancho Bernardo Inn, El Bizcocho seamlessly combines elegance with warmth and comfort in its newly redesigned dining room. The eloquence of the cuisine, service, and atmosphere is complemented by one of California's most extensive wine lists.

Fine French cuisine

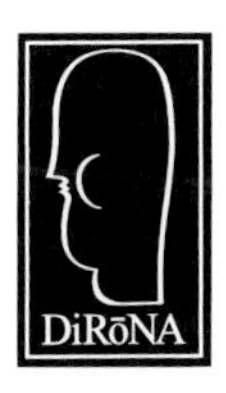

AWARD WINNER
SINCE 1992

Directions

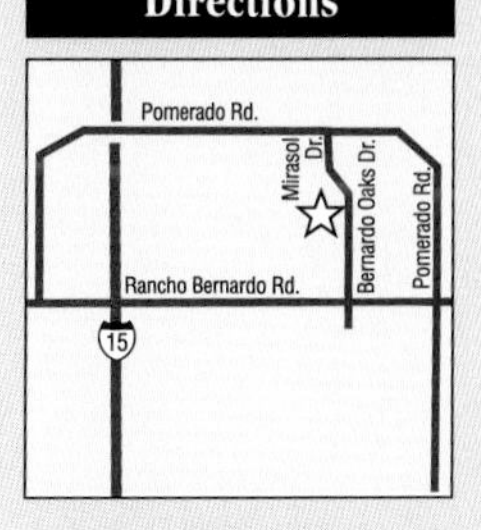

At Rancho Bernardo Inn off Interstate 15, 25 min. from San Diego International Airport

17550 Bernardo Oaks Drive
San Diego, CA 92128
PH: (858) 675-8550
FAX: (858) 675-8443
www.jcresorts.com

Owners
JC Resorts

Cuisine
Gourmet French

Days Open
Open Sun. for brunch, daily for dinner

Pricing
Dinner for one,
without tax, tip, or drinks:
$40-$60

Dress Code
Jacket and tie required

Reservations
Recommended

Parking
Free on site, valet

Credit Cards
AE, VC, MC, DC, DS

Grant Grill

Directions

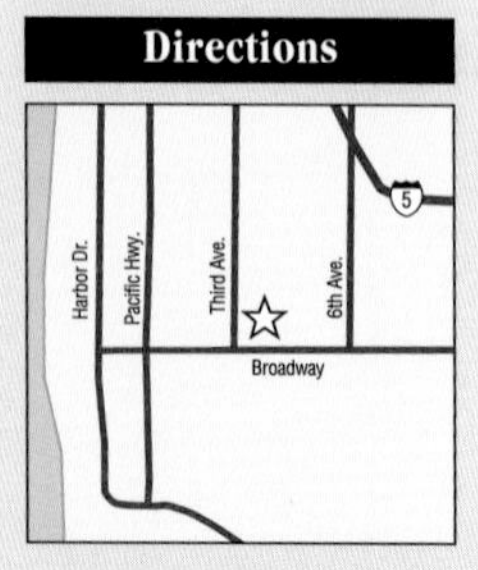

On Broadway between Third and Fourth avenues, 10 min. from San Diego International Airport

326 Broadway
San Diego, CA 92101
PH: (619) 239-6806
FAX: (619) 239-9517
www.usgranthotel.com

Owners
U.S. Grant Hotel

Cuisine
Moderate French Continental

Days Open
Open daily for breakfast, lunch, and dinner

Pricing
Dinner for one, without tax, tip, or drinks: $20-$40

Dress Code
Jacket and tie appropriate

Reservations
Recommended

Parking
Free on site, garage nearby

Credit Cards
AE, VC, MC, DC, DS

Chef de Cuisine Marc Gomez

A San Diego institution since 1910, the Grant Grill, in the historic U.S. Grant Hotel, evokes a New York chop house and was recently rated as "The Best Place to Bring a Client" by *San Diego Magazine*. Executive Chef Marc Gomez orchestrates a menu that includes such specialties as prime rib, beef carpaccio, veal sweetbreads, and the Grant Grill's signature dish, mock turtle soup. Diners can enjoy San Diego's vibrant downtown scene at the sidewalk cafe.

Seared ahi Provencal

Christopher DiNofia and Chef Marc Gomez

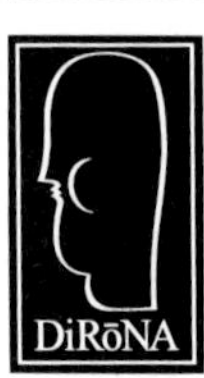

AWARD WINNER
SINCE 1992

Rainwater's on Kettner

Elegant dining

Since 1985 San Diego's only Eastern-style chophouse has exuded warmth and subdued elegance with rich wood paneling, intimate leather booths, and crisp white linen. Rainwater's on Kettner features prime, Midwestern, corn-fed aged beef, the finest and freshest seafood from around the world, veal, lamb, and pork chops. *Wine Spectator* has honored Rainwater's with its Best of Excellence Award since 1986, and the restaurant was chosen as one of the top steakhouses in America by *Gourmet* magazine.

Prime beef

Creative fish entrees

Dining room

AWARD WINNER
SINCE 1999

Directions

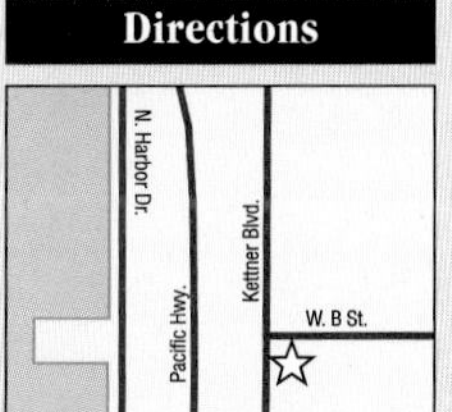

On Kettner Boulevard downtown, 5 min. from San Diego International Airport

1202 Kettner Boulevard
San Diego, CA 92101
PH: (619) 233-5757
FAX: (619) 233-6722
www.rainwaters.com

Owners
Laurel and Paddy Rainwater

Cuisine
American

Days Open
Open Mon.-Fri. for lunch, daily for dinner

Pricing
Dinner for one, without tax, tip, or drinks: $40-$60

Dress Code
Business casual

Reservations
Recommended

Parking
Free on site, valet, lot nearby

Features
Private room/partico, near theater

Credit Cards
AE, VC, MC, CB, DC

Downey's

Directions

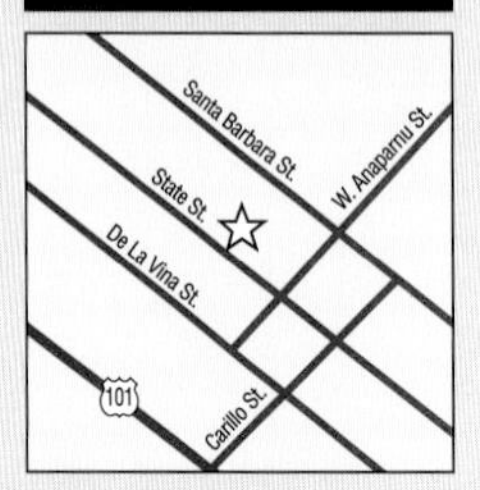

On State Street near Victoria, 15 minutes from Santa Barbara Airport

1305 State Street
Santa Barbara, CA 93101
PH: (805) 966-5006
FAX: (805) 966-5000
www.downeyssb.com

Owners
John and Liz Downey

Cuisine
California-French

Days Open
Open Tues.-Sun. for dinner

Pricing
Dinner for one,
without tax, tip or drinks:
$40-$60

Dress Code
Business casual

Reservations
Recommended

Parking
On-street parking nearby

Features
Near theater

Credit Cards
VC, MC, DS

The dining room

When John Downey opened his namesake restaurant in 1982, the concept was simple: Serve the very best food available, and serve it in a comfortable, unpretentious setting where it would be easy to drop in for an exquisite dinner. The idea worked so well that 18 years later the same tenet still applies. It has not gone unnoticed by the dining press, which over the years has consistently awarded Downey's top honors for fine dining.

John and Liz Downey

Roast squab with garlic cloves and mustard greens

AWARD WINNER
SINCE 1992

Renaissance

Main dining room

Celebrating its 10th anniversary, Renaissance has gained international renown for its innovative cuisine, casually elegant service, and extensive wine program — all in a relaxed and cozy room. Chef-owner Charles Dale delights diners with such specialties as espresso-blackened tenderloin of beef, crispy Chilean sea bass with artichokes, shiitakes, and foie gras, and two tasting menus that change nightly. Don't miss the fabulous desserts!

Espresso-blackened tenderloin of beef

Chef-owner Charles Dale

Maine lobster salad with melon and fiery peanuts

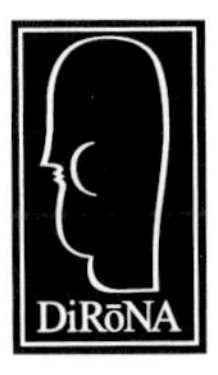

AWARD WINNER
SINCE 1999

Directions

S. Monarch
S. Mill
Main St.
E. Hopkins Ave.

At E. Hopkins and S. Monarch in Aspen, 10 min. from Aspen Airport

304 E. Hopkins
Aspen, CO 81611
PH: (970) 925-2402
FAX: (970) 925-6634
www.renaissancerestaurant.com

Owners
Charles Dale

Cuisine
Modern French, haute rustic

Days Open
Open daily for dinner (closed May and October)

Pricing
Dinner for one, without tax, tip, or drinks: $60-$80

Dress Code
Casual

Reservations
Recommended

Parking
Valet nearby

Features
Private room/parties, outdoor dining, near theater

Credit Cards
AE, VC, MC, DC

Beano's Cabin

Directions

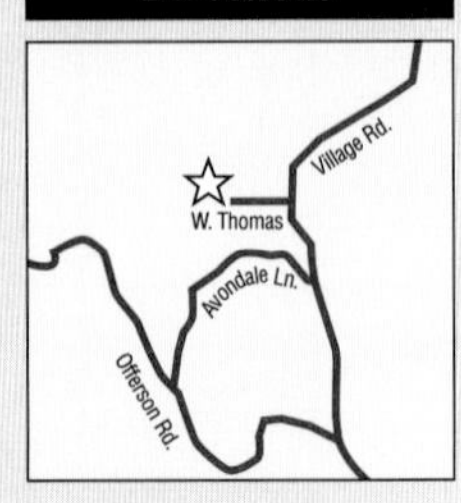

On Beaver Creek Mountain, 30 min. from Eagle County Airport

Post Office Box 915
Avon, CO 81620
PH: (970) 845-5770
Reservations: (970) 949-9090
FAX: (970) 845-5769
www.beavercreek.com
www.mountainevents.com

Owners
Vail Resorts

Cuisine
Colorado cuisine

Days Open
Open daily for dinner Dec.-mid-April, Wed.-Sun. for dinner June-Sept.

Pricing
Dinner for one, without tax, tip, or drinks: $60-$80

Dress Code
Casual

Reservations
Required

Parking
Garage nearby

Features
Semi-private room/parties, live entertainment

Credit Cards
AE, VC, MC, DC, DS

Beano's Cabin is a destination restaurant high in the Rocky Mountains. This AAA Three-Diamond eatery combines spectacular views with a memorable dining adventure in the Larkspur Bowl of Beaver Creek, Colorado. In the winter months your experience begins with a snowcat-drawn sleigh ride up Beaver Creek Mountain. In the summertime, guests may arrive on horseback or take a wagon ride pulled by antique tractors. Once there, diners delight in the five-course menu offering unique choices paired with award-winning wine selections and excellent service.

Executive Chef David J. Clark

Beano's dining room

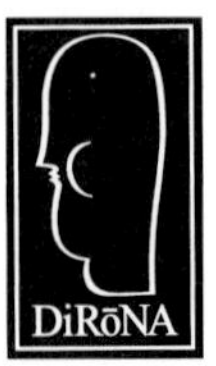

AWARD WINNER
SINCE 1993

Mirabelle Restaurant at Beaver Creek

Dining room

Tucked away amid the blue spruce and quaking aspen at the base of Beaver Creek Resort, Mirabelle Restaurant is housed in a restored 19th century farmhouse. Master Chef Daniel Joly has created a menu using only the freshest ingredients. Selections range from rabbit stewed with prunes in Belgian monks beer and roasted garlic potatoes to roasted elk gateau with poached baby pear, potato gnocchi, and rhubarb coulis. Exacting service and an award-winning wine list make Mirabelle Restaurant the perfect setting for a romantic evening.

Roasted elk with black truffle mashed potatoes

Master Chef Daniel Joly

AWARD WINNER
SINCE 1994

Directions

Exit 163
70
6
Beaver Creek Resort

Across from Welcome Center at the Beaver Creek ski resort, 20 min. from Eagle County Airport and 2 hrs. from Denver International

55 Village Road
Avon, CO 81620
PH: (970) 949-7728
FAX: (970) 845-9578

Owners
Daniel and Nathalie Joly

Cuisine
Contemporary European/Belgian

Days Open
Open Mon.-Sat. for dinner (closed late April through late May and late October through late November)

Pricing
Dinner for one, without tax, tip, or drinks: $40-$60

Dress Code
Casual

Reservations
Recommended

Parking
Garage nearby

Features
Private room/parties, outdoor dining

Credit Cards
AE, VC, MC, DS

Charles Court

Directions

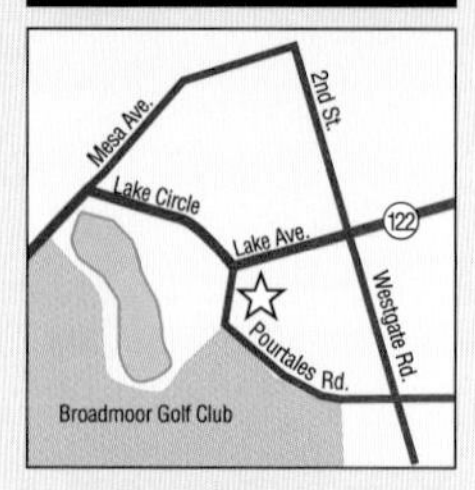

At The Broadmoor resort, 25 min. from Colorado Springs Municipal Airport

One Lake Avenue
Colorado Springs, CO 80906
PH: (719) 577-5774
FAX: (719) 577-5709
www.broadmoor.com

Owners
Oklahoma Publishing Company

Cuisine
American regional

Days Open
Open daily for dinner

Pricing
Dinner for one, without tax, tip, or drinks: $40-$60

Dress Code
Business casual

Reservations
Recommended

Parking
Free on site, valet

Features
Private parties, outdoor dining, cigar/cognac events, chef's table

Credit Cards
AE, VC, MC, CB, DC, DS

Main dining room

Ideal for intimate dinners and entertaining clients, Charles Court at Broadmoor West offers fine dining without the formality. Impeccable service complements exceptional American regional cuisine, such as the Colorado game mixed grill, which comprises caribou chop with lingonberry pepper butter, loin of venison with cassis and roasted shallots, and seared buffalo sausage. For parties of 10, the Chef's table is a culinary world unto itself, with a specially created menu and complementing wines.

Roast loin of Colorado elk

Chef's table

AWARD WINNER
SINCE 1999

Primitivo Wine Bar

Located in the heart of downtown Colorado Springs, Primitivo serves world-class meals with friendly, relaxed service. Chef John Broening's menus change monthly, and feature the finest seasonal ingredients from around the world, as well as from local ranches and growers. The award-winning wine list of about 1,000 selections features top bottles from premier regions of California, Italy, Spain, and France.

Chef John's menus change monthly

World-class entrees

The elegant bar and dining room

AWARD WINNER SINCE 1999

Directions

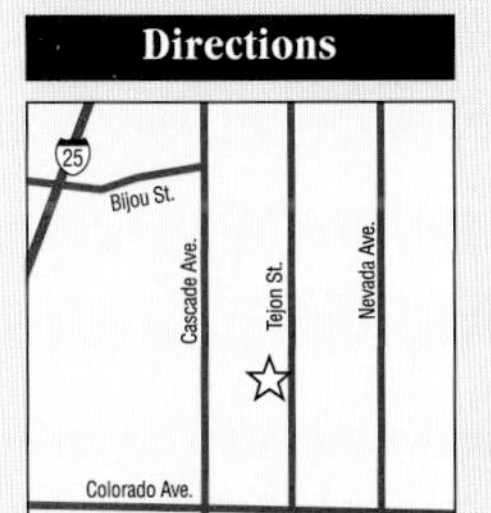

At S. Tejon Street near E. Pikes Peak Avenue in downtown, 15 min. from Colorado Springs Airport

28 S. Tejon Street
Colorado Springs, CO
80903
PH: (719) 473-4900
FAX: (719) 442-6644
www.primitivo.com

Owners
Alan Manley

Cuisine
Mediterranean/American

Days Open
Open Tues.-Fri. for lunch, Mon.-Sat. for dinner

Pricing
Dinner for one, without tax, tip, or drinks: $20-$40

Dress Code
Casual

Reservations
Recommended

Parking
Lot nearby

Features
Private room/parties, outdoor dining

Credit Cards
AE, VC, MC, DS

Strings

Directions

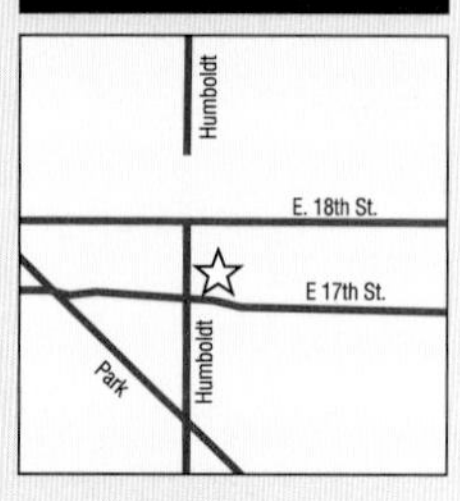

11 blocks from downtown, 25 min. from Denver International Airport

1700 Humboldt Street
Denver, CO 80218
PH: (303) 831-7310
FAX: (303) 860-8812
www.eatatstrings.com

Owners
Noel Cunningham

Cuisine
Casual contemporary

Days Open
Open Mon.-Sat. for lunch, daily for dinner

Pricing
Dinner for one, without tax, tip, or drinks: $20-$40

Dress Code
Casual

Reservations
Recommended

Parking
Complimentary valet

Features
Private room/parties, outdoor dining, near theater

Credit Cards
AE, VC, MC, DC, DS

The Atrium

Bright and cheerful, Strings is a happy place where every guest is made to feel welcome. The menu features old favorites and a weekly specials page where Chef/Owner Noel Cunningham and Executive Chef Sean Farley show their creativity. There's something for everyone, or the kitchen will whip up what you want or even match smaller portions if you can't decide. Carpaccio is a signature appetizer, crab cakes with chutney are a must, and the gazpacho soup with a scoop of tomato sorbet is a warm-weather delight. The wine list is excellent, and so is the lemonade.

Char-grilled raspberry salmon

Chef/Owner Noel Cunningham

Main dining room

AWARD WINNER SINCE 1993

Restaurant Picasso

Table with a mountain view

Serving up light interpretations of European fare, Restaurant Picasso, at the Lodge and Spa at Cordillera, allows guests to enjoy world-class cuisine and breathtaking views of New York Mountain and the Sawatch Range. The ultimate touch before dining is a tour of the wine cellar, completely renovated with customized racks and wine memorabilia. Come dine with Executive Chef Fabrice Beaudoin and allow him to create true "works of art for the palate."

Executive Chef Fabrice Beaudoin

Sliced elk tenderloin

RESTAURANT Picasso

AWARD WINNER
SINCE 1993

Directions

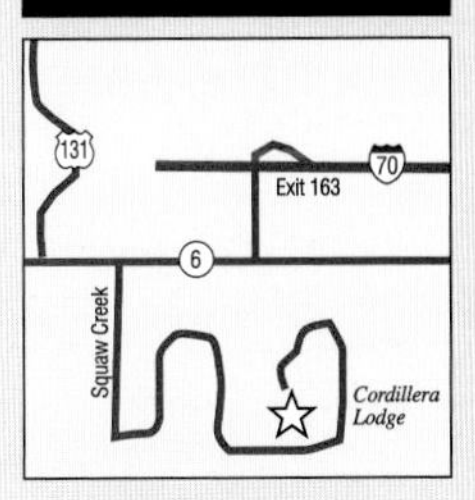

At Lodge and Spa at Cordillera, 25 min. from Eagle County Airport

2205 Cordillera Way
Edwards, CO 81632
PH: (970) 926-2200
FAX: (970) 926-2486
www.cordillera-vail.com

Owners
Felix Posen

Cuisine
European/Continental

Days Open
Open daily for breakfast, lunch, and dinner

Pricing
Dinner for one, without tax, tip, or drinks: $40-$60

Dress Code
Jacket and tie suggested

Reservations
Required

Parking
Free on site, valet

Features
Private room/portico, entertainment, cigar/cognac events, wine cellar dining

Credit Cards
AE, VC, MC, DC, DS

Briarhurst Manor

Directions

10 min. west of downtown Colorado Springs and 25 min. from Colorado Springs Regional Airport

404 Manitou Avenue
Manitou Springs, CO 80829
PH: (719) 685-1864
and (877) 685-1448
FAX: (719) 685-9638
www.briarhurst.com

Owners
Sigi and Candace Krauss

Cuisine
American and Continental

Days Open
Open Mon.-Sat. for dinner (Sun. during summer)

Pricing
Dinner for one,
without tax, tip, or drinks:
$20-$40

Dress Code
Business casual

Reservations
Recommended

Parking
Free on site

Features
Private room/parties, outdoor dining, gourmet take-out

Credit Cards
AE, VC, MC, CB, DC

Victorian splendor

Celebrating its 25th year, Briarhurst Manor is located in a tudor manor built in 1876 by the founder of Manitou Springs. The affordably priced, award-winning menu features Colorado beef, premium prime rib, lamb, and Rocky Mountain rainbow trout. The Wednesday night Candlelight Buffet is a local tradition. Summer dining is available on the terrace, and the Conservatory Ballroom seats up to 300 for banquets.

Chef-owner Sigi Krauss

Casual elegance

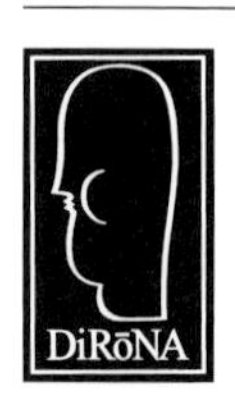

AWARD WINNER
SINCE 1999

Left Bank Restaurant

The dining room

Owned and operated since 1970 by Chef Luc Meyer and his wife Liz, this landmark restaurant presents consistently fine French/Mediterranean cuisine in surroundings warmed by family antiques and paintings. Specialties include bouillabaisse, Colorado lamb, trout, salmon, elk, and soufflés. The service is prompt and courteous, and the award-winning wine list features vintages from France and California.

Owners Luc and Liz Meyer

Fine art, fine dining

AWARD WINNER
SINCE 1992

Directions

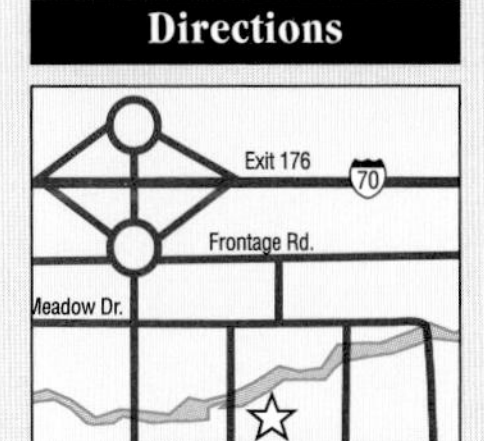

In Vail Village, 30 min. from Eagle County Airport and 2 hrs. from Denver International

183 Gore Creek Drive
Vail, CO 81657
PH: (970) 476-3696
FAX: (970) 476-3723

Owners
Liz and Luc Meyer

Cuisine
French

Days Open
Open daily except Wednesday (closed mid-April through mid-June and October through mid-November)

Pricing
Dinner for one, without tax, tip, or drinks: $20-$40

Dress Code
Casual

Reservations
Recommended

Parking
Garage nearby

Features
Private parties, near theater

Credit Cards
None accepted

Ludwig's

Directions

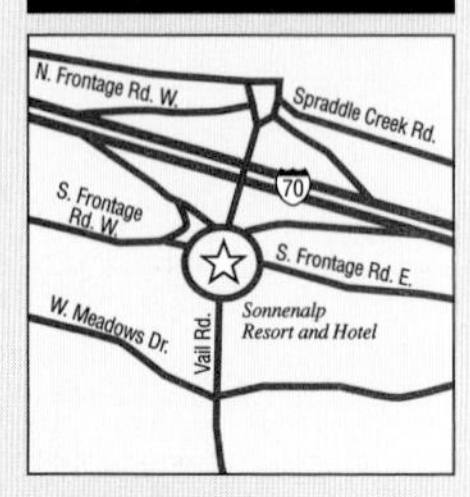

In Vail Village, 30 min. from Eagle County Airport and 2 hr. from Denver International

20 Vail Road
Vail, CO 81657
PH: (970) 476-5656
FAX: (970) 476-1639
www.sonnenalp.com

Owners
Johannes Faessler

Cuisine
International

Days Open
Open daily for dinner

Pricing
Dinner for one,
without tax, tip, or drinks:
$20-$40

Dress Code
Jacket and tie optional

Reservations
Recommended

Parking
Valet

Features
Private room/parties, outdoor dining on terrace

Credit Cards
AE, VC, MC, DC

Located at the Sonnenalp Resort of Vail in the heart of Vail Village, Ludwig's is a gourmet dining experience. The cozy decor, hand-painted ceilings, and terrace overlooking Gore Creek make for truly inviting surroundings. The chef's innovative international cuisine is accompanied by an award-winning wine list. Come dine in a candlelit setting fit for royalty.

A gourmet retreat

Sonnenalp Resort at Vail suite

The library

AWARD WINNER
SINCE 1993

Terra Bistro

Main dining room at Terra Bistro

Terra Bistro, located at the Vail Athletic Club Hotel and Spa, continues to win accolades for its creative and healthy contemporary American cuisine served in an upbeat dining room. Executive Chef Kevin Nelson uses organic produce, poultry, and meats in fashioning his diverse menu. Vegetarians and steak lovers alike will enjoy the artistic and flavorful dishes. The menu is complemented by an extensive wine and champagne list.

Creative and healthy cuisine

Chef Kevin Nelson and Jennifer Appleman, manager

AWARD WINNER SINCE 1999

Directions

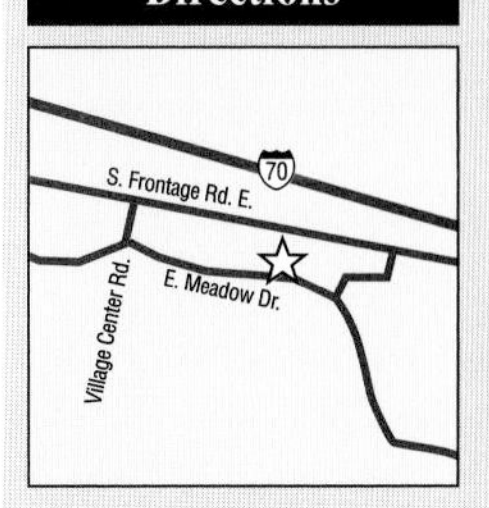

At the Vail Athletic Club Hotel & Spa on East Meadow Drive, 1 hr. 45 min. from Denver International Airport

352 East Meadow Drive
Vail, CO 81657
PH: (970) 476-6836
FAX: (970) 476-6451

Owners
Ron Byrne

Cuisine
Contemporary American/fusion

Days Open
Open daily for breakfast, lunch, and dinner

Pricing
Dinner for one, without tax, tip, or drinks: $40-$60

Dress Code
Casual

Reservations
Recommended

Parking
Garage nearby, valet

Features
Private room/parties, near theater

Credit Cards
AE, VC, MC, DC, DS

The Tyrolean

Directions

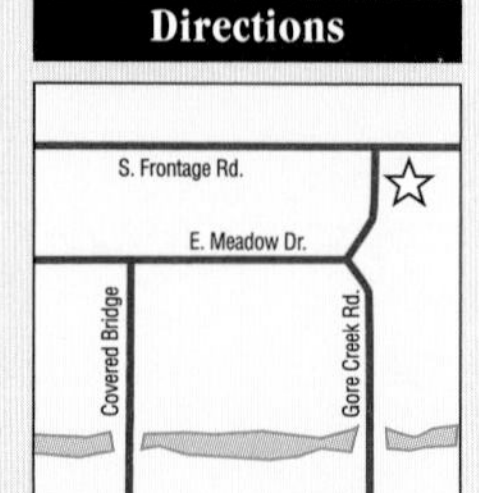

Steps from Vail Village parking structure, 30 min. from Eagle County Airport and 2 hrs. from Denver International Airport.

400 E. Meadow Drive
Vail, CO 81657
PH: (970) 476-2204
FAX: (970) 476-3652
www.tyrolean.net

Owners
Sig Langegger

Cuisine
Creative European and American

Days Open
Open daily for dinner (closed Tues. during summer)

Pricing
Dinner for one, without tax, tip, or drinks: $20-$40

Dress Code
Casual

Reservations
Recommended

Parking
Garage nearby

Features
Private room/parties, outdoor dining

Credit Cards
AE, VC, MC

The dining room

Overlooking the ski slopes and scenic Gore Creek, The Tyrolean, family-owned since 1972, offers a dining experience unique to the Vail Valley. The restaurant's rustic Alpine ambience is softened by white tablecloths and silver table settings. The eclectic menu gives a creative American twist to classic European cuisine. Favorites include grilled elk loin with marsala sauce, and trout crusted with pine nuts and painted with orange basil aioli. The extensive wine list has received *Wine Spectator's* Award of Excellence since 1994.

Rack of lamb with a mint and roasted garlic jus

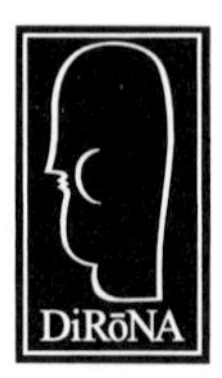

AWARD WINNER
SINCE 1999

Wildflower

Vail's No. 1 restaurant in the *Zagat Survey*, Wildflower — at The Lodge at Vail — is an eternal celebration of spring with giant flower arrangements in bloom year-round. Executive Chef Tom Gay and Chef de Cuisine Perry Katsapis serve creative interpretations of contemporary American cuisine, ranging from green peppercorn and herb crusted swordfish with baby spinach and sherry jus to grilled Colorado lamb T-bone with butternut squash, cinnamon mushrooms, and potato gnocchi.

Garden-like ambience

Wildflower-filled patio

AWARD WINNER
SINCE 1993

Directions

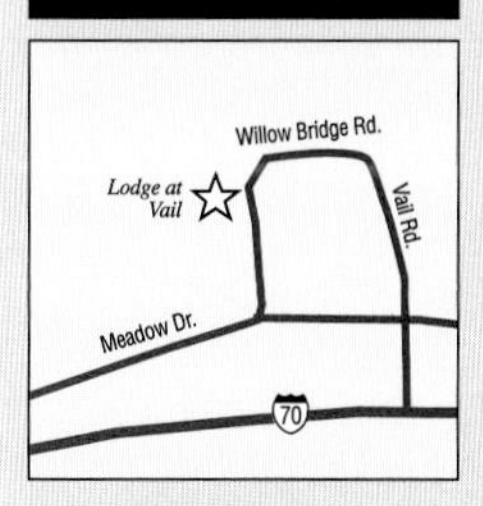

In Vail Village, 30 min. from Eagle County Airport and 2 hrs. from Denver International

174 E. Gore Creek Drive
Vail, CO 81657
PH: (970) 476-5011
FAX: (970) 476-7425
www.lodgeatvail.com

Owners
The Lodge at Vail/Vail Resorts Inc.

Cuisine
Creative American

Days Open
Open daily for dinner

Pricing
Dinner for one,
without tax, tip, or drinks:
$40-$60

Dress Code
Casual

Reservations
Highly recommended

Parking
Valet

Features
Outdoor dining,
entertainment

Credit Cards
AE, VC, MC, DC, DS

Cavey's Restaurant

The bar

Directions

On E. Center Street just off Main Street, 20 min. from Bradley International Airport

45 E. Center Street
Manchester, CT 06040
PH: (860) 643-2751
FAX: (860) 649-0344

Owners
Steve Cavagnaro

Cuisine
Modern French and Northern Italian

Days Open
Open Tues.-Sat. for lunch and dinner

Pricing
Dinner for one, without tax, tip, or drinks: $40-$60

Dress Code
Business casual

Reservations
Recommended

Parking
Free on site

Features
Private room/parties, entertainment

Credit Cards
AE, VC, MC

Cavey's is actually two restaurants in one building — an elegant French restaurant on the lower level, and a more casual Northern Italian restaurant upstairs, offering jazz piano on weekends. Both are furnished with art and antiques, and in the French restaurant, fabric wall coverings and a profusion of fresh flowers. Both restaurants have earned critical acclaim, including *Wine Spectator*'s Best of Award of Excellence.

Private dining room

Dining room

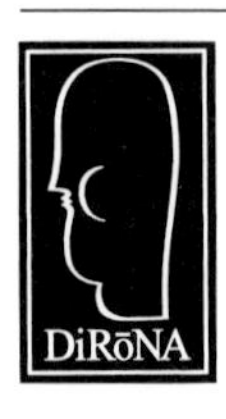

AWARD WINNER
SINCE 1993

Columbus Inn

Patio dining

The flagship of the 1492 Hospitality Group, the Columbus Inn, housed in a beautiful and historic stone building, serves up a memorable dining experience in Delaware's largest city. Attentive service and a wine list cited for excellence by *Wine Spectator* complement the kitchen's innovative creations, such as calypso spiced grilled free range chicken breast and sauteed jumbo lump crab cake. Cigars, single malt scotches, and fireplaces in each dining room add to the ambience.

Davis Sezna

Gracious hospitality

Private dining room

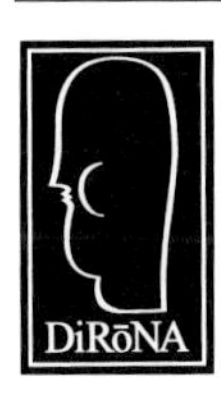

AWARD WINNER
SINCE 1997

Directions

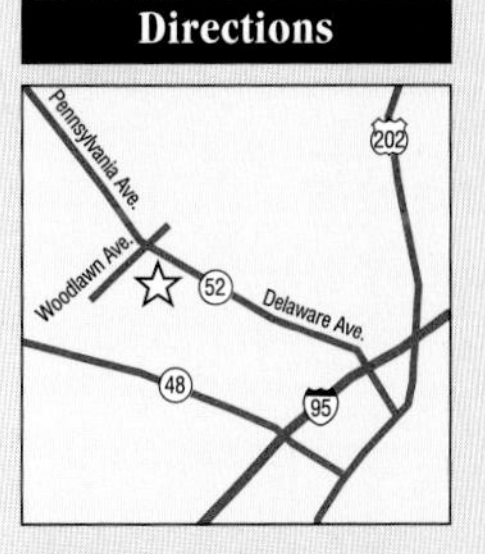

Off Interstate 95 in Wilmington, 20 min. from Philadelphia International Airport

2216 Pennsylvania Avenue
Wilmington, DE 19806
PH: (302) 571-1492
FAX: (302) 571-1111
www.columbusinn.com

Owners
Davis Sezna, David Peterson, and Joe Van Horn

Cuisine
American regional

Days Open
Open Mon.-Fri. for lunch, daily for dinner (brunch on Sun.)

Pricing
Dinner for one, without tax, tip, or drinks: $20-$40

Dress Code
Upscale casual

Reservations
Suggested

Parking
Free on site, valet

Features
Private room/parties, outdoor dining, entertainment, near theater, cigar/cognac events

Credit Cards
AE, VC, MC, DC, DS

Bombay Club

Directions

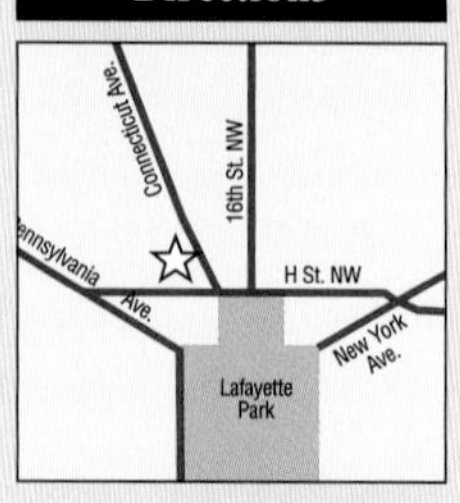

Located on Connecticut Ave. near Farragut Square, across from the White House, 15 min. from Reagan National Airport

815 Connecticut Ave. NW
Washington, DC 20006
PH: (202) 659-3727
FAX: (202) 659-5012

Owners
Ashok Bajaj

Cuisine
Indian

Days Open
Open daily for lunch and dinner, brunch served on Sunday

Pricing
Dinner for one, without tax, tip or drinks: $20-$40

Dress Code
Business casual

Reservations
Recommended

Parking
Valet

Features
Outdoor dining, pianist, near theater

Credit Cards
AE, VC, MC, DC

Elegant dining

The Bombay Club emulates characteristics of the old clubs of India. The elegant environment with pale pastels, ceiling fans, and a profusion of greenery is designed to create a warm and inviting gathering place for relaxation and regeneration. The cuisine is the finest of India, utilizing only the best quality ingredients to create a harmony of subtle flavors. Specialties, prepared by Executive Chef Ramesh Kaundal, include tandoori salmon and green chili chicken. The sophisticated cuisine is enhanced by refined service and live piano music.

AWARD WINNER
SINCE 1993

Galileo

Dining room

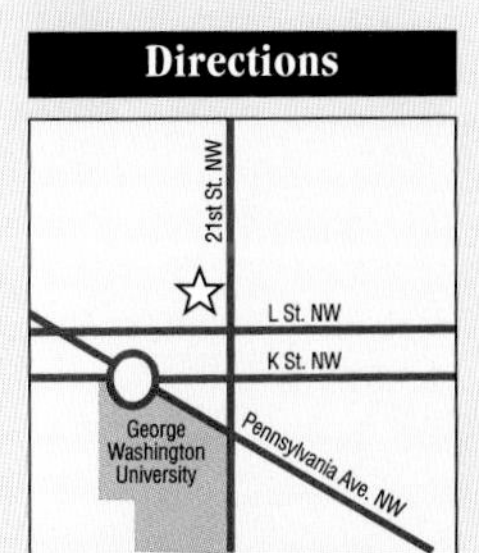

Directions

On 21st Street NW off Washington Circle, 20 min. from Reagan National Airport

1110 21st Street NW
Washington DC 20036
PH: (202) 293-7191
FAX: (202) 331-9364
www.robertodonna.com

Owners
Roberto Donna

Cuisine
Northern Italian

Days Open
Open Mon.-Fri. for lunch and daily for dinner

Pricing
Dinner for one,
Without tax, tip, or drinks:
$40-$60

Dress Code
Business Casual

Reservations
Recommended

Parking
Valet–Mon.-Sat.

Features
Private room/parties, outdoor dining, near theater, wine events

Credit Cards
AE, VC, MC, DC

Chef Roberto Donna's four-star restaurant, Galileo, features award winning contemporary and traditional cuisine of northern Italy, his native Piedmont region. The newly redesigned restaurant has an elegant dining room and two private wine rooms. There is also a private "chef's table" for eight in the kitchen and a covered terrace by the garden. Donna's new showcase kitchen "Laboratorio del Galileo" has been added, where he personally cooks for up to 30 guests. There is also a cheese cellar, which features over 75 wonderful cheeses from around the world.

"Laboratorio del Galileo"

Chef/Owner Roberto Donna

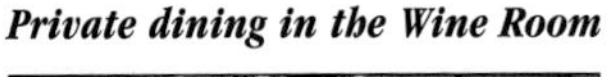
Private dining in the Wine Room

AWARD WINNER
SINCE 1992

Ristorante i Ricchi

Directions

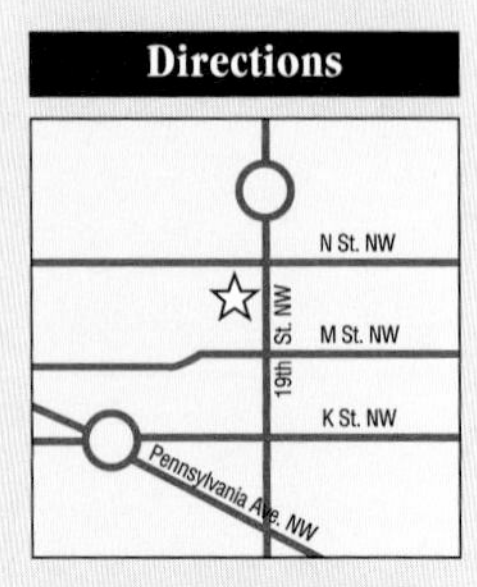

One block south of Dupont Circle on 19th Street, 10 min. from Reagan National Airport

1220 19th Street NW
Washington, DC 20036
PH: (202) 835-0459
FAX: (202) 872-1220
www.iricchi.net

Owners
Christianne Ricchi

Cuisine
Italian, Tuscan, and regional

Days Open
Open Mon.-Fri. for lunch and Mon.-Sat. for dinner

Pricing
Dinner for one,
without tax, tip, or drinks:
$40-$60

Dress Code
Business casual

Reservations
Recommended

Parking
Valet

Features
Private room/parties

Credit Cards
AE, VC, MC, CB, DC

Tuscan dining room

Ristorante i Ricchi is designed to resemble a Florentine country villa, with its open kitchen and roaring wood-burning oven as the focal point. Owner and Executive Chef Christianne Ricchi invites you to savor the authentic flavors of Tuscany, from hearty pastas and risottos to succulent Florentine-style steaks and chops, savory grilled fish and fowl, and freshly baked Tuscan-style bread. All this and an award-winning wine list make this restaurant a must-go.

Tortelloni

Intimate dining

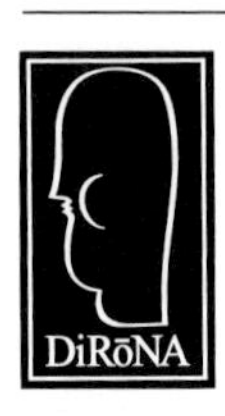

AWARD WINNER
SINCE 1992

Kinkead's, An American Brasserie

Signature seafood entrees

This four-star restaurant is led by one of the brightest stars in American cuisine, Chef Bob Kinkead. Its setting is elegance spiced with jazz. Its food is a world of fresh tastes brought together in imaginative creations. The dazzling menu changes daily, with an emphasis always on seafood. Dishes range from spectacular grilled fish selections to unique specialties, such as rare pepper-crusted tuna with grilled portabellas and pepita-crusted salmon with crab, chilies, and a corn relish.

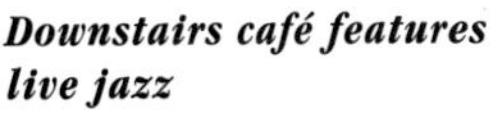

Downstairs café features live jazz

Catalan grilled whole fish

Chef/Owner Bob Kinkead

AWARD WINNER SINCE 1996

Directions

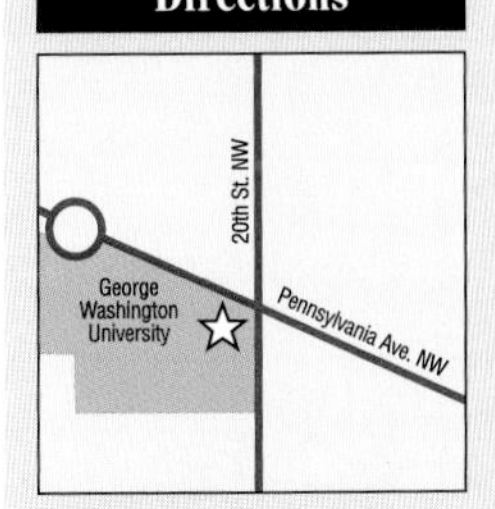

On I Street between 20th and 21st streets, near George Washington Univ., 15 min. from Ronald Reagan International Airport

2000 Pennsylvania Avenue NW
Washington, DC 20006
PH: (202) 296-7700
FAX: (202) 296-7688
www.kinkead.com

Owners
Robert Kinkead

Cuisine
American brasserie

Days Open
Open daily for lunch and dinner

Pricing
Dinner for one, without tax, tip, or drinks: $40-$60

Dress Code
Business casual

Reservations
Recommended

Parking
Valet, garage nearby

Features
Private room/parties, outdoor dining, entertainment, near theater

Credit Cards
AE, VC, MC, CB, DC, DS

Morrison-Clark Inn

Directions

11th St. NW
10th St. NW
L St. NW
K St. NW
Mt. Vernon Square
New York Ave.

Two blocks from the convention center downtown, 15 min. from Reagan National Airport

1015 L Street NW
Washington, DC 20001
PH: (202) 898-1200
FAX: (202) 289-8576
www.morrisonclark.com

Owners
Classic Hospitality

Cuisine
American with regional influences

Days Open
Open Mon.-Fri. for breakfast and lunch, daily for dinner (brunch on Sun.)

Pricing
Dinner for one,
without tax, tip, or drinks:
$20-$40

Dress Code
Business casual

Reservations
Recommended

Parking
Complimentary valet

Features
Private room/parties, outdoor dining

Credit Cards
AE, VC, MC, CB, DC, DS

A Victorian mansion dating to Abraham Lincoln's administration, Morrison-Clark is the only inn in the nation's capital listed on the National Register of Historic Places, and its restaurant is consistently rated among Washington's finest. The main dining room is highlighted by gilded mirrors, Italian marble fireplaces, and lace curtains. The chef's new American cuisine has regional influences, and changes seasonally. During pleasant weather, guests can dine in the brick courtyard.

Historic charm

AWARD WINNER
SINCE 1994

The Oval Room

Sophisticated dining

The Oval Room is an elegant and sophisticated restaurant, near Farragut Square across from the White House, which accounts for its popularity among politicians, journalists, lobbyists, and lawyers. The setting is refined but cozy with a whimsical mural of celebrities and former occupants of 1600 Pennsylvania Avenue. George Vetsch's seasonal American cuisine has charmed critics and connoisseurs alike. Among the favorites are the crab cake, which comes with zucchini and potato, fried to a crisp, and accompanied by naturally sweet corn relish. *USA Today* said The Oval Room's flower-bedecked patio is one of the best outdoor dining experiences in the United States.

AWARD WINNER
SINCE 1999

Directions

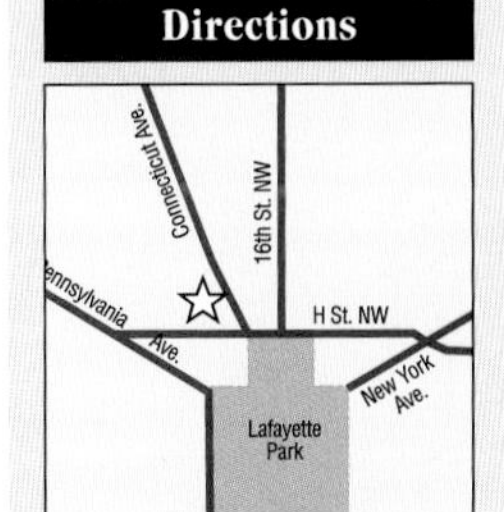

Located on Connecticut Ave. near Farragut Square, across from the White House, 15 min. from Reagan National Airport

800 Connecticut Ave. NW
Washington, DC 20004
PH: (202) 463-8700
FAX: (202) 785-9863

Owners
Ashok Bajaj

Cuisine
Modern American

Days Open
Open Mon.-Fri. for lunch, Mon.-Sat. for dinner

Pricing
Dinner for one, without tax, tip, or drinks: $20-$40

Dress Code
Business casual

Reservations
Recommended

Parking
Valet

Features
Private room/parties, outdoor dining, entertainment, near theater

Credit Cards
AE, VC, MC, DC

Sam & Harry's

Main dining room

Directions

Connecticut Ave.
New Hampshire Ave.
22 St. NW
DuPont Circle
23 St. NW
19th St. NW
M St. NW
K St.

Near Dupont Circle, 15 min. from Reagan National Airport

1200 19th Street NW
Washington, DC 20036
PH: (202) 296-4333
FAX: (202) 785-1070
www.samandharrys.com

Owners
Michael Sternberg and Larry Work

Cuisine
Classic American steakhouse

Days Open
Open Mon.-Fri. for lunch, Mon.-Sat. for dinner

Pricing
Dinner for one, without tax, tip, or drinks: $60-$80

Dress Code
Business casual

Reservations
Recommended

Parking
Complimentary valet

Features
Private room/parties

Credit Cards
AE, VC, MC, CB, DC, DS

A classic American steakhouse and a longtime favorite among Washingtonians, Sam & Harry's offers exceptional food, fine wines, great cigars, and personalized service. The menu features prime aged steaks, a veal T-bone, pristinely grilled fish, and fresh Maine lobster, all in generous portions. Colorful jazz paintings, animated jazz sculptures, a visible wine cellar, and intimate private dining rooms create a romantic and clubby atmosphere.

Classic entrees and an award-winning wine selection

Owners Larry Work and Michael Steinberg

Club-like atmosphere

AWARD WINNER SINCE 1995

701 Restaurant

Supper club dining

701 Restaurant overlooks the cascading fountains of the US Naval Memorial, and features international cuisine in a supper club setting. Tuna tartare is one specialty served by Chef Trent Conry. The interior is divided by a series of fluid curves in materials as rich and eclectic as etched glass held within chrome panels, polished walnut, granite, and layered torn silk paper. Well-spaced tables and comfortable chairs create an atmosphere of intimacy. There is nightly entertainment and a vodka, caviar and champagne lounge tucked behind the piano.

Vodka and caviar bar

Live jazz

International Bar

AWARD WINNER
SINCE 1997

Directions

On Pennsylvania Ave. near the U.S. Naval Memorial, 15 min. from Reagan National Airport

701 Pennsylvania Ave. NW
Washington, DC 20004
PH: (202) 393-0701
FAX: (202) 393-0242

Owners
Ashok Bajaj

Cuisine
Continental/American

Days Open
Open Mon.-Fri. for lunch and daily for dinner

Pricing
Dinner for one,
without tax, tip, or drinks:
$20-$40

Dress Code
Business casual

Reservations
Recommended

Parking
Valet

Features
Private room/parties, outdoor dining, live jazz, near theater

Credit Cards
AE, VC, MC, DC

1789 Restaurant

Directions

N St.
37th St.
36th St.
35th St.
34th St.
33rd St.
Prospect St.
M St.
Key Bridge

At 36th and Prospect streets in Georgetown, 10 min. from Reagan National Airport

1226 36th Street NW
Washington, DC 20007
PH: (202) 965-1789
FAX: (202) 337-1541
www.1789restaurant.com

Owners
Stuart C. Davidson and John G. Laytham

Cuisine
Seasonal American

Days Open
Open daily for dinner

Pricing
Dinner for one, without tax, tip, or drinks: $40-$60

Dress Code
Jacket required

Reservations
Recommended

Parking
Complimentary valet

Features
Private room/parties, near theater

Credit Cards
AE, VC, MC, CB, DC, DS

Georgetown elegance

Tucked away on one of Georgetown's quiet residential streets, 1789 feels like an elegant country inn. Beyond the curbside valet of the two-story Federal townhouse, the setting is refined yet cozy, with Limoges and crystal-clad tables before a blazing fire. Chef Ris Lacoste's seasonal American menu has charmed critics and connoisseurs alike. Every bit as tempting are the fresh breads and desserts by Pastry Chef Terri Horn. Dinner specialties include grilled macadamia-crusted shrimp, Maryland crab cakes with leek vinaigrette, and roasted rack of American lamb with creamy feta potatoes.

Fireside dining

Middleburg Room

Chef Ris Lacoste

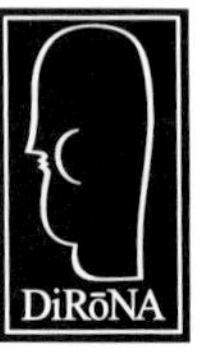

AWARD WINNER
SINCE 1992

Taberna Del Alabardero

Rio Frio Room

Bringing a sophisticated Spanish kitchen to the Nation's Capital, Taberna Del Alabardero offers an abundance of regional specialties. Under executive chef Josu Zubikarai, the menu features such authentic dishes such as tapas, fried squid and salted codfish as well as surprises like a leek terrine with wild mushrooms or hake with roasted peppers. The restaurant regularly plays host to diplomats and dignitaries.

Elegant dining

La Granja Room

AWARD WINNER
SINCE 1999

Directions

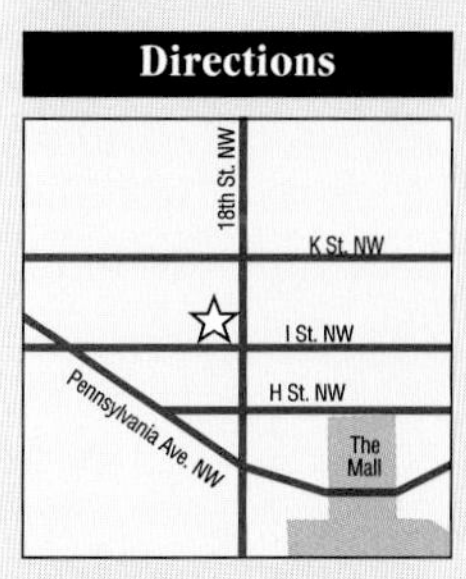

Located four blocks from the White House on I Street (entrance on 18th Street), 10 min. from Reagan National Airport

1776 I Street, NW
Washington, DC 20006
PH: (202) 429-2200
FAX: (202) 775-3713
www.alabardero.com

Owners
Luis de Lezama

Cuisine
Spanish

Days Open
Open Mon.-Fri. for lunch and Mon.-Sat. for dinner

Pricing
Dinner for one, without tax, tip, or drinks: $40-$60

Dress Code
Jacket and tie required

Reservations
Recommended

Parking
Valet, garage nearby

Features
Private room/parties, entertainment, near theater

Credit Cards
AE, VC, MC, DC, JCB, DS

Vidalia

Directions

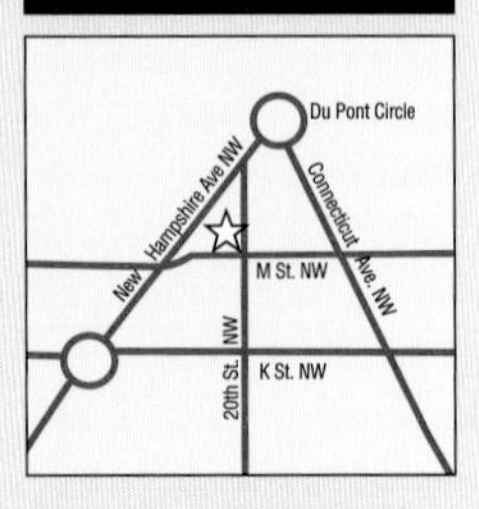

On M Street NW between 19th and 20th, 20 min. from Reagan National Airport

1990 M Street NW
Washington, DC 20036
PH: (202) 659-1990
FAX: (202) 223-8572

Owners
Jeffrey and Sallie Buben

Cuisine
Regional American with a Southern accent

Days Open
Open Mon.-Fri. for lunch, daily for dinner (call for summer Sunday hours)

Pricing
Dinner for one, without tax, tip or drinks: $40-$60

Dress Code
Business casual

Reservations
Recommended

Parking
Valet after 5:30 p.m.

Features
Semi-private room/parties

Credit Cards
AE, VC, MC, DC, DS

Vidalia's upscale, country manor house decor beautifully complements the restaurant's unique regional American menu. James Beard award winning Chef/Owner Jeffrey Buben, together with Executive Chef Peter Smith, incorporates a myriad of fresh ingredients indigenous to the area, such as Chesapeake rockfish, blue crab, and fresh produce hand picked daily from local farmers. Favorites include the seasonal baked Vidalia onion, sauteed shrimp with creamy grits, and lemon chess pie.

Intimate dining

AWARD WINNER
SINCE 1996

Maison & Jardin

A central Florida favorite since 1958

Oriental rugs, Austrian crystal, and antique, Venetian framed mirrors help create the exquisite atmosphere that is the hallmark of Mason & Jardin. The cuisine is of classical European style but with a distinct American touch. Selections include prime veal, lamb, and aged beef, as well as exotic fresh game and fowl and local seafood, all prepared by Executive Chef Hans Spirig. Maison & Jardin's impressive wine cellar contains over 1,300 different selections from around the world.

Main dining room

Owner William R. Beuret and Executive Chef Hans Spirig

Creative entrees

AWARD WINNER
SINCE 1993

Directions

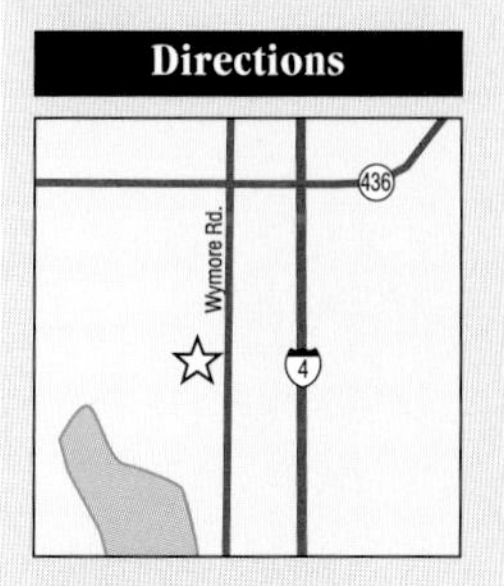

On S. Wymore Road, 25 min. from Orlando International Airport

430 S. Wymore Road
Altamonte Springs, FL 32714
PH: (407) 862-4410
FAX: (407) 862-5507
www.maisonjardin.com

Owners
William R. Beuret

Cuisine
Contempory Continental

Days Open
Open daily for dinner, seasonal Sunday brunch (closed Sundays during the summer)

Pricing
Dinner for one, without tax, tip, or drinks: $60-$80

Dress Code
Business casual

Reservations
Required

Parking
Free on site

Features
Private room/parties, near theater

Credit Cards
AE, VC, MC, CB, DC

Chef Allen's

Directions

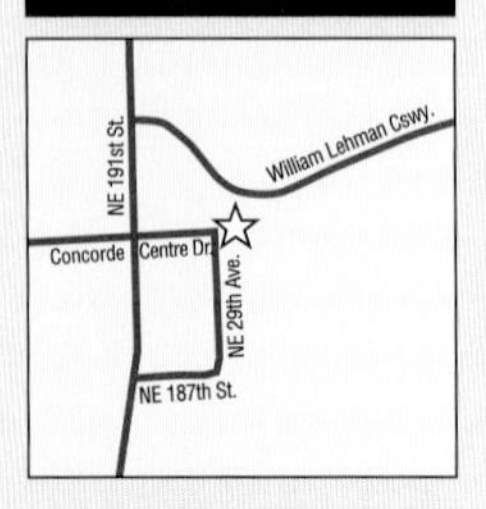

At N.E. 191st Street, 1 block east of Biscayne Blvd., 15 min. from Ft. Lauderdale Hollywood International Airport

19088 N.E. 29th Avenue
Aventura, FL 33180
PH: (305) 935-2900
FAX: (305) 935-9062
www.chefallen.com

Owners
Allen and Judi Susser

Cuisine
New world/new era

Days Open
Open daily for dinner

Pricing
Dinner for one,
without tax, tip or drinks:
$40-$60

Dress Code
Business casual

Reservations Policy
Recommended

Parking
Free on site, valet

Features
Private parties

Credit Cards
AE, VC, MC, CB, DC

Front view of restaurant

Chef Allen's is South Florida's top table, winner of a passel of awards and voted the region's best restaurant by *Gourmet* magazine in 1999. Chef Allen Susser blends the flavors of the Caribbean, Latin America, and Europe, offering a unique New World cuisine. The most gifted chef in the region, he specializes in fresh local seafood, game fish, and dessert soufflés.

Chef Allen Susser

Reception at the bar

Rack of shrimp

AWARD WINNER
SINCE 1992

Arturo's Ristorante Italiano

Arturo's Ristorante is one of South Florida's most acclaimed dining establishments. The cuisine is authentic Italian, and the display window allows guests to view pastas, breads, and desserts being prepared on the premises. Executive Chef Elisa Gismondi's repertoire ranges from osso buco to lobster Fradiavolo. In addition to the bar and elegantly furnished main dining room, Arturo's has the beautiful Garden Room and the intimate Wine Cellar for small parties.

The Garden Room

The Wine Cellar

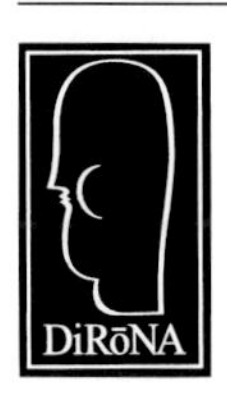

AWARD WINNER
SINCE 1999

Directions

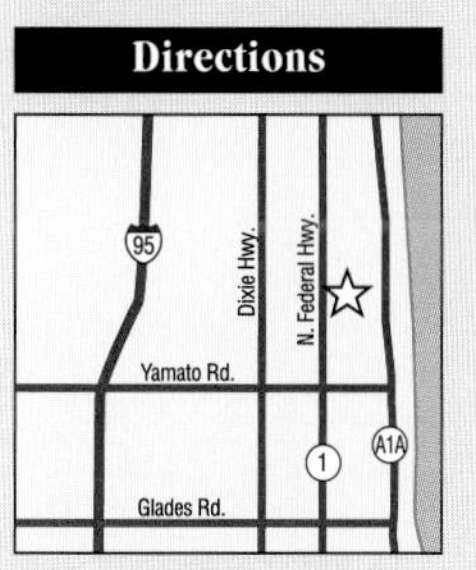

On N. Federal Highway, 30 min. from Palm Beach International Airport and 30 min. north of Fort Lauderdale International Airport

6750 N. Federal Highway
Boca Raton, FL 33487
PH: (561) 997-7373
FAX: (561) 997-7374

Owners
Vincent and Rosaria Gismondi

Cuisine
Italian Continental

Days Open
Open Mon.-Fri. for lunch, daily for dinner

Pricing
Dinner for one, without tax, tip, or drinks: $20-$40

Dress Code
Jacket required

Reservations
Recommended

Parking
Valet

Features
Private room/parties, entertainment, cigar/cognac events

Credit Cards
AE, VC, MC, CB, DC, DS

La Finestra Restaurant

Directions

Florida Turnpike
95
Federal Hwy.
NE 1st Ave.
Palmetto Park Rd.

On E. Palmetto Park Road, 25 min. from both West Palm Beach and Fort Lauderdale International Airports

171 E. Palmetto Park Road
Boca Raton, FL 33432
PH: (561) 392-1838
FAX: (561) 392-0632

Owners
Antoine Pepaj

Cuisine
Northern Italian

Days Open
Open daily for dinner

Pricing
Dinner for one,
without tax, tip, or drinks:
$40-$60

Dress Code
Business casual

Reservations
Recommended

Parking
Free on site, valet

Features
Private room/parties, outdoor dining, pianist

Credit Cards
AE, VC, MC, DC, DS

Piano bar and dining room

Soft lighting and a romantic atmosphere create an intimate dining experience for guests at La Finestra Restaurant. No less enchanting is the cuisine of owner and Executive Chef Antoine Pepaj. His light style is evident in his misto griglia, a toss of grilled fish fillets, scallops, and shrimp with a concassee of tomatoes. The dessert menu features soufflé of raspberry cream in Calvado sauce, espresso-chocolate torte, and creme brulée.

Chef-owner Antoine Pepaj

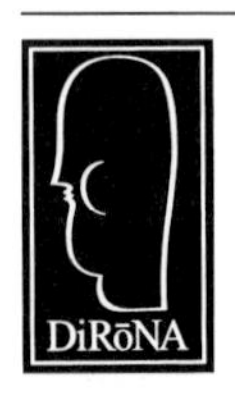

AWARD WINNER
SINCE 1997

Restaurant St. Michel

Main dining room

Housed in the beautifully restored Hotel Place St. Michel, Restaurant St. Michel offers superb contemporary American and light French cuisine, served in a beautiful art deco-style dining room. Executive Chef Jack Miranda prepares an eclectic mix of international cuisines featuring fresh, local seafood, aged prime meats, wild game, pastas, and homemade desserts. The wine list complements the varied menu, and nightly piano music enhances the dining ambience.

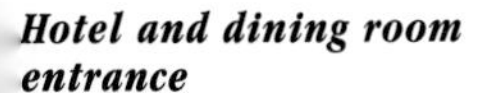

Hotel and dining room entrance

Rack of lamb

Owner Stuart Bornstein

AWARD WINNER SINCE 1993

Directions

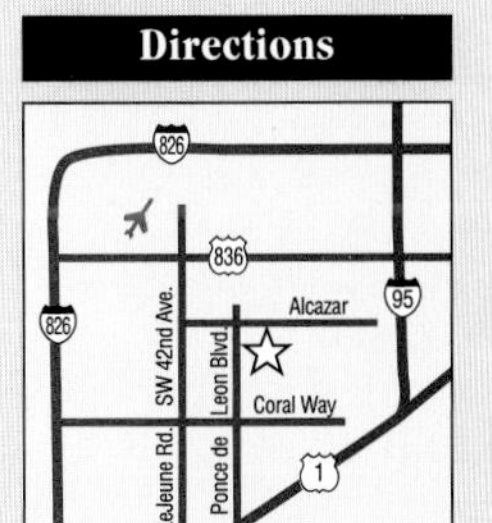

At the Hotel Place St. Michel, 10 min. from Miami International Airport

162 Alcazar Avenue
Coral Gables, FL 33134
PH: (305) 444-1666
FAX: (305) 529-0074
www.hotelplacestmichel.com

Owners
Stuart Bornstein

Cuisine
Contemporary American and light French

Days Open
Open daily for breakfast, lunch, and dinner

Pricing
Dinner for one, without tax, tip, or drinks: $20-$40

Dress Code
Business casual

Reservations
Recommended

Parking
Garage nearby

Features
Private room/parties, entertainment, near theater

Credit Cards
AE, VC, MC, DC

Ristorante La Bussola

Directions

Lejuene Rd.
Salzedo St.
Giralda
Ponce de Leon Blvd.
Miracle Mile
Valencia

On Giralda Avenue, 15 min. from Miami International Airport

264 Giralda Avenue
Coral Gables, FL 33134
PH: (305) 445-8783
FAX: (305) 441-6435

Owners
Elizabeth Giordano and Tino Ponticorvo

Cuisine
Northern Italian

Days Open
Open Mon.-Fri. for lunch, daily for dinner

Pricing
Dinner for one, without tax, tip, or drinks: $20-$40

Dress Code
Business casual

Reservations
Recommended

Parking
Valet, self-parking

Features
Private room/parties, live piano, near theater

Credit Cards
AE, VC, MC, CB, DC

An elegant setting

Ristorante La Bussola offers some of the finest Italian cuisine in Florida. The dining room is elegant and the service is impeccable. The specialties, prepared by Executive Chef Roberto Rimari, include fresh homemade pastas, fresh local fish, prime steaks and chops, and Ristorante La Bussola's memorable mango cheesecake. The imaginative menu, extensive wine list, and intimate cocktail lounge featuring live piano music make for the perfect setting for a special occasion.

The finest cuisine

Artistic decor

AWARD WINNE
SINCE 1996

Brooks Restaurant

Your wine is served

In the capable hands of the second generation managing this South Florida landmark, Brooks Restaurant makes either an intimate dinner for two or a lavish party an experience to remember. The dining rooms are adorned with Queen Anne chairs, crisp linens, and soft candlelight, the perfect backdrop for inspired Continental American cuisine featuring such standards as individual rack of lamb and sweet soufflés. The imaginative wine list has more than 300 selections.

Main dining room

Intimate dining

AWARD WINNER
SINCE 1999

Directions

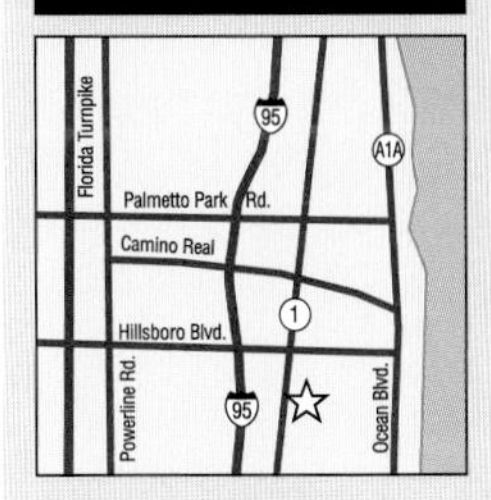

On S. Federal Highway, 30 min. from Fort Lauderdale-Hollywood International Airport

500 S. Federal Highway
Deerfield Beach, FL 33441
PH: (954) 427-9302
FAX: (954) 427-9811
www.brooks-restaurant.com

Owners
Perron, Howe, and Gaudree families

Cuisine
Continenal, American

Days Open
Open Tues.-Sun. for dinner

Pricing
Dinner for one, without tax, tip, or drinks: $20-$40

Dress Code
Business casual

Reservations
Recommended

Parking
Free on site, valet

Features
Private room/parties

Credit Cards
AE, VC, MC, DC, DS

The Black Pearl

Cozy small town atmosphere

The Black Pearl offers a total dining experience: intimate setting, professional service, and the finest New American cuisine. This combination has led to numerous accolades, including: Top 20 New Florida Restaurants, *Florida Trend* magazine, 1998; one of Tampa Bay's Top Ten Resturants 1998, *Tampa Tribune*; Best Upscale Restaurant/1998, Best Chef/ 1999, and Best Restaurant to Celebrate a Special Occasion/1999, 2000, *Tampa Bay* magazine. Oven-steamed Prince Edward Island mussels with coconut milk, red Thai curry and lime, and veal paillards with vanilla bean and mushroom sauce are house specialties.

Homemade vanilla bean ice cream

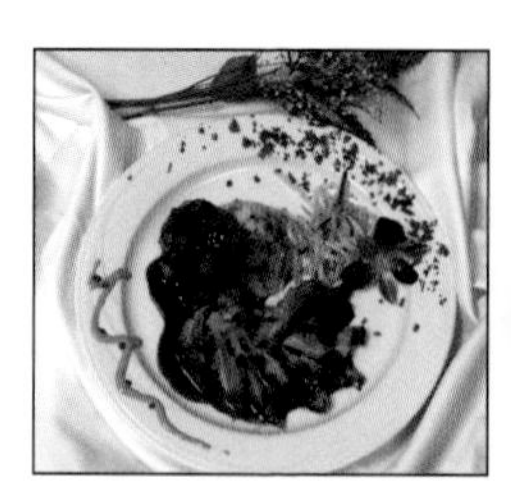
Award-winning entrees

Art deco dining intimacy

AWARD WINNER
SINCE 2001

Directions

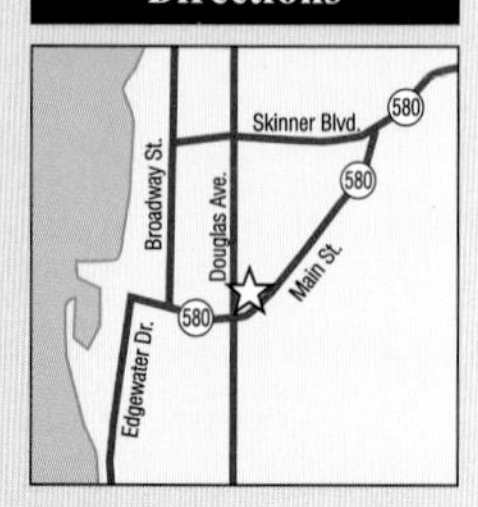

On Main Street, two blocks east of the Dunedin marina, 35 min. from Tampa International Airport

315 Main Street
Dunedin, FL 34698
PH: (727) 734-3463
FAX: (727) 771-8086

Owners
Kathleen La Roche

Cuisine
New American

Days Open
Open daily for dinner

Pricing
Dinner for one,
without tax, tip, or drinks:
$20-$40

Dress Code
Business casual

Reservations
Recommended

Parking
Free on site

Features
Private parties

Credit Cards
AE, VC, MC, CB, DC, DS

Burt & Jacks

Beautiful views

Burt & Jacks is the award-winning collaboration of actor Burt Reynolds and restaurateur Jack Jackson. The dramatic Mediterranean villa overlooks the spectacular Port Everglades, with cruise ships and yachts from all over the world. The menu features USDA Prime steaks and chops, fresh seafood, and jumbo live Maine lobsters. The extensive wine list, an outside patio, and the intimate cocktail lounge featuring live piano music provide the perfect setting for a special occasion.

Maine lobster

Intimate waterfront dining

AWARD WINNER
SINCE 1997

Directions

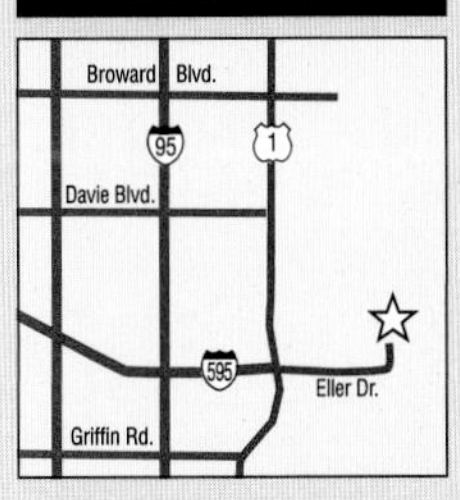

Overlooking Port Everglades, 5 min. from Fort Lauderdale International Airport

Berth 23, Port Everglades
Fort Lauderdale, FL 33316
PH: (954) 522-5225
FAX: (954) 522-2048
www.burtandjacks.com

Owners
Jack Jackson and Burt Reynolds

Cuisine
Sophisticated American

Days Open
Open daily for dinner

Pricing
Dinner for one,
without tax, tip, or drinks:
$40-$60

Dress Code
Jacket and tie required

Reservations
Recommended

Parking
Valet

Features
Private room/parties, entertainment

Credit Cards
AE, VC, MC, CB, DC

Il Tartufo on Las Olas

Directions

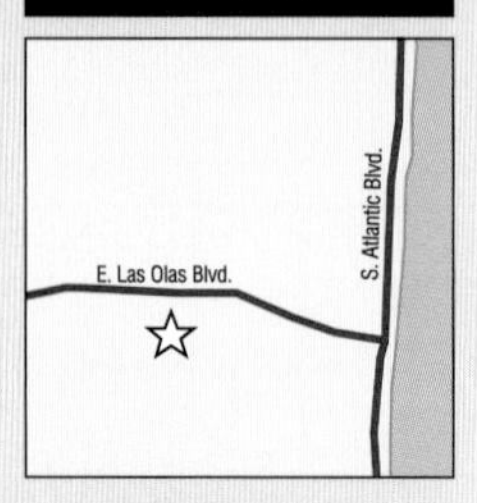

In downtown Fort Lauderdale, 20 min. from Fort Lauderdale International Airport

2400 E. Las Olas Boulevard
Ft. Lauderdale, FL 33301
PH: (954) 767-9190
FAX: (954) 767-9821
www.iltartufo.com

Owners
Gianni and AnnMarie Minervini

Cuisine
Italian

Days Open
Open daily for dinner

Pricing
Dinner for one, without tax, tip, or drinks: $20-$40

Dress Code
Business casual

Reservations
Recommended

Parking
Valet

Features
Private room/parties, outdoor dining, entertainment, near theater, cigar/cognac events

Credit Cards
AE, VC, MC, DC

Alba Room

Located on popular Las Olas Boulevard, Il Tartufo is one of the most elegant and picturesque restaurants in South Florida. Enter through the charming courtyard with its two magnificent 100-year-old banyan trees. Tiny white lights twinkle everywhere — guests feel like they're dining under a star- spangled sky. The dining room is a blend of rich forest greens, mahogany, cozy leather booths, and beautifully appointed tables where innovative northern Italian cuisine is served.

Fine Italian cuisine

Owners Gianni and AnnMarie Minervini

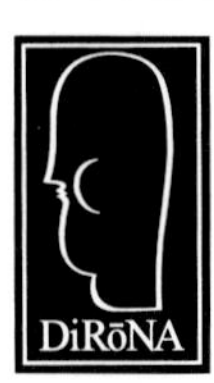

AWARD WINNER
SINCE 1994

Marker 88 Restaurant

Dining room, with view of Florida Bay

Located on Plantation Key, Marker 88 Restaurant offers waterfront dining with dockside views of spectacular sunsets overlooking Florida Bay. Executive Chef Andre Mueller's menu specializes in classical Continental cuisine featuring fresh native seafood such as yellowtail, snapper, pink shrimp, and lobster.

Dockside dining and bar

Creative seafood specialties

From left, Chef Wes, dining room manager Denise, and Chef Jim

AWARD WINNER
SINCE 1997

Directions

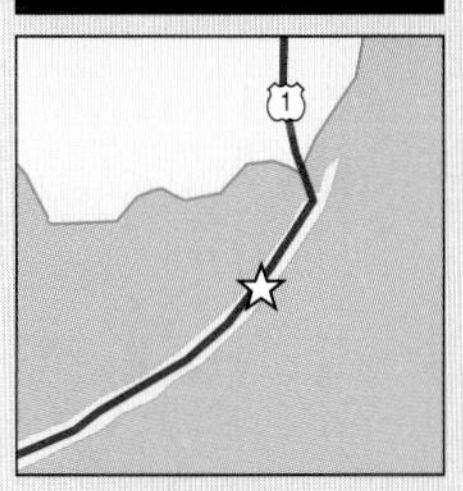

Overlooking Florida Bay on Plantation Key, 1 hr. 20 min. from Miami International Airport

Mile Marker 88, Plantation Key
Islamorada, FL 33036
PH: (305) 852-9315
FAX: (305) 852-9069

Owners
Andre Mueller

Cuisine
Seafood/Continental

Days Open
Open Tues.-Sun. for dinner

Pricing
Dinner for one, without tax, tip, or drinks: $20-$40

Dress Code
Casual

Reservations
Recommended

Parking
Free on site

Features
Private room/parties, outdoor dining

Credit Cards
AE, MC, CB, DC, DS

Square One Restaurant

Main dining room

Directions

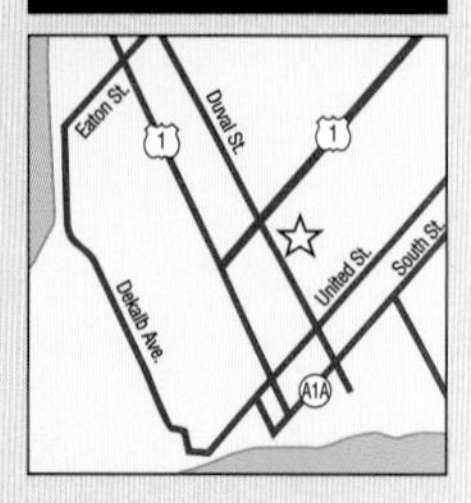

At Duval Square, 10 min. from Key West Airport

1075 Duval Street, C12
Duval Square
Key West, FL 33040
PH: (305) 296-4300
FAX: (305) 292-5039
www.squareonerestaurant.com

Owners
Michael Stewart

Cuisine
New American

Days Open
Open daily for dinner

Pricing
Dinner for one,
without tax, tip, or drinks:
$20-$40

Dress Code
Casual

Reservations
Recommended

Parking
Free on site

Features
Private parties, outdoor dining, entertainment

Credit Cards
AE, VC, MC, CB, DC, DS

Square One Restaurant is a Key West favorite that features a classic baby grand piano by the door and candlelit tables set with stemware on white linens. The cuisine, created by Executive Chef Timothy Reynolds, is New American classic with Caribbean influences. The menu changes with the chef's creativity and the availability of fresh products. Entrees include Long Island duck, grilled New Zealand rack of lamb, and Angus filet of beef.

Sea scallops

Courtyard dining

AWARD WINNER
SINCE 1996

Victoria & Albert's

American regional cuisine with classical influences is how Chef Scott Hunnel describes the highly creative menu at Victoria & Albert's at Disney's Grand Floridian Resort & Spa. Entrees include yellowtail snapper, olive-crusted rubbed veal tenderloin, and smoked black pepper polenta. A waitress-waiter team expertly serves each table. Dining here is an experience of elegance and indulgence.

Chef Scott Hunnel

Heirloom tomato napolean

Timbale of cold smoked salmon

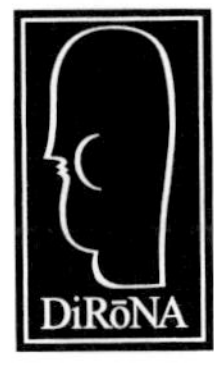

AWARD WINNER
SINCE 1994

Directions

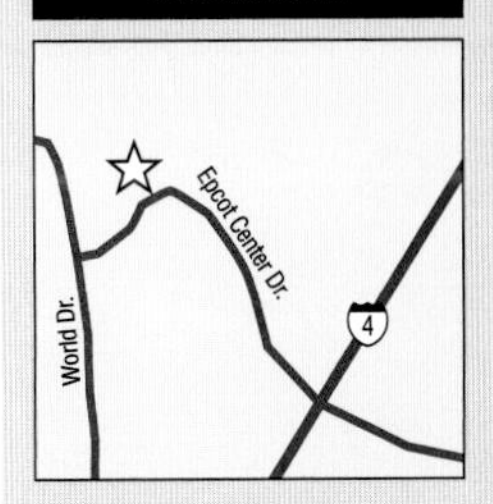

At Disney's Grand Floridian Resort & Spa, 25 min. from Orlando International Airport

4401 Grand Floridian Way
Lake Buena Vista, FL
32830
PH: (407) 939-3463
www.disneyworld.com

Owners
Walt Disney Company

Cuisine
American regional

Days Open
Open daily for dinner

Pricing
Dinner for one,
without tax, tip, or drinks:
$80+

Dress Code
Jacket required

Reservations Policy
Required

Parking
Valet

Features
Food and wine pairings, exclusive Chef's Table

Credit Cards
AE, VC, MC, DC, JCB, DS, Disney Charge

The Colony Dining Room

Colony Dining Room

Nestled on a pristine Gulf of Mexico beach, The Colony Dining Room is located in the world-famous Colony Beach & Tennis Resort. For more than 30 years, The Colony has set the standard for fine dining in Sarasota, featuring contemporary Continental cuisine. Director of Food and Beverage Operations Thomas Klauber and his culinary team prepare fresh and innovative entrees such as crispy fried lobster tail with sweet potato fries, and pan-roasted American snapper.

Florida crab cake with key lime beurre blanc

President and General Manager Katherine Klauber Moulton and Executive Vice President Michael Moulton

AWARD WINNER SINCE 1992

Directions

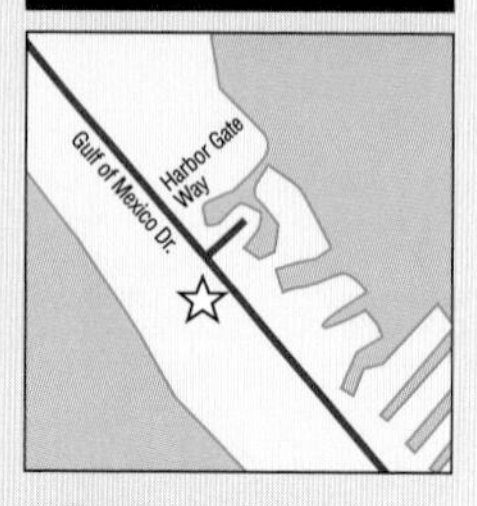

At The Colony Beach & Tennis Resort, 15 min. from Sarasota-Bradenton International Airport

1620 Gulf of Mexico Drive
Longboat Key, FL 34228
PH: (941) 383-5558
FAX: (941) 387-0250
www.colonybeachresort.com

Owners
Dr. Murf Klauber

Cuisine
Regional Continental

Days Open
Open daily for breakfast, lunch, and dinner

Pricing
Dinner for one, without tax, tip, or drinks: $40-$60

Dress Code
Business casual

Reservations
Recommended

Parking
Valet

Features
Private room/parties, outdoor dining, entertainment, cigar/cognac events

Credit Cards
AE, VC, MC, CB, DC, DS

Euphemia Haye

The Hayeloft Lounge

Euphemia Haye's menu is as inspired and eclectic as the art, antiques, and music that adorn this award-winning restaurant. Owner and Executive Chef Raymond Arpke turns out consistently extraordinary cuisine - roast duck, flambéed prime peppered steak, fresh seafood, and classic Caesar salad. A comprehensive wine list complements this varied menu. Complete your dining in the HayeLoft, an upstairs lounge and dessert room serving dessert wines and vintage ports, with live music nightly.

Main dining room

The owners, Chef Raymond and D'Arcy Arpke

Dessert selection

AWARD WINNER
SINCE 1994

Directions

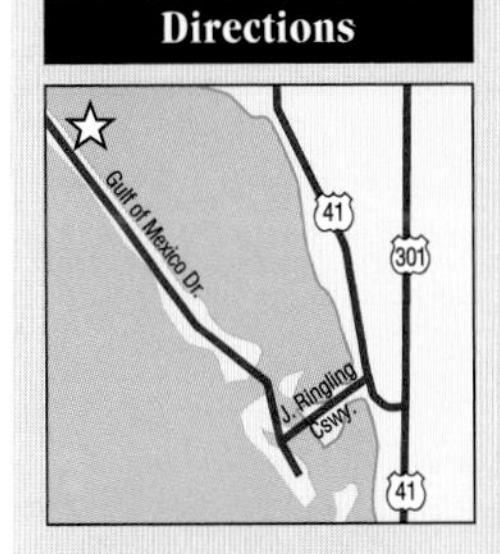

On the northern end of Longboat Key, 30 min. from Sarasota-Bradenton International Airport

5540 Gulf of Mexico Drive
Longboat Key, FL 34228
PH: (941) 383-3633
FAX: (941) 387-8336
www.euphemiahaye.com

Owners
Raymond and D'Arcy Arpke

Cuisine
Global eclectic

Days Open
Open daily for dinner

Pricing
Dinner for one, without tax, tip, or drinks: $40-$60

Dress Code
Resort casual

Reservations
Recommended

Parking
Free on site

Features
Lounge and dessert room, lesson luncheons

Credit Cards
VC, MC, CB, DC, DS

Peter Scott's

Directions

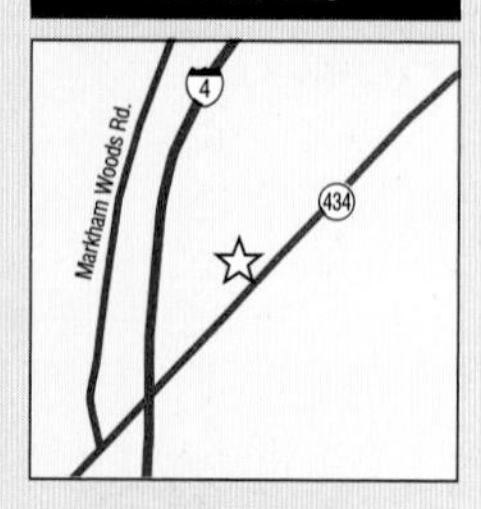

In Longwoods Village Shoppes (Jacobson's Plaza), off Exit 49 of Interstate 4, 45 min. from Orlando International Airport

1811 West State Road 434
Longwood, FL 32750
PH: (407) 834-4477
FAX: (407) 834-2414
www.peterscotts.com

Owners
Peter Scott Cahall

Cuisine
Continental

Days Open
Open Tues.-Sat. for dinner

Pricing
Dinner for one, without tax, tip, or drinks: $40-$60

Dress Code
Business casual

Reservations
Recommended

Parking
Free on site

Features
Entertainment

Credit Cards
AE, VC, MC, CB, DC, DS

Dining and dancing

The name Peter Scott's has become synonymous with excellent food, service, and entertainment. Chef Scott's cutting-edge cuisine has made this restaurant a must-stop in Central Florida. Signature items include imported Dover sole, Chilean sea bass, and flaming chateaubriand. The restaurant, which also offers live music and dancing nightly, received *Wine Spectator's* Award of Excellence and earned Five Stars from the American Association of Hospitality Services and four diamonds from AAA.

Frankie Avalon performing

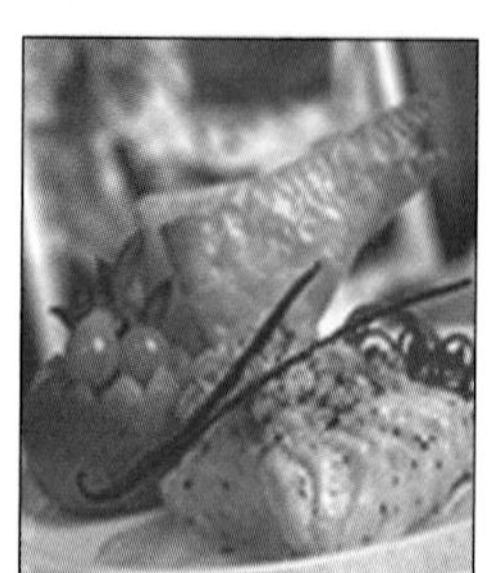

Chilean sea bass

David J. Miles, general manager

AWARD WINNER SINCE 1995

Lafite

Main dining room

Lafite, at the Registry Resort in Naples, is southwest Florida's most exclusive restaurant and is rapidly gaining national acclaim for its superb Continental cuisine and outstanding international wines. Savor the special creations of Executive Chef Neil Griffin amid the delicious aromas and elegant decor of the intimate dining areas. Entrees include sauteed almond-coated fillet of Dover sole, and slow roasted Oriental spiced duckling with candied plum wine tamarind sauce.

Asian seafood salad

Executive Chef Neil Griffin

An experience to remember

AWARD WINNER
SINCE 1992

Directions

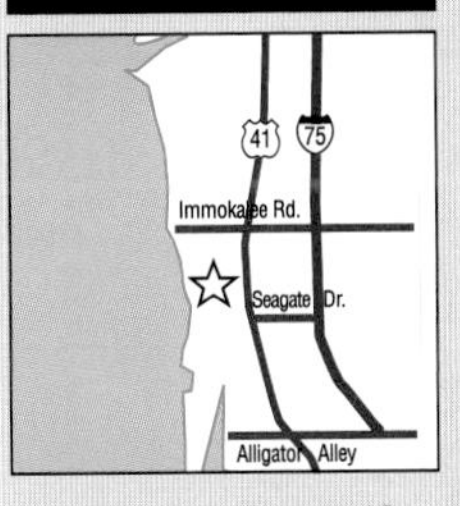

At the Registry Resort, 10 min. from Naples Airport

475 Seagate Drive
Naples, FL 34103
PH: (941) 597-3232
FAX: (941) 597-7168
www.registryhotels.com

Owners
Boca Resorts Inc.

Cuisine
American regional, Continental

Days Open
Open daily for dinner

Pricing
Dinner for one, without tax, tip, or drinks: $60-$80

Dress Code
Jacket required

Reservations
Required

Parking
Valet

Features
Private room/parties, entertainment, near theater

Credit Cards
AE, VC, MC, CB, DC, ER, JCB, DS

Restaurant On The Bay

Directions

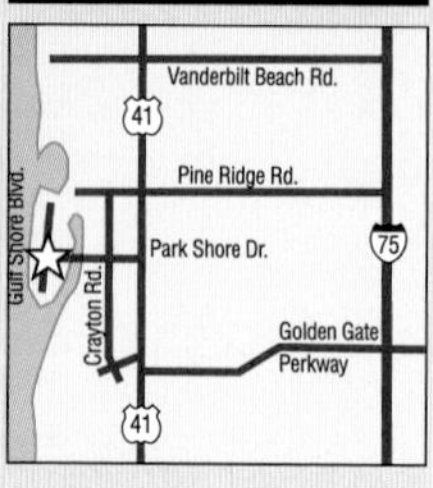

On Gulf Shore Boulevard North, in Venetian Village, 10 min. from Naples Airport

4236 Gulf Shore Boulevard N.
Naples, FL 34103
PH: (941) 263-0900
FAX: (941) 263-0850

Owners
Marie-Michelle Rey

Cuisine
Mediterranean Cuisine

Days Open
Open daily for lunch and dinner

Pricing
Dinner for one, without tax, tip, or drinks: $20-$40

Dress Code
Casual

Reservations
Recommended

Parking
Free on site

Features
Outdoor dining, entertainment

Credit Cards
AE, VC, MC

Owner Marie-Michelle Rey

With her charming, flower-filled outdoor terrace, owner Marie-Michelle Rey brings a little corner of the French Riviera to the heart of Naples. Overlooking Venetian Bay, you will experience the "joie de vivre" of the South of France. The restaurant offers a rare combination of stunning views and superb French food, characterized by Executive Chef Kyle Hughes' light and tasty sauces. There's live music nightly on the terrace.

AWARD WINNER
SINCE 1999

Ruth's Chris Steak House

Filet mignon

This is the steak that steak lovers rave about! Ruth's Chris Steak House specializes in USDA Prime beef. Strips, filets, ribeyes, T-bones, and porterhouses are aged to exacting standards, broiled to perfection, and served sizzling. An award-winning wine list features premium vintages by the glass. The service is attentive, knowledgeable, and friendly.

The place for great steaks

AWARD WINNER
SINCE 2001

Directions

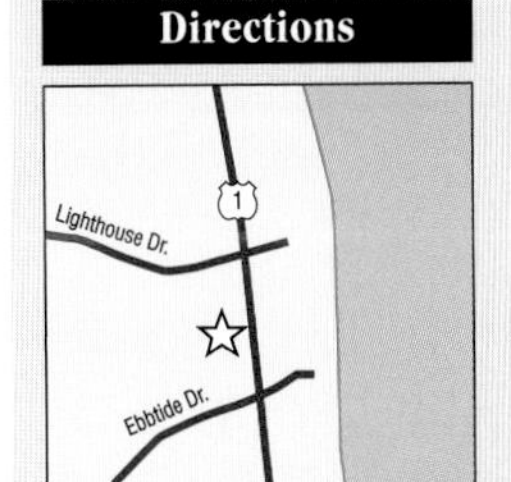

On U.S. 1, 25 min. from Palm Beach International Airport

661 U.S. 1
North Palm Beach, FL
33408
PH: (561) 863-0660
FAX: (561) 863-3670
www.ruthschris.com

Owners
Ruth's Chris Steak House

Cuisine
Steaks, seafood

Days Open
Open daily for dinner

Pricing
Dinner for one,
without tax, tip, or drinks:
$40-$60

Dress Code
Business casual

Reservations
Recommended

Parking
Valet

Features
Private rooms/portico,
cigar/cognac events

Credit Cards
AE, VC, MC, CB, DC, DS

Atlantis

Intimate dining

Atlantis, located at the Renaissance Orlando Resort, offers an elegant, intimate atmosphere where you can enjoy the finest fresh seafood entrees prepared by Executive Chef Mitsuo Miyashita. The menu is complemented by an extensive wine list, and dinner is served by a gracious and accommodating staff. The restaurant has won the AAA Four Diamond award annually since 1988.

Directions

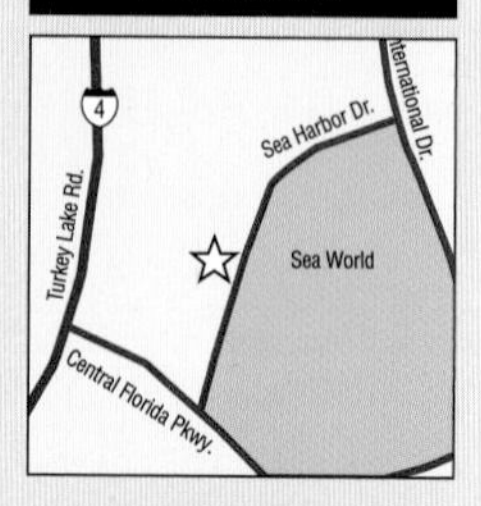

At the Renaissance Orlando Resort, 17 min. from Orlando International Airport

6677 Sea Harbor Drive
Orlando, FL 32821
PH: (407) 351-5555
FAX: (407) 363-9247
www.renaissancehotels.com

Owners
The Renaissance Orlando Resort

Cuisine
Seafood

Days Open
Open Mon.-Sat. for dinner

Pricing
Dinner for one,
without tax, tip, or drinks:
$20-$40

Dress Code
Casual

Reservations
Recommended

Parking
Free on site, valet

Features
Private room/parties, entertainment, cigar/cognac events

Credit Cards
AE, VC, MC, CB, DC, JCB, DS

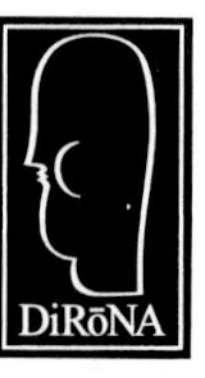

AWARD WINNER
SINCE 1992

DUX

The Peabody Orlando's signature restaurant, DUX, offers traditional Southern hospitality at its finest. The menu changes throughout the year, allowing Executive Chef Christophe Gerad to prepare dishes using seasonal vegetables and fruits to accompany the varied fish, meat, and game entrees. Recommended delicacies include seared foie gras with fresh grapefruit and preserved citrus zests, roulade of lightly smoked salmon with caviar and potato vinaigrette, and pan-seared medallions of farm-raised venison with peppered pineapple.

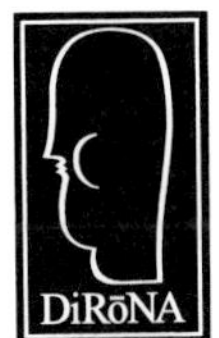

AWARD WINNER
SINCE 1994

Directions

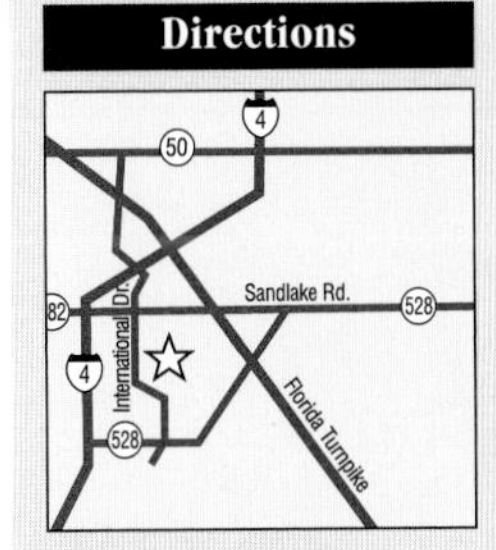

At The Peabody Orlando, 15 min. from Orlando International Airport

9801 International Drive
Orlando, FL 32819
PH: (407) 352-4000
FAX: (407) 363-1505
www.peabodyorlando.com

Owners
The Peabody Hotel Group

Cuisine
Global American

Days Open
Open Mon.-Sat. for dinner

Pricing
Dinner for one,
without tax, tip, or drinks:
$40-$60

Dress Code
Business casual

Reservations
Recommended

Parking
Free on site, valet

Features
Private parties

Credit Cards
AE, VC, MC, CB, DC, DS

Haifeng

Directions

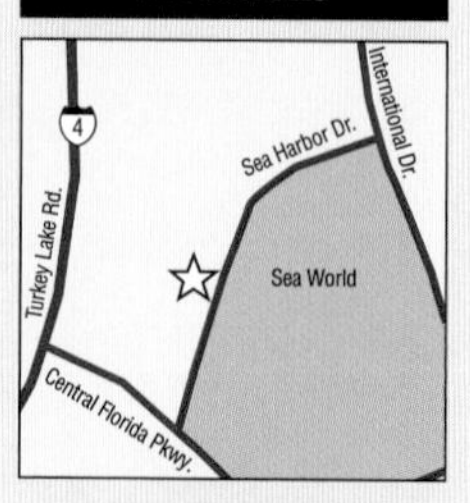

At the Renaissance Orlando Resort, 17 min. from Orlando International Airport

6677 Sea Harbor Drive
Orlando, FL 32821
PH: (407) 351-5555
FAX: (407) 363-9247
www.renaissancehotels.com

Owners
The Renaissance Orlando Resort

Cuisine
Asian

Days Open
Open Tues.-Sun. for dinner

Pricing
Dinner for one,
without tax, tip, or drinks:
$20-$40

Dress Code
Casual

Reservations
Recommended

Parking
Free on site, valet

Features
Private room/parties

Credit Cards
AE, VC, MC, CB, DC, JCB, DS

Far East flavor

At Haifeng in the Renaissance Orlando Resort, savor the secrets of the Far East and enjoy authentic cuisine from China, Japan, and Korea prepared by Executive Chef Eric Tran. The service is invariably impeccable and gracious, and the atmosphere is one of soothing Oriental elegance.

AWARD WINNER
SINCE 1997

La Coquina

La Coquina, located in the award-winning Hyatt Regency Grand Cypress, features New World cuisine with a view of Lake Windsong. Executive Chef Kenneth Juran invites you into his kitchen, where he personally prepares specialties, such as seared loin of tuna wrapped in prosciutto, lobster ravioli with avocado and citrus beurre blanc, and smoked salmon and crisp straw potatoes. The Sunday champagne brunch is not to be missed.

Main dining room

Poolside elegance

AWARD WINNER
SINCE 1992

Directions

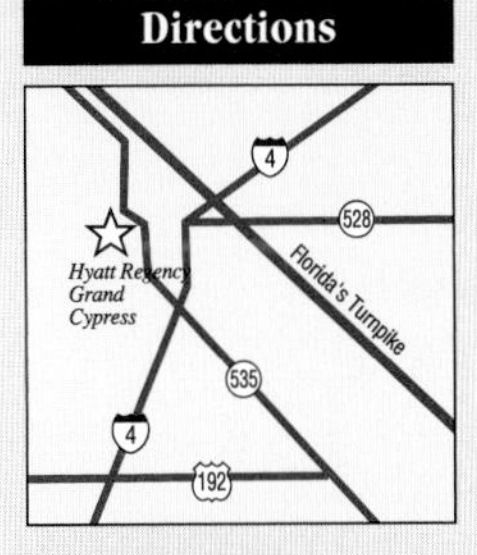

At the Hyatt Regency Grand Cypress, 20 min. from Orlando International Airport

1 Grand Cypress Boulevard
Orlando, FL 32836
PH: (407) 239-1234
FAX: (407) 239-3800
www.hyattgrandcypress.com

Owners
Grand Cypress Florida Inc.

Cuisine
New World

Days Open
Open Thurs.-Mon. for dinner and Sun. for brunch

Pricing
Dinner for one,
without tax, tip, or drinks:
$40-$60

Dress Code
Resort upscale

Reservations
Recommended

Parking
Free on site, valet

Features
Private parties, cigar/cognac events

Credit Cards
AE, VC, MC, CB, DC, JCB, DS

Manuel's on the 28th

Directions

Corner of Livingston and Orange, 25 min. from Orlando International Airport

390 N. Orange Avenue
Bank of America Building
Suite 2800
Orlando, FL 32801
PH: (407) 246-0633
FAX: (407) 246-6575
www.culinaryconceptsinc.com

Owners
Hal Valdes, Chef Tony Pace, and Manny Garcia

Cuisine
Contemporary world

Days Open
Open Tues.-Sat. for dinner

Pricing
Dinner for one,
without tax, tip, or drinks:
$40-$60

Dress Code
Business casual, jacket and tie preferred

Reservations
Recommended

Parking
Garage nearby

Features
Private parties, near theater, cognac events

Credit Cards
AE, VC, MC, CB, DC, DS

Main dining room

Located atop the Bank of America Building, Manuel's on the 28th offers a breathtaking view of Orlando through floor-to-ceiling windows. The contemporary world menu has nightly specialties of exotic game and seafood. Complementing the cuisine is world-class service and a wine list with the finest California and international selections. Celebrate a special occasion, close a business deal, or simply enjoy an elegant evening 28 stories up, where all the elements come together for a majestic dining experience.

Exotic game

Intimate dining

From left, Chef Tony Pace, Manny Garcia, and Hal Valdez

AWARD WINNER
SINCE 1997

Café L'Europe

Bistro dining

Café L'Europe continues a tradition of excellence in quality cuisine, superior service, and unique ambience. This romantic, flower-filled restaurant is one of the most beautiful and elegant in Palm Beach. Enjoy selections from the caviar bar, and any of the menu specialties prepared by co-owner and Executive Chef Norbert Goldner, including fresh spinach and potato gnocchi, pecan-crusted black pearl salmon, and filet mignon in a Cabernet mushroom sauce. The wine list has more than 2,000 labels.

Filet mignon of swordfish

Dining room

Private room

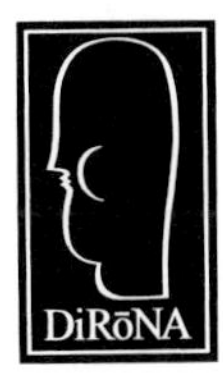

AWARD WINNER
SINCE 1993

Directions

S. Ocean Blvd.
S. County Rd.
Cocoanut Row
Royal Palm Way
Brazilian Ave.
Australian Ave.

Corner of Brazilian Avenue and South County Road, 20 min. from Palm Beach International Airport

331 South County Road
Palm Beach, Florida 33480
PH: (561) 655-4020
FAX: (561) 659-6619
www.cafeleurope.com

Owners
Norbert and Lidia Goldner

Cuisine
French, with contemporary American influence

Days Open
Open Tues.-Fri. for lunch, daily for dinner

Pricing
Dinner for one, without tax, tip, or drinks: $40-$60

Dress Code
Business casual

Reservations
Recommended

Parking
Valet

Features
Private room/parties

Credit Cards
AE, VC, MC, DC

Chancellor Grille Room

At your service

Directions

95
Flagler Dr.
Cocoanut Row
Ocean Blvd.
Okeechobee Blvd.
Royal Palm Way
Brazilian Ave.
Australian Ave.
Hibiscus
Worth Ave.

In the Brazilian Court Hotel on Austrailian Ave. at Hibiscus Ave., 10 min. from Palm Beach International Airport

301 Australian Avenue
Palm Beach, FL 33480
PH: (561) 655-7740
FAX: (561) 655-9615
www.braziliancourt.com

Cuisine
Continental

Days Open
Open daily for breakfast, lunch, and dinner

Pricing
Dinner for one, without tax, tip or drinks: $20-$40

Dress Code
Business Casual

Reservations Policy
Recommended

Parking
Free on site, valet

Features
Private room/parties, outdoor dining, entertainment, near theater, cigar/cognac events

Credit Cards
AE, VC, MC, CB, DC, DS

The Brazilian Court Hotel's formal dining room, which overlooks the famous Fountain Courtyard, offers the classic French touch of Executive Chef Jerome Nicholas, who prepares a variety of dishes to please the simple or sophisticated palate. Patrons dine sumptuously on continental cuisine with an elegant regional influence and then dance to the Brazilian Court Trio. An additional feature: the superb wine list, which *Wine Spectator* has recognized with its Award of Excellence.

Signature luncheon Maryland jumbo lump crab meat platter

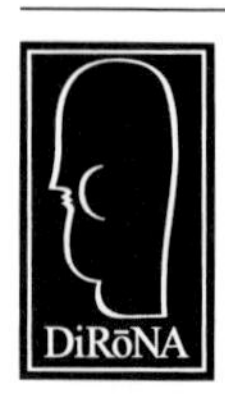

AWARD WINNER
SINCE 2001

The Florentine

The Breakers

The Florentine, located in venerable Palm Beach, offers one of the country's most unforgettable dining experiences. Reminiscent of the dining rooms of France's most elegant chateaus, the room is accented by antique mirror panels, lush fabrics, and exquisite tapestries. Passionately committed master chefs infuse two new exhibition kitchens with innovation and vitality. The foie gras of the day is a menu highlight, with such changing daily selections as pan-seared foie gras with caramelized crab apples, and roasted foie gras with braised turnips, wilted Swiss chard, and natural jus. The masterful servers have flawless tableside knowledge, and the 5,700-bottle wine cellar is one of the world's most acclaimed collections.

Rack of lamb

Pan-seared lobster

Main dining room

AWARD WINNER
SINCE 2001

Directions

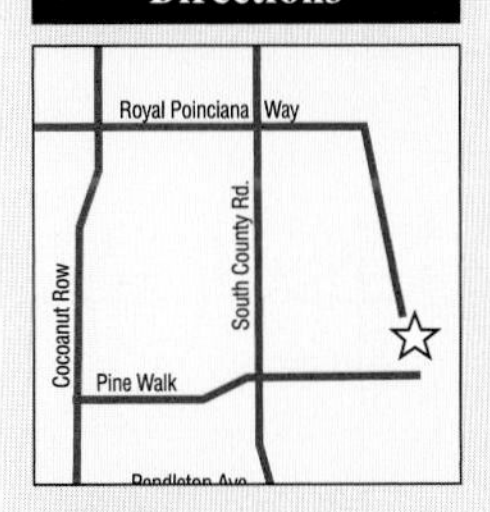

At The Breakers on South County Road, 15 min. from Palm Beach International Airport

One South County Road
Palm Beach, FL 33480
PH: (561) 659-8488
FAX: (561) 653-6328
www.thebreakers.com

Owners
Flagler System Management, Inc.

Cuisine
French

Days Open
Open daily for dinner (closed Tues. and Wed. during summer)

Pricing
Dinner for one, without tax, tip, or drinks: $40-$60

Dress Code
Jacket and tie required

Reservations
Recommended

Parking
Valet

Features
Private parties, near theater

Credit Cards
AE, VC, MC, CB, DC, DS

Capriccio Ristorante

Directions

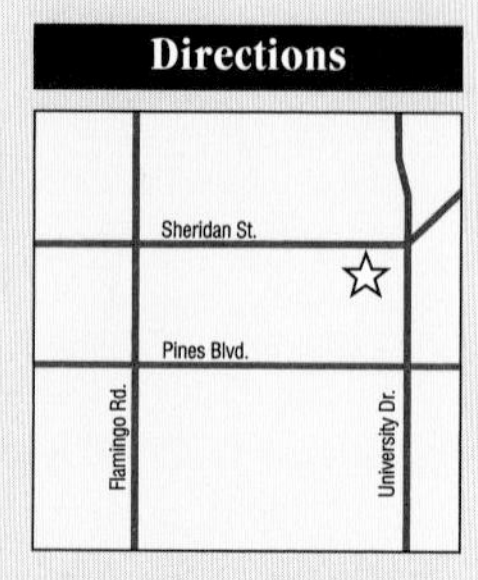

At N. University Drive and Sheridan Street, 15 min. from Fort Lauderdale-Hollywood International Airport

2424 N. Univeristy Drive
Pembroke Pines, FL 33024
PH: (954) 432-7001
FAX: (954) 432-7560
www.capriccio-online.com

Owners
Gianpiero and Karen Cangelosi

Cuisine
Fine Italian

Days Open
Open daily for dinner

Pricing
Dinner for one, without tax, tip, or drinks: $20-$40

Dress Code
Business casual

Reservations
Recommended

Parking
Free on site

Features
Private parties, entertainment, cigar/cognac events

Credit Cards
AE, VC, MC, DS

Superb food and friendly service have won Capriccio's a loyal following in its 13 years in Pembroke Pines. The restaurant has a moderately priced menu with dishes to suit any appetite, such as veal with mushrooms and baby artichokes served with sherry and lemon sauce, and shrimp sauteed in tomato, cream, vodka, and onions over penne pasta. The garlic bread is addictive, the tossed salad is the best in town, and a pianist, violinist, and vocalist add to the dining experience. There is also dancing in the lounge.

AWARD WINNER
SINCE 1998

Darrel & Oliver's Cafe Maxx

A landmark in Pompano Beach

Cafe Maxx has a 17-year history of presenting consistently fresh, innovative regional Floridian cuisine. The menu may change daily, allowing Executive Chef Oliver Saucy to prepare only the freshest entrees, which might include lobster from Maine, Key West dolphin, salmon from Norway, Midwestern beef, or free-range chicken from Colorado. Mediterranean, Asian, tropical, or Southwestern are among the seasoning choices. A cozy wine bar is a popular pre-dinner gathering spot.

Nori-wrapped salmon

Darrel Broek and Oliver Saucy

AWARD WINNER
SINCE 1993

Directions

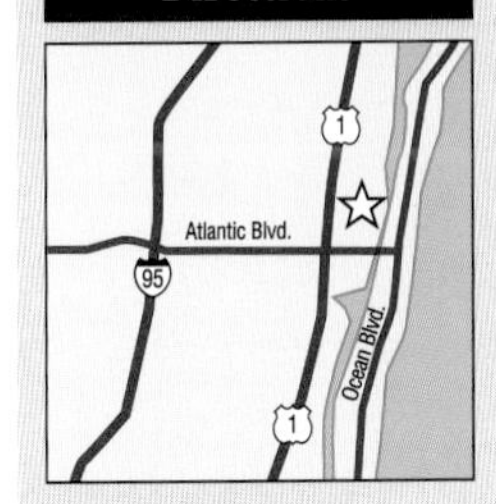

On E. Atlantic Boulevard, 25 min. from Fort Lauderdale/Hollywood International Airport

2601 E. Atlantic Boulevard
Pompano Beach, FL 33062
PH: (954) 782-0606
FAX: (954) 782-0648
www.cafemaxx.com

Owners
Darrel Broek, Oliver Saucy, Nikolai Battoo, and Gianni Respinto

Cuisine
Regional Floridian

Days Open
Open daily for dinner

Pricing
Dinner for one, without tax, tip, or drinks: $60-$80

Dress Code
Tastefully casual

Reservations
Recommended

Parking
Valet

Features
Private room/parties

Credit Cards
AE, VC, MC, DC, DS

La Parisienne

Directions

At Hypolita and Spanish streets downtown, 1 hr. 15 min. from Orlando International Airport

60 Hypolita Street
St. Augustine, FL 32084
PH: (904) 829-0055
FAX: (904) 829-1806
www.laparisienne.net

Owners
Len and Kristy Weeks

Cuisine
Contemporary French

Days Open
Open daily except Wednesday for lunch and dinner

Pricing
Dinner for one, without tax, tip, or drinks: $20-$40

Dress Code
Business casual

Reservations
Recommended

Parking
Parking lot nearby

Features
Private parties

Credit Cards
AE, VC, MC, DS

Wine from our special selections

Nestled in the heart of the nation's oldest city, La Parisienne offers an exciting selection of contemporary French cuisine. Using the freshest ingredients the seasons have to offer, from local organic farms to European delicacies, the staff creates an amazing dining experience with a five-course tasting menu. Diners may also choose one of the many wonderful dishes on the seasonally changing menu.

Flourless chocolate torte

Rack of lamb

AWARD WINNER SINCE 1999

Café L'Europe

St. Armands Circle

For better than 25 years, Café L'Europe has thrilled even the most sophisticated of palates. Located on beautiful St. Armands Circle, the restaurant has a fresh look and an exciting new menu. After studying the current culinary trends in Europe, Executive Chef Jeff Trefry has added his own nuances and created a unique "new European" cuisine. Long considered the "grande dame" of Sarasota restaurants, this establishment has virtually reinvented itself, much to the delight of locals and tourists.

Bon appetit!

General Manager Michael Garey and Chef Jeff Trefry

AWARD WINNER
SINCE 1992

Directions

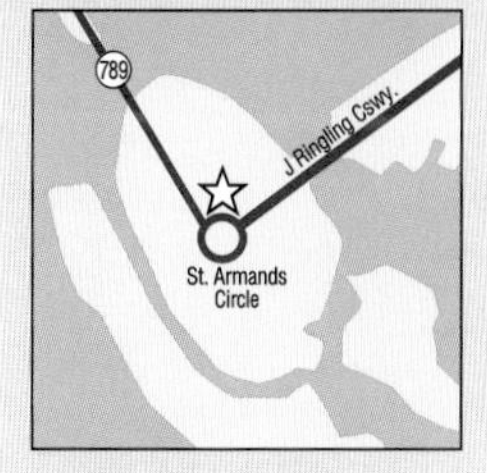

On St. Armands Circle, 20 min. from Sarasota-Bradenton International Airport

431 St. Armands Circle
Sarasota, FL 34236
PH: (941) 388-4415
FAX: (941) 388-2362
www.neweuropeancuisine.com

Owners
Titus Letschert

Cuisine
Continental European

Days Open
Open daily for lunch and dinner

Pricing
Dinner for one, without tax, tip, or drinks: $20-$40

Dress Code
Resort casual

Reservations
Recommended

Parking
Valet

Features
Private room/parties, outdoor dining, entertainment, near theater

Credit Cards
AE, VC, MC, CB, DC, DS

Michael's on East

Directions

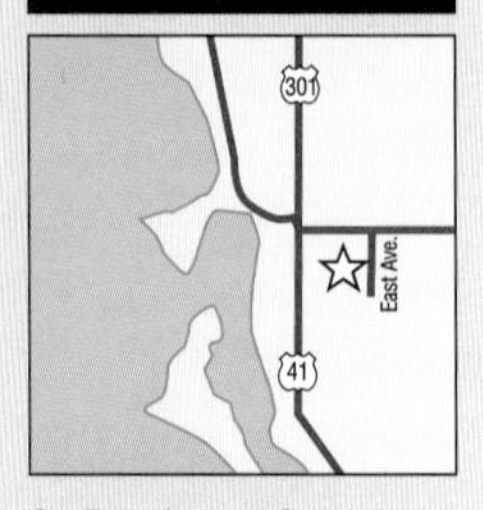

On East Avenue South in Midtown Plaza, 15 min. from Sarasota-Bradenton International Airport

1212 East Avenue South
Midtown Plaza
Sarasota, FL 34239
PH: (941) 366-0007
FAX: (941) 953-9501
www.bestfood.com

Owners
Michael Klauber and Philip Mancini

Cuisine
American Continental

Days Open
Open Mon.-Fri. for lunch, daily for dinner

Pricing
Dinner for one, without tax, tip, or drinks: $40-$60

Dress Code
Business casual

Reservations
Recommended

Parking
Valet

Features
Private room/parties, near theater

Credit Cards
AE, VC, MC, DC

Dining room

Sarasota's most celebrated restaurant is dazzling guests with its vibrant decor, reminiscent of a 1930s private dining club. The look is matched by the restaurant's inspired Continental cuisine, impeccable service, and distinguished wine list—just what you would expect from this recipient of nine consecutive Golden Spoon Awards.

Sarasota's finest Continental cuisine

Co-proprietors Michael Klauber and Philip Mancini

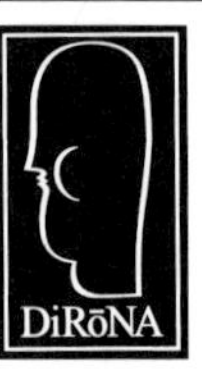

AWARD WINNER SINCE 1993

Armani's

Main dining room

Located on top of the Hyatt Regency Westshore, Armani's is the classic embodiment of a beautiful, tranquil place to dine, enjoyed by both visitors and Tampa residents alike. A rich harvest of northern Italian selections and an extravagant antipasti bar awaits diners' contemplation. The chef and his staff prepare a variety of traditional entrees with tantalizing poultry, beef, and seafood. Succulent veal is the house specialty.

Antipasti Misto

Antipasti bar

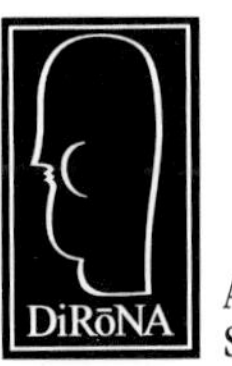

AWARD WINNER
SINCE 1992

Directions

At the Hyatt Regency Westshore on Tampa Bay, 5 min. from Tampa International Airport

Hyatt Regency Westshore
6200 Courtney Campbell Causeway
Tampa, FL 33607
PH: (813) 874-1234, ext. 165
FAX: (813) 288-0374
www.hyatt.com

Owners
Hyatt Hotels Corporation

Cuisine
Northern Italian

Days Open
Open Mon.-Sat. for dinner

Pricing
Dinner for one, without tax, tip, or drinks: $40-$60

Dress Code
Jacket and tie required

Reservations
Required

Parking
Free on site, valet

Features
Entertainment, cigar/cognac events, wine dinners

Credit Cards
AE, VC, MC, CB, DC, ER, JCB, DS

Bern's Steak House

Classical elegance in lobby

Directions

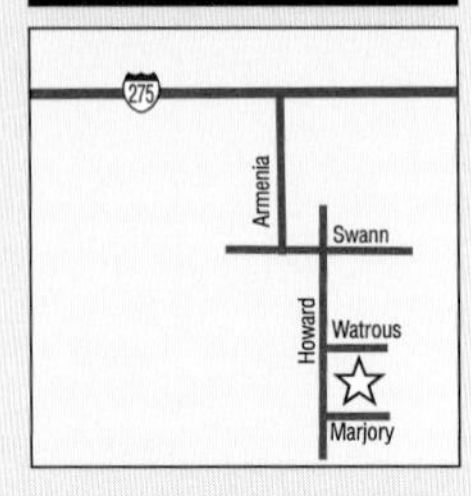

On S. Howard Avenue, 20 min. from Tampa International Airport

1208 S. Howard Avenue
Tampa, FL 33606
PH: (813) 251-2421
FAX: (813) 251-5001
www.bernssteakhouse.com

Owners
David and Christina Laxer

Cuisine
Steakhouse

Days Open
Open daily for dinner

Pricing
Dinner for one, without tax, tip, or drinks: $40-$60

Dress Code
Business casual

Reservations
Recommended

Parking
Free on site, valet

Features
Entertainment

Credit Cards
AE, VC, MC, CB, DC, DS

Since its humble beginnings in 1956, Bern's Steak House has been driven by the perfectionism of Bern Laxer, resulting in an exceptional steakhouse with an impressive reputation. From organically grown vegetables, to the hand-sorted coffee beans roasted fresh daily, to a service staff trained for over a year, every effort has been made to ensure the most memorable evening. Specialties include steak tartare Bern, escargot, and aged USDA Prime beef.

Extensive wine cellar

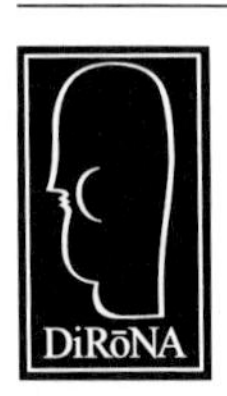

AWARD WINNER SINCE 1992

Donatello

Main dining room

Donatello, named after the famous Florentine sculptor, has been a Tampa tradition since 1984, serving the finest Northern Italian cuisine. Immediately as guests step inside, they are welcomed and catered to from the first sip of wine to the roses that are given at the end of every meal. Exquisite culinary creations include fresh oysters cooked in the shell with spinach and cream and fresh hand-rolled pasta, and osso bucco.

Owner Guido Tiozzo

Dessert table

AWARD WINNER
SINCE 2001

Directions

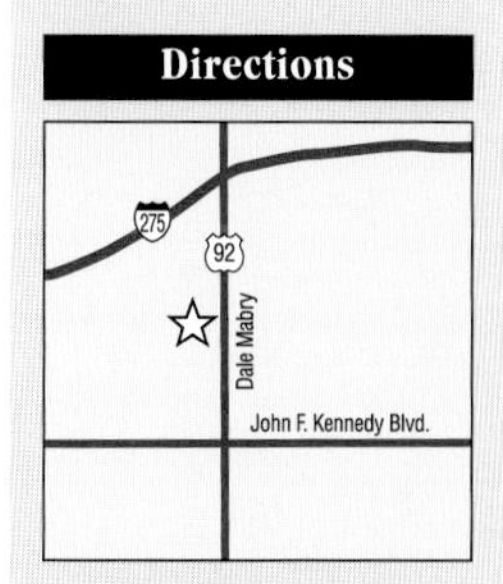

One block north of Kennedy Blvd., 5 min. from Tampa International Airport

232 North Dale Mabry Highway
Tampa, FL 33609
PH: (813) 875-6660
FAX: (813) 876-3644
www.donatellorestaurant.com

Owners
Guido Tiozzo

Cuisine
Northern Italian

Days Open
Open Mon.-Fri. for lunch, daily for dinner

Pricing
Dinner for one, without tax, tip or drinks: $40-$60

Dress Code
Business casual

Reservations Policy
Recommended

Parking
Free on site, valet

Features
Private room/parties, live music, cigar/cognac events

Credit Cards
AE, VC, MC, CB, DC, JCB, DS

Café du Soir

Directions

At the end of Royal Palm Boulevard, east of Indian River Boulevard, 1 hr. 45 min. from both Orlando International and Palm Beach International Airports

21 Royal Palm Boulevard
Vero Beach, FL 32960
PH: (561) 569-4607
FAX: (561) 569-4607

Owners
Yannick and Valerie Martin

Cuisine
French

Days Open
Open daily for dinner (closed Sun. and Mon. during summer)

Pricing
Dinner for one, without tax, tip, or drinks: $20-$40

Dress Code
Business casual

Reservations
Recommended

Parking
Free on site

Features
Private room/parties, outdoor dining

Credit Cards
AE, VC, MC, DC

Dining room

Recognized as one of Vero Beach's best restaurants, Valerie and Yannick Martin's Café du Soir offers an elegant country French setting paired with the skillfully prepared cuisine of French-born Yannick. A distinctive air of authenticity and a true European feel entices diners to relax and enjoy a wide array of dishes, such as sauteéd Dover sole with white butter sauce, onion-encrusted grouper with a caramelized onion-bacon confit, and one dozen snails in puff pastry with spinach creamy garlic sauce. Café du Soir is a well-established restaurant with a solid reputation for quality cuisine and service — a true destination.

One of three dining rooms

Daily preparation of bread

Yannick and his staff

AWARD WINNER
SINCE 1997

Ruth's Chris Steak House

Filet mignon

This is the steak that steak lovers rave about! Ruth's Chris Steak House specializes in USDA Prime beef. Strips, filets, ribeyes, T-bones, and porterhouses are aged to exacting standards, broiled to perfection, and served sizzling. An award-winning wine list features premium vintages by the glass. The service is attentive, knowledgeable, and friendly.

AWARD WINNER SINCE 1998

Directions

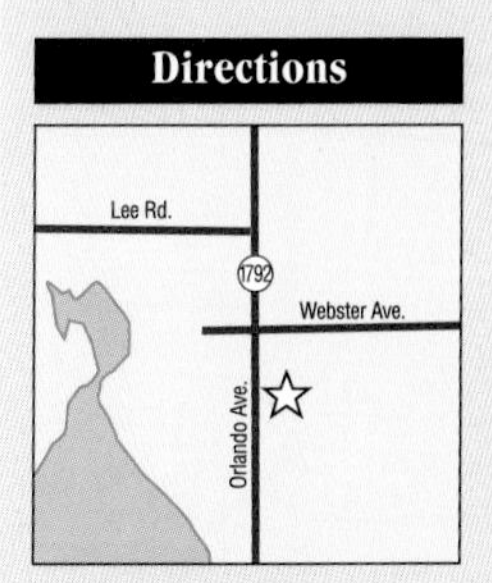

In the Winter Park Mall, 25 min. from Orlando International Airport

610 N. Orlando Avenue
Winter Park, FL 32789
PH: (407) 622-2444
FAX: (407) 622-4455
www.ruthschris.com

Owners
Ruth's Chris Steak House

Cuisine
Steaks, seafood

Days Open
Open daily for dinner

Pricing
Dinner for one, without tax, tip, or drinks: $40-$60

Dress Code
Business casual

Reservations
Recommended

Parking
Valet

Features
Private rooms/parties

Credit Cards
AE, VC, MC, DC, DS

The Abbey

Established in 1968, The Abbey is a gothic church converted into Atlanta's most-honored restaurant. Vaulted ceilings, massive stained glass windows, and waiters in monk robes create a medieval atmosphere. Executive Chef Philippe Haddad prepares a varied, contemporary classic cuisine which includes seared Maine sea scallops with rock shrimp, portabella vegetarian Napoleon, and grilled elk chops. An award-winning wine list complements the dinner menu.

Fine cuisine

Romantic setting

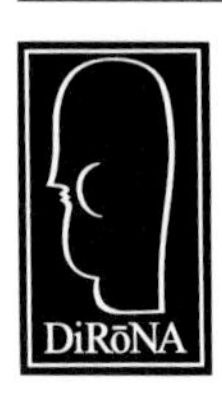

AWARD WINNER
SINCE 1999

Directions

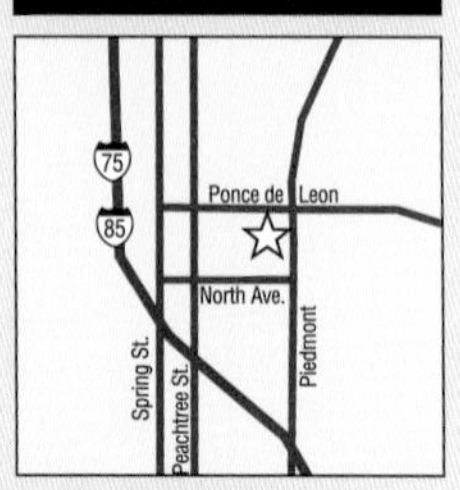

On Ponce de Leon Avenue in midtown, 15 min. from Hartsfield Atlanta International Airport

163 Ponce de Leon Avenue
Atlanta, GA 30308
PH: (404) 876-8532
FAX: (404) 876-8832
www.theabbeyrestaurant.com

Owners
Bill Swearingen

Cuisine
Contemporary classic

Days Open
Open daily for dinner

Pricing
Dinner for one,
without tax, tip, or drinks:
$40-$60

Dress Code
Business casual

Reservations
Recommended

Parking
Free on site

Features
Entertainment/pianist

Credit Cards
AE, VC, MC, CB, DC, JCB, DS

Bone's Restaurant

Main dining room

Bone's has long been a "must visit" in Buckhead. Its clubby atmosphere, award-winning food, and 10,000-bottle wine cellar have made it a favorite choice for local diners. The walls are covered with photographs of Atlanta landmarks and caricatures of local personalities. Executive Chef Gregory Gammage prepares such specialties as prime beef, live Maine lobster, and lamb chops.

The Back Room

Menu specialties

AWARD WINNER
SINCE 1996

Directions

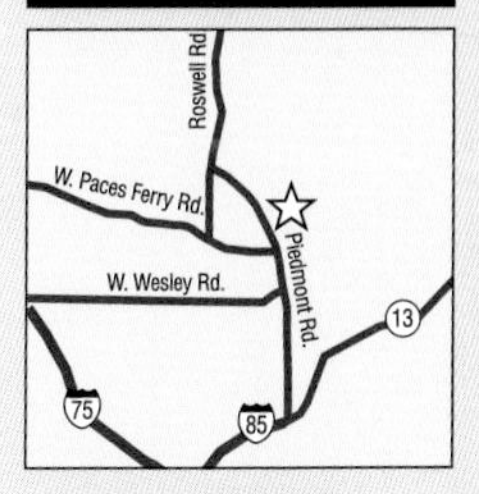

On Piedmont Road in Buckhead, 30 min. from Hartsfield Atlanta International Airport

3130 Piedmont Road
Atlanta, GA 30305
PH: (404) 237-2663
FAX: (404) 233-5704

Owners
Susan DeRose and Richard Lewis

Cuisine
Steakhouse

Days Open
Open Mon.-Fri. for lunch, daily for dinner

Pricing
Dinner for one, without tax, tip, or drinks: $40-$60

Dress Code
Casual upscale

Reservations
Recommended

Parking
Valet

Features
Private room/parties

Credit Cards
AE, VC, MC, CB, DC, DS

Directions

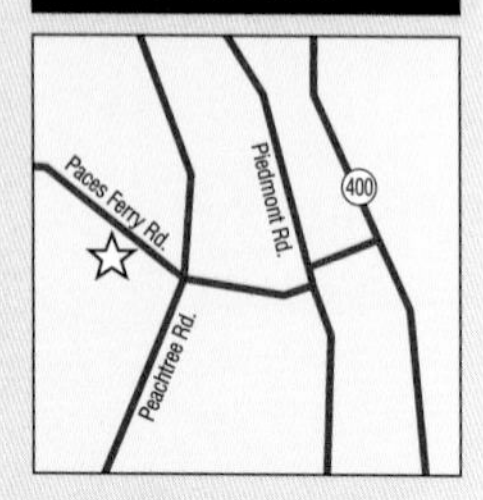

In Buckhead on W. Paces Ferry Road, 25 min. from Hartsfield Atlanta International Airport

70 W. Paces Ferry Road
Atlanta, GA 30305
PH: (404) 262-2675
FAX: (404) 240-6645
www.buckheadrestaurants.com

Owner
Pano Karatassos

Cuisine
Classic steakhouse and seafood

Days Open
Open daily for lunch and dinner

Pricing
Dinner for one, without tax, tip, or drinks: $20-$40

Dress Code
Business casual

Reservations
Recommended

Parking
Valet, or validated parking

Features
Private room/parties

Credit Cards
AE, VC, MC, DC, DS

Chops

Chops is a classic yet state-of-the-art restaurant, consistently ranked one of the country's top 10 steak houses. The architecture and interior are an integral part of the overall dining experience. Executive Chef Rickey Figueroa prepares exceptional seafood and uses only the very best USDA prime aged beef — all served with attentive style. An award-winning wine list complements the classic menu.

AWARD WINNER
SINCE 1995

The Dining Room at The Ritz-Carlton, Buckhead

Intimate dining

Executive Chef Joel Antunes creates a new menu daily at The Dining Room, Georgia's only Mobil Five-Star, AAA Five-Diamond restaurant. For a dining experience unmatched in the Southeast, try the tasting menu, paired with premium wines suggested by the sommelier. A counterpoint to the intimate setting — silk-upholstered seating at tables surrounded by museum-quality art on mahogany paneled walls — is the open kitchen where the chef and his 10 assistants prepare each course. Uncompromising personal service is orchestrated by a professional staff under the direction of manager Peter Krehan.

Executive Chef Joel Antunes

AWARD WINNER
SINCE 1992

Directions

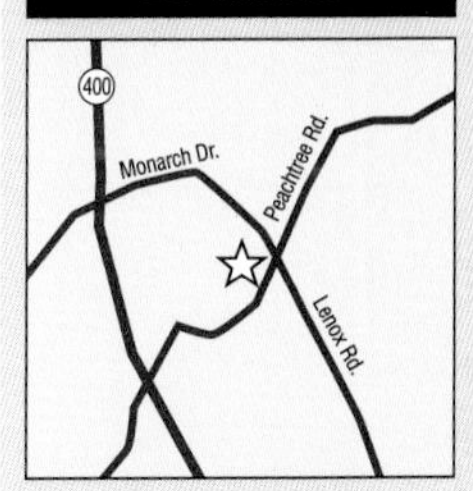

At Peachtree and Lenox roads in the heart of Buckhead, 25 min. from Atlanta Hartsfield International Airport

3434 Peachtree Road NE
Atlanta GA 30326
PH: (404) 237-2700
FAX: (404) 262-2888
www.ritzcarlton.com

Owners
The Ritz-Carlton, Buckhead

Cuisine
French-Mediterranean with Thai influences

Days Open
Open Mon.-Sat. for dinner

Pricing
Dinner for one, without tax, tip, or drinks: $80+

Dress Code
Jacket and tie required

Reservations
Required

Parking
Valet

Credit Cards
AE, VC, MC, DC

The 1848 House

Directions

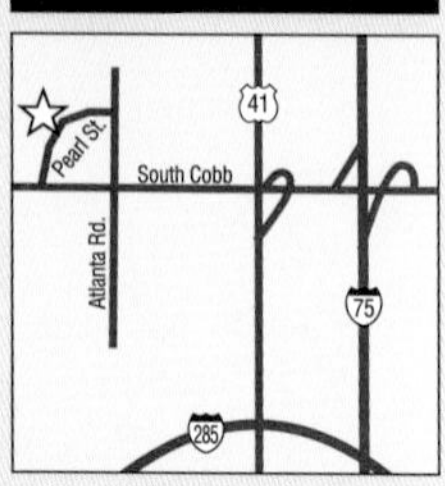

In Marietta, off I-75 at exit 261, 30 min. from Hartsfield Atlanta International Airport

780 S. Cobb Drive
Marietta, GA 30060
PH: (770) 428-1848
FAX: (770) 427-5886
www.1848House.com

Owners
William B. Dunaway

Cuisine
Contemporary Southern

Days Open
Open Tues.-Sun. for dinner, jazz brunch on Sun.

Pricing
Dinner for one, without tax, tip, or drinks: $20-$40

Dress Code
Business casual

Reservations
Recommended

Parking
Free on site, free valet

Features
Private room/parties, outdoor dining, near theater, Sunday jazz brunch

Credit Cards
AE, VC, MC, CB, DC, JCB, DS

The 1848 House

The 1848 House, a bastion of fine Southern cooking, is located in a National Historic Register plantation home on a Civil War battle site. It earned its "Best Southern Cuisine" commendation from *Atlanta Magazine* for such mouthwatering dishes as Charleston she-crab soup, and maple-pecan crusted boneless Georgia trout pan fried with a mess of greens and orange-vanilla Chardonnay sauce. Don't miss the Sunday jazz brunch.

Chef Tom McEachern

Produce from our garden

The Back Yard

AWARD WINNER
SINCE 1997

La Grotta Ristorante Italiano

Delightful dining atmosphere

For over two decades, La Grotta Ristorante Italiano has been known for its classic Northern and regional Italian cuisine. The atmosphere is private and elegant yet relaxed. Co-owner and Executive Chef Antonio Abizanda prepares grilled specialties and vegetarian dishes, as well as homemade pastas, fresh seafood, veal, and beef. Complementing the varied menu is an extensive wine list. There is also a private terrace overlooking a beautiful garden for outside dining.

Owners Antonio Abizanda and Sergio Favalli

Hearty Italian cuisine

Imaginative creations

AWARD WINNER
SINCE 1997

Directions

In Buckhead on Peachtree Road NE, 25 min. from Hartsfield Atlanta International Airport

2637 Peachtree Road NE
Atlanta, GA 30305
PH: (404) 231-1368
FAX: (404) 231-1274
www.la-grotta.com

Owners
Sergio Favalli and Antonio Abizanda

Cuisine
Northern and regional Italian

Days Open
Open Mon.-Sat. for dinner

Pricing
Dinner for one, without tax, tip, or drinks: $20-$40

Dress Code
Jacket suggested

Reservations
Recommended

Parking
Valet

Features
Private parties, outdoor dining, near theaters

Credit Cards
AE, VC, MC, CB, DC, JCB, DS

Nava

Directions

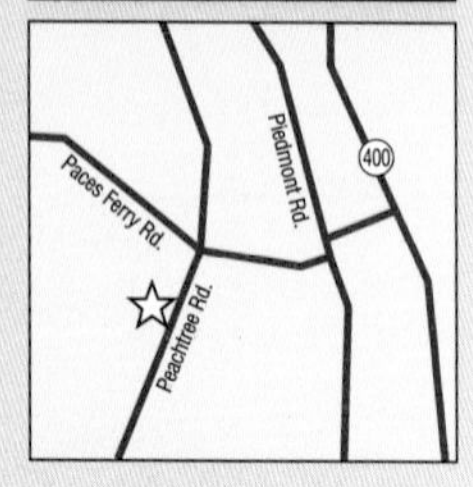

In Buckhead on Peachtree Road, 25 min. from Hartsfield Atlanta International Airport

3060 Peachtree Road
Suite 160
Atlanta, GA 30305
PH: (404) 240-1984
FAX: (404) 240-1831
www.buckheadrestaurants.com

Owner
Pano Karatassos

Cuisine
Upscale Southwestern

Days Open
Open daily for lunch and dinner

Pricing
Dinner for one, without tax, tip, or drinks: $20-$40

Dress Code
Business casual

Reservations
Recommended

Parking
Valet

Features
Outdoor dining

Credit Cards
AE, VC, MC, DC, DS

Main dining room at Nava

Nava is an upscale, dramatically decorated restaurant that serves its Southwestern cuisine with theatrical flair. The innovative menu features a variety of seafood, meat, and game dishes, with Latin and Native American influences. Executive Chef Brian Krell creates bold flavors, vibrant colors, and unusual textures by using ingredients indigenous to the South and Southwest. Menu items include green chili lobster tacos, suncorn crusted snapper, and red chili seared scallops. The entrees can be prepared mild or robust, as the guest desires.

AWARD WINNER
SINCE 1998

Nikolai's Roof

Main dining room

Nikolai's Roof, gracing the top floor of the downtown Hilton, offers guests a spectacular view, striking interior, and delectable French Continental cuisine. Executive Chef Johannes Klapdohr's meticulously executed menu also features Russian specialties. Special marinated Russian vodkas and caviar from the Caspian Sea are popular items. The cuisine, the wine list, and the outstanding service orchestrated by maitre d' Michel Sauvage have proven to be an unparalleled combination, earning Nikolai's Roof four stars from Mobil.

Take the outside elevator to Nikolai's Roof.

AWARD WINNER
SINCE 1992

Directions

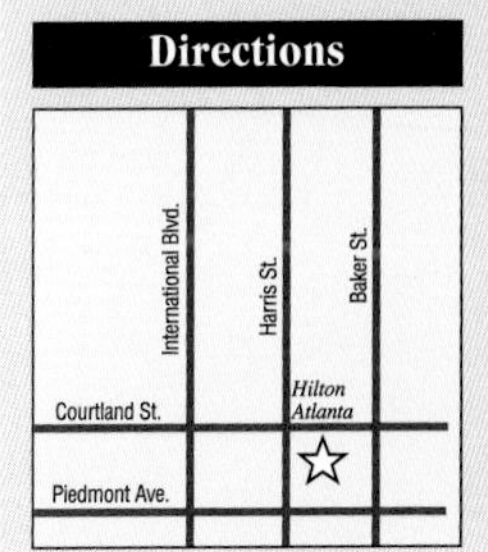

Atop the Hilton Atlanta & Towers downtown, 20 min. from Hartsfield Atlanta International Airport

Hilton Atlanta & Towers
255 Courtland Street NE
Atlanta, GA 30303
PH: (404) 221-6362
FAX: (404) 221-6811
www.atlanta.hilton.com

Owners
Hilton Hotel Corp.

Cuisine
French Continental

Days Open
Open daily for dinner

Pricing
Dinner for one,
without tax, tip, and drinks:
$60-$80

Dress Code
Jacket and tie required

Reservations
Required

Parking
Free on site, valet, garage nearby

Features
Private room/parties, near theater, cigar/cognac events

Credit Cards
AE, VC, MC, CB, DC, DS

103 West

Directions

Near the Governor's Mansion on W. Paces Ferry Road, 20 min. from Hartsfield Atlanta International Airport

103 W. Paces Ferry Road
Atlanta, GA 30305
PH: (404) 233-5993
FAX: (404) 240-6619
www.buckheadrestaurants.com

Owners
Pano Karatassos

Cuisine
Continental with French influence

Days Open
Open Mon.-Sat. for dinner

Pricing
Dinner for one, without tax, tip, or drinks: $20-$40

Dress Code
Jacket required, tie optional

Reservations
Recommended

Parking
Free on site, valet

Features
Private room/parties, entertainment, cigar/cognac events

The main dining room

103 West is one of Atlanta's most glamorous restaurants, featuring continental cuisine with a French influence. Executive Chef Gary Donlick prepares entrees such as sauteed Atlantic salmon with toasted sesame crust, rosemary and garlic roasted lamb chops, roasted farm-raised ostrich loin, and cold water lobster tail in thin-crisped batter. The award-winning wine list is extensive.

Unique decor

Cozy elegance

Intimate dining

AWARD WINNER
SINCE 1992

Pano's & Paul's

This Atlanta institution is known as the standard for luxury dining. Pano's & Paul's features creative American/ Continental fare in an elegant, club-like environment. The service is exceptional. Under the direction of Executive Chef Peter Kaiser, the varied menu includes such entrees as the "famous" cold water lobster tail, breast of Peking duck, and broiled filet mignon.

Executive Chef
Peter Kaiser

AWARD WINNER
SINCE 1992

Directions

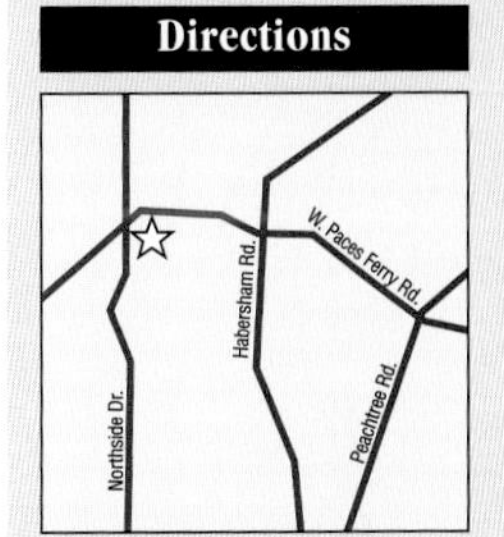

On W. Paces Ferry Road near the Governor's Mansion, 25 min. from Hartsfield Atlanta International Airport

1232 W. Paces Ferry Road
Atlanta, GA 30327
PH: (404) 261-3662
FAX: (404) 261-4512
www.buckheadrestaurants.com

Owners
Pano Karatassos

Cuisine
Creative American/ Continental

Days Open
Open Mon.-Sat. for dinner

Pricing
Dinner for one, without tax, tip, or drinks: $20-$40

Dress Code
Business casual

Reservations
Recommended

Parking
Free on site

Features
Private room/parties

Credit Cards
AE, VC, MC, DC, DS

Pricci

Dining room at Pricci

An up-to-the-moment outrageous yet authentic Italian restaurant, Pricci boasts a creative menu, a dramatically fun interior, and beautiful private rooms. The architecture and furniture are stunning, and the service is excellent. Pricci has an open kitchen, with wood-burning pizza ovens and even an herb garden. Executive Chef Marc Sublette has created a diverse menu which includes unique pizzas, home-style pastas, salads, regional seafoods, and specialty desserts.

Executive Chef Marc Sublette

Directions

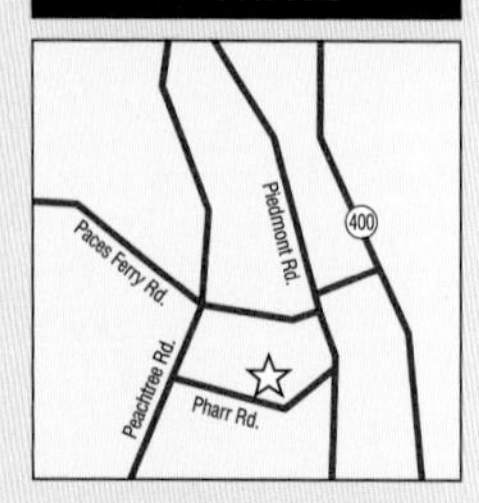

In Buckhead on Pharr Road, 25 min. from Hartsfield Atlanta International Airport

500 Pharr Road
Atlanta, GA 30305
PH: (404) 237-2941
FAX: (404) 261-0058
www.buckheadrestaurants.com

Owner
Pano Karatassos

Cuisine
Modernly, authentic Italian

Days Open
Open daily for lunch and dinner

Pricing
Dinner for one, without tax, tip, or drinks: $20-$40

Dress Code
Business casual

Reservations
Recommended

Parking
Valet

Features
Private room/parties

Credit Cards
AE, VC, MC, DC, DS

AWARD WINNER SINCE 1997

Veni Vidi Vici

Dining room

Veni Vidi Vici offers hearty, flavorful Italian cuisine, served with style in a chic Midtown location. Executive Chef Michael Persichetti has created a varied menu. Highlights include antipasti piccoli, wood-burning rotisserie-roasted pork, lamb, duck, and chicken; and handmade pastas. The outdoor terrace beckons during the warm-weather months.

AWARD WINNER SINCE 1995

Directions

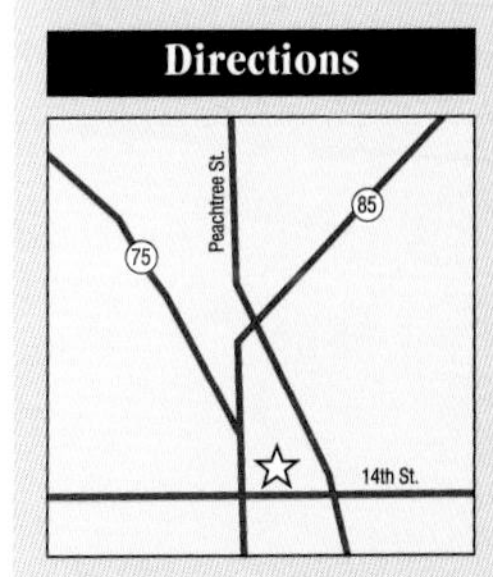

In Midtown on 14th Street, 20 min. from Hartsfield Atlanta International Airport

41-14th Street
Atlanta, GA 30309
PH: (404) 875-8424
FAX: (404) 875-6533
www.buckheadrestaurants.com

Owner
Pano Karatassos

Cuisine
Authentic, rustic Italian

Days Open
Open for lunch Mon.-Fri., daily for dinner

Pricing
Dinner for one, without tax, tip, or drinks: $20-$40

Dress Code
Business casual

Reservations
Recommended

Parking
Valet, or self-parking

Features
Private room/parties, outdoor dining

Credit Cards
AE, VC, MC, DC, DS

Bali by-the-Sea

A memorable dining experience

Overlooking Waikiki Beach, Bali by-the-Sea offers a memorable dining experience with delicious, island-inspired cuisine, elegant surroundings on the mezzanine level of the Hilton Hawaiian Village's Rainbow Tower, and friendly service. Executive Chef Jean Luc Voegele applies French and Asian techniques to the best seafoods and meats from Hawaii and around the world. His signature dishes include opakapaka with kaffir lime sauce, and rack of lamb encrusted with macadamia nuts and herbs. An excellent wine list has numerous selections from celebrated European and American vineyards.

Elegant surroundings

Chef Jean Luc Voegele

AWARD WINNER
SINCE 1993

Directions

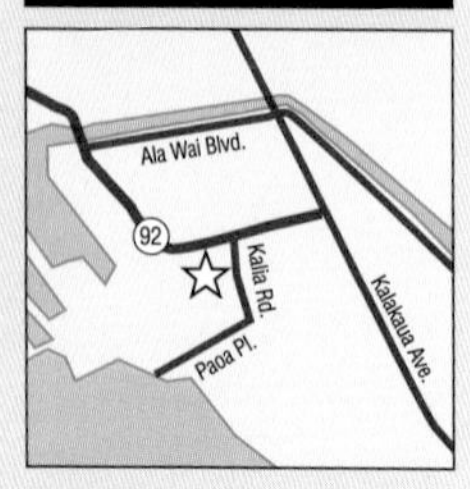

At the Hilton Hawaiian Village in Waikiki, 30 min. from Honolulu International Airport

Hilton Hawaiian Village
2005 Kalia Road
Honolulu, HI 96815
PH: (808) 949-4321
FAX: (808) 947-7898

Owners
Hilton Hotels Corporation

Cuisine
Pacific Rim, with European flair

Days Open
Open Mon.-Sat. for dinner

Pricing
Dinner for one,
without tax, tip, or drinks:
$40-$60

Dress Code
Evening casual

Reservations
Recommended

Parking
Valet

Features
Private room

Credit Cards
AE, VC, MC, CB, DC, JCB, DS

Cafe Portofino

Come and enjoy true authentic Italian cuisine at the award-winning Cafe Portofino. Its hardworking owners, settlers from Italy, are committed to high food quality and professional service. The bright, spacious, and cheerful restaurant offers a variety of tasty and generous entrees, including fine pastas, fresh seafood, great osso buco, sensational ahi carpaccio and many other specialties. The restaurant also features heavenly homemade gelati that is prepared daily.

Owner Giuseppe Avocadi

Elegant selections

Main dining room

AWARD WINNER
SINCE 1999

Directions

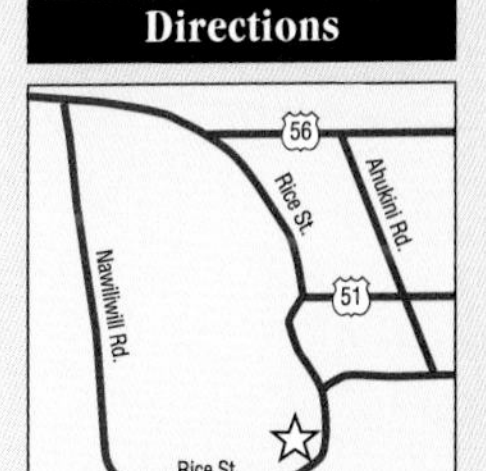

In New Harbor Mall across from the Kauai Marriott, 5 minutes from Lihue Airport

3501 Rice Street #208
Lihue, HI 96766
PH: (808) 245-2121
FAX: (808) 246-0553
www.cafeportofino.com

Owners
Giuseppe Avocadi

Cuisine
Classic Northern Italian

Days Open
Open daily for dinner

Pricing
Dinner for one, without tax, tip, or drinks: $20-$40

Dress Code
Business casual

Reservations
Recommended

Parking
Free on site

Features
Private parties, outdoor dining, entertainment, near theater, cigar/cognac events

Credit Cards
AE, VC, MC, CB, DC, JCB

The Anuenue Room

Directions

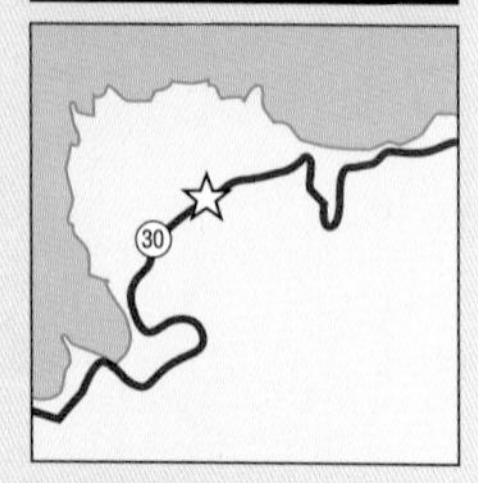

At The Ritz-Carlton, Kapalua, 5 min. from West Maui-Kapalua Airport

One Ritz-Carlton Drive
Kapalua, Maui, HI 96761
PH: (808) 669-6200
FAX: (808) 665-0026
www.ritzcarlton.com

Owners
NI Hawaii Resort

Cuisine
Contemporary Hawaiian

Days Open
Open Tues.-Sat. for dinner

Pricing
Dinner for one,
without tax, tip, or drinks:
$60-$80

Dress Code
Resort business casual

Reservations
Recommended

Parking
Free on site, valet

Features
Private room/parties, outdoor dining, entertainment, cigar/cognac events

Credit Cards
AE, VC, MC, CB, DC, ER, JCB, DS

Terrace with ocean view

Warm and intimate, The Anuenue Room at The Ritz-Carlton, Kapalua, commands spectacular views of the Bay Golf Course, Pailolo Channel, and the island of Molokai. This award-winning restaurant features contemporary island cuisine emphasizing local bounty. Among the innovative offerings are barbecued rack of lamb with ohi a ai (mountain apple) glaze and inamona (kukui nut) crust, and sauteed Kona crab cake with watercress and sun-dried guava butter.

Warm elegance

AWARD WINNER
SINCE 1997

Beverly's Restaurant

Rick Powers, Director of Food and Beverage, with Executive Chefs Rod Jessick (left) and Jim Barrett

Overlooking Lake Coeur d'Alene, Beverly's Restaurant features distinctive entrees ranging from Midwestern Prime Grade beef and fresh seafood flown in daily to such exotic fare as Priest River buffalo and Idaho ostrich. Guests dine amid casual elegance in comfortable surroundings and are pampered by an attentive staff. The wine cellar has been consistently cited for excellence by *Wine Spectator*.

Beverly's dining room

Lake Coeur d'Alene

AWARD WINNER
SINCE 1992

Directions

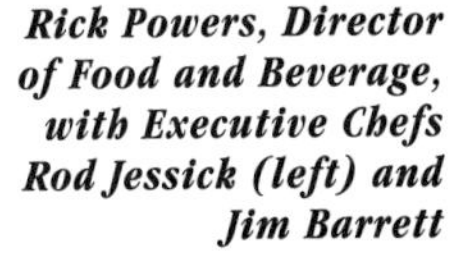

At the Coeur d'Alene Resort, off Exit 11 of Interstate 90, 40 min. from Spokane (Wash.) International Airport

The Coeur d'Alene Resort
P.O. Box 7200
115 Front Street
Coeur d'Alene, ID 83814
PH: (208) 765-4000, ext. 23
or (800) 688-4142
FAX: (208) 664-7220
www.cdaresort.com

Owners
Duane B. Hagadone and Jerald J. Jaeger

Cuisine
Seafood and beef with a Northwest flair

Days Open
Open daily for lunch and dinner

Pricing
Dinner for one, without tax, tip, or drinks: $20-$40

Dress Code
Resort casual

Reservations
Recommended

Parking
Free on site, valet

Features
Private room/parties, entertainment in lounge

Credit Cards
AE, VC, MC, CB, DC, DS

Le Titi de Paris

Directions

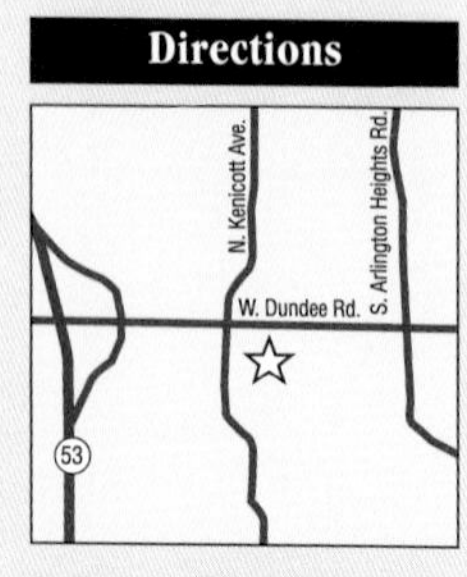

At Dundee Road (Route 68) and Kennicott Avenue, two blocks east of Route 53 and 30 min. from O'Hare International Airport

1015 W. Dundee Road
Arlington Heights, IL 60004
PH: (847) 506-0222
FAX: (847) 506-0474
www.letitideparis.com

Owners
Pierre and Judith Pollin

Cuisine
Innovative French

Days Open
Open Tues.-Fri for lunch, Tues.-Sat. for dinner

Pricing
Dinner for one, without tax, tip, or drinks: $40-$60

Dress Code
Jacket preferred

Reservations
Required

Parking
Free on site

Features
Private room/parties

Credit Cards
AE, VC, MC, CB, DC, JCB, DS

Main dining room

Proprietor and Executive Chef Pierre Pollin and Chef de Cuisine Michael Maddox serve innovative French cuisine — sauteed salmon with cider sauce is a signature dish — in a comfortably elegant setting. The main dining room is tailored somewhat formally with upholstered seating and hues of plum and gold. The wine list offers more than 1,100 selections, and a degustation dinner with wine flight is available.

Creative entrees

Sophisticated elegance

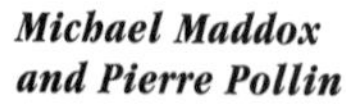

Michael Maddox and Pierre Pollin

AWARD WINNER
SINCE 1992

Ambria

At Ambria, deep-toned woods and crystalline etched glass are combined with art nouveau architectural touches, such as tiny shaded lamps on each table and massive urns of flowers. But this restaurant is noted as much for its cuisine as its high style. Owner Gabino Sotelino innovates with an approach that relies on the freshest ingredients and cooking techniques that enhance food's light, natural flavors.

Chef-owner Gabino Sotelino

AWARD WINNER
SINCE 1992

Directions

N. Lake Shore Dr.
Lincoln Park
W. Fullerton Pkwy.
W. Belden Ave.
N. Lincoln Park W.
N. Lincoln Ave.
Oz Park

In the Lincoln Park neighborhood north of the Loop, 30 min. from O'Hare International Airport

2300 N. Lincoln Park West
Chicago, IL 60614
PH: (773) 472-5959
FAX: (773) 472-9077
www.leye09.com

Owner
Gabino Sotelino

Cuisine
Fine French

Days Open
Open Mon.-Sat. for dinner

Pricing
Dinner for one,
without tax, tip, or drinks:
$80+

Dress Code
Jacket required, tie optional

Reservations
Required

Parking
Valet

Features
Private room, chef's table

Credit Cards
AE, VC, MC, CB, DC, DS

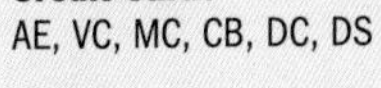

Arun's Restaurant

Directions

Montrose Ave.
Berteau Ave.
Belle Plaine Ave.
Kimball Ave.
Kedzie Ave.
Irving Park

At N. Kedzie Avenue and W. Irving Park Road in northwest Chicago, 20 min. from O'Hare International Airport

4156 N. Kedzie Avenue
Chicago, IL 60618
PH: (773) 539-1909
FAX: (773) 539-2125

Owners
Arun Sampanthavivat

Cuisine
Thai

Days Open
Open Tues.-Sun. for dinner

Pricing
Dinner for one,
without tax, tip, or drinks:
$60-$80

Dress Code
Business casual

Reservations
Required

Parking
Valet

Features
Private room

Credit Cards
AE, VC, MC, CB, DC, DS

Main dining room

Arun's exclusive "chef's design menu" is a fixed-price, 12-course dinner that gives customers the chance to explore the many tantalizing flavors (including the various degrees of spiciness) and exciting textures of refined Thai cuisine. In addition to the most prominent award, (James Beard Foundation's Best Chef, Midwest), *The New York Times* called Arun's "America's best Thai restaurant" and the *Chicago Tribune* pronounced it "a civic treasure." Arun's interior reflects the harmonious balance of contemporary simplicity and classical elegance, with cut and patterned panels of deep mahogany as well as lustrous Thai silks and exquisite paintings. A variety of fine wines, a full-service bar, and the popular Thai Singha lager add to the unforgettable dining experience.

A magnificant display of classical Thai cuisine

Chef/Owner Arun Sampanthavivat

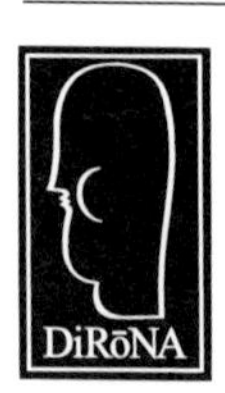

AWARD WINNER
SINCE 1998

Coco Pazzo

Coco Pazzo serves authentic regional Italian cuisine with an emphasis on Tuscan specialties as well as pastas and pizzas. Among the entrees are stewed spinach with shrimp and calamari, and wood-roasted quail with baby spinach and oyster mushrooms. The casually elegant restaurant is housed in a converted loft building with beamed ceilings, Australian cypress floors, brick walls, and large bay windows. Blue velvet drapes and theatrical lighting enhance the setting, and customers can see beyond the 80-foot antique bar into the open kitchen, which is dominated by a ceramic-tiled wood-burning oven.

Spaghetti aglio

Jack Weiss, vice president, operations and Pino Luongo, owner

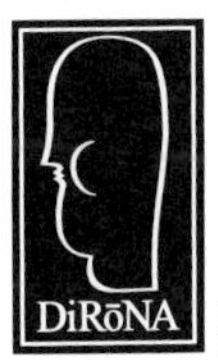

AWARD WINNER
SINCE 1998

Directions

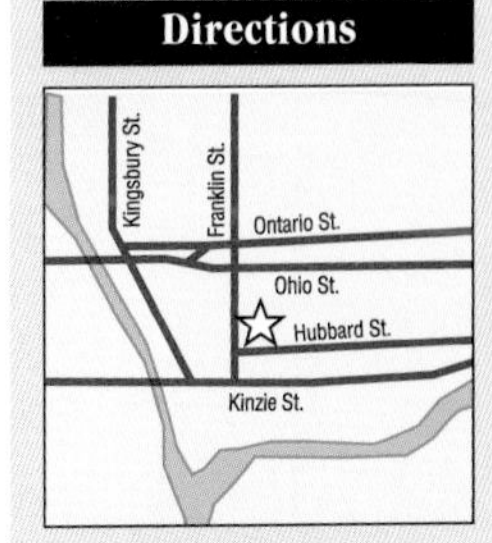

Near the Merchandise Mart in the River North area, 30 min. from O'Hare International and Midway airports

300 W. Hubbard Street
Chicago, IL 60610
PH: (312) 836-0900
FAX: (312) 836-0257
www.tribads.com/cocopazzo

Owners
Pino Luongo

Cuisine
Italian

Days Open
Open Mon.-Fri. for lunch, daily for dinner

Pricing
Dinner for one, without tax, tip, or drinks: $40-$60

Dress Code
Business casual

Reservations
Recommended

Parking
Valet

Features
Private parties, near theater, cigar/cognac events

Credit Cards
AE, VC, MC, CB, DC

The Pump Room

The bar

Directions

Schiller
Goethe
Division
State St.
Lake Shore Drive
Michigan Ave.

In the Omni Ambassador East Hotel, 45 min. from O'Hare International Airport and 30 min. from Midway Airport

1301 N. State Parkway
Chicago, IL 60610
PH: (312) 266-0360
FAX: (312) 266-1798
www.omnihotels.com

Owners
Dallas Restaurant Management Co.

Cuisine
Contemporary French

Days Open
Open daily for breakfast, lunch, and dinner (brunch on Sun.)

Pricing
Dinner for one, without tax, tip, or drinks: $40-$60

Dress Code
Business casual

Reservations
Recommended

Parking
Valet, garage nearby

Features
Private room/parties, entertainment, cigar/cognac events

Credit Cards
AE, VC, MC, CB, DC

Inventive French-inspired American cuisine, an incomparable wine list, and premier service are hallmarks of this revitalized Chicago landmark with Fariborz Rouchi as General Manager. A $2-million restoration in 1998 returned the Pump Room to its original luster and color scheme of blue and gold. Menu highlights include sauteed peppered tuna with bok choy, grilled green onions, fried lotus and ponzu sauce, and Colorado rack of lamb.

Chef Martial Noguier

The dining room

Roasted Muscovy duck

AWARD WINNER SINCE 1999

Vivere

Main dining room

One of a trio of restaurants in the Italian Village complex, Vivere is both a feast for the eyes and palate. Conical light fixtures, gilded scrolls, wrought iron stair rails, and a stained glass ceiling are hallmarks of the classy, recently redesigned dining room. The eclectic surroundings perfectly complement Executive Chef Marcelo Gallegos' innovative cuisine, which runs along the lines of pheasant-filled pasta with butter, sage, and parmesan cheese, and salmon with tomato gazpacho sauce, zucchini rosettes, and infused sweet herb oil. The wine list is a *Wine Spectator* Grand Award winner.

Frank, Gina, and Alfredo Capitanini

Duck breast with fruit and balsamic reduction

AWARD WINNER
SINCE 1998

Directions

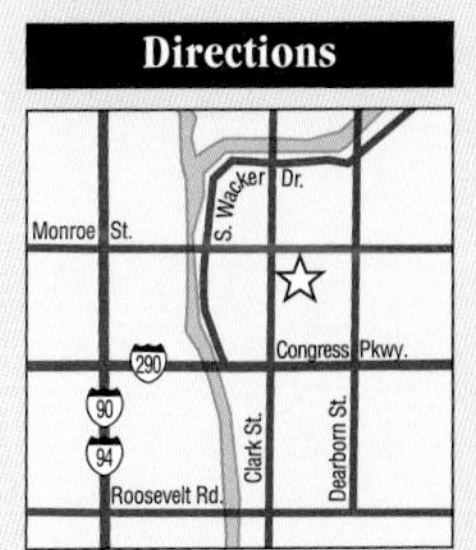

On W. Monroe between Clark and Dearborn in the Loop, 30 min. from O'Hare International Airport

71 W. Monroe
Chicago, IL 60603
PH: (312) 332-4040
FAX: (312) 332-2656
www.italianvillage-chicago.com

Owners
Capitanini family

Cuisine
Regional contemporary Italian

Days Open
Open Mon.-Fri. for lunch, Mon.-Sat. for dinner

Pricing
$20-$40

Dress Code
Business casual

Reservations
Recommended

Parking
Valet, garage nearby

Features
Private room/parties, near theater

Credit Cards
AE, VC, MC, CB, DC, JCB, DS

Carlos' Restaurant

Dining room

Directions

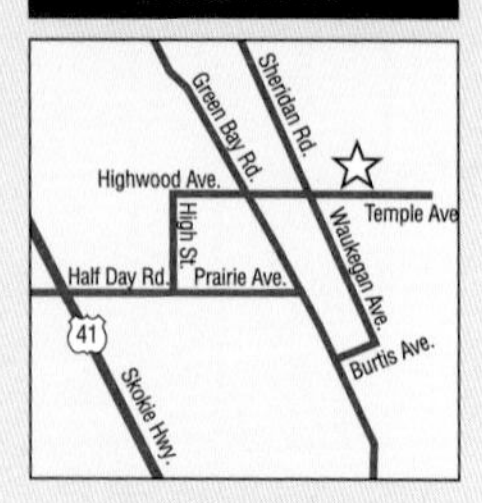

North of Chicago in Highland Park, 40 min. from O'Hare International Airport

429 Temple Avenue
Highland Park, IL 60035
PH: (847) 432-0770
FAX: (847) 432-2047
www.carlos-restaurant.com

Owners
Carlos and Debbie Nieto

Cuisine
Contemporary French

Days Open
Open Wed.-Mon. for dinner

Pricing
Dinner for one,
without tax, tip, or drinks:
$60-$80

Dress Code
Jacket required

Reservations
Required

Parking
Valet

Features
Private room/parties

Credit Cards
AE, VC, MC, CB, DC, JCB, DS

For more than a decade and a half, residents of Chicago's North Shore have been coming to Carlos' for those significant celebrations that call for a memorable meal. They come for the comfortable, understated elegance of the intimate dining room, accented by mirrors and flowers, and for the stylish, satisfying, beautifully presented fare, such as grilled loin of Scottish venison, and pan-caramelized red snapper on lemon grass. The wine list is a winner of *Wine Spectator's* Grand Award.

Stately elegance

Strawberry almond tart

Pinenut-crusted rack of Austrailian baby lamb

AWARD WINNER
SINCE 1992

Café 36

Dining room

Reinhard Barthel Sr. and his son, Reinhard Jr., impress customers and critics alike with exceptional cuisine and outstanding service in their charming French-style restaurant. Acclaimed by the *Chicago Tribune* and *Chicago Sun-Times*, Café 36 maintains high standards to ensure a memorable experience with each visit. Expect such tempting specialties as braised stuffed leg and tenderloin of rabbit in lingonberry Cabernet jus, and sauteed ostrich medallions with pink peppercorns, wild mushrooms, and brandy demi-glace. The wine list is extensive.

Venison ragout in puff pastry

Owners Reinhard Barthel Sr. and Reinhard Barthel Jr.

Chef Reinhard Barthel Jr.

AWARD WINNER
SINCE 1997

Directions

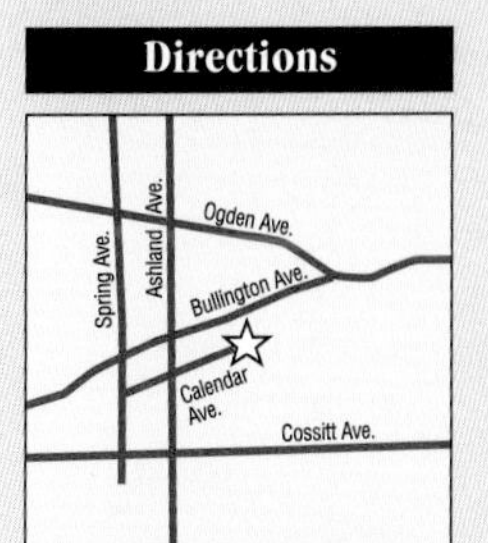

Seven miles north of the Stevenson Expressway in the southeast suburb of LaGrange, 20 min. from O'Hare International Airport

22 Calendar Court
LaGrange, IL 60525
PH: (708) 354-5722
FAX: (708) 354-5042

Owners
Reinhard Barthel Sr. and Reinhard Barthel Jr.

Cuisine
French bistro

Days Open
Open Mon.-Fri. for lunch, daily for dinner

Pricing
Dinner for one, without tax, tip, or drinks: $20-$40

Dress Code
Business casual

Reservations
Recommended

Parking
Free on site

Features
Private room/parties

Credit Cards
AE, VC, MC, DC, DS

The English Room at the Deer Path Inn

Directions

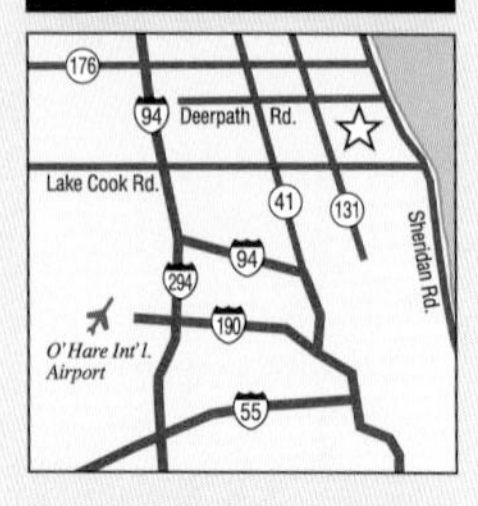

In the North Shore community of Lake Forest, 30 min. from O'Hare International Airport

225 E. Illinois Road
Lake Forest, IL 60045
PH: (847) 234-2280
FAX: (847) 234-3352
www.dpihotels.com

Owners
Michel T. Lama, General Manager

Cuisine
Continental

Days Open
Open daily for breakfast, lunch, and dinner

Pricing
Dinner for one, without tax, tip, or drinks: $20-$40

Dress Code
Business casual

Reservations
Recommended

Parking
Free on site

Features
Private room/parties, outdoor dining

Credit Cards
AE, VC, MC, DC, DC, DS

The dining room

For patrons accustomed to elegance, The English Room at the Deer Path Inn has been a dining destination since 1929. International culinary experience is paired with the finest seasonal foods to suit discriminating tastes. Move from starters, such as Maine lobster roll or foie gras, to seared sea bass with "forbidden" black rice, prime New York strip steak, or grilled veal chop. Complement these with a selection from the award-winning wine cellar.

Bass with tomato coulis

Chef Khellil Abbderezik and General Manager Michel T. Lama

AWARD WINNER SINCE 1999

Le Vichyssois

A popular Lakemoor destination

Enjoy a day in the country and then relax with a delicious dinner prepared by Chef Bernard Cretier at his French country inn, now in its 25th year. Fresh fish, steak, veal, and duck are the bill of fare at Le Vichyssois, where the specialties of the house include mushroom cigar, salmon en croute, and, of course, the namesake soup, served hot or cold. Le Vichyssois is equidistant from both Chicago and Milwaukee.

The main dining room

The bar

Understated elegance

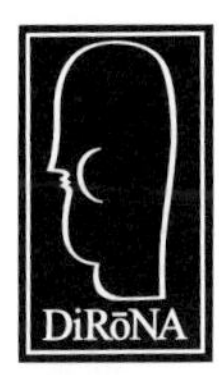

AWARD WINNER
SINCE 1992

Directions

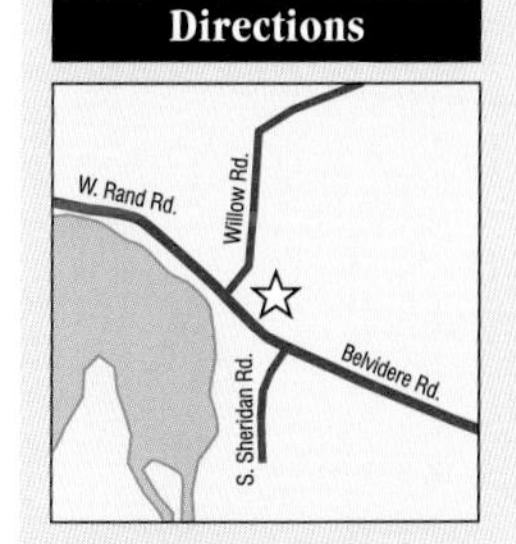

On Route 120, 2 miles west of Route 12, 45 min. from O'Hare International Airport

220 W. Route 120
Lakemoor, IL 60050
PH: (815) 385-8221
Fax: (815) 385-8223
www.levichyssois.com

Owners
Bernard and Priscilla Cretier

Cuisine
French

Days Open
Open Wed.-Sun. for dinner

Pricing
Dinner for one,
without tax, tip, or drinks:
$40-$60

Dress Code
Business casual

Reservations
Recommended

Parking
Free on site

Features
Private room/parties

Credit Cards
VC, MC, CB, DC, JCB

The Glass Chimney Restaurant

Directions

131st St.
W. Main St.
31
Pennsylvania St.
Old Meridian St.
Carmel Dr.

Off U.S. 31 north of Indianapolis, 15 min. from Indianapolis International Airport

12901 Old Meridian Street
Carmel, IN 46032
PH: (317) 844-0921
FAX: (317) 574-1360

Owners
Dieter G. Puska

Cuisine
Continental

Days Open
Open Mon.-Sat. for dinner

Pricing
Dinner for one,
without tax, tip, or drinks:
$40-$60

Dress Code
Business casual

Reservations
Recommended

Parking
Free on site

Features
Private room/parties, outdoor dining, cigar/cognac events

Credit Cards
AE, VC, MC, DC

Glass Chimney lounge

Established in 1976 by Dieter G. Puska, The Glass Chimney serves classical French and Viennese cuisine along with hearty steaks and seafood flown in daily. The restaurant has an extensive wine list and an equally comprehensive bar selection, and the mahogany lounge and bar is an inviting gathering place in its own right. “If you have time for only one meal in Indianapolis,” one restaurant critic wrote, “you must try The Glass Chimney.”

From left: maitre d' Gabriele Piron, owner Dieter G. Puska, and Executive Chef Dan Noble

Creative entrees

AWARD WINNER
SINCE 1995

Restaurant at the Canterbury

Atrium

The Restaurant at the Canterbury is just off the lobby of the historic Canterbury Hotel in the heart of downtown Indianapolis. The intimate ambience and unobtrusive, professional service are sure to exceed the expectations of the most discriminating guests. Expect American and Continental cuisine expertly prepared by Executive Chef Volker Rudolph.

Dining room

Lounge

AWARD WINNER
SINCE 1995

Directions

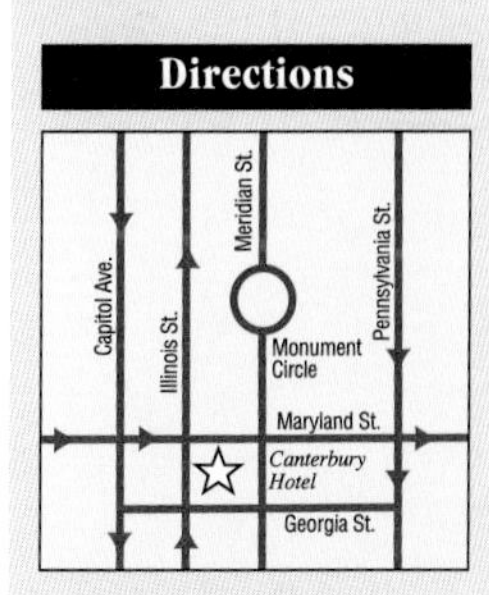

On Illinois Street, one block from the Indiana Convention Center and RCA Dome and 10 min. from Indianapolis International Airport

123 S. Illinois Street
Indianapolis, IN 46225
PH: (317) 634-3000
FAX: (317) 262-8111
www.canterburyhotel.com

Owners
DND

Cuisine
American and Continental

Days Open
Open daily for breakfast, lunch, and dinner

Pricing
$40-$60

Dress Code
Jacket and tie required

Reservations
Recommended

Parking
Valet

Features
Private room/parties, cigar/cognac events

Credit Cards
AE, VC, MC, CB, DC, JCB, DS

The Oakroom at the Seelbach Hilton

Directions

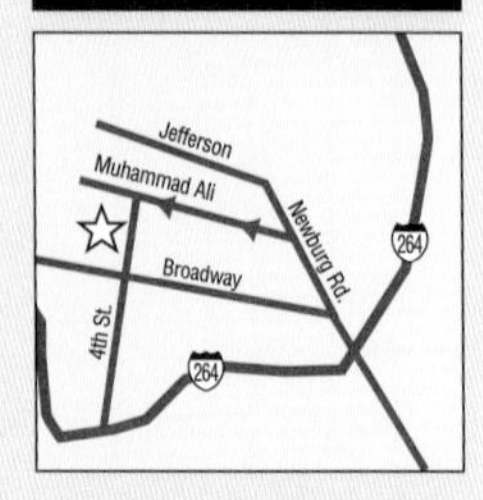

In downtown Louisville, 10 min. from Standiford Field Airport

The Seelbach Hilton
500 4th Avenue
Louisville, KY 40202
PH: (502) 807-3463
FAX: (502) 585-9240
www.hilton.com

Owners
Meristar Hotels and Resorts

Cuisine
Kentucky fine dining

Days Open
Open Fri. for lunch, Mon.-Fri. for afternoon tea, daily for dinner

Pricing
Dinner for one, without tax, tip, or drinks
$40-$60

Dress Code
Business casual

Reservations
Recommended

Parking
Complimentary valet

Features
Private rooms/parties, near theater, cigar/cognac events

Credit Cards
AE, VC, MC, DC, JCB, DS

Director Adam Seger in the wine cellar

Kentucky's first and only AAA Five-Diamond restaurant is located in the historic Seelbach Hilton. Come savor the best of Bluegrass Country. French rib chop of pork with green tomato pawpaw relish and country ham jus is just one of the many irresistible creations that emerge from the kitchen of award-winning Executive Chef Jim Gerhardt. The wine cellar has more than 1,000 selections, and the bar, cited by *The Independent* of London as one of the top 50 bars in the world, is stocked with more than 40 varieties of bourbon.

Chef de Cusine Michael Cunha

Bourbon French rib of pork

Executive Chef Jim Gerhardt

AWARD WINNER SINCE 1999

Vincenzo's

Owners Agostino and Vincenzo Gabriele

Vincenzo's represents brothers Agostino and Vincenzo Gabriele's personal dreams for a place of hospitality where friends old and new can come for a truly special evening, whether a simple meal or a multicourse tour de force. The menu reflects the owners' European heritage and training. In addition to Continental classics, Vincenzo's offers "Eurospa" heart-healthy cuisine to meet a growing preference among guests for lighter fare.

Your host

Your chef

AWARD WINNER
SINCE 1993

Directions

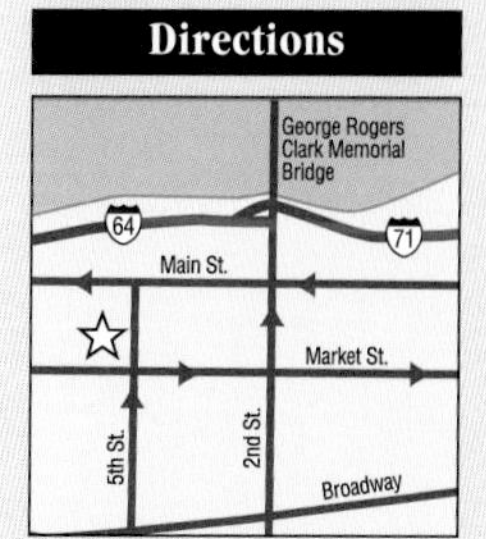

At S. 5th and Market streets in downtown Louisville, 15 min. from Louisville International Airport

150 S. 5th Street
Louisville, KY 40202
PH: (502) 580-1350
FAX: (502) 580-1355

Owners
Vincenzo Gabriele and Agostino Gabriele

Cuisine
Continental, Italian

Days Open
Open Mon.-Fri. for lunch, Mon.-Sat. for dinner

Pricing
Dinner for one, without tax, tip, or drinks: $20-$40

Dress Code
Business casual

Reservations
Recommended

Parking
Valet

Features
Private room/parties, outdoor dining, near theater, cigar/cognac events

Credit Cards
AE, VC, MC, CB, DC

Lafitte's Landing Restaurant At Bittersweet Plantation

Directions

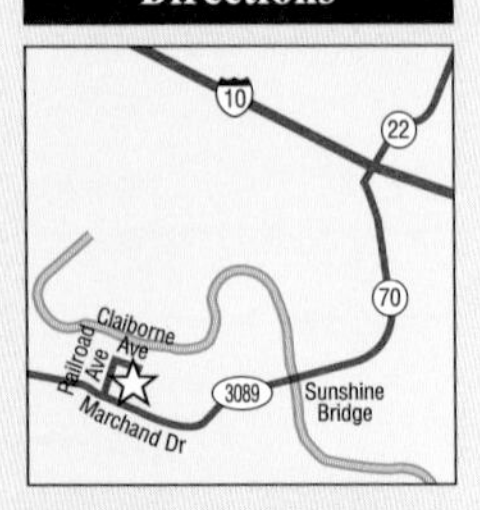

At Clairborne and Railroad avenues, 1 hr. from New Orleans International Airport and 1 hr. from Baton Rouge Regional Airport

404 Claiborne Avenue
Donaldsonville, LA 70346
PH: (225) 473-1232
FAX: (225) 473-1161
www.jfolse.com

Owner
Chef John D. Folse, CEC, AAC

Cuisine
Cajun and Creole

Days Open
Open Sun. for lunch, Tues.-Sat. for dinner

Pricing
Dinner for one, without tax, tip, or drinks: $30-$40

Dress Code
Upscale casual

Reservations
Recommended

Parking
Free on site, valet

Features
Outdoor dining, cigar/cognac events

Credit Cards
AE, VC, MC, DS

The Gingry Board Room

Located in the heart of plantation country, Lafitte's Landing Restaurant is one of the most renowned eateries in South Louisiana. The restaurant is housed in the former home of Chef John Folse, Bittersweet Plantation. Lafitte's Landing has won numerous national and international awards, including induction into the Fine Dining Hall of Fame in 1989.

Venison Carencro

Chef John Folse and staff

Bed-and-breakfast accommodations

AWARD WINN
SINCE 1996

Andrea's Restaurant

Chef Andrea Apuzzo offers the finest Northern Italian and Continental cuisine, with a great variety of selections. An array of tempting appetizers beckons from an antipasto display table as diners enter the restaurant. They include veal Tonnato, shrimp Caprese, and fresh Nova Scotia salmon. For an entree, patrons prefer white veal or fresh seafood: red snapper, speckled trout, pompano, or lobster, served with a choice of sauce.

Chef Andrea Appuzzo at antipasto table

Chicken Michelangelo

Quail Princess Anne

Pompano pesto

AWARD WINNER
SINCE 2001

Directions

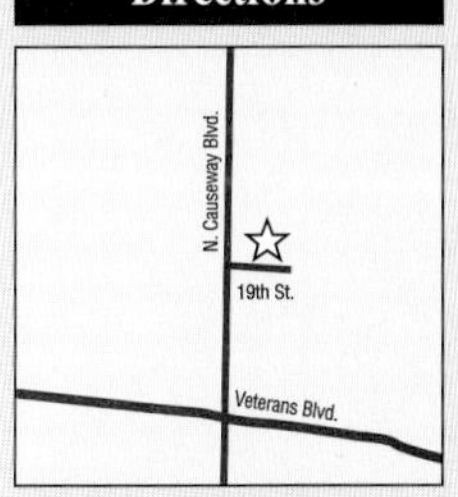

Off Causeway Boulevard in suburban Metairie, LA 15 min. from New Orleans International Airport

3100 19th Street
Metairie, LA 70002
PH: (504) 834-8583
Fax: (504) 834-6698
www.andreasrestaurant.com

Owners
Andrea and Cathie Apuzzo

Cuisine
Northern Italian, seafood

Days Open
Open Mon.-Fri. for lunch, daily for dinner, champagne brunch on Sun.

Pricing
Dinner for one, without tax, tip or drinks: $20-$40

Dress Code
Business casual

Reservations Policy
Recommended

Parking
Free on site

Features
Private room/parties, cigar/cognac events

Credit Cards
AE, VC, MC, CB, DC, DS

Arnaud's Restaurant

Arnaud's Creole cuisine excites today just as it has since 1918, with world-famous originals prepared by Executive Chef Tommy DiGiovanni. Shrimp Arnaud, oysters Bienville, trout meuniere, and grilled Louisiana quail are among the specialties. Savor lunch or dinner in quiet elegance, or dine less formally in the Richelieu Room with live jazz nightly. Superb wines complement your meal. Sunday brunch is a lively occasion set to the rhythm of a traditional Dixieland band.

Mardi Gras Museum

Pompano duarte

Owners Jane and Archie Casbarian

AWARD WINNER
SINCE 1992

Directions

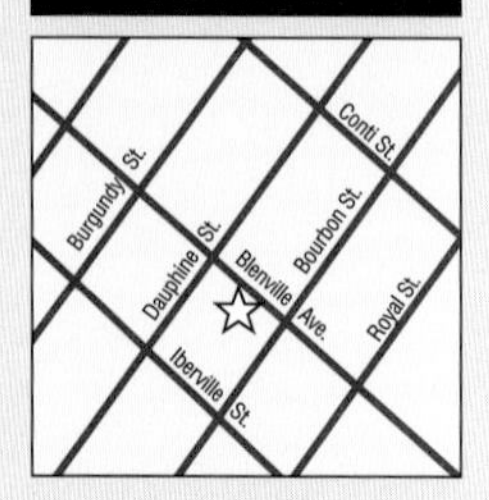

In the heart of the French Quarter at Bourbon Street, 30 min. from New Orleans International Airport

813 Rue Bienville
New Orleans, LA 70112
PH: (504) 523-5433
FAX: (504) 581-7908
www.arnauds.com

Owners
Archie and Jane Casbarian

Cuisine
Classic Creole and French

Days Open
Open Sun.-Fri. for lunch, daily for dinner, Sun. for brunch

Pricing
Dinner for one, without tax, tip or drinks: $20-$40

Dress Code
Business casual at lunch, jacket and tie preferred at dinner

Reservations
Recommended

Parking
Validated at garage nearby

Features
Private room/parties, entertainment, near theater

Credit Cards
AE, VC, MC, CB, DC, DS

Bayona

In the French Quarter

Housed in a 200-year old cottage in the heart of the French Quarter, Bayona offers a casually elegant dining atmosphere and consistently outstanding service. Co-owner and Executive Chef Susan Spicer emphasizes the flavors of the Mediterranean but also incorporates Alsace, Asia, India, and the American Southwest. Specialties include grilled shrimp with coriander sauce and black bean cakes, and grilled pork chops with wilted greens and garlic-almond sauce. Select the perfect bottle of wine from Bayona's extensive wine list.

Dinner in the courtyard

Lemon-buttermilk tart

Co-owner and Executive Chef, Susan Spicer

AWARD WINNER
SINCE 1993

Directions

Bourbon St.
Dauphine St.
Conti St.
St. Louis St.
Toulouse St.

On Dauphine Street in the French Quarter, 30 min. from New Orleans International Airport

430 Dauphine Street
New Orleans, LA 70112
PH: (504) 525-4455
FAX: (504) 522-0589
www.bayona.com

Owners
Regina Keever and Susan Spicer

Cuisine
French/Mediterranean

Days Open
Open Mon.-Fri. for lunch, Mon.-Sat. for dinner

Pricing
Dinner for one, without tax, tip, or drinks: $20-$40

Dress Code
Casual

Reservations
Required

Parking
Garage nearby

Features
Private room/parties, outdoor dining, near theater

Credit Cards
AE, VC, MC, CB, DC, JCB, DS

Bistro at Maison de Ville

Directions

Toulouse
St. Peter
Bourbon St.
Royal
Decatur

In the heart of the French Quarter, 30 min. from New Orleans International Airport

727 Toulouse St.
New Orleans, LA 70130
PH: (504) 528-9206
FAX: (504) 589-9939
www.maisondeville.com

Owners
Meristar

Cuisine
Nouvelle Creole

Days Open
Open daily for lunch and dinner

Pricing
Dinner for one, without tax, tip or drinks: $20-$40

Dress Code
Business casual

Reservations
Recommended

Parking
Garage nearby

Features
Outdoor dining

Credit Cards
AE, VC, MC, DC, DS

Courtyard fountain

Located in the luxurious Hotel Maison de Ville, this bistro has a justly deserved reputation for introducing bright young culinary talent to an enthusiastic and appreciative public. Most recently recognized as "Top Haute Restaurant" by the Zagat Guide and "America's Top Tables" by Gourmet magazine, the eatery has a loyal following among local and national gourmands. Diners order from an innovative seasonal menu of traditional French bistro selections and New Orleans culinary favorites.

Chef Greg Picolo

Exquisite entrees

Bistro dining

AWARD WINNER
SINCE 1994

Broussard's Restaurant

French Quarter landmark since 1920

In a city that joyously celebrates fine dining as an art form, Broussard's has been a fixture for nearly a century. Located in the heart of the French Quarter, Broussard's blends old architecture, classic food, and tradition to achieve a dining experience one is not likely to forget. Co-owner and Executive Chef Gunter Preuss is a master of traditional Creole cooking. Try the veal Broussard or the seafood bouillabaisse.

Delice

Soft-shell crabs Doré

Victorian bar

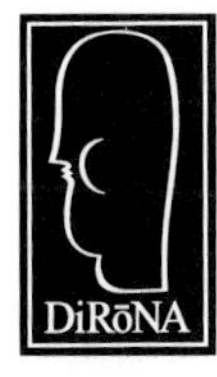

AWARD WINNER
SINCE 1998

Directions

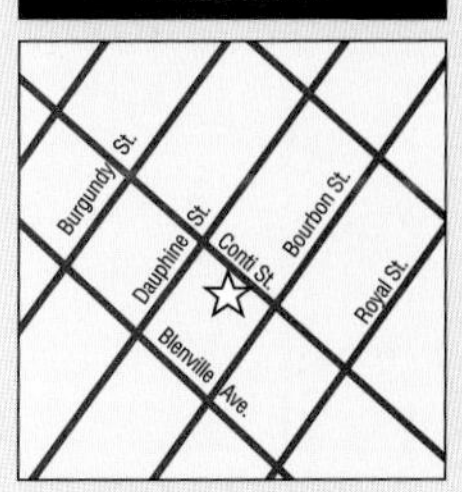

In the French Quarter, 30 min. from New Orleans International Airport

819 Conti Street
New Orleans, LA 70112
PH: (504) 581-3866
FAX: (504) 581-3873
www.broussards.com

Owners
Gunter and Evelyn Preuss

Cuisine
French Creole

Days Open
Open daily for dinner

Pricing
Dinner for one,
without tax, tip or drinks:
$40-$60

Dress Code
Business casual

Reservations
Recommended

Parking
Garage and lot nearby

Features
Private room/parties, outdoor dining, entertainment, near theater, cigar/cognac events

Credit Cards
AE, VC, MC

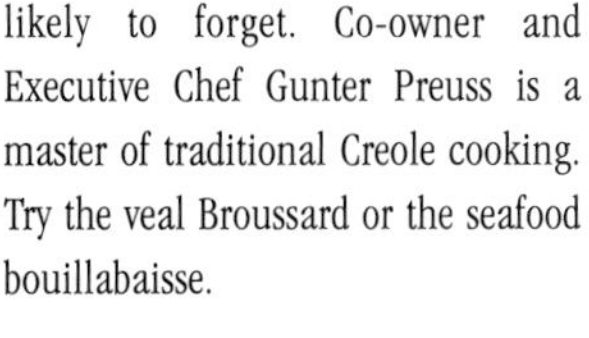

Christian's Restaurant

A New Orleans landmark

Christian's Restaurant is located in an old church, one of the most unusual restaurant settings in this eclectic city. The dining room has beautiful stained glass windows, cathedral ceilings, and greenery, which offers a charming atmosphere for dining. Chef Jared Hutto combines New Orleans Creole and classical French cuisine creating such entrees as filet au poivre, bouillabaisse Marseillaise, and stuffed eggplant.

An extensive wine selection complements the culinary excellence

A unique setting for elegant dining

AWARD WINNER
SINCE 1992

Directions

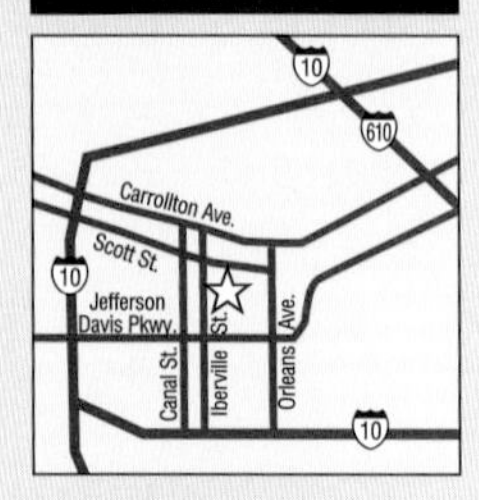

At Iberville and Scott streets one block from Canal Street, 25 min. from New Orleans International Airport

3835 Iberville Street
New Orleans, LA 70119
PH: (504) 482-4924
FAX: (504) 482-6852
www.
neworleansrestaurants.
com

Owners
Hank Bergeron

Cuisine
New Orleans Creole and classical French

Days Open
Open Tues.-Fri. for lunch, Tues.-Sat. for dinner

Pricing
Dinner for one, wthout tax, tip or drinks: $20-$40

Dress Code
Business casual

Reservations
Recommended

Parking
Free on site

Credit Cards
AE, VC, MC, DC

Galatoire's Restaurant

Main dining room

Everything old is new again at Galatoire's, the restaurant that defines New Orleans. Since 1905, this establishment has served authentic French Creole cuisine in the historic atmosphere of the Vieux Carré. Now a renovated Galatoire's awaits you with two floors of fine dining overlooking Bourbon Street. Specialties include oysters Rockefeller, shrimp remoulade, and lamb chops Bernaise. Don't miss this gastronomic tradition in the Big Easy.

Trout amandine

Shrimp remoulade

Oysters Rockefeller

AWARD WINNER
SINCE 2001

Directions

Bourbon St.
Iberville St.
Bienville St.

In the French Quarter, 25 min. from New Orleans International Airport

209 Bourbon Street
New Orleans, LA 70130
PH: (504) 525-2021
FAX: (504) 525-5900
www.galatoires.com

Owners
The Galatoire family

Cuisine
French Creole

Days Open
Open Tues.-Sun. for lunch and dinner

Pricing
Dinner for one, without tax, tip or drinks: $20-$40

Dress Code
Jacket required at dinner and on Sunday

Reservations Policy
Taken for second floor only

Parking
Garage nearby

Features
Private room/parties

Credit Cards
AE, VC, MC, DC, DS

Ruth's Chris Steak House

Directions

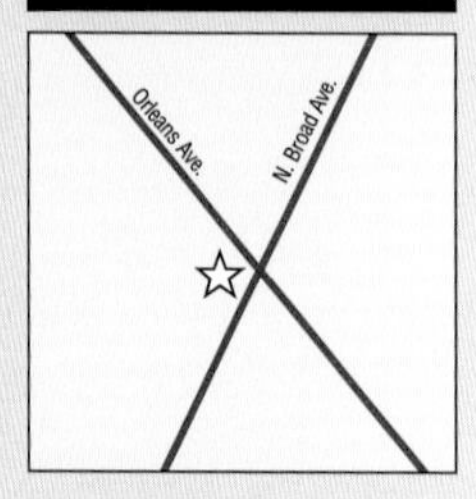

At N. Broad and Orleans avenues, convenient to the French Quarter and convention center and 20 min. from New Orleans International Airport

711 N. Broad Street
New Orleans, LA 70119
PH: (504) 486-0810
FAX: (504) 486-1324
www.ruthschris.com

Owners
Ruth's Chris Steak House

Cuisine
Steaks, seafood

Days Open
Open Sun.-Fri. for lunch, daily for dinner

Pricing
Dinner for one,
without tax, tip, or drinks:
$40-$60

Dress Code
Business casual

Reservations
Recommended

Parking
Valet

Features
Private rooms/parties

Credit Cards
AE, VC, MC, DC, DS

Filet mignon

This is the steak that steak lovers rave about! Ruth's Chris Steak House specializes in USDA Prime beef. Strips, filets, ribeyes, T-bones, and porterhouses are aged to exacting standards, broiled to perfection, and served sizzling. An award-winning wine list features premium vintages by the glass. The service is attentive, knowledgeable, and friendly.

Elegant dining

AWARD WINNER
SINCE 1999

Smith's Louis XVI Restaurant Français

Courtyard at Christmas

In a city famous for food, Louis XVI has maintained its commitment to style, refinement, and quality for more than a quarter century. Executive Chef Agnes Bellet and Chef de Cuisine Dominique Rizzo apply today's techniques to the French classics, creating beautiful dishes immersed in natural flavors. A romantic evening spent overlooking the Mediterranean courtyard, complete with tropical foliage and picturesque fountain, has become an integral part of the New Orleans experience.

Host/Proprietor Antoine Camenzuli and Executive Chef Agnes Bellet

Exquisite French cuisine

Clients enjoy fine dining

AWARD WINNER SINCE 1993

Directions

Iberville
Bienville
Bourbon
Royal

In the St. Louis Hotel in the French Quarter, 20 min. from New Orleans International Airport

730 Bienville Street
New Orleans, LA 70130
PH: (504) 581-7000
FAX: (504) 524-8925
www.louisxvi.com

Owners
Mark C. Smith III

Cuisine
French

Days Open
Open daily for breakfast and dinner

Pricing
Dinner for one, without tax, tip, or drinks: $40-$60

Dress Code
Business casual

Reservations
Recommended

Parking
Free on site

Credit Card
AE, VC, MC, CB, DC

The White Barn Inn

Directions

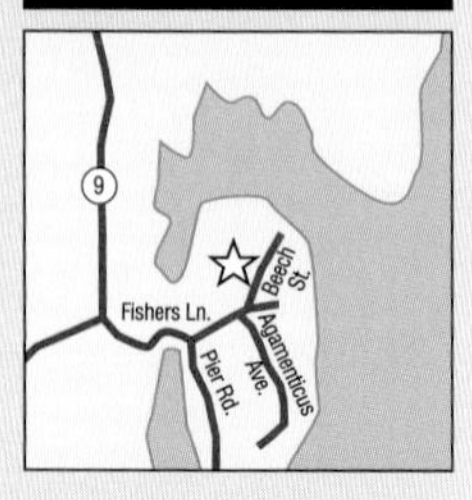

80 min. from Logan Airport; 25 miles from Portland, ME

P.O. Box 560 C
37 Beach Avenue
Kennebunkport, ME 04046
PH: (207) 967-2321
FAX: (207) 967-1100
www.whitebarninn.com

Owner
Laurence Bongiorno

Cuisine
Contemporary American with New England influences

Days Open
Daily for dinner

Pricing
Dinner for one, without tax, tip, or drinks: $60-$80

Dress Code
Jacket required

Reservations
Required

Parking
Complimentary valet

Features
Private wine room

Credit Cards
AE, VC, MC

The White Barn Inn in full bloom

The White Barn Inn is the only restaurant in New England to be honored with the AAA Five Diamond Award for eight consecutive years. The restaurant, housed in two meticulously restored barns, seats 120 guests for dinner. Antiques, 19th-century oil paintings., and soft candlelight provide an ideal setting for celebrating life's memorable occasions. Specialties of the house include Maine seafood, farm-raised venison, and quail.

Executive Chef Jonathan Cartwright

Romantic dining

AWARD WINNER
SINCE 1993

Clay Hill Farm

Wooded retreat

Clay Hill Farm's menu of New American Cuisine combines traditional New England favorites with contemporary specials. Start with the award-winning lobster bisque, followed by entrée specialties like roast duckling, French-cut rack of lamb, and a wide variety of fresh local seafood preparations. Over 200 wine varietals from around the world complement any meal. For dessert, try the white chocolate crème brulée, then conclude your special evening with a stroll through the beautiful gardens and bird sanctuary.

Ambience of yesteryear

Chef Melissa Ettinger

Artisitc presentations

AWARD WINNER
SINCE 1999

Directions

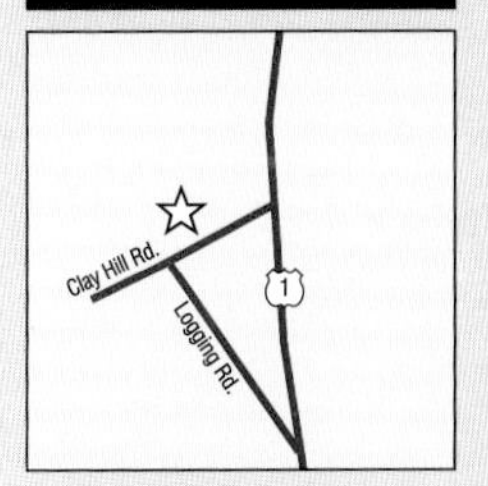

Two miles west of Ogunquit Square in York; 75 mins. from Boston's Logan International Airport

220 Clay Hill Road
York, ME 03907
PH: (207) 361-2272
FAX: (207) 646-0938
www.clayhillfarm.com

Owners
The Lewis Family

Cuisine
New American

Days Open
Daily for dinner, in season

Pricing
Dinner for one,
without tax, tip, or drinks:
$20-$40

Dress Code
Business casual

Reservations
Recommended

Parking
Valet

Features
Entertainment, near theater, private room/parties

Credit Cards
AE, VC, MC, DS

Northwoods

Directions

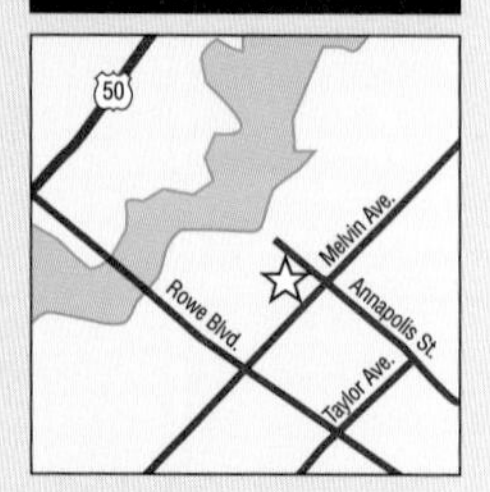

At Melvin and Ridgely avenues, 30 min. from Baltimore-Washington International Airport

609 Melvin Avenue
Annapolis, MD 21401
PH: (410) 268-2609
FAX: (410) 268-0930

Owners
Russell and Leslie Brown

Cuisine
Continental

Days Open
Open daily for dinner

Pricing
Dinner for one,
without tax, tip or drinks:
$20-$40

Dress Code
Business casual

Reservations
Recommended

Parking
Free on site

Features
Outdoor dining

Credit Cards
AE, VC, MC, CB, DC, DS

Northwoods

Located in the quaint West Annapolis shopping district, this eatery features a menu that seamlessly combines Northern Italian, French, and American culinary cultures and focuses on the abundant local seafood. Hosts Russell and Leslie Brown welcome diners into their lovely restaurant to experience Zuppa de Pesce, Tournedoes Cezanne, or one of the wonderful daily fresh fish specials. An award-winning wine list and a garden terrace for al fresco dining complete the experience.

Fresh shellfish selection

Owners Russell and Leslie Brown

The dining room

AWARD WINNER
SINCE 1992

Da Mimmo Finest Italian Cuisine

La Dolce Vita Dining Room

For more than two decades, Chef Mimmo Cricchio has prepared gourmet Italian food cooked to order in Baltimore's Little Italy. In addition to the delectable cuisine—dishes such as tortellini Pavarotti, lobster Tetrazzini, and red snapper Adriatica—this family-run restaurant offers a casually intimate atmosphere, fine service, and a memorable wine list. While the locals love Da Mimmo, it also draws many visitors, and offers complimentary limo service to and from hotels.

The tradition lives on in Baltimore's Little Italy

Co-owners/Chefs Mimmo and Mary Ann Cricchio and staff

Best veal chop in Baltimore

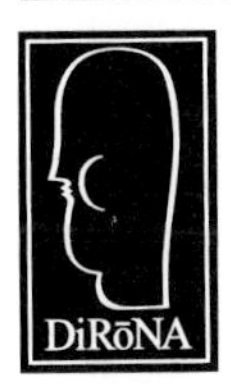

AWARD WINNER SINCE 1999

Directions

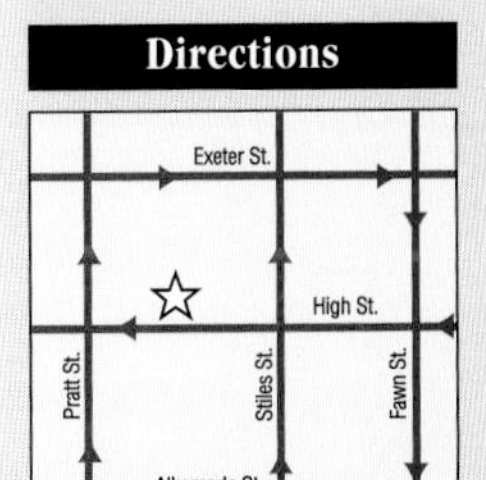

In Little Italy, a short walk from the Inner Harbor and 20 min. from Baltimore-Washington International Airport

217 South High Street
Baltimore, MD 21202
PH: (410) 727-6876
FAX: (410) 727-1927

Owners
Mimmo and Mary Ann Cricchio

Cuisine
Gourmet Italian

Days Open
Open daily for lunch and dinner

Pricing
Dinner for one, without tax, tip, or drinks: $20-$40

Dress Code
Elegant casual

Reservations
Recommended

Parking
Free on site, valet

Features
Private room/parties, entertainment, cigar/cognac events in lounge

Credit Cards
AE, VC, MC, CB, DC

Hampton's

Directions

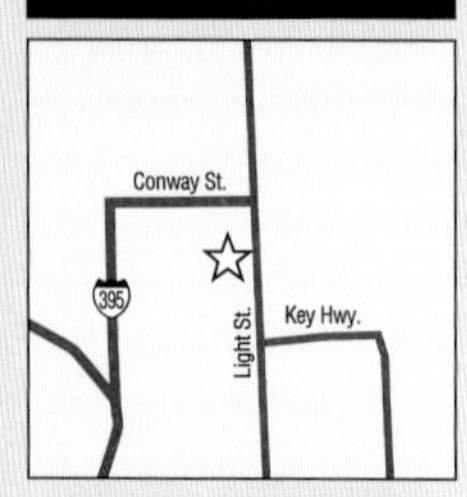

In the Harbor Court Hotel in downtown Baltimore, 20 min. from Baltimore-Washington International Airport

550 Light Street
Baltimore MD 21202
PH: (410) 234-0550, ext. 3424
FAX: (410) 385-6194
www.harborcourt.com

Owner
David Murdock

Cuisine
New American

Days Open
Open Tues.-Sun. for dinner, Sun. for brunch

Pricing
Dinner for one, without tax, tip, or diinks: $40-$60

Dress Code
Jacket and tie required

Reservation
Recommended

Parking
Complimentary valet

Features
Entertainment

Credit Cards
AE, VC, MC, DC

The city's only Mobil four-star and AAHS five-star-diamond restaurant

Located at the Harbor Court Hotel in Baltimore's scenic Inner Harbor, Hampton's serves innovative American cuisine in an elegant Edwardian setting. "Dining at Hampton's is a four-star experience all the way around," *Baltimore Magazine* declared. An award-winning wine list, ample table privacy, and a breathtaking view of the harbor contribute to the elegance. The Sunday champagne brunch has become a Baltimore tradition.

A feast for the eyes as the well as the palate

Seasonal menus emphasize classic cooking techniques with interesting flavors.

Lightly scented gardenia are a signature part of each table setting.

AWARD WINNER
SINCE 1992

Stone Manor

18th century charm

Directions

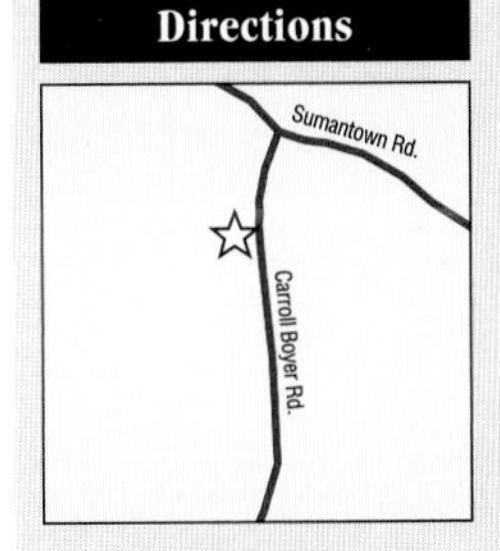

Just outside Fredrick, MD conveniently located from both Baltimore and Washington D.C., 25 min. from Harrisburg International Airport

5820 Carroll Boyer Road
Middletown, MD 21769
PH: (301) 473-5454
FAX: (301) 371-5622
www.stonemanor.com

Cuisine
Contemporary American

Days Open
Open Tues.-Sun. for lunch and dinner

Pricing
Dinner for one,
without tax, tip, or drinks:
$60-$80

Dress Code
Business casual

Reservations
Required

Parking
Free on site

Features
Private room/parties

Credit Cards
AE, VC, MC, DS

Savor the magic of exceptional cuisine, luxurious suites, and 18th century charm at this 114-acre country estate. The chef's contemporary American cuisine is presented in two prix fixe menus with suggested wine packages. The fare changes frequently with the seasons and the whims of the chef, but expect such entrees as prime beef filet with wild mushroom and black olive bread pudding, or grilled wahoo with tropical paella and Madras curry oil.

Creative entrees

Sumptuous desserts

Extensive wine list

AWARD WINNER
SINCE 1998

208 Talbot

Directions

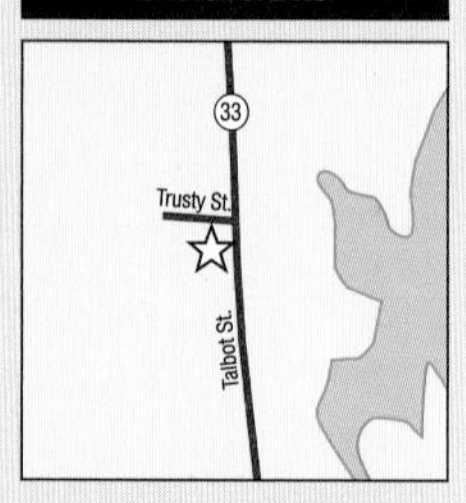

On Route 33 in St. Michaels on Maryland's Eastern Shore, 1 hr. from Baltimore-Washington International Airport

208 N. Talbot Street
St. Michaels, MD 21663
PH: (410) 745-3838
FAX: (410) 745-6507
www.208talbot.com

Owners
Paul Milne and
Candace Chiaruttini

Cuisine
Innovative American

Days Open
Open Wed.-Sun. for dinner (closed mid-February to mid-March)

Pricing
Dinner for one,
without tax, tip, or drinks:
$40-$60

Dress Code
Casual

Reservations
Recommended

Parking
Free on site

Credit Cards
VC, MC, DS

Historic charm

Chef-owned and operated, 208 Talbot is located in historic St. Michaels, just minutes from Chesapeake Bay. The innovative cuisine served in this charming establishment reflects the Eastern Shore's bounty of fresh seafood and produce. *Travel and Leisure* included the roasted oysters and crispy soft-shell crabs at 208 Talbot among the "Seven Wonders of the Eastern Shore." The atmosphere is casually elegant, and the excellent food, well-chosen wine list, and exceptional service guarantee a wonderful dining experience.

AWARD WINNER
SINCE 1996

Antrim 1844

Discover the genteel spirit of 19th century America in this restored country-inn resort nestled in the rolling mountains of central Maryland. Guests enjoy the inn's superb cuisine, starting at breakfast with Belgian waffles, the house specialty. At dinnertime, after passed hors d'oeuvres, diners enjoy a sumptuous five-course meal, with selections from the French-influenced Continental menu the chef creates daily. Choosing a bottle from the nationally acclaimed wine list, boasting over 800 selections, completes the dining experience.

Rack of lamb Dijonnaise

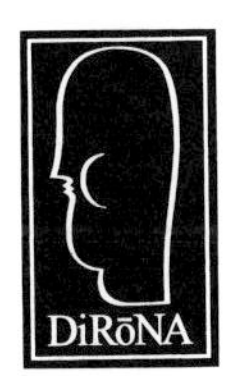

AWARD WINNER SINCE 1999

Directions

In Taneytown, 1 hr. from Baltimore-Washington International Airport and 1 hr. 15 min. from Reagan National Airport

30 Trevanion Road
Taneytown, MD 21787
PH: (800) 858-1844
FAX: (410) 756-2744
www.antrim1844.com

Owner
Richard Mollett

Cuisine
American with Continental flair

Days Open
Open daily for dinner

Pricing
Dinner for one, without tax, tip, or drinks: $40-$60

Dress Code
Business casual

Reservations
Required

Parking
Free on site

Features
Private room/parties, entertainment, cigar-cognac events

Credit Cards
AE, VC, MC, DC, DS

Anthony's Pier 4

Directions

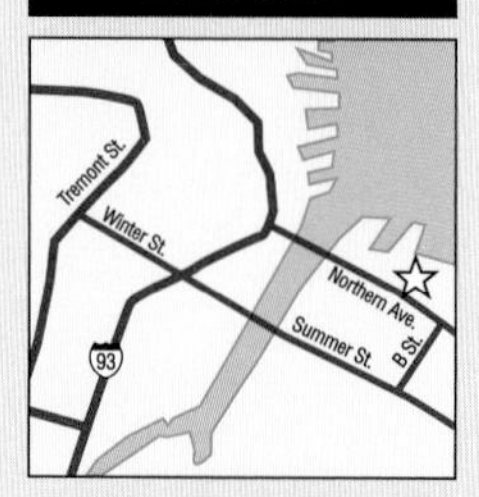

On Northern Ave., 5 min. from Logan International Airport.

140 Northern Avenue
Boston, MA 02110
PH: (617) 482-6262
FAX: (617) 426-2324
www.pier4.com

Owners
Anthony Athanas and sons: Anthony Athanas, Jr., Michael Athanas, Robert Athanas, Paul Athanas

Cuisine
New England regional and international, with emphasis on seafood and lobster

Days Open
Open daily for lunch and dinner

Pricing
Dinner for one, without tax, tip, or drinks: $20-$40

Dress Code
Business casual

Reservations
Recommended

Parking
Free on-site, valet

Features
Private room/parties, outdoor dining, cigar and wine events

Credit Cards
AE, VC, MC, CB, DC, JCB, DS

Spectacular city and harbor views

Anthony's Pier 4 is one of Boston's most prestigious culinary landmarks. This world-renowned restaurant has catered to a local, national, and international clientele for 38 years with its incomparable selections and innovative preparations, such as lobster from its own lobster company in Maine, fresh New England seafood, imported Dover sole, prime steaks, and an award-winning wine list of more than 500 selections. The lobby is lined with photographs of the heads of state, famous athletes, and Hollywood stars who have dined here.

Anthony's Pier 4 Clambake Special

Founder Anthony Athanas

Alfresco dining overlooking Boston Harbor

AWARD WINNER SINCE 1996

The Café Budapest

Experience European elegance at this world-famous restaurant located in the Copley Square Hotel in the heart of the Back Bay section of Boston. The Café Budapest has been the city's most romantic restaurant since it came on the Boston dining scene. Enjoy enchanting Hungarian and European delicacies in a charming, Old World setting. Specialties include iced tart cherry soup, chicken paprikas, beef Stroganoff, veal Gulyas, and the world-famous strudel.

Directions

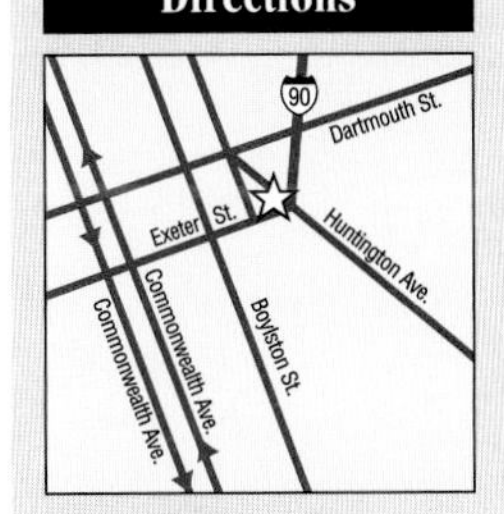

In Back Bay, 1 block from the Hynes Convention Center and 30 min. from Logan International Airport

90 Exeter Street
Boston, MA 02116
PH: (617) 266-1979
FAX: (617) 266-1395

Owners
Dr. Livia Hedda Rev-Kury

Cuisine
Hungarian, European

Days Open
Open Mon.-Sat. for lunch, daily for dinner

Pricing
Dinner for one, without tax, tip or drinks: $20-$40

Dress Code
Jacket and tie required

Reservations
Required

Parking
Garage nearby

Features
Private room/parties, near theater

Credit Cards
AE, VC, MC, DS

AWARD WINNER
SINCE 1990

The Dining Room at The Ritz-Carlton, Boston

Directions

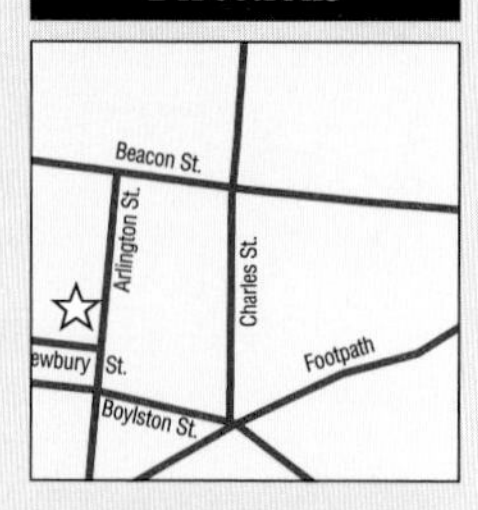

At The Ritz-Carlton, Boston, downtown, across from the Public Garden, 15 min. from Logan International Airport

The Ritz-Carlton, Boston
15 Arlington Street
Boston, MA 02117
PH: (617) 536-5700
FAX: (617) 536-1335
www.ritzcarlton.com

Owners
Millennium Partners

Cuisine
Contemporary French with Asian, Mediterranean, and California influences

Days Open
Open Tues.-Sun. for dinner, Sun. for brunch

Pricing
Dinner for one, without tax, tip, or drinks: $60-$80

Dress Code
Jacket and tie required

Reservations
Required

Parking
Valet, garage nearby

Features
Private room, entertainment, near theater

Credit Cards
AE, VC, MC, CB, DC, DS

Dining Room

Since The Ritz-Carlton, Boston, opened in 1927, The Dining Room has been recognized as one of the city's culinary classics. Executive Chef Mark Allen gives a fresh twist to contemporary French cuisine, accenting rich flavors and a defining lighter style. Recent enhancements at The Dining Room include two new private dining rooms and seasonal and weekly tasting menus. Among the acclaimed specialties are potato-wrapped turbot with braised artichokes and beans and lobster jus, and braised rabbit with forest mushrooms, duck liver, and Boulanger potatoes. A pianist sets the mood for dinner and Sunday brunch.

Chef de Cuisine Mark Allen

Maine lobster with fresh tomato consumme sevruga cavier

Auguste Escoffier private dining room

AWARD WINNER
SINCE 1992

Icarus

A romantic setting for an intimate dinner

For nearly 20 years, Chef and Co-owner Chris Douglass' American regional menu has continued to set the standard for fine dining in Boston's exciting South End. Locally grown produce, the finest farm-raised meat and poultry, and the freshest New England seafood complemented by sumptuous desserts and an award-winning wine list assure a memorable dining experience. Icarus features a lovely two-level dining room appointed in rich woods and mission furniture, accented by soft lighting and spacious seating.

Private dining room is the perfect spot for a business or social function.

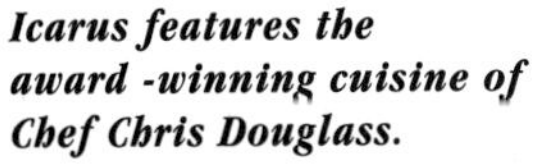

Icarus features the award -winning cuisine of Chef Chris Douglass.

AWARD WINNER
SINCE 1994

Directions

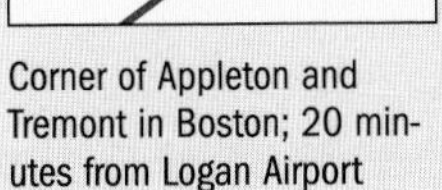

Corner of Appleton and Tremont in Boston; 20 minutes from Logan Airport

3 Appleton St.
Boston MA 02116
PH: (617) 426-1790
FAX: (617) 426-2150
www.icarusrestaurant.com

Owners
Chris Douglass

Cuisine
American regional

Days Open
Daily for dinner

Pricing
Dinner for one,
without tax, tip, or drinks:
$40-$60

Dress Code
Business casual

Reservations
Recommended

Parking
Valet

Features
Private room/parties, live jazz on Fridays

Credit Cards
AE, VC, MC, DC

L'Espalier

Directions

In the heart of Back Bay, 20 min. from Logan International Airport

30 Gloucester Street
Boston, MA 02115
PH: (617) 262-3023
FAX: (617) 375-9297
www.lespalier.com

Owners
Frank and Catherine McClelland

Cuisine
New England French

Days Open
Open Mon.-Sat. for dinner

Pricing
Dinner for one,
without tax, tip, or drinks:
$60-$80

Dress Code
Business casual

Reservations
Required

Parking
Valet

Features
Private room/parties

Credit Cards
AE, VC, MC, DC

A beautiful setting

A culinary exploration in an 1886 Back Bay townhouse, L'Espalier was the first independently owned restaurant to bring haute cuisine to Boston. Twenty years later, it remains a chic and modern restaurant featuring Chef/Proprietor Frank McClelland's innovative New England-French cooking based on local ingredients. Three beautifully appointed rooms provide the setting for your dining experience. L'Espalier is one block from the Hynes Convention Center, the Prudential Center, and Copley Place, and within walking distance of Symphony Hall.

Quiet atmosphere

Slow roasted Muscovy duck breast

Chef/Proprietor Frank McClelland

AWARD WINNER
SINCE 1993

Locke-Ober

The Men's Cafe

A landmark restaurant rich in tradition, impervious to trends, yet always in style, Locke-Ober's very name is synonymous with Boston. A beloved institution, generation after generation comes to Locke-Ober to initiate, celebrate, negotiate, and commiserate. At this timeless refuge from the modern world, gentility is the rule rather than the exception. Specialties include baked lobster Savannah, Nantucket bay scallops, Black Angus Sirloin, Châteaubriand for two, and roast rack of lamb Persillade.

Splendid seafood

Chef Trevor Nelson

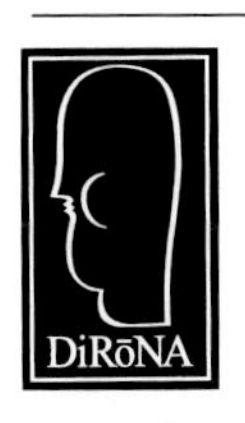

AWARD WINNER
SINCE 1993

Directions

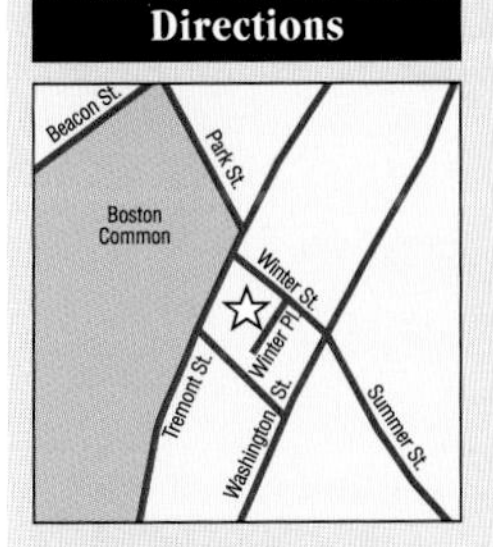

Off Tremont St. across from Park Street T Station; 20 min. from Logan Airport

3-4 Winter Place
Boston, MA 02108
PH: (617) 542-1340
FAX: (617) 542-6452
www.locke-ober.com

Owners
David W. Ray

Cuisine
Traditional American

Days Open
Open Mon. - Fri. for lunch, Mon.-Sat. for dinner

Pricing
Dinner for one, without tax, tip, or drinks: $20-$40

Dress Code
Business casual

Reservations
Recommended

Parking
Valet

Features
Entertainment, near theater, private rooms/parties, cigar/cognac events

Credit Cards
AE, VC, MC, CB, DC, DS, JCB

Maison Robert

Directions

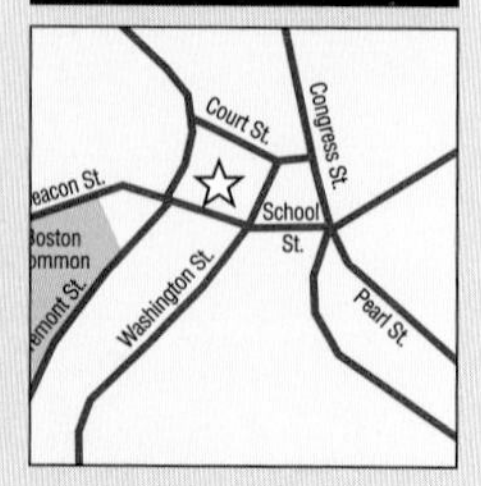

Between Tremont and Washington streets; 15 minutes from Logan Airport

45 School St.
Boston, MA 02108
PH: (617) 227-3370
FAX: (617) 227-5977
www.maisonrobert.com

Owners
Lucien Robert, Ann Robert, Andrée Robert

Cuisine
Classical and contemporary French

Days Open
Mon.-Fri.. lunch and dinner, Sat. dinner only, Sun. private parties only.

Pricing
Dinner for one, without tax, tip, or drinks: $20-$40 Café, $40-$60 main dining room

Dress Code
Business casual, jacket and tie requested

Reservations
Required

Parking
Valet, garage nearby

Features
Outdoor dining, near theater, private room/parties

Credit Cards
AE, VC, MC, CB, DC

Main dining room

Offering fine cuisine and fine wine in Boston's historic old city hall, Maison Robert allows diners a choice of two restaurants, the elegant Bonhomme Richard and Ben's Café, a less formal, airy bar and restaurant that features outdoor dining in summer months. The Bonhomme Richard maintains the grace of Old World dining in its high-ceilinged Second Empire-style room. In both restaurants, chefs prepare exquisite dishes that, coupled with an award-wining wine list, have given Maison Robert its reputation for first-class dining.

Faisan en chartreuse

Outdoor Ben's Café

AWARD WINNER
SINCE 1993

Top of the Hub

At Top of the Hub, the breathtaking panorama is matched only by the award-winning new American cuisine of Executive Chef Dean Moore. Elegantly presented and exquisitely prepared, each entree at the Top of the Hub is a meal to remember. Located atop the landmark Prudential Tower in the fashionable Back Bay, the Top of the Hub is life on a whole different level.

At Top of the Hub, every dining experience is memorable.

The finest cuisine

Live jazz nightly

AWARD WINNER
SINCE 1998

Directions

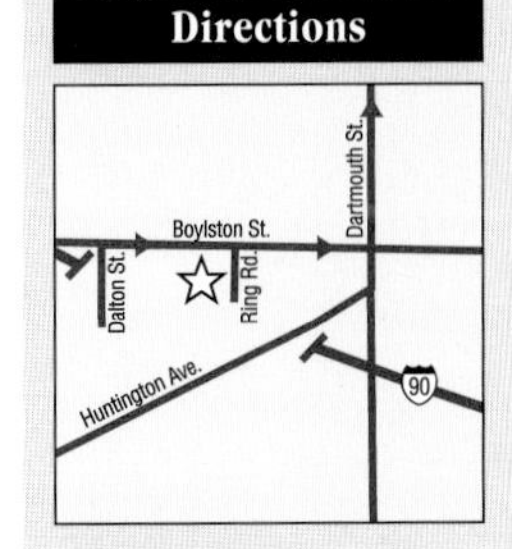

In the Prudential Building, at Boylston and Ring Road, 15 minutes from Logan Airport

800 Boylston Street
Prudential Tower, 52nd Fl.
Boston, MA 02119
PH: (617) 536-1775
FAX: (617) 859-8298
www.topofthehub.net

Owners
Select Restaurants

Cuisine
Creative American

Days Open
Open daily for lunch and dinner, Sunday brunch

Pricing
Dinner for one,
Without tax, tip, or drinks:
$20-$40

Dress Code
Business casual

Reservations
Recommended

Parking
Garage in building, validated parking

Features
Entertainment, near theater, private room/parties, cognac events

Credit Cards
AE, VC, MC, CB, DC, DS

Chillingsworth

Directions

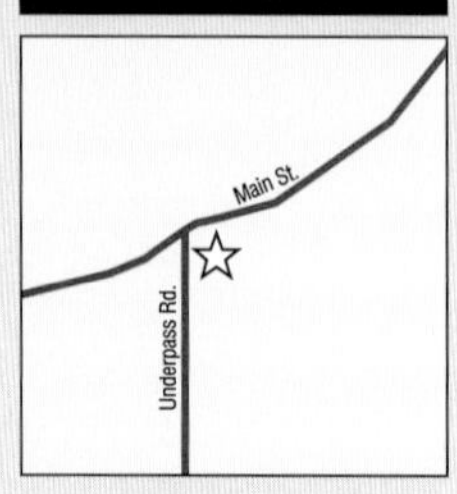

On Route 6A (Main St.) in Brewster, 1.1 miles east of the Route124 intersection; 20 mins. from Hyannis Airport

2449 Main Street
Brewster, MA 02631
PH: (508) 896-3640
FAX: (508) 896-7540

Owners
Nitzi and Pat Rabin

Cuisine
Modern French

Days Open
Tues.-Sun. for bistro lunch, brunch and dinner

Pricing
Dinner for one, without tax, tip, or drinks: $60-$80; bistro entrees from $15

Dress Code
Business casual

Reservations
Recommended

Parking
Free on site

Features
Private dining

Credit Cards
AE, VC, MC, DC,

Chillingsworth restaurant, inn, and bistro

An antique cape house surrounded by six acres of lawns and gardens provides the enchanting setting for this landmark restaurant on Cape Cod. Modern French cuisine with California flair is served in a six-course table in the flower-filled, antique-appointed dining rooms of the main house. Specialties include native fish and shellfish and fine meats and poultry. An airy solarium and brick patio offer casual à la carte luncheons and a bistro dinner menu in the evening. There are several antique-filled guest rooms and an eclectic gourmet shop.

Chef Nitzi Rabin in front of the Gazebo

Foie gras raviolis

The Alcove Table overlooks the Terrace Room

AWARD WINNER SINCE 1993

Wheatleigh

Directions

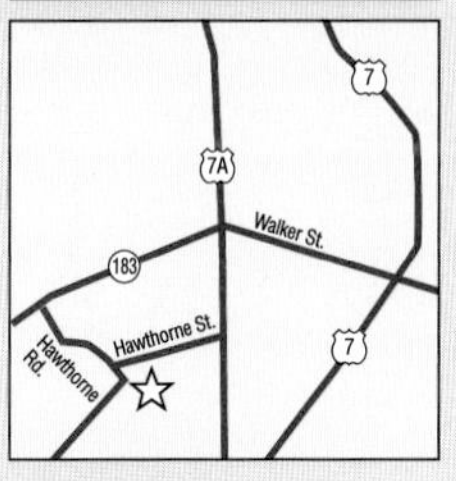

In the Berkshires town of Lenox, 1 hr. from Connecticut's Bradley International Airport

According to *The New York Times*, the Wheatleigh dining experience is "a table fit for a prince." The small luxury hotel with a European flavor is a replica of a 16th century Florentine palazzo, built in the Berkshires by an American industrialist as a wedding gift for his daughter. Guests enjoy the chef's contemporary interpretation of classical French food utilizing a large network of local organic farmers.

Chef Peter Platt

Clementine sorbet

The dining room

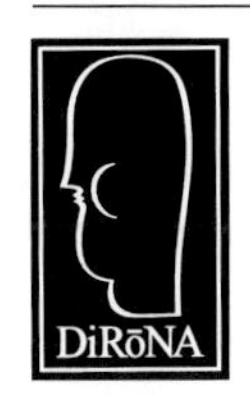

AWARD WINNER
SINCE 1992

Hawthorne Road,
P.O. Box 824
Lenox, MA 01240
PH: (413) 637-0610
FAX: (413) 637-4507
www.wheatleigh.com

Cuisine
Eclectic American

Days Open
Open daily for breakfast, lunch,and dinner

Pricing
Dinner for one, wthout tax, tip or drinks: $60-$80

Dress Code
Jacket and tie preferred

Reservations Policy
Required

Parking
Free on site, valet

Features
Private room/parties, near theater, cigar/cognac events

Credit Cards
AE, VC, MC, DC

The Dan'l Webster Inn

The Dan'l Webster Inn

Directions

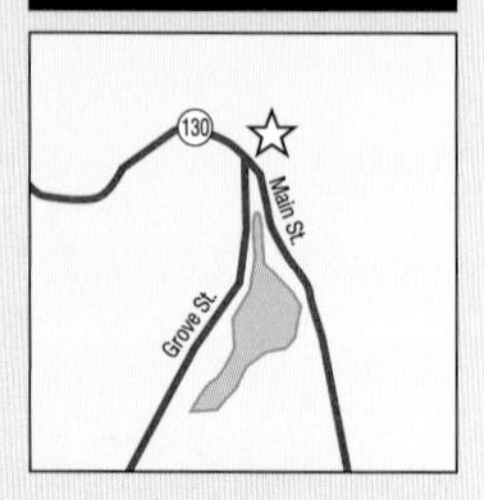

On Main St. in Sandwich; 20 min. from Hyannis Municipal Airport, 95 min. from Logan Airport

149 Main Street
Sandwich, MA 02563
PH: (800) 444-3566;
(508) 888-3622
FAX: (508) 888-5156
www.danlwebsterinn.com

Owners
The Catania family

Cuisine
Contemporary/American

Days Open
Daily for lunch and dinner, Sunday brunch

Pricing
Dinner for one, without tax, tip, or drinks: $20-$40

Dress Code
Casual

Reservations
Recommended

Parking
Free on-site

Features
Entertainment, private room/parties, cigar/cognac events

Credit Cards
AE, VC, MC, CB, DC, DS

The centerpiece of Cape Cod's oldest village, the inn is the essence of elegance, featuring 54 individually appointed guest rooms. Dine fireside or in the sunlit conservatory, enveloped in an extraordinary ambiance and enjoy the courtesy of the finest staff. The menu reflects distinctive selections representing both traditional and contemporary tastes. Creative chef's selections are complemented by decadent desserts by the expert pastry chef. The inn is also home to one of the most acclaimed wine cellars in the region

The Conservatory

Fine dining

The Music Room

AWARD WINNER SINCE 1995

The Chanticleer

Our main dining room

Directions

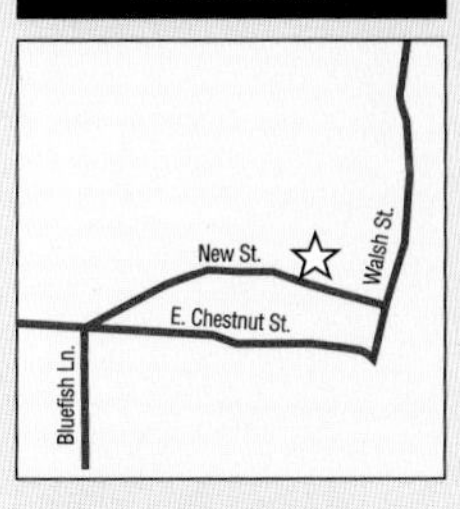

In the village of Siasconset at the eastern end of Nantucket Island, 7 min. from Nantucket Airport

Celebrating its 30th year of excellence, The Chanticleer, under the loving direction of Chef/Proprietor Jean-Charles Berruet and his wife, Anne, is a restaurant without peer. Certainly the setting is about as perfect as anyone could wish for: multipaned windows looking out to gardens full of climbing roses and a delightful carousel horse. The cuisine is traditional French, with an emphasis on local fruits and vegetables, Nantucket seafood, game birds, and prime meats. The wine cellar is amazing: 1,200 French and California selections, more than 40,000 bottles in all.

Chocolate soufflé

Chef/Proprietor Jean Charles Berruet

Rose garden entrance

AWARD WINNER SINCE 1993

9 New Street
Box 601
Siasconset, MA 02564
PH: (508) 257-6231
FAX: (508) 257-4154
www.thechanticleerinn.com

Owners
Jean-Charles and Anne Berruet

Cuisine
French, seafood

Days Open
Open Tues.-Sun. for lunch and dinner

Pricing
Dinner for one, without tax, tip, or drinks: $60-$80

Dress Code
Jacket required

Reservations
Required

Parking
Free on site

Features
Private room/parties, outdoor dining, cigar/cognac events

Credit Cards
AE, VC, MC, DC

Silks at Stonehedge Inn

Directions

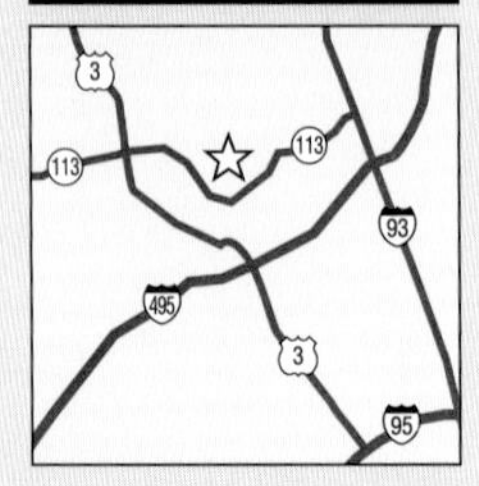

On Route 113 east of Route 3; 45 min. from Logan Airport, 25 min. from Manchester, NH Airport

160 Pawtucket Blvd.
Tyngsboro, MA 01879
PH: (978) 649-4400
FAX: (978) 649-9256
www.stonehedgeinn.com

Owners
Levent Bozkurt

Cuisine
New French

Days Open
Open daily for breakfast, Mon.-Sat. for lunch, Tues.-Sun. for dinner

Pricing
Dinner for one, without tax, tip, or drinks: $40-$60

Dress Code
Jacket required

Reservations
Recommended

Parking
Valet, free on site

Features
Outdoor dining, private parties, cigar/cognac events, monthly wine dinners

Credit Cards
AE, VC, MC, CB, DC, JCB, DS

French cuisine in the country

Chef Jon Mathieson, formerly of Lespinasse in New York, creates extraordinary French cuisine with fresh New England fish, game, and produce. *Food & Wine*, the *Boston Globe* and *USA Today* have praised Mathieson's cuisine as "elegant cooking in the country." General Manager Levent Bozkurt hosts "Celebration of Wine," a monthly dinner series with guest winemakers from around the world. Awarded *Wine Spectator*'s Grand Award for Outstanding Wine, Stonehedge Inn also offers impeccable cuisine and European service.

Grilled lobster with summer fondue

Owner Levent Bozkurt

Impeccable cuisine and European service

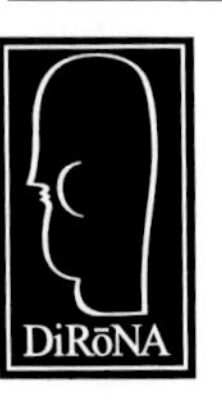

AWARD WINNER SINCE 1992

Giovanni's Ristorante

Giovanni's has been a family-owned business for 30 years, from its humble beginnings as a pizzeria to the fine-dining establishment of today. The eatery offers the greatest level of quality and authenticity possible, from the bistecca calamari fritta and the homemade gnocchi di patate verde, to the fresh seafood flown in from Boston. Its old-world charm and elegance, combined with a comfortable, congenial atmosphere make even the most distant stranger feel at home.

Randy Truant and his mother, Frances Truant

A gracious setting

Intimate main dining room

AWARD WINNER
SINCE 2001

Directions

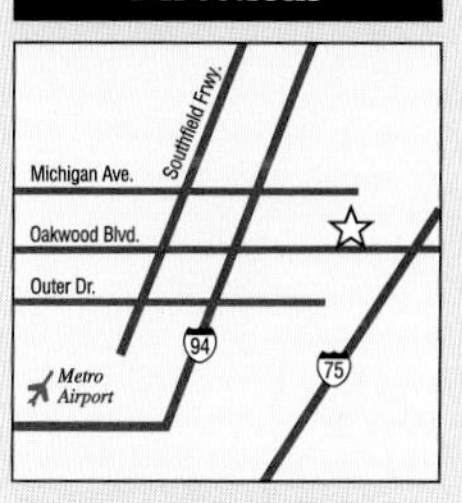

Near the Rouge River and Bridge, 15 min. from Detroit Metro International Airport

330 S. Oakwood Boulevard
Detroit, MI 48217
PH: (313) 841-0122
FAX: (313) 841-3947
www.giovannisristorante.com

Owners
Frances C. and
Randy J. Truant

Cuisine
Italian

Days Open
Open Tues.-Fri. for lunch,
Tues.-Sat. for dinner

Pricing
Dinner for one,
without tax, tip or drinks:
$20-$40

Dress Code
Business casual

Reservations
Recommended

Parking
Free on site

Features
Private room/parties,
near theater

Credit Cards
AE, VC, MC, DC

Opus One

Elegant dining

American cuisine with a Continental flair" describes Opus One's signature style at lunch, dinner, and a wide range of private banquets and events. The restaurant's interior is a blend of deep woods, marble, etched glass, and eye-catching artwork, reflecting an attention to detail that is even more evident in the food and service. Specialties include filo-encased shrimp Helene and, for dessert, warm Michigan apple harvest flan with cinnamon ice cream and house-made caramel sauce.

Front dining room

Jim Kokas and Ed Mandziara

AWARD WINNER
SINCE 1992

Directions

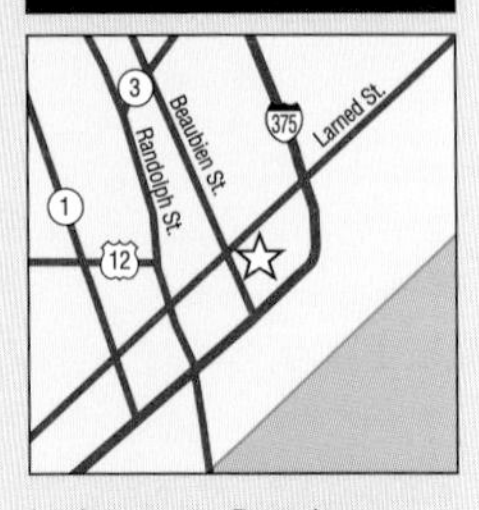

In downtown Detroit two blocks from the Renaissance Center, 35 min. from Detroit Metropolitan Airport

565 E. Larned Street
Detroit, MI 48226
PH: (313) 961-7766
FAX: (313) 961-9243
www.opus-one.com

Owners
James C. Kokas and Edward R. Mandziara

Cuisine
American with Continental flair

Days Open
Open Mon.-Fri. for lunch, Mon.-Sat. for dinner

Pricing
Dinner for one, without tax, tip, or drinks: $40-$60

Dress Code
Business casual

Reservations
Recommended

Parking
Valet

Features
Private room/parties, entertainment, shuttle service to theaters

Credit Cards
AE, VC, MC, CB, DC, DS

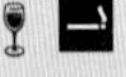

The Rattlesnake Club

Chef/Owner Jimmy Schmidt

Chef/Owner Jimmy Schmidt transformed a warehouse space into a carefully appointed, beautifully designed restaurant with breathtaking views of the Detroit skyline and the Windsor, Ontario, waterfront. Works by noted artists Jasper Johns, Jim Dine, and Frank Stella adorn the restaurant and private dining rooms. Jimmy Schmidt's food, too, is a work of art. Among his signature dishes are Lake Ontario pickerel, rack of Michigan lamb, and white chocolate ravioli.

Lake Ontario perch sauteed with watercress sauce

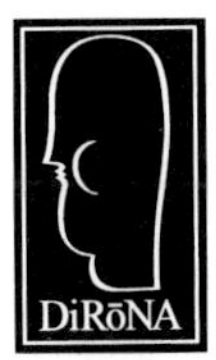

AWARD WINNER SINCE 1993

Directions

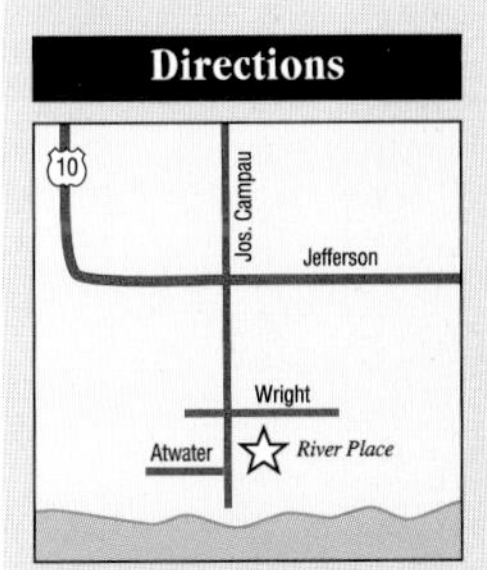

At the foot of Jos. Campau in downtown, 2 1/2 miles east of the Renaissance Center and 20 min. from Detroit Metropolitan Airport

300 River Place
Detroit, MI 48207
PH: (313) 567-4400
FAX: (313) 567-2063

Owner
Jimmy Schmidt

Cuisine
New American

Days Open
Open Mon.-Fri. for lunch, Mon.-Sat. for dinner

Pricing
Dinner for one:
without tax, tip, or drinks:
$40-$60

Dress Code
Business casual

Reservations
Recommended

Parking
Valet

Features
Private parties, catering services, outdoor dining, entertainment, near theater

Credit Cards
AE, VC, MC, CB, DC, DS

Directions

11 Mile Rd.
10 Mile Rd.
Orchard Lake Rd.
Middlebelt Rd.
696

On W. 10 Mile Road east of Orchard Lake Road, 20 min. from Detroit Metropolitan Airport

30715 W. 10 Mile Road
Farmington Hills, MI 48336
PH: (248) 474-3033
FAX: (248) 474-9064
www.cafecortina.com

Owners
Tonon family

Cuisine
Regional Italian

Days Open
Open Mon.-Fri. for lunch, Mon.-Sat. for dinner

Pricing
Dinner for one,
without tax, tip, or drinks:
$40-$60

Dress Code
Business casual

Reservations
Suggested

Parking
Valet

Features
Private room/parties, outdoor dining, entertainment, cigar/cognac events

Credit Cards
AE, VC, MC, CB, DC, DS

Ristorante Café Cortina

Private party room with outside courtyard

After 24 years, Ristorante Café Cortina continues to present the true heart and soul of Italian cooking. The proprietors hail from Italy's Veneto region, known for its earthy polentas, risottos, wild game, and beautiful wines. That distinctive cuisine is re-created here. Formerly an apple orchard, the restaurant's grounds are used for farming the aromatic herbs and vegetables that make their way to the signature grilled dishes. An award-winning wine list features premium vintages by the glass. The service is attentive, knowledgeable, and warm.

Il giardino

Italian desserts

La famiglia Tonon

AWARD WINNER
SINCE 1997

Tribute

Main dining room

This first-class destination restaurant in the lovely suburb of Farmington Hills offers top-rated Asian-fusion food in a dynamic contemporary setting. Classically trained chef Takashi Yagihashi has created a menu that features such items as wild mushroom-crusted beef tenderloin served with fingerling potatoes and beef marrow-filled tortellini, sashimi dressed in tangy yuzu (Asian citrus fruit) vinaigrette, and the locally familiar Lake Superior walleye, served on rock shrimp risotto.

Seared scallops

Chef Takashi Yagihashi

Chilled Maine lobster

AWARD WINNER
SINCE 2001

Directions

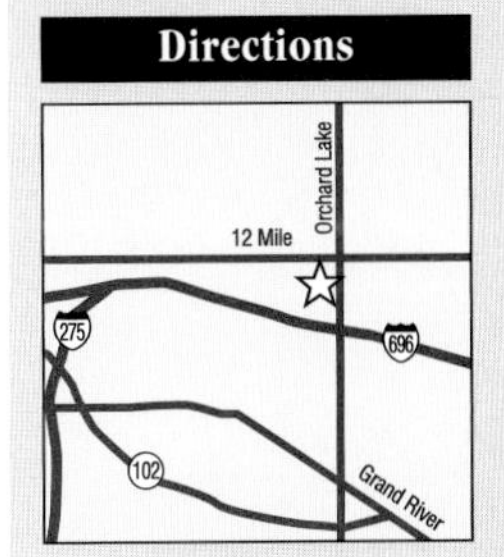

On 12 Mile Road just west of Orchard Lake Road, 25 min. from Detroit Metro International Airport

31425 West 12 Mile Road
Farmington Hills, MI 48334
PH: (248) 848-9393
FAX: (248) 848-1919
www.tribute-restaurant.com

Owners
Epoch Restaurant Group

Cuisine
Contemporary French with Asian Influences

Days Open
Open Tues.-Sat. for dinner

Pricing
Dinner for one,
without tax, tip, or drinks:
$60-$80

Dress Code
Business casual

Reservations
Required

Parking
Valet

Features
Private room/parties

Credit Cards
AE, VC, MC, CB, DC, DS

The Golden Mushroom

Directions

Corner of West 10 Mile and Southfield roads, 35 min. from Detroit Metropolitan Airport

18100 W. 10 Mile Road
Southfield, MI 48075
PH: (248) 559-4230
FAX: (248) 559-7312
www.thegoldenmushroom.com

Owner
Reid L. Ashton

Cuisine
Continental

Days Open
Open Mon.-Fri. for lunch, Mon.-Sat. for dinner

Pricing
Dinner for one:
without tax, tip, or drinks:
$40-$60

Dress Code
Business casual

Reservations
Recommended

Parking
Free on site, valet

Features
Private room/private parties, cigar/cognac events

Credit Cards
AE, VC, MC, CB, DC, JCB, DS

Lobby and dining room

A suburban landmark for 28 years, The Golden Mushroom is famed for its Continental cuisine, wild game dishes, and innovative use of wild mushrooms. Diners can expect knowledgeable service, comfortable surroundings, and an extensive wine list of more than 800 selections. Little wonder that over the years The Golden Mushroom, its owner, chefs, and staff have received more culinary awards than any other restaurant in Michigan. Try the cookbook, *The Golden Mushroom Kitchen, 25 Years of Chefs and Recipes* (see Web site). Very interesting.

Continental cuisine

700-seat Banquet Hall

Owner Reid L. Ashton

AWARD WINNER
SINCE 1993

The Lark

A country inn

Consistently named Michigan's most romantic restaurant, The Lark also was first-place winner in *Gourmet's* Top Table Awards and the best restaurant in North America in *Condé Nast Traveler's* readers poll. A European-style country inn with outdoor tables in season, The Lark presents an eclectic menu, ranging from the latest French creations to Maine lobsters and steak. An award-winning wine cellar houses 1,000 selections.

Dining room

Jim and Mary Lark

Walled garden

AWARD WINNER
SINCE 1992

Directions

At Farmington and Maple roads, 40 min. from Detroit Metropolitan Airport

6430 Farmington Road
West Bloomfield, MI 48322
PH: (248) 661-4466
FAX: (248) 661-8891
www.thelark.com

Owners
James D. Lark

Cuisine
Continental

Days Open
Open Tues.-Sat. for dinner

Pricing
Dinner for one,
without tax, tip, or drinks:
$60-$80

Dress Code
Jacket and tie required

Reservations
Required

Parking
Free on site

Features
Private parties,
outdoor dining

Credit Cards
AE, VC, MC, DC

D'Amico Cucina

Directions

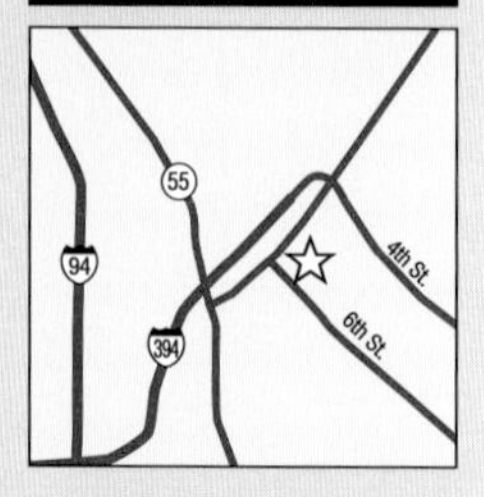

In Butler Square downtown, 20 min. from Minneapolis-St. Paul International Airport

100 N. 6th Street
Minneapolis, MN 55403
PH: (612) 338-2401
FAX: (612) 337-5130
www.damico.com

Owners
Richard and Larry D'Amico

Cuisine
Contemporary Italian

Days Open
Open daily for dinner

Pricing
Dinner for one, without tax, tip, or drinks: $40-$60

Dress Code
Business casual

Reservations
Recommended

Parking
Valet, garage nearby

Features
Private room/parties, entertainment, near theater

Credit Cards
AE, VC, MC, CB, DC, JCB, DS

Elegant surroundings

Established in 1987, D'Amico Cucina serves world-class Italian cuisine with a contemporary accent. The restaurant features an outstanding, Italian-only wine list, along with an extensive selection of Italian grappas and other liqueurs. Specialties include butternut squash cappelletti with pistachio and sage — a wintertime entree — and pangrattato crusted pork tenderloin with soft polenta. D'Amico Cucina's innovative fare, extensive wine list, and stunning interior have won the restaurant numerous local and national awards.

Chef J.P. Samuelson

Private dining room

Main dining room

AWARD WINNER SINCE 1993

Goodfellow's

Dining room

At Goodfellow's, award-winning regional American cooking is served in a historic art-deco environment — the former Forum Cafeteria. Specialties include roast Glenwood pheasant and Wisconsin veal chop. This premier restaurant, conveniently located in the heart of downtown Minneapolis, has received numerous accolades, including induction into *Nation's Restaurant News*' Hall of Fame. Private dining and meeting facilities are available for groups of eight to 80.

Lounge

Bar

AWARD WINNER
SINCE 1992

Directions

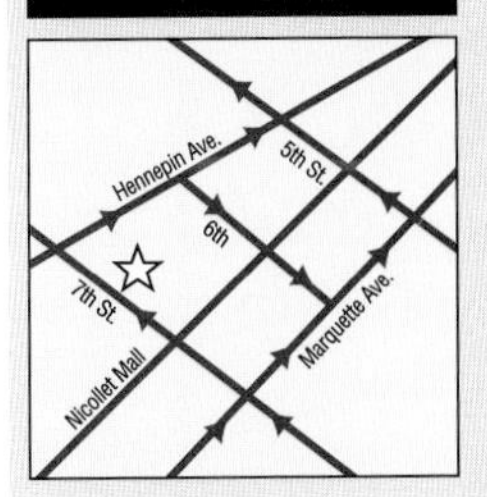

On Second Avenue S. between Sixth and Seventh streets in downtown, 20 min. from Minneapolis-St. Paul International Airport

40 S. Seventh Street
Minneapolis, MN 55402
PH: (612) 332-4800
FAX: (612) 332-1274
www.goodfellowsrestaurant.com

Owners
John Dayton and Wayne Kostroski

Cuisine
Regional seasonal American

Days Open
Open Mon.-Fri. for lunch, Mon.-Sat. for dinner

Pricing
Dinner for one, without tax, tip, or drinks: $40-$60

Dress Code
Business casual

Reservations
Recommended

Parking
Valet for dinner only, garage nearby

Features
Private room/parties, near theater

Credit Cards
AE, VC, MC, CB, DC, DS

The St. Paul Grill

Directions

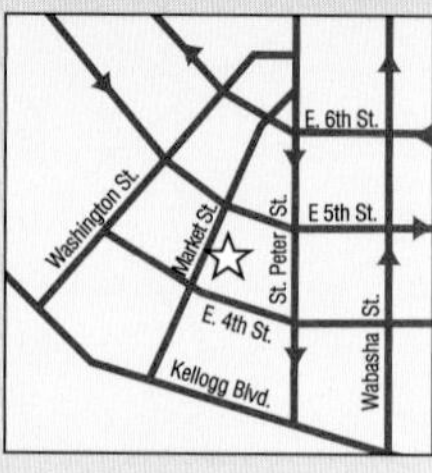

At the Saint Paul Hotel near Market and Fifth streets, 20 min. from Minneapolis-St. Paul International Airport

---

350 Market Street
St. Paul, MN 55102
PH: (651) 224-7455
FAX: (651) 228-3810
www.stpaulhotel.com

Owners
350 Market St., Inc., managed by Morrissey Hospitality Cos.

Cuisine
American

Days Open
Open daily for lunch and dinner

Pricing
Dinner for one, without tax, tip, or drinks: $20-$40

Dress Code
Business casual

Reservations
Recommended

Parking
Valet, garage nearby

Features
Near theater and sports

Credit Cards
AE, VC, MC, DC, DS

The English Garden

The charming views of Rice Park are surpassed only by the food and service at this popular Twin Cities restaurant. The menu reflects the best of American cuisine — the freshest fish, aged beef, fresh poultry and game — prepared simply and then finished with a cutting-edge culinary element. You'll find such classic regional favorites as beer-battered walleye and roast beef hash with fried eggs. There is an impressive wine list and a collection of single malt scotches.

The Grill Bar

Bill Morrissey and Ray Toth

Porter house with fresh asparagus

AWARD WINNER
SINCE 1999

Lord Fletcher's on Lake Minnetonka

A beautiful day at Lord Fletcher's

Warm hospitality and creative cuisine abound while dining amid the beautiful lakeside surroundings of Lord Fletcher's on Lake Minnetonka. *Minneapolis-St.Paul* magazine says Lord Fletcher's has the best view of any restaurant in the Twin Cities. The service is second to none, and the fare is creatively and beautifully prepared: Dijon roast rack of lamb, traditional walleye, and Szechuan grilled rare ahi tuna steak are representative of Lord Fletcher's entrees. *Wine Spectator* has recognized Lord Fletcher's with its Best of Excellence Award since 1998.

Outdoor dining at its best

Delightful lamb presentation

A global specialty

AWARD WINNER
SINCE 1999

Directions

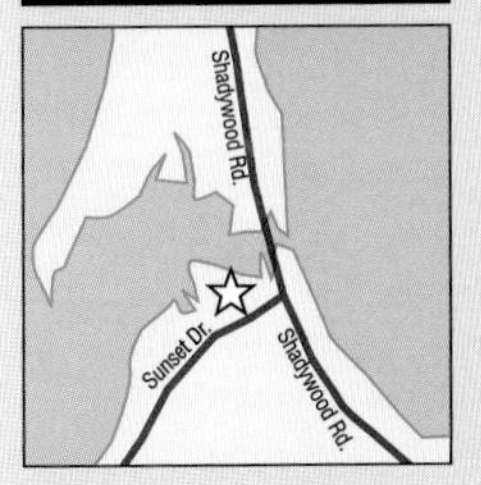

On Lake Minnetonka, 30 min. from Minneapolis-St. Paul International Airport

3746 Sunset Drive
Spring Park, MN 55384
PH: (952) 471-8513
FAX: (952) 471-8937
www.lordfletchers.com

Owners
William O. Naegele

Cuisine
American with global flair

Days Open
Open Mon.-Sat. for lunch, daily for dinner, Sun. for brunch

Pricing
Dinner for one, without tax, tip, or drinks: $20-$40

Dress Code
Business casual

Reservations
Recommended

Parking
Free on site, valet

Features
Private parties, outdoor dining, entertainment

Credit Cards
AE, VC, MC, DC, DS

Fairbanks Steakhouse

Safari Lounge

Directions

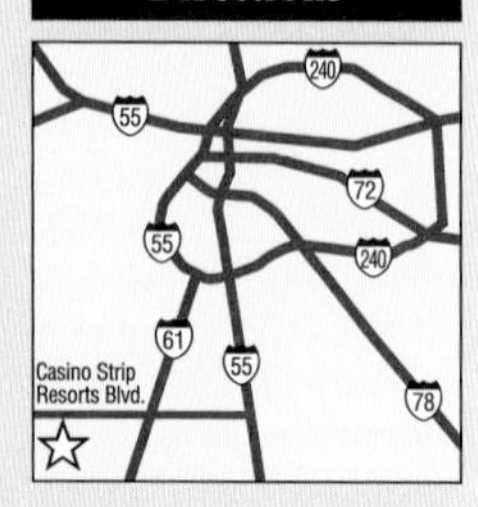

Located south of Memphis off I-61 on Hwy. 304, 30 min. from Memphis International Airport

1150 Casino Strip Resorts Boulevard
Robinsonville, MS 38664
PH: (800) 871-0711
FAX: (662) 357-7831
www.hollywoodtunica.com

Owners
Hollywood Casino Corporation

Cuisine
Steakhouse

Days Open
Open daily for dinner

Pricing
Dinner for one, without tax, tip, or drinks: $40-$60

Dress Code
Business casual

Reservations
Required

Parking
Free on site, valet

Features
Entertainment

Credit Cards
AE, VC, MC, DS

Fairbanks Steakhouse, in the Hollywood Casino, serves up a premier dining experience with mouthwatering certified Black Angus beef, lobsters, and gourmet specialty dishes. The restaurant is a delight for the eye, with motion picture memorabilia from the Douglas Fairbanks era and the amazing Fairbanks Wall of Wine, which holds 1,500 bottles. A humidor fully stocked with premium cigars will satisfy the most discriminating customers.

Hollywood Casino

Casino view

Fairbanks Steakhouse dining room

AWARD WINNER
SINCE 1998

Cafe Allegro

"Urban sophistication" best describes this intimate bistro-style restaurant in the heart of the chic 39th Street dining district. Exposed brick walls, warm mahogany accents, and eclectic art create a casually elegant atmosphere and warmly intimate dining experience. The contemporary menu changes monthly with an emphasis on locally grown produce, using the finest seasonal ingredients available. All breads, desserts, and most pastas are prepared in house daily. The restaurant smokes its own meats, fish, and game and grills all items over a pecan wood fire.

The bar

The front door

The dining room

AWARD WINNER
SINCE 1992

Directions

Just off State Line Road, 30 min. from Kansas City International Airport

1815 W. 39th Street
Kansas City, MO 64111
PH: (816) 561-3663
FAX: (816) 756-3265
www.cafe-allegro.com

Owner
Stephen Cole

Cuisine
Contemporary seasonal

Days Open
Open Mon.-Fri. for lunch, Mon.-Sat. for dinner

Pricing
Dinner for one, without tax, tip, or drinks: $20-$40

Dress Code
Business casual

Reservations
Recommended

Parking
Free on site

Features
Private parties

Credit Cards
AE, VC, MC, DC

Al's

Intimate dining

Al's, after more than 75 years of family operation at the same location, is a beloved institution in the Gateway City. Instead of a printed menu, the day's available seafoods and meats are presented to you on a silver platter, while an amiable table captain describes the preparation of each entree and suggests suitable accompaniments. Drinks in the riverboat lounge are a delightful interlude.

Courteous service

Cocktail lounge

AWARD WINNER
SINCE 1996

Directions

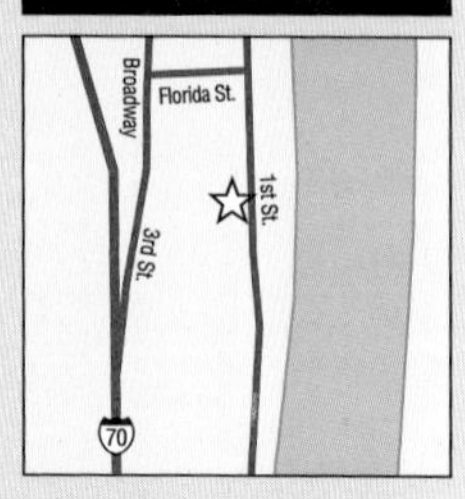

At N. First and Biddle streets near the river in downtown, 20 min. from Lambert-St. Louis International Airport

1200 N. First Street
St. Louis, MO 63102
PH: (314) 421-6399

Owners
Al Barroni

Cuisine
Italian American

Days Open
Open Mon.-Sat. for dinner

Pricing
Dinner for one,
without tax, tip, or drinks:
$40-$60

Dress Code
Jacket required

Reservations Policy
Recommended

Parking
Valet

Features
Private room/parties

Credit Cards
AE, VC, MC

Benedetto's Ristorante

Main dining room

One of St. Louis' premier Italian gourmet restaurants, this formal and intimate establishment offers patrons the true definition of European flair. Benedetto Buzzetta's hard work and dedication is evident in every dish that is prepared. Service is refined but friendly, ensuring the ultimate Italian dining experience. Tantalizing specialties include parpadella paesana and filetto ripieno.

The atrium

Indoor garden

AWARD WINNER
SINCE 1997

Directions

S. Forty Dr.
61
64
Clayton Rd.
Lindbergh Blvd.

In Frontenac, 15 minutes from Lambert St. Louis International Airport

10411 Clayton Road
Frontenac, MO 63131
PH: (314) 432-8585
FAX: (314) 432-3199

Owners
Benedetto Buzzetta

Cuisine
Gourmet Italian

Days Open
Open Mon.-Fri. for lunch, daily for dinner

Pricing
Dinner for one, without tax, tip or drinks: $20-$40

Dress Code
Jacket and tie required

Reservations
Recommended

Parking
Free on site

Features
Entertainment, live music, private room/parties

Credit Cards
AE, VC, MC, DC, DS

Directions

Daggett Ave.
Wilson Ave.
Hereford St.
Kingshighway Blvd.
Bischoff Ave.
Marconi Ave.
Cuggiono Pl.

At Wilson Avenue and Hereford Street on the Hill, 20 min. from Lambert-St. Louis International Airport

5101 Wilson Avenue
St. Louis, MO 63110
PH: (314) 771-1632
FAX: (314) 771-1695

Owners
Dominic Galati

Cuisine
Classic Northern Italian

Days Open
Open Mon.-Sat. for dinner

Pricing
Dinner for one, without tax, tip, or drinks: $20-$40

Dress Code
Jacket preferred

Reservations
Recommended

Parking
Free on site, valet

Features
Private room/parties, cigar/cognac events

Credit Cards
AE, VC, MC, DC, DS

Dominic's

Welcome to Dominic's

Superior food, exquisite tableside service, and meticulous attention to detail has helped build a dedicated following at Dominic's. There is an open yet cozy feel to the dining room. Owner and Executive Chef Dominic Galati prepares such Northern Italian specialties as fettuccine Verdi with shrimps and sweet peppers, and veal chops with truffles. Dominic's also boasts one of St. Louis' most generous wine cellars.

Dominic and Jackie Galati

Veal scallopine alla crema

Elegant dining

AWARD WINNER
SINCE 1992

Giovanni's

Dining room

Giovanni's on the Hill is the epitome of Italian dining in St. Louis. Executive Chef Francesco Gabriele prepares a classic Italian menu, including such unique entrees as veal saltimboca alla Giovanni, and swordfish alla Ghiotta. A pasta and eggplant dish called melanzana alla Conca D'Oro was created some years ago for former Beatle Paul McCartney and his vegetarian wife Linda; it remains on the menu as a tribute to the McCartneys. Other notable diners over the years include Ronald Reagan, George Bush, and Al Gore; the latter repaired to Giovanni's for a celebration after announcing his 2000 candidacy for President. Giovanni's is listed in the Millenium Issue of *America's Elite 1000*.

Wall of awards

Special for the McCartneys

Owner Giovanni Gabriele flanked by sons Carmelo (left), and Francesco

AWARD WINNER
SINCE 1992

Directions

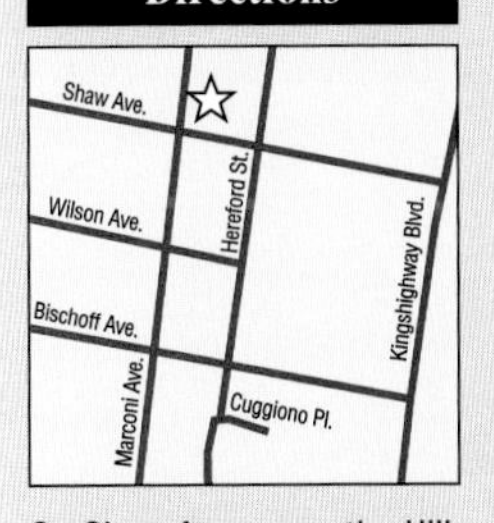

On Shaw Avenue on the Hill, 20 min. from Lambert-St. Louis International Airport

5201 Shaw Avenue
St. Louis, MO 63110
PH: (314) 772-5958
FAX: (314) 772-0343

Owners
Giovanni Gabriele

Cuisine
Classic Italian

Days Open
Open Mon.-Sat. for dinner

Pricing
Dinner for one,
without tax, tip, or drinks:
$40-$60

Dress Code
Business casual

Reservations
Recommended

Parking
Free on site, valet

Features
Private rooms/parties

Credit Cards
AE, VC, MC, DC

G.P. Agostino's

Directions

In the western suburbs of St. Louis, 20 min. from Lambert-St. Louis International Airport

15846 Manchester Road
Ellisville, MO 63011
PH: (636) 391-5480
FAX: (636) 391-3892

Owners
Rosa Gabriele Agostino and family

Cuisine
Northern Italian

Days Open
Open Tues.-Fri. for lunch, daily for dinner

Pricing
Dinner for one, without tax, tip, or drinks: $20-$40

Dress Code
Jacket and tie optional

Reservations
Recommended

Parking
Free on site

Features
Private room/parties, outdoor dining, cigar/cognac events

Credit Cards
AE, VC, MC, CB, DC, JCB, DS

Luxurious exterior

At G.P. Agostino's, love for delicious, well-presented food, served in elegant surroundings, has been an Agostino family tradition for two generations. Executive Chef Paul Gabriele uses only the freshest ingredients, finest spices, and purest Italian cheeses when preparing the menu, which highlights Northern Italian specialties. A varied wine list and delicious desserts complete a memorable meal.

Elegant presentation

Founder Agostino Gabriele, who died in 1999, as a young chef.

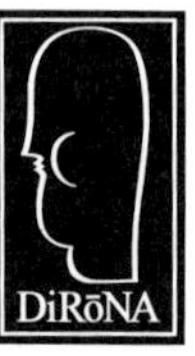

AWARD WINNER
SINCE 1995

John Mineo's Italian Restaurant

Owned and operated by John and Anna Mineo since 1973, John Mineo's Italian Restaurant serves top-notch Italian cuisine with five-star service. Chefs and servers alike finish the preparation of many dishes table-side. The sea bass, Dover sole, and veal chop are among the most popular entrees. Don't miss John Mineo's heavenly dessert drink, made from French vanilla ice cream, creme de cacao, and Amaretto. Four main dining areas accommodate all manner of social and business gatherings.

John Mineo Sr. and John Jr.

AWARD WINNER
SINCE 1994

Directions

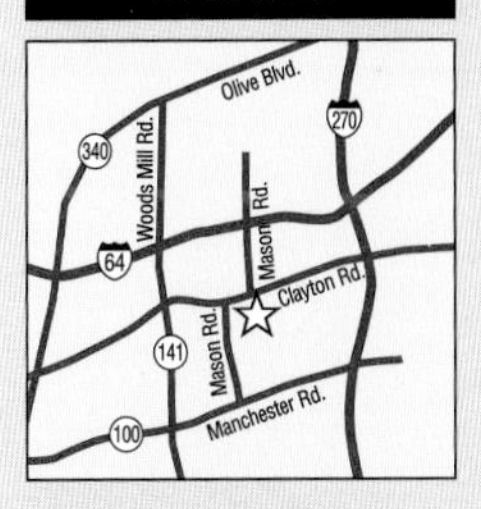

On the corner of Clayton and Mason, 20 min. from Lambert St. Louis International Airport

13490 Clayton Road
St. Louis, MO 63131
PH: (314) 434-5244
FAX: (314) 434-0714

Owners
John Mineo

Cuisine
Italian

Days Open
Open daily for dinner

Pricing
Dinner for one, without tax, tip or drinks: $20-$40

Dress Code
Business casual

Reservations
Recommended

Parking
Free on site

Features
Private room/parties

Credit Cards
AE, VC, MC, CB, DC, DS

The Seventh Inn

Directions

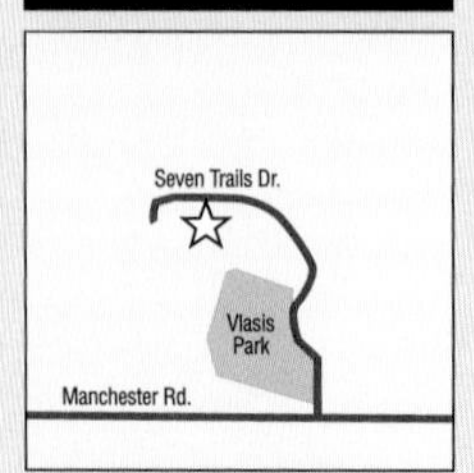

In Ballwin, 30 min. from Lambert-St. Louis International Airport

100 Seven Trails Drive
St. Louis, MO 63011
PH: (636) 227-6686
FAX: (636) 227-6595

Owners
Else M. Barth

Cuisine
Continental

Days Open
Open Tues.-Sat. for dinner

Pricing
Dinner for one,
without tax, tip, or drinks:
$20-$40

Dress Code
Jacket and tie required

Reservations
Required

Parking
Valet

Features
Private room/parties, entertainment

Credit Cards
AE, VC, MC, DC, DS

Private dining room

Experience distinguished Continental dining in elegant, relaxed surroundings at The Seventh Inn, a St. Louis landmark for more than 30 years. The glow of candlelight and the fragrance of fresh flowers enhance the mood, while professional servers attend to one's every need. Under the direction of Executive Chef Else Barth, the menu is varied, featuring more than 150 entrees. Fresh fish and aged beef are specialties.

Excellent cuisine in an elegant setting

A team of outstanding chefs

AWARD WINNER
SINCE 1994

Tony's

Wine Room

Tony's, within the shadow of the mighty Gateway Arch, welcomes guests from all over to an evening of elegant dining. The restaurant has a reputation for fine service—captains and waiters indulge the most discriminating diner with tableside preparation. The Italian menu, prepared by owner and Executive Chef Vincent J. Bommarito, emphasizes prime beef and veal and fresh seafood. An extensive wine collection and an array of mouthwatering desserts complete the meal.

Rack of lamb

Main dining room

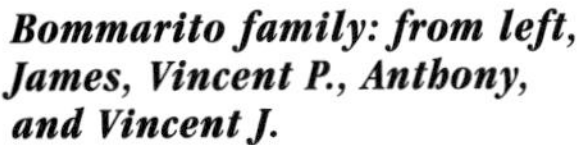
Bommarito family: from left, James, Vincent P., Anthony, and Vincent J.

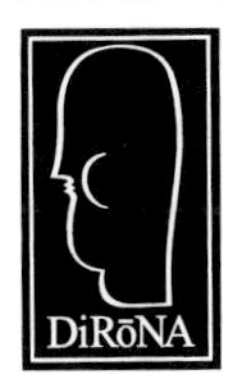

AWARD WINNER
SINCE 1992

Directions

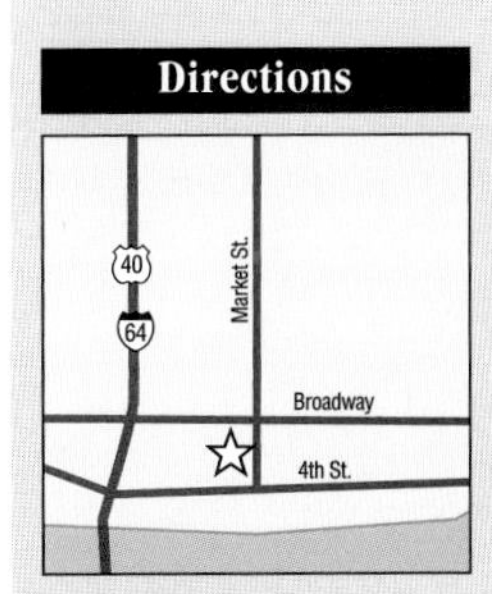

In downtown St. Louis near the base of the Gateway Arch, 30 min. from Lambert-St. Louis International Airport

410 Market Street
St. Louis, MO 63102
PH: (314) 231-7007
FAX: (314) 231-4740

Owner
Vincent J. Bommarito

Cuisine
Italian

Days Open
Open Mon.-Sat. for dinner

Pricing
Dinner for one,
without tax, tip, or drinks:
$40-$60

Dress Code
Jacket required

Reservations
Recommended

Parking
Valet

Features
Private room/parties,
cigar/cognac events

Credit Cards
AE, VC, MC, CB, DC, DS

Directions

95
S. 6th St.
Bridger Ave.
S. Las Vegas Blvd.
Clark Ave.

Just off the Strip, 25 min. from McCarran International Airport

401 S. 6th Street
Las Vegas, NV 89101
PH: (702) 385-5016
FAX: (702) 384-8574
www.andresfrenchrest.com

Owner
Andre Rochat, Norbert Koblitz, and Mary Jane Jarvis

Cuisine
French

Days Open
Open Mon.-Sat. for dinner

Pricing
Dinner for one, without tax, tip, or drinks: $40-$60

Dress Code
Business casual

Reservations
Recommended

Parking
Free on site, valet

Features
Private room/parties, outdoor dining, cigar/cognac events

Credit Cards
AE, VC, MC, CB, DC, JCB

Andre's French Restaurant

Andre's original downtown location

Housed in a 1930 home in a quiet residential neighborhood one block east of the Strip, Andre's is Las Vegas' most honored French restaurant — the best French restaurant and best gourmet restaurant in the city, according to the *Las Vegas Review-Journal* — and has attracted a loyal local following as well as an international clientele. They come for Andre's exquisite Classic French cuisine, superior service, and extensive wine list.

Intimate, elegant atmosphere

Owner and Executive Chef Andre Rochat

AWARD WINNER
SINCE 1992

Ferraro's Restaurant

The home of great Italian cooking

To dine at Ferraro's is to dine at a special place. Upon entering, a soft, pink light radiates a misty presence. Since 1985, Gino Ferraro and his family have overseen this environment of elegance and great Italian cooking. From the kitchens, presided over by Chef Mario Andreoni, come time-honored family recipes: superb pasta dishes, homemade breads, exquisitely fresh seafood dishes, and Ferraro's renowned osso buco.

Award-winning cuisine

The dining room

AWARD WINNER
SINCE 1999

Directions

Jones Blvd.
W. Flamingo Rd.

On W. Flamingo Road near the Bellagio, 20 min. from McCarran International Airport

5900 W. Flamingo Road
Las Vegas, NV 89103
PH: (702) 364-5300
FAX: (702) 871-2721
www.lasvegasdirectory.com/Ferraros

Owners
Gino and Rosalba Ferraro

Cuisine
Contemporary Northern and Southern Italian

Days Open
Open Mon.-Fri. for lunch, daily for dinner

Pricing
Dinner for one, without tax, tip, or drinks: $40-$60

Dress Code
Business casual

Reservations
Recommended

Parking
Free on site

Features
Private parties, entertainment, cigar/cognac events

Credit Cards
AE, VC, MC, DC, JCB, DS

Michael's

Directions

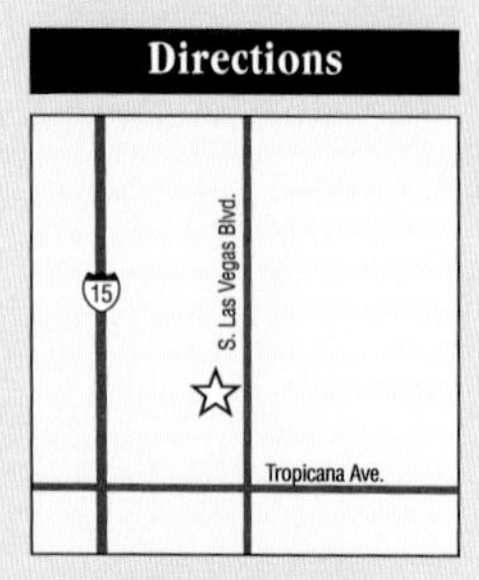

On the Strip at Flamingo Road, 10 min. from McCarran International Airport

3595 Las Vegas Boulevard S.
Las Vegas, NV 89109
PH: (702) 737-7111
FAX: (702) 737-6304
www.barbarycoastcasino.com

Owner
Michael Gaughan

Cuisine
Continental

Days Open
Open daily for dinner

Pricing
Dinner for one,
without tax, tip, or drinks:
$80+

Dress Code
Business casual

Reservations
Required

Parking
Free on site, valet

Features
Private room/parties

Credit Cards
AE, VC, MC, CB, DC,
ER, JCB, DS

Intimate dining

For nearly two decades, Michael's Restaurant, inside the charming, stained glass-laden Barbary Coast Hotel & Casino, has provided Las Vegas with elegance and distinction in fine dining. The intimate, 50-seat gourmet room will appeal to the truly enlightened, with an abundance of red velvet and deep mahogany, an Italian marble floor, and an elaborate crystal chandelier. Quite a stage for the cuisine: "We have carefully selected the finest recipes and we use only the highest quality fresh foods available," says Executive Chef Fred Bielak.

Fine Continental cuisine

Chef Fred Bielak

At your service

AWARD WINNER
SINCE 1993

Monte Carlo

The Desert Inn

Gracious ambience, reminiscent of the legendary Cote D'Azur, awaits in The Desert Inn's signature restaurant, Monte Carlo, frequented over its 34 years by celebrities ranging from Frank Sinatra and Shirley MacLaine to David Letterman and Wayne Gretzky. The exquisite menu features such French classics as roasted duck l'orange with a touch of vanilla; quails stuffed with honey, green apples, and raisins; and lamb chops draped with Roquefort sauce, almonds, fruit, and rosemary.

A majestic lobby

Golf on site

Elegant dining

AWARD WINNER
SINCE 1995

Directions

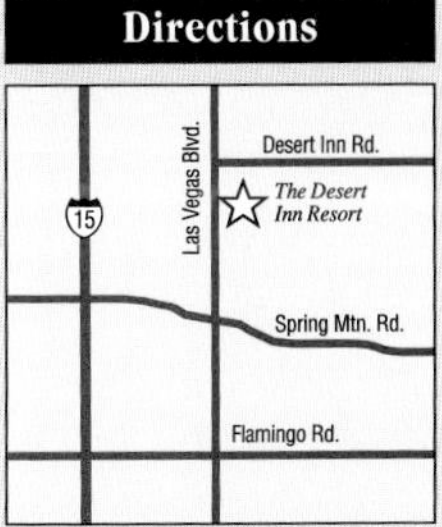

At the Desert Inn Resort on the Strip, 10 min. from McCarran International Airport

The Desert Inn Resort
3145 Las Vegas Boulevard S.
Las Vegas, NV 89109
PH: (702) 733-4524
FAX: (702) 733-4588
www.thedesertinn.com

Owner
The Desert Inn Resort

Cuisine
French

Days Open
Open Thurs.-Mon. for dinner

Pricing
Dinner for one,
without tax, tip, or drinks:
$80+

Dress Code
Business casual

Reservations
Recommended

Parking
Free on site, valet

Features
Private room

Credit Cards
AE, VC, MC, DC, DS

Piero's

Sumptuous decor

Fine food, an extensive wine list, and caring service that starts at the door make Piero's a consistent winner and a favorite with locals, celebrities, and convention center attendees alike. Executive Chef Gilbert Fetaz's osso buco is world renowned, as are his seafood preparations, notably Florida stone crab (in season) served with a mouthwatering mustard sauce. The delicious desserts are lovingly prepared every morning.

Delicious osso buco

Owner Fred Glusman

Beautiful presentation

AWARD WINNER
SINCE 1995

Directions

Sahara Ave.
15
Las Vegas Blvd.
Paradise Rd.
Convention Center Dr.
Desert Inn Rd.

Next to the Las Vegas Convention Center, 10 min. from McCarran International Airport

355 Convention Center Drive
Las Vegas, NV 89109
PH: (702) 369-2305
FAX: (702) 735-5699
www.pieroscuisine.com

Owner
Fred Glusman

Cuisine
Northern Italian

Days Open
Open daily for dinner

Pricing
Dinner for one,
without tax, tip, or drinks:
$40-$60

Dress Code
Business casual

Reservations
Recommended

Parking
Free on site, valet

Features
Private room/parties, entertainment

Credit Cards
AE, VC, MC, DC, JCB, DS

Harrah's Steak House

Harrah's Reno Hotel Casino

Signature items that will take your breath away, tableside preparation, and attention to the smallest of details have made the award-winning Harrah's Steak House one of Reno's best restaurants for over 30 years. The commitment to creating an outstanding and elegant dining experience makes Harrah's Steak House the perfect place for an intimate dinner or special celebration. Be sure to experience the Creamy Five Onion Soup, which is baked in a Carruso onion and crusted with Gruyere cheese.

Tableside preparation

Continental Entrees

Steak House delights

AWARD WINNER
SINCE 1996

Directions

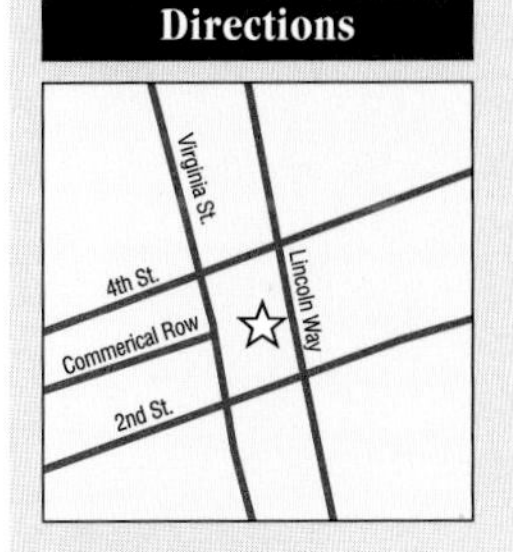

In downtown Reno, 5 min. from Reno/Tahoe International Airport

219 N. Center Street
Reno, NV 89501
PH: (775) 788-2929
FAX: (775) 788-3575
www.harrahsreno.com

Owners
Harrah's Hotel Casino

Cuisine
Steakhouse, Continental

Days Open
Open Mon.-Fri. for lunch, daily for dinner

Pricing
Dinner for one, without tax, tip, or drinks: $20-$40

Dress Code
Casual

Reservations
Recommended

Parking
Free on site, valet

Features
Private room, tableside cooking

Credit Cards
AE, VC, MC, CB, DC, DS

Peppermill's White Orchid

Directions

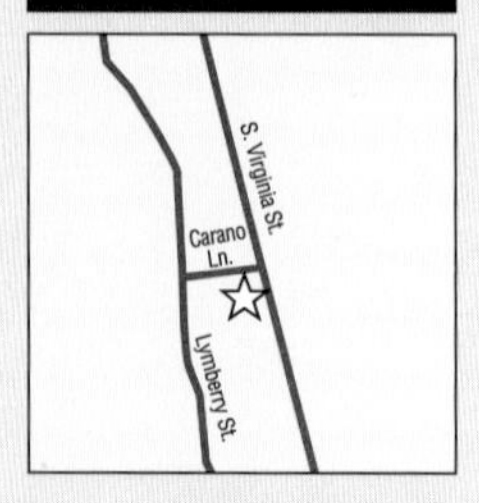

In the Peppermill Hotel Casino, 10 min. from Reno-Tahoe International Airport

2707 South Virginia Street
Reno, NV 89502
PH: (775) 689-7300
FAX: (775) 689-7189
www.peppermillcasinos.com

Owners
Peppermill Hotel Casino

Cuisine
Contemporary Continental

Days Open
Open daily for dinner

Pricing
Dinner for one,
without tax, tip or drinks:
$40-$60

Dress Code
Business casual

Reservations
Recommended

Parking
Free on site, valet

Features
Private room/parties

Credit Cards
AE, VC, MC, DC, DS

1,070 luxurious rooms and jacuzzi suites

The luxurious White Orchid offers Reno's finest dining experience. Chef de Cuisine Roger Moore and his team excel at creating cuisine-as-fine-art: original, delectable, and rich in texture and complexity. With 1,000 labels, the wine list is spectacular, and servers' knowledge is extensive. Nestled into the majestic Sierra Nevada Mountains as part of the vibrant Peppermill Hotel Casino, this restaurant can be one stop in a stay of supreme luxury and play.

Complex, original entrees

The main dining room

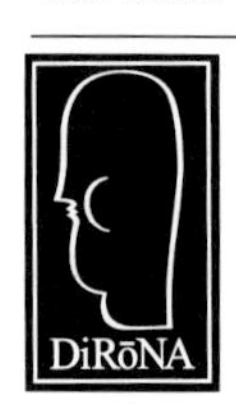

AWARD WINNER
SINCE 2001

Llewellyn's

Scenic dining

Innovative Continental cuisine, impeccable service, and panoramic views of Lake Tahoe provide a magical and exceptionally memorable dining experience at Llewellyn's, on the 19th floor of Harveys Resort & Casino. Guests who return time and again have voted Llewellyn's view, wine list, and fabulous Sunday brunch as the best of Tahoe. The restaurant is named for Llewellyn Gross, who with her husband Harvey established the hotel in 1944.

Tempting cuisine

Panoramic views

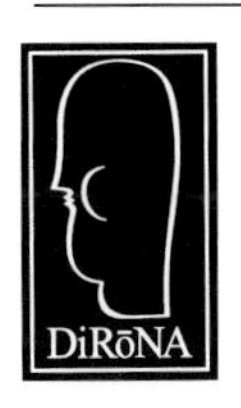

AWARD WINNER
SINCE 1997

Directions

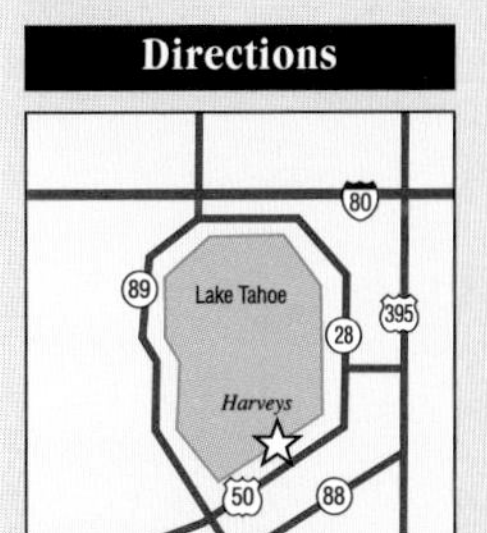

On Route 50 on Lake Tahoe's South Shore, 1 hr. from Reno/Tahoe International Airport

Harveys Resort & Casino
Highway 50 and Stateline Avenue
Stateline, NV 89449
PH: (775) 588-2411
FAX: (775) 588-6643

Owner
Harveys Resort & Casino

Type of Cuisine
Continental

Days Open
Open Wed.-Sat. for lunch, daily for dinner (brunch on Sun.)

Pricing
Dinner for one, without tax, tip, or drinks: $20-$40

Dress Code
Business casual

Reservations
Recommended

Parking
Free on site, valet, garage nearby

Features
Private parties, entertainment

Credit Cards
AE, VC, MC, CB, DC, JCB, DS

Bedford Village Inn

The Porch Garden

The Bedford Village Inn, a multi-million-dollar farm estate restoration that received the Four Diamond Award rating for dining and lodging, features its award-winning cuisine in eight intimate dining rooms–each graced with exotic orchids and fresh flower arrangements–and casual fare in The Tap Room. Executive Chef Nathan Baldwin leads a notable culinary team. Beginning with perhaps an appetizer of pan-seared Jonah crab cakes and continuing on to grilled tenderloin of ostrich, everything that emerges from the kitchen will delight even the most discriminating palate. An expanded wine cellar houses more than 8,000 bottles. The Inn's 14 luxury suites are bathed in Italian marble and have whirlpools and spacious sitting areas.

Overlook dining

The Tap Room

AWARD WINNER
SINCE 1996

Directions

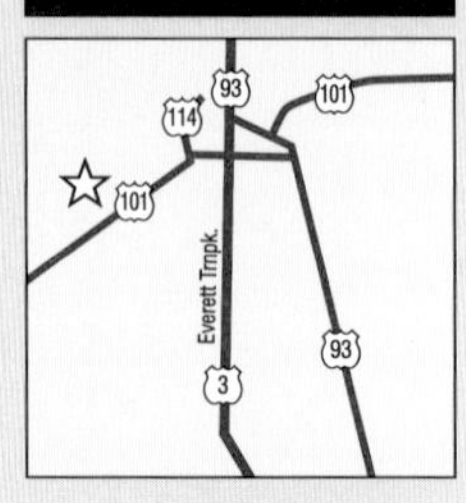

Off Highway 101, 10 min. from Manchester Airport and 1 hr. 15 min. from Boston's Logan International

2 Village Inn Lane
Bedford, NH 03110
PH: (603) 472-2001
FAX: (603) 472-2379
www.bedfordvillageinn.com

Owners
Jack and Andrea Carnevale

Cuisine
Regional New England

Days Open
Open daily for breakfast, lunch, and dinner

Pricing
Dinner for one, without tax, tip, or drinks: $20-$40

Dress Code
Business casual

Reservations
Recommended

Parking
Free on site

Features
Private room/parties

Credit Cards
AE, VC, MC, CB, DC

Ram's Head Inn

Gracious courtyard

Ram's Head Inn offers quiet, distinctively American dining in an elegant country atmosphere. This delightful restaurant is filled with authentic antiques and augmented by a gracious courtyard. Set on five country acres with sprawling gardens and flower-lined fences, the property has received the AAA Four Diamond Award, "Best of the Shore" (*Atlantic City Magazine*), and "Best of the Best" (*New Jersey Monthly*).

Private dining room

Phyllo purse of portobello mushroom

From garden to table

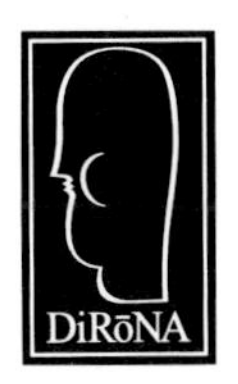

AWARD WINNER
SINCE 1994

Directions

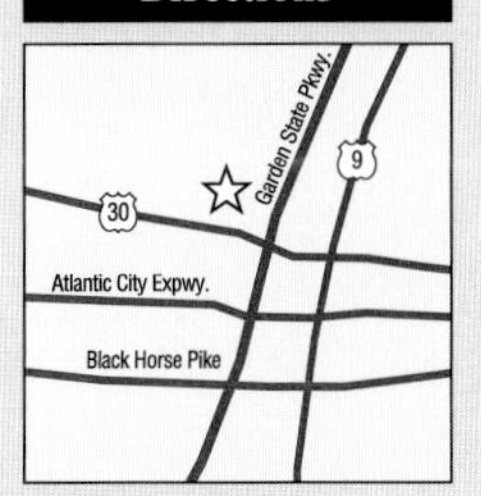

Seven miles from the casinos of Atlantic City and 10 min. from Atlantic City International Airport

9 West White Horse Pike
Absecon, NJ 08201
PH: (609) 652-1700
FAX: (609) 748-1588
www.ramsheadinn.com

Owners
The Knowles family

Cuisine
American

Days Open
Open Tues.-Fri. for lunch, Tues.-Sun. for dinner

Pricing
Dinner for one, without tax, tip, or drinks: $20-$40

Dress Code
Jackets required, ties optional

Reservations
Recommended

Parking
Free on site, valet

Features
Private room/parties, entertainment, near theater, cigar/cognac events

Credit Cards
AE, VC, MC, CB, DC, DS

Peregrines'

Main dining room

This exclusive five-star culinary centerpiece is an award-winning achievement with an exquisite sense of excellence. Named for the Peregrine falcons that have made the Atlantic City Hilton's penthouse ledge their annual summer home, this establishment offers regional and international contemporary cuisine featuring gourmet seafood.

Elegance at the Hilton

Directions

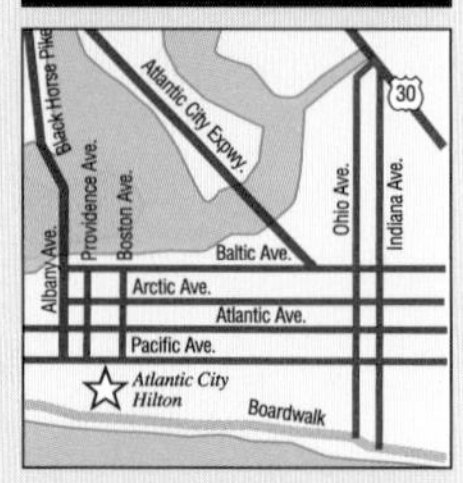

At the Atlantic City Hilton Casino Resort, 20 min. from Atlantic City International Airport

Boston Avenue at the Boardwalk
Atlantic City, NJ 08401
PH: (609) 340-7400
FAX: (609) 340-4879
www.ballys.com

Owners
Park Place Entertainment

Cuisine
Regional and international contemporary

Days Open
Open Thurs.-Sun. for dinner

Pricing
Dinner for one,
without tax, tip, or drinks:
$40-$60

Dress Code
Business casual

Reservations
Recommended

Parking
Valet, garage nearby

Credit Cards
AE, VC, MC

AWARD WINNER
SINCE 1997

The Bernards Inn

The Great Room

The Bernards Inn was created as a sumptuous retreat for discerning travelers, first welcoming guests in 1907. It is a tranquil retreat where history surrounds you, graceful architecture shelters you, privacy comforts you, and gracious hospitality envelops you. Chef and co-owner Edward Stone's fine menu of contemporary American fare reflects nature's seasonal bounty. His culinary innovations are enhanced by an award-winning wine list with over 450 selections and 9,000 bottles in inventory.

Executive Chef Edward Stone

Maine lobster and prawns

Lobby fireplace

AWARD WINNER
SINCE 1999

Directions

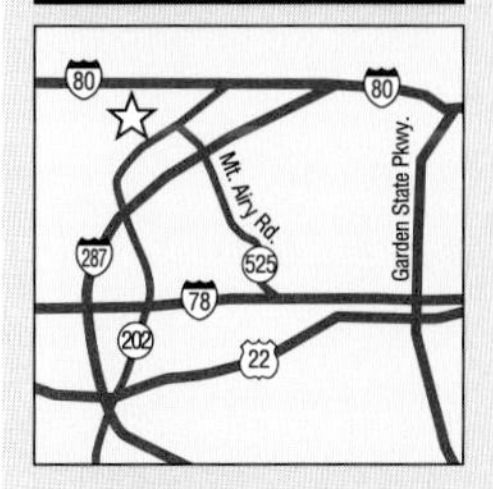

On southbound Route 202 in downtown Bernardsville, 40 min. from Newark International Airport

27 Mine Brook Road
Bernardsville, NJ 07924
PH: (908) 766-0002
FAX: (908) 766-4604
www.bernardsinn.com

Owners
Alice and George Rochat, Edward Stone

Cuisine
Progressive American

Days Open
Open Mon.-Fri. for lunch, Mon.-Sat. for dinner

Pricing
Dinner for one, without tax, tip, or drinks: $40-$60

Dress Code
Business casual; jacket required on Saturday only

Reservations
Recommended

Parking
Free on site

Features
Private room/parties, outdoor dining, wine cellar, entertainment, near theater

Credit Cards
AE, VC, MC, DC

Beau Rivage

Directions

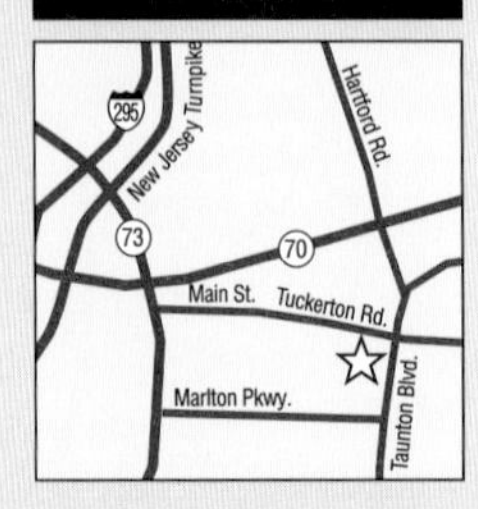

In woods overlooking Lake Pine, 30 min. from Philadelphia International Airport

128 Taunton Boulevard
Medford, NJ 08055
PH: (856) 983-1999
FAX: (856) 988-1136
www.beau-rivage.com

Owners
Gerard P. Gehin

Cuisine
French provincial

Days Open
Open Tues.-Fri. for lunch, Tues.-Sun. for dinner

Pricing
Dinner for one, without tax, tip, or drinks: $40-$60

Dress Code
Business casual

Reservations
Required

Parking
Free on site, valet on Saturday

Features
Private room/parties

Credit Cards
VC, MC, CB, DC

Main dining room

Nestled in tranquil woods overlooking Lake Pine, this Jersey jewel was created by Gerard Gehin, a master chef from Lorraine, France. Whether you choose to dine in a rustic atmosphere on the first floor or in the elegance of the Louis XVI Room upstairs, you will experience French cuisine at its best. Dishes range from the traditional to the daring, and the impeccable service and extensive wine list contribute to a truly memorable dining adventure.

Chef-owner Gerard P. Gehin

Lobster bisque

Wine cellar

AWARD WINNER
SINCE 1992

Panico's

Owner Frank Panico

Noted for fine wines and innovative Italian cuisine, Panico's has received raves from *The Star Ledger* of Newark and *The New York Times.* Executive Chef Gregg Freda uses only the very best and freshest ingredients, and his creations are brought to the table by a legion of formally dressed, unobtrusive servers. Entrees include Chilean sea bass wrapped in Parma ham, pan seared, and served over lemon thyme couscous with a brown butter vinaigrette; and grilled beef tenderloin topped with a Chippolini crust and served with a garlic and shallot red wine sauce.

Fresh Maine lobster tail wrapped with spinach and filet of sole

Stone crab risotto

Porcini and black trumpet sformato

AWARD WINNER
SINCE 1994

Directions

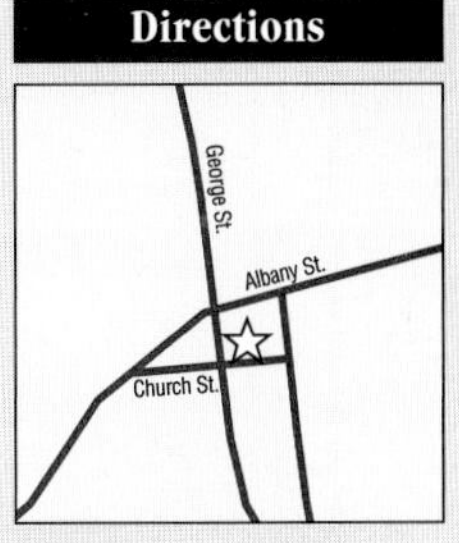

At Church and George streets in New Brunswick, near Route 18 and 25 min. from Newark International Airport

103 Church Street
New Brunswick, NJ 08901
PH: (732) 545-6100
FAX: (732) 545-7346

Owners
Frank Panico

Cuisine
Italian

Days Open
Open Mon.-Fri, for lunch, Mon.-Sat. dinner

Pricing
Dinner for one, without tax, tip or drinks: $80+

Dress Code
Jacket required

Reservations
Recommended

Parking
Garage nearby

Features
Private room/parties, near theater

Credit Cards
AE, VC, MC, DC, DS

The Dining Room

Directions

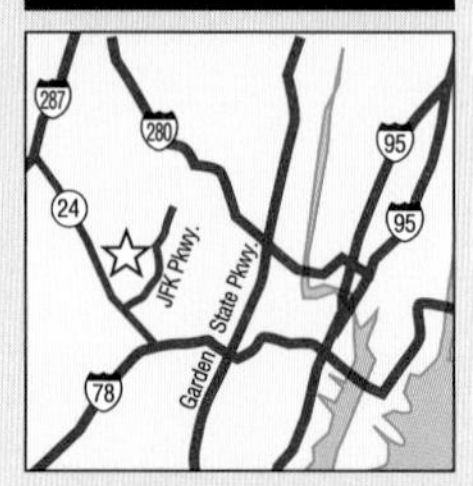

At the Hilton Short Hills, 20 min. from Newark International Airport

Hilton Short Hills
41 John F. Kennedy Parkway
Short Hills, NJ 07078
PH: (973) 379-0100
FAX: (973) 379-6870
www.hiltonshorthills.com

Owners
Hilton Hotels Corporation

Cuisine
American with French country accents

Days Open
Open Mon.-Sat. for dinner

Pricing
Dinner for one,
without tax, tip, or drinks:
$60-$80

Dress Code
Jacket/tie required

Reservations
Required

Parking
Free on site

Features
Private room, harpist, cigar/cognac events

Credit Cards
AE, VC, MC, CB, DC, ER, JCB, DS

Sophisticated charm, exquisite cuisine

The Dining Room at the Hilton Short Hills, led by Executive Chef Walter Leffler and Chef de Cuisine James Haurey, is New Jersey's only AAA Five Diamond restaurant. It offers imaginative French country cuisine, an extensive wine cellar, expert wine pairing, a refreshingly friendly staff, and soothing harp music. A private dining room is available for celebrations with 12 or 14 guests.

AWARD WINNER
SINCE 1999

Diamond's

Diamond's, nestled on a block of immaculate, working-class homes, is the crown jewel of the historic Chambersburg Restaurant District in New Jersey's capital city. The restaurant's understated exterior yields to a plush cocktail lounge and dining room that combine Old World grace with accents of contemporary chic. Anthony J. and Thomas M. Zucchetti, the brothers who own Diamond's and were born just two doors away, specialize in authentic Italian cuisine, as well as prime dry-aged steaks and fresh seafood. The wine list is legendary, and the lounge has a fully stocked humidor.

Plenty of room for events

Tempting Italian cuisine

A friendly place to gather

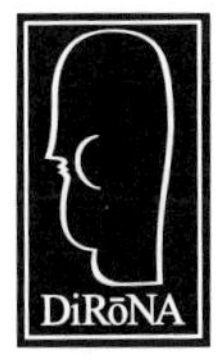

AWARD WINNER
SINCE 1998

Directions

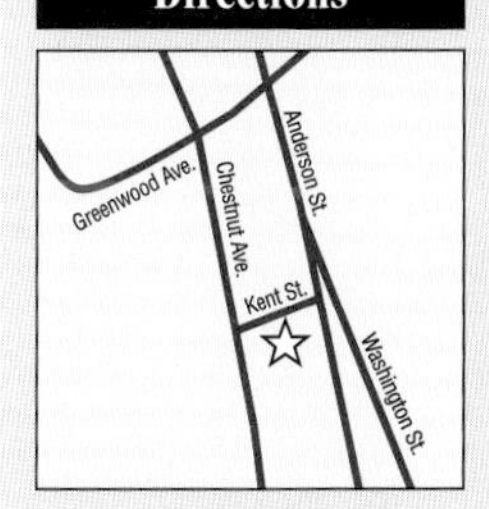

On Kent Street in the Chambersburg Restaurant District, 10 min. from Mercer County Airport, 35 min. from Philadelphia International, and 50 min. from Newark International

132 Kent Street
Trenton, NJ 08611
PH: (609) 393-1000
FAX: (609) 393-1672
www.diamondsrestaurant.com

Owners
Anthony J. Zucchetti and Thomas M. Zucchetti

Cuisine
Italian

Days Open
Open Mon.-Fri. for lunch, daily for dinner

Pricing
Dinner for one, without tax, tip, or drinks: $20-$40

Dress Code
Business casual

Reservations
Recommended

Parking
Free on site, valet

Features
Private room/parties, near theater, cigar/cognac events

Credit Cards
AE, VC, MC, CB, DC, DS

Highlawn Pavilion

Main dining room

Directions

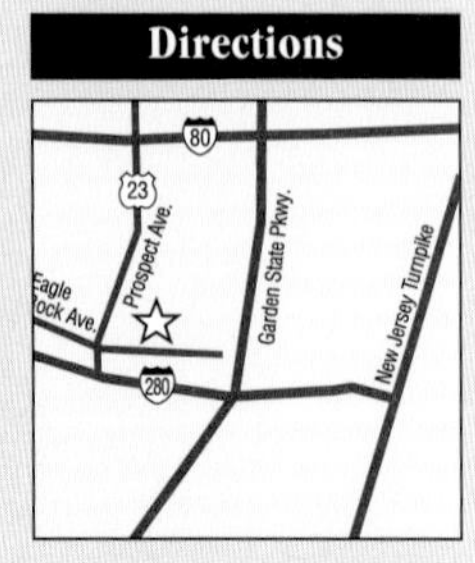

On Eagle Rock Reservation's scenic overlook, 15 min. from Newark International Airport

Eagle Rock Reservation
West Orange, NJ 07052
PH: (973) 731-3463
FAX: (973) 731-0034
www.highlawn.com

Owners
The Knowles family

Cuisine
American with European flair

Days Open
Open Mon.-Fri. for lunch, daily for dinner

Pricing
Dinner for one,
without tax, tip, or drinks:
$20-$40

Dress Code
Jacket required, tie preferred

Reservations
Recommended

Parking
Free on site, valet

Features
Private room/parties, near theater, cigar/cognac events

Credit Cards
AE, VC, MC, CB, DC, DS

Highlawn Pavilion offers an unmatched view of Manhattan's skyline. Distinctive American cuisine with European accents is served in a turn-of-the-century Florentine-style villa with a unique open kitchen. Voted among "America's Top Tables" by readers of *Gourmet*, it has become one of the area's most exciting restaurants. *New Jersey Monthly* awarded Highlawn Pavilion its "best atmosphere" and "most romantic dining" accolades.

A view of Manhattan

Chocolate bombe

Executive Chef Ossama Mickail

AWARD WINNER
SINCE 1995

The Manor

Terrace garden

A gracious manor house set amid acres of magnificent gardens, The Manor combines distinctive gourmet cuisine, superb service, and elegant decor. Bob Lape of *Crain's New York Business* declares its Terrace Lounge "outstanding dining — perfect for a business lunch." Voted among "America's Top Tables" by readers of *Gourmet*, the restaurant is also the recipient of the AAA Four Diamond Award as well as *Wine Spectator's* Grand Award.

Herb-crusted rack of lamb

The Knowles family: Doris and, from left, Harry, Kurt, and Wade K.

AWARD WINNER
SINCE 1992

Directions

Bordering Montclair Golf Club and Eagle Rock Reservation, 15 min. from Newark International Airport

111 Prospect Avenue
West Orange, NJ 07052
PH: (973) 731-2360
FAX: (973) 731-5168
www.themanorrestaurant.com

Owners
The Knowles family

Cuisine
New World

Days Open
Open Wed.-Fri. for lunch, Tues.-Sun. for dinner

Pricing
Dinner for one, wthout tax, tip, or drinks: $20-$40

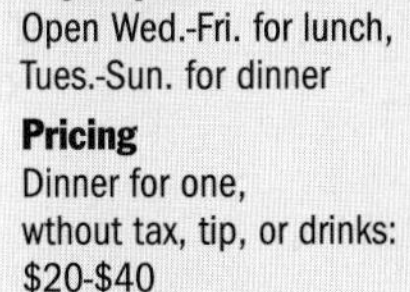

Dress Code
Jacket required, tie preferred

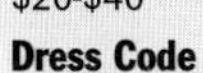

Reservations
Recommended

Parking
Free on site, valet

Features
Private room/parties, entertainment, near theater, cigar/cognac events

Credit Cards
AE, VC, MC, CB, DC, DS

The Ryland Inn

Directions

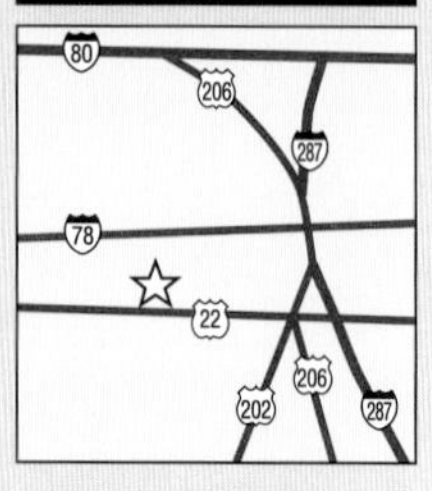

On Route 22 west, 1 hr. from New York City and Philadelphia, 35 min. from Newark International Airport

Route 22 west
Whitehouse, NJ 08888
PH: (908) 534-4011
FAX: (908) 534-6592
www.therylandinn.com

Owners
Craig Shelton

Cuisine
Contemporary American-French

Days Open
Open Tues.-Fri. for lunch, Tues.-Sun. for dinner

Pricing
Dinner for one, without tax, tip, or drinks: $60-$80

Dress Code
Business casual

Reservations
Recommended

Parking
Valet

Features
Private room/parties, cigar/cognac events, wine events

Credit Cards
AE, VC, MC, CB, DC, DS

Country restaurant

Dining takes on new meaning at The Ryland Inn, as Craig Shelton offers guests a creative and delightful approach to culinary artistry through his award-winning contemporary American-French cuisine. This gracious 200-year-old inn set amid rolling hills provides the venue that defines the ultimate dining experience. It has also earned worldwide recognition that extends beyond food to a selection of fine wines, and an unerring attention to presentation and service. The chef maintains a 3-acre organic herb and vegetable garden.

Warm tart of lobster

Chef-owner Craig Shelton

AWARD WINNER
SINCE 1996

Ranchers Club of New Mexico

Ranchers Club Lounge

The Ranchers Club is a dining experience that no visitor to the Land of Enchantment should miss. It offers food prepared on an authentic gridiron grill over a variety of aromatic wood embers, such as mesquite, hickory, sassafras, and apple. The eatery specializes in ample portions of corn-fed, dry-aged USDA prime beef. House specialties also include certified American bison and roasted venison loin. An award-winning wine list complements the mouthwatering selections.

Enjoy five-star dining

Let the culinary sensations entice you.

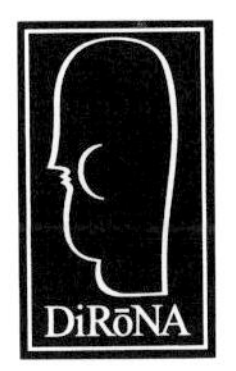

AWARD WINNER SINCE 1994

Directions

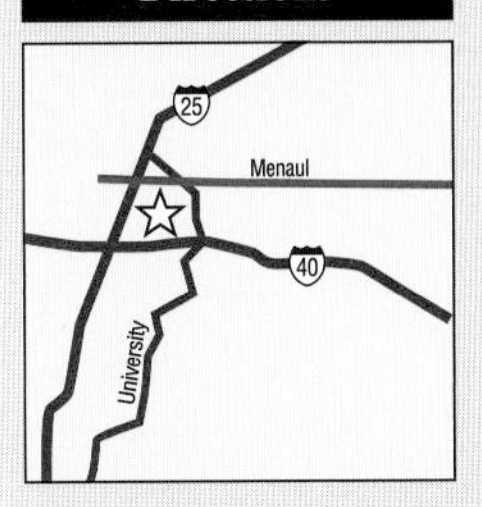

In the Albuquerque Hilton at Menaul and University, 10 minutes from Albuquerque International Sunport

1901 University Boulevard NE
Albuquerque, NM 87102
PH: (505) 889-8071
FAX: (505) 837-1715
www.albuquerquehilton.com

Owners
Ocean Properties

Cuisine
Authentic grill/classic American

Days Open
Open Mon.-Fri. for lunch, daily for dinner

Pricing
Dinner for one, without tax, tip or drinks: $40-$60

Dress Code
Business casual

Reservations Policy
Required

Parking
Free on site

Features
Private room/parties, entertainment

Credit Cards
AE, VC, MC, CB, DC, DS

Coyote Cafe

Directions

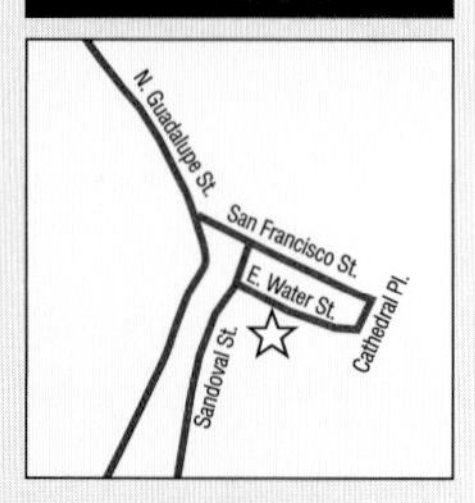

In downtown Santa Fe between Galisteo and Don Gaspar, 1 hr. 15 min. from Albuquerque International Sunport

132 W. Water Street
Santa Fe, NM 87501
PH: (505) 983-1615
FAX: (505) 989-9026
www.coyote-cafe.com

Owner
Mark Miller

Cuisine
Modern Southwestern

Days Open
Open daily for lunch and dinner

Pricing
Dinner for one, without tax, tip, or drinks: $20-$40

Dress Code
Casual

Reservations
Recommended

Parking
Garage nearby

Features
Outdoor dining

Credit Cards
AE, VC, MC, DC, DS

The Rooftop Cantina

Discover Mark Miller's celebrated modern Southwestern cuisine at Santa Fe's most popular and most honored restaurant, a 1999 *Wine Spectator* Award of Excellence winner. Signature dishes include buttermilk corn cakes with chipotle shrimp and the famous "cowboy" rib chop with ancho chile onion rings. The decor is unmatched in Santa Fe — whimsical with an open-view kitchen. During the summer, the Rooftop Cantina serves Mexican specialties and your favorite cocktails.

Creative Southwestern fare

Owner Mark Miller

Spectacular setting

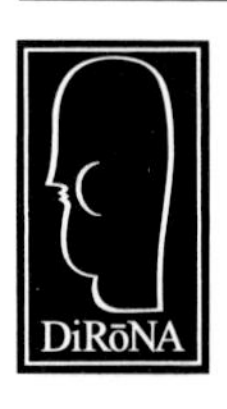

AWARD WINNER
SINCE 1992

Geronimo

Intimate dining room

In its celebrated 10 years, Geronimo has established a reputation as the place to dine in Santa Fe. Tradition and innovation merge at this Canyon Road legend, where simplicity and understatement reign. Owners Cliff Skoglund and Chris Harvey have succeeded in bringing unparalleled sophistication to the 1756 adobe home. The restaurant's romantic, elegant atmosphere creates a fabulous backdrop for the exquisite regional American and Southwest-influenced creations of Chef Eric DiStefano.

Cold water baby lobster

Chef Eric DiStefano with owners Cliff Skoglund (left) and Chris Harvey

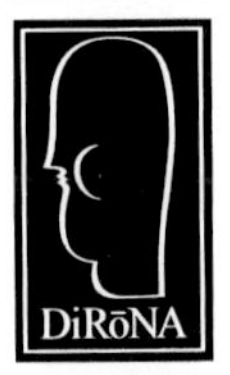

AWARD WINNER
SINCE 2001

Directions

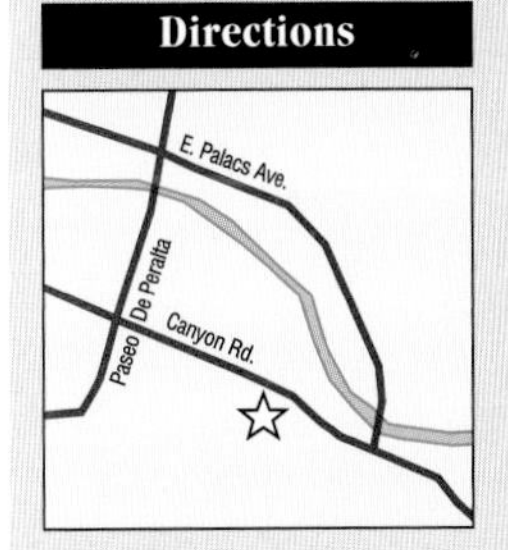

2 blocks from The Plaza downtown, 1 hr. from Albuquerque International Sunport

724 Canyon Road
Santa Fe, NM 87501
PH: (505) 982-1500
FAX: (505) 820-2083

Owners
Cliff Skoglund, Chris Harvey

Cuisine
Global American/Southwest

Days Open
Open daily for lunch and dinner

Pricing
Dinner for one, without tax, tip or drinks: $40-$60

Dress Code
Business casual

Reservations
Recommended

Parking
Free on site, garage nearby

Features
Outdoor dining, private room

Credit Cards
AE, VC, MC

Villa Fontana

Directions

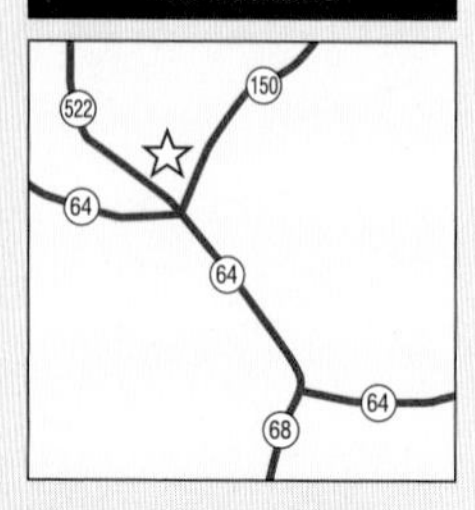

Five miles north of Taos on Highway 522, 2 hr. from Albuquerque International Sunport

71 Highway 522
Taos, NM 87571
PH: (505) 758-5800
FAX: (505) 758-0301
www.silverhawk.com/taos/villafontana

Owners
Carlo and Siobhan Gislimberti

Cuisine
Northern Italian

Days Open
Open Tues.-Sat. for dinner

Pricing
Dinner for one,
without tax, tip, or drinks:
$20-$40

Dress Code
Casual

Reservations
Recommended

Parking
Free on site

Features
Private room/parties, outdoor dining

Credit Cards
AE, VC, MC, CB, DC, JCB, DS

Charming Southwestern setting

A charming atmosphere, sophisticated presentations, and traditional European service make for a memorable experience at Villa Fontana, situated amid the majestic Sangre de Cristo Mountains of northern New Mexico. Local wild mushrooms gathered by Chef/Owner Carlo Gislimberti himself are just one of the house specialties. Expect such exceptional entrees as beef tenderloin with green peppercorns and brandy, and roasted duck with chanterelles, brandy, and cream. A summer garden provides a pleasant spot for outdoor dining.

Regional specialties

Homey interiors

Chef/Owner Carlo Gislimberti

AWARD WINNER SINCE 1994

Friends Lake Inn

Main dining room

Enjoy acclaimed contemporary American cuisine, personable service, and an award-winning wine list at this cozy, candlelit dining room with original tin ceiling and chestnut woodwork, located in a historic inn in the foothills of the Adirondacks. House specialties include sauteed lobster and scallop crepes with vanilla beurre blanc and toasted macadamia nuts, roasted venison loin with red currant sauce, and pomegranate-lacquered beast of duckling.

Greg and Sharon Taylor

River Rock Room

Sauteed lobster and scallop crepe, left, and roasted venison loin

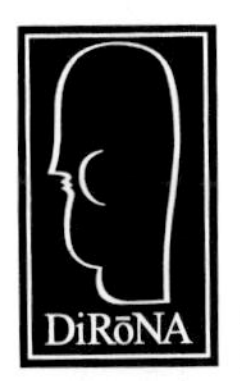

AWARD WINNER
SINCE 1998

Directions

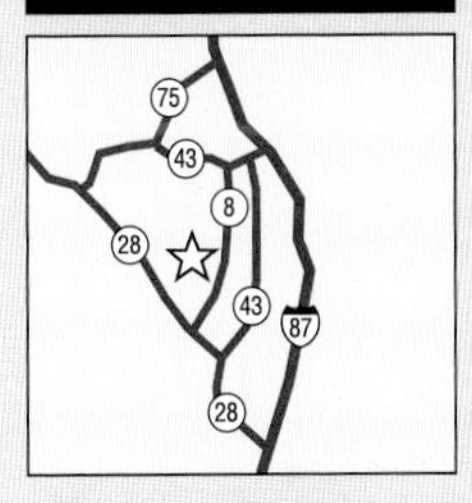

20 min. north of Lake George, 1 hr. from Albany International Airport

963 Friends Lake Road
Chestertown, NY 12817
PH: (518) 494-4751
FAX: (518) 494-4616
www.friendlsake.com

Owners
Sharon and Greg Taylor

Cuisine
New American

Days Open
Open daily for breakfast and dinner (lunch in winter only)

Pricing
Dinner for one, without tax, tip, or drinks: $20-$40

Dress Code
Casual

Reservations
Recommended

Parking
Free on site

Features
Private room/parties, wine cellar dining

Credit Cards
AE, VC, MC, CB, DC

Alison on Dominick Street

Romantic dining in SoHo

Directions

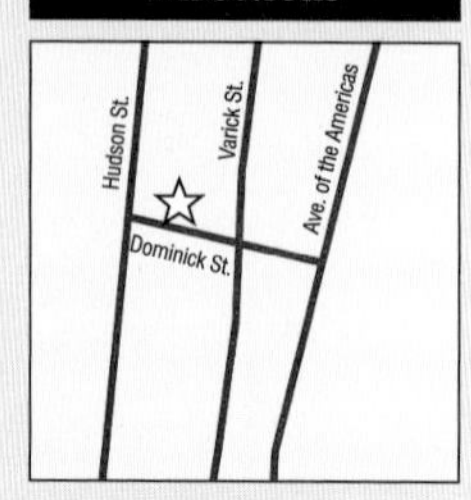

On Dominick Street between Hudson and Varick streets in SoHo, 20 min. from Newark International Airport

38 Dominick Street
New York, NY 10013
PH: (212) 727-1188
FAX: (212) 727-1005
www.alisonondominick.com

Owners
Alison Becker-Hurt

Cuisine
Country French

Days Open
Open daily for dinner

Pricing
Dinner for one,
without tax, tip, or drinks:
$40-$60

Dress Code
Business casual

Reservations
Recommended

Parking
Garage nearby

Features
Private room/parties

Credit Cards
AE, VC, MC, DC

Alison on Dominick Street, in SoHo, is one of Manhattan's most romantic and elegant restaurants. The seasonally changing menu features fare from southwest France and Spain, with such dishes as braised lamb shank, roasted squab, and applewood smoked lobster. An award-winning wine list complements the cuisine. Come experience the restaurant that *The New York Times* described as a "simple, harmonious place to dine."

Country French elegance

AWARD WINNER
SINCE 1993

Aquavit

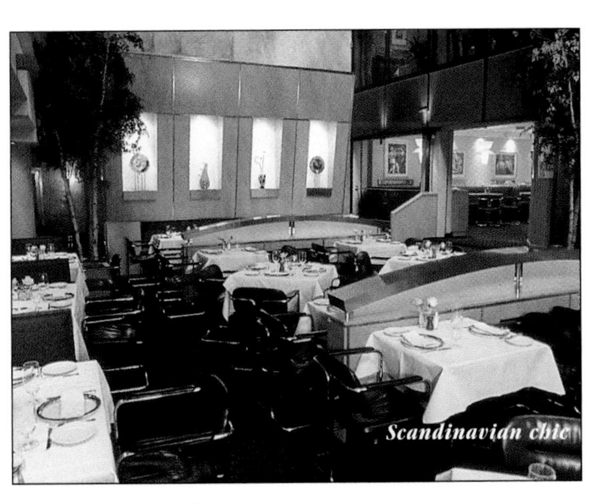

Scandinavian chic

Named for a popular icy neutral spirit (which the restaurant serves in a variety of flavorful incarnations), Aquavit showcases the culinary creations of Co-owner and Chef Marcus Samuelsson, who brings a world of influences and dynamic talent to the bustling kitchen. The distinctive eatery occupies the lower floors of the Rockefeller townhouses across the street from the Museum of Modern Art's sculpture garden. Specialties include gravlax, fois gras ganache, and sorrel-crusted char.

Creative specialties

Marcus Samuelsson

Hakan Swahn

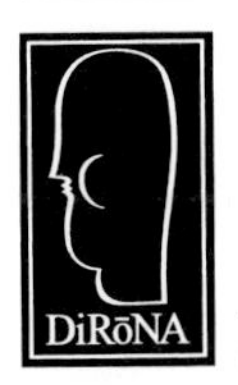

AWARD WINNER
SINCE 1992

Directions

Central Park
Madison Ave.
58th St.
56th St.
54th St.
Seventh Ave.
Sixth Ave.
Fifth Ave.

On 54th Street just off Fifth Avenue in midtown, 30 min. from LaGuardia Airport

13 West 54th Street
New York, NY 10019
PH: (212) 307-7311
FAX: (212) 957-9043
www.aquavit.org

Owners
Hakan Swahn, Marcus Samuelsson

Cuisine
Scandinavian

Days Open
Open daily for lunch and dinner

Pricing
Dinner for one, without tax, tip, or drinks: $60-$80

Dress Code
Business casual

Reservations
Recommended

Parking
Garage nearby (in same building)

Features
Private room/parties, near theater

Credit Cards
AE, VC, MC, CB, DC, JCB

Aureole

Townhouse glamour

Directions

E. 63rd St.
Central Park
E. 61st St.
Madison Ave.
Park Ave.
59th St.
E. 58th St.
Fifth Ave.

On 61st Street between Park and Madison avenues, 30 min. from LaGuardia Airport

34 E. 61st Street
New York, NY 10021
PH: (212) 319-1660
FAX: (212) 750-3126
www.aureolerestaurant.com

Owners
Charlie Palmer

Cuisine
Progressive American

Days Open
Open Mon.-Fri. for lunch, Mon.-Sat. for dinner

Pricing
Dinner for one, without tax, tip, or drinks: $60-$80

Dress Code
Jacket/tie required

Reservations
Required

Parking
Garage nearby

Features
Outdoor dining

Credit Cards
AE, VC, MC, DC, DS

Step into the understated elegance of the newly renovated Aureole, Charlie Palmer's Upper East Side town-house restaurant. For 11 years, this beautiful establishment has been known for its warm service and Palmer's distinctive contemporary American cuisine. New features include a six-course tasting menu and a vegetarian menu. Not to be missed are the ever-changing desserts for a grand finale. In warmer months, the picturesque garden is one of New York's most romantic secrets.

Wine bar

Herb-poached guinea fowl

Charlie Palmer

AWARD WINNER
SINCE 1992

Barbetta

Dining room

Barbetta, opened in 1906 by Sebastiano Maioglio and now owned by his daughter Laura, is the oldest restaurant in Manhattan still in the hands of its founding family. Amid 18th century Italian antiques, diners feast on the delicious cuisine of Piemonte. In summer, patrons can enjoy a meal in the lush, romantic flowering garden. Wine aficionados greatly appreciate this *Wine Spectator* Award of Excellence winner.

Owner Laura Maioglio

Garden

Quail's nest of Fonduta

AWARD WINNER
SINCE 1997

Directions

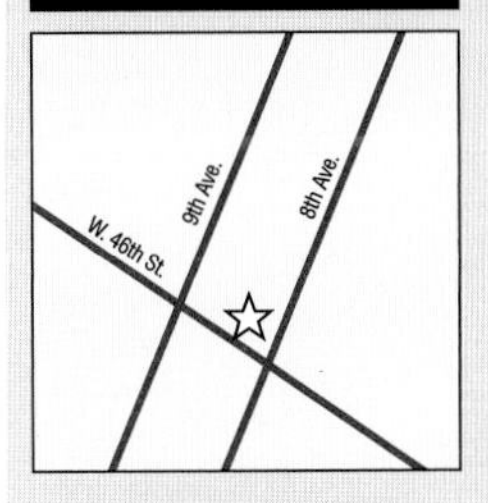

On Restaurant Row in the theater district, 30 min. from LaGuardia Airport

321 W. 46th Street
New York, NY 10036
PH: (212) 246-9171
FAX: (212) 246-1279
www.barbettarestaurant.com

Owners
Laura Maioglio

Cuisine
Northern Italian

Days Open
Open daily for lunch and dinner

Pricing
Dinner for one,
without tax, tip, or drinks:
$40-$60

Dress Code
Business casual,
jacket preferred

Reservations
Recommended

Parking
Adjacent lots

Features
Private room/parties, outdoor dining, entertainment, near theater

Credit Cards
AE, VC, MC, CB, DC, JCB, DS

Ciao Europa

Northside Dining Room

Directions

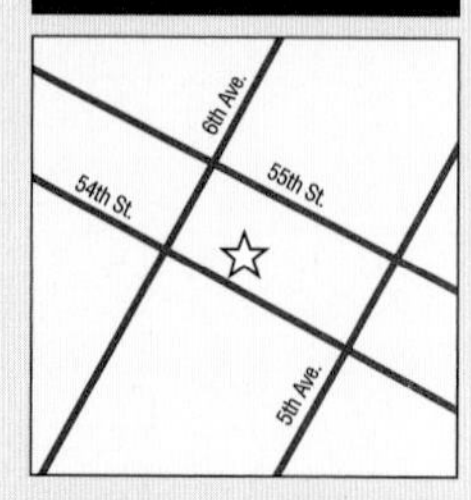

In the Warwick Hotel in the Theater District, 30 min. from Newark International Airport and 40 min. from LaGuardia Airport

63 W. 54th Street
New York, NY 10019
PH: (212) 247-1200
FAX: (212) 247-2184

Owners
Tony Pecora, Frank Pecora, and Michele Orsino

Cuisine
Italian

Days Open
Open daily for breakfast, lunch, and dinner

Pricing
Dinner for one, without tax, tip, or drinks: $40-$60

Dress Code
Business casual

Reservations
Recommended

Parking
Garage nearby

Features
Private parties, entertainment, near theater

Credit Cards
AE, VC, MC, DC, JCB

Whether it's breakfast, a business lunch, or an intimate dinner, Ciao Europa offers superb cuisine in a dramatic setting in the Warwick Hotel. Among the chef's personal favorites are red snapper cooked in parchment, shrimps wrapped with prosciutto, and half-moon pasta filled with broccoli rabe and shrimp. The menu has a generous selection of gourmet pastas with often exotic ingredients and there is a highly recommended pre-theater menu.

Superb cuisine

Owners Tony Pecora and Chef Michele Orsino

Eastside Main Dining Room

AWARD WINNER SINCE 1999

Cité

Main dining room

This steakhouse with a French accent specializes in succulent steaks, chops, and seafood and luscious home-baked desserts, and features an extensive wine cellar containing over 9,000 bottles. Located in the Time-Life Building at Rockefeller Center, the restaurant is filled with hand-painted tiles, marble walkways, and deep leather banquettes. Art deco grillwork and architectural embellishments that once graced Paris' Au Bon Marche department store now give Cité an atmosphere of casual elegance.

The Bacchus Mouth

The bar at The Grill

AWARD WINNER
SINCE 1995

Directions

Central Park
Central Park South
Madison Ave.
E. 58th St.
Seventh Ave.
51st St.
Ave. of the Americas
Fifth Ave.

At W. 51st Street between Sixth and Seventh avenues, 40 min. from LaGuardia Airport

120 West 51st Street
New York, NY 10020
PH: (212) 956-7100
FAX: (212) 956-7157
www.citerestaurant.com

Owners
Alan Stillman

Cuisine
American

Days Open
Open daily for lunch and dinner

Pricing
Dinner for one, without tax, tip, or drinks: $40-$60

Dress Code
Business casual

Reservations
Recommended

Parking
Garage nearby

Features
Private room/parties, prix-fixe wine dinner nightly

Credit Cards
AE, VC, MC, DC, DS

Daniel

The bar

Daniel offers a dining experience that awakens all the senses, from the elegant ambience and gracious service, to the delectable food and wines that epitomize la grande restauration francaise in the heart of Manhattan's Upper East Side. Savor Chef Daniel Boulud's seasonal French cuisine inspired by the market in a setting reminiscent of a Venetian Renaissance palazzo. Signature dishes include roasted squab stuffed with foie gras and morels, and creamy oyster velouté with lemongrass and caviar.

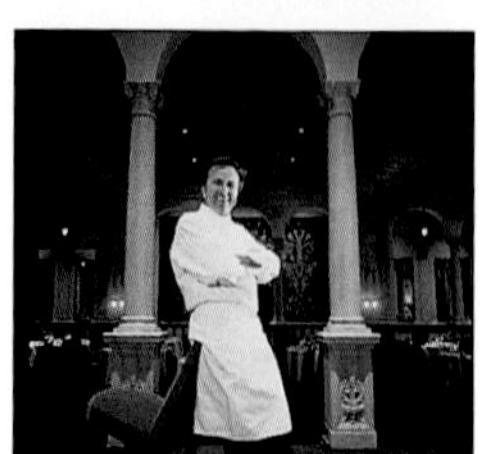

Chef/Owner Daniel Boulud

Maine crab in green-apple gelée

The dining room

AWARD WINNER
SINCE 1996

Directions

Central Park
E. 66th St.
E. 65th St.
E. 63rd St.
E. 62nd St.
Fifth Ave.
Madison Ave.
Park Ave.

On 65th St. between Park and Madison avenues, 30 min. from LaGuardia Airport

60 E. 65th Street
New York, NY 10021
PH: (212) 288-0033
FAX: (212) 396-9014
www.danielnyc.com

Owners
Daniel Boulud, Joel Smilow

Cuisine
Seasonal contemporary French

Days Open
Open Tues.-Sat. for lunch, Mon.-Sat. for dinner

Pricing
Dinner for one, without tax, tip, or drinks: $60-$80

Dress Code
Jacket and tie required

Reservations
Required

Parking
Garage nearby

Features
Private rooms/parties, lounge and bar

Credit Cards
AE, VC, MC

The Four Seasons

The Pool Room

The Four Seasons is one of Manhattan's most delicious restaurants. In addition to the sleek design and outstanding service, diners always remember Chef Christian Albin's adventurous new flavors. For lunch, visit the airy Pool Room and taste the seasonal American specialties that won *Where* magazine's Best Food award. In the evening, try the warm and cozy Grill Room for the truly spectacular prix-fixe menu.

Executive Chef Christian Albin

The bar

Seasonal dishes

AWARD WINNER
SINCE 1992

Directions

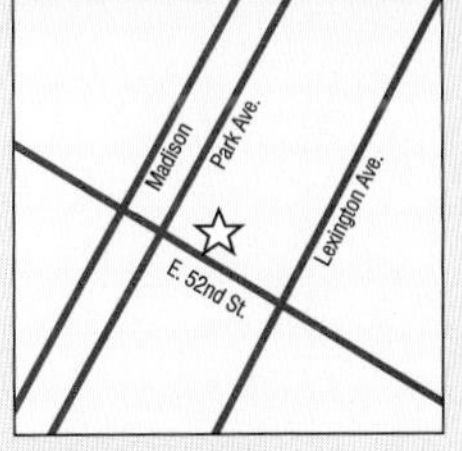

Between Park and Lexington Avenues, 30 min. from LaGuardia Airport

99 East 52nd St.
New York, NY 10022
PH: (212) 754-9494
FAX: (212) 754-1077
www.fourseasonsrestaurant.com

Owners
Alex von Bidder,
Julian Niccolini

Cuisine
American seasonal

Days Open
Open Mon.-Fri. for lunch, Mon.-Sat. for dinner

Pricing
Dinner for one,
without tax, tip, or drinks:
$40-$60

Dress Code
Jacket required, tie optional

Reservations
Recommended

Parking
Garage nearby

Features
Private room/parties, near theater

Credit Cards
AE, VC, MC, DC, JCB, DS

Gramercy Tavern

Directions

On E. 20th Street between Broadway and Park Avenue South, 40 min. from LaGuardia Airport

42 E. 20th Street
New York, NY 10003
PH: (212) 477-0777
FAX: (212) 477-1160

Owners
Danny Meyer and Tom Colicchio

Cuisine
Contemporary American

Days Open
Open Mon.-Fri. for lunch, daily for dinner

Pricing
Dinner for one, without tax, tip, or drinks: $60-$80

Dress Code
Business casual

Reservations
Required in main dining room; no reservations taken in Tavern Room

Parking
Garage nearby

Features
Private room/parties

Credit Cards
AE, VC, MC, DC

Full of urban and rustic charm, Danny Meyer's Gramercy Tavern was New Yorkers' second-favorite restaurant in the 2000 Zagat Survey. The restaurant is divided into two parts: casual Tavern Room and the pricier main dining room, which presents an ambitious and winning contemporary American menu. Tuna tartare with cucumber and sea urchin vinaigrette; salt-baked salmon with chanterelles, baby spinach, and roast garlic cream; and roasted rabbit with black olives and sherry vinegar are among the specialties than have won over New Yorkers and visiting food cognoscenti alike.

Private dining room

The Tavern

Main dining room

AWARD WINNER SINCE 1998

Halcyon

Elegant dining at the Rihga Royal Hotel

Delectable contemporary American cuisine and impeccable service continues to attract faithful patrons, celebrities, and CEOs to Halycon, the Rihga Royal Hotel's beautiful dining room. Try the smoked and roasted lamb with mascarpone risotto, or one of the many fresh seafood dishes. On Sundays, the Marketplace in the Sky brunch occupies the hotel's 54th floor, offering savory fixings and panoramic views of the Manhattan skyline.

AWARD WINNER
SINCE 1999

Directions

Central Park
Central Park South
Madison Ave.
58th St.
57th St.
56th St.
55th St.
Seventh Ave.
Sixth Ave.
Fifth Ave.

At the Rihga Royal Hotel, 54th Street between Sixth and Seventh avenues, 30 min. from all New York airports

151 W. 54th Street
New York, NY 10019
PH: (212) 468-8888
FAX: (212) 468-8816
www.rihga.com

Owners
Rihga Royal Hotels

Cuisine
American

Days Open
Open daily for breakfast, lunch, and dinner

Pricing
Dinner for one, without tax, tip, or drinks: $20-$40

Dress Code
Business casual

Reservations
Recommended

Parking
Valet, garage nearby

Features
Private parties, entertainment, near theater

Credit Cards
AE, VC, MC, CB, DC, DS

Jo Jo

Directions

Central Park
E. 64th St.
Third Ave.
Second Ave.
Central Park South
E. 58th St.
Fifth Ave.

On 64th Street between Lexington and Third avenues on the Upper East Side, 30 min. from LaGuardia Airport

160 East 64th Street
New York, NY 10021
PH: (212) 223-5656
FAX: (212) 755-9038
www.jean-georges.com

Owners
Jean-Georges Vongerichten, Phil Suarez, Bob Giraldi

Cuisine
Contemporary French

Days Open
Open Mon.-Sat. for lunch and dinner

Pricing
Dinner for one, without tax, tip, or drinks: $40-$60

Dress Code
Business casual

Reservations
Required

Parking
Garage nearby

Credit Cards
AE, VC, MC, DC

This charmingly elegant bistro serves Chef Jean-Georges Vongerichten's innovative interpretation of classic French cuisine. Jo Jo (Jean-Georges' childhood nickname) offers vibrant dishes created with intense flavors and satisfying textures made with vegetable juices and fruit essences, light broths, and herbal vinaigrettes. Sample such signature dishes as tuna spring roll with fresh soybean coulis, Day Boat lobster tartine in a pumpkin seed broth, and the famed melting Valrhona chocolate cake.

Bistro dining

AWARD WINNER
SINCE 1997

La Caravelle

Main dining room

La Caravelle has reigned as one of Manhattan's finest French restaurants since 1960. The elegant hand-painted murals by Jean Pagès evoke charming and colorful Parisian street scenes. La Caravelle's graceful setting is the ideal backdrop for the menu's brilliant integration of classical and contemporary French cuisine. Guests receive excellent, professional care under the watchful eye of owners Rita and André Jammet. Private dining for parties up to 30 guests is also available.

Private dining room

Mint chocolate soufflé

Owners Rita and André Jammet

AWARD WINNER
SINCE 1994

Directions

Central Park
Madison Ave.
58th St.
56th St.
Seventh Ave.
Sixth Ave.
Fifth Ave.
55th St.

On West 55th Street between 5th and 6th Ave., 30 min. from LaGuardia, 50 min. from Kennedy International Airport

33 W. 55th Street
New York, NY 10019
PH: (212) 586-4252
FAX: (212) 956-8269
www.lacaravelle.org

Owners
André and Rita Jammet

Cuisine
Classic and contemporary French

Days Open
Open Mon.-Fri. for lunch, Mon.-Sat. for dinner

Pricing
Dinner for one, without tax, tip, or drinks: $60-$80

Dress Code
Jacket and tie optional

Reservations
Recommended

Parking
Garage nearby

Features
Private room/parties, near theater, wine-tasting events and fashion show lunches

Credit Cards
AE, VC, MC, CB, DC

La Cote Basque

Directions

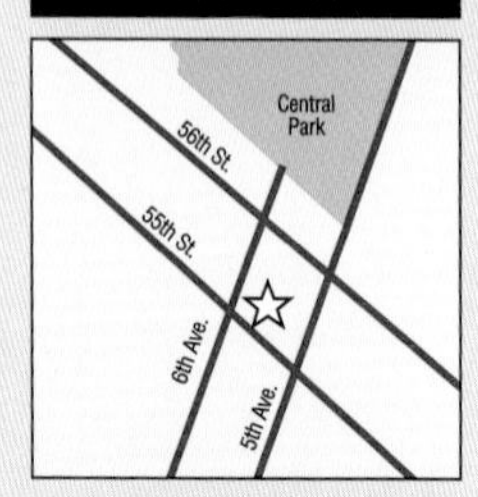

On W. 55th Street between 5th and 6th avenues in midtown Manhattan, 40 min. from LaGuardia Airport

60 W. 55th Street
New York, NY 10019
PH: (212) 688-6525
FAX: (212) 258-2493

Owners
Jean-Jacques Rachou

Cuisine
Updated classic French

Days Open
Open Mon.-Sat. for lunch, daily for dinner

Pricing
Dinner for one, without tax, tip, or drinks: $60-$80

Dress Code
Jacket and tie required

Reservations
Recommended

Parking
Garage nearby

Features
Private room, near theater

Credit Cards
AE, VC, MC, CB, DC, JCB, DS

Main dining room

"I may be a businessman but I am first an idealist. Because I treat everyone on my staff with the same care I give my customers, they give all they can," says Jean-Jacques Rachou, Chef/Proprietor of La Cote Basque, known for its sumptuous decor and sunny murals of the Basque coast and countryside. A new menu reflects the restaurant's recent modernization. In addition to Rachou's revered cassoulet Toulousain, the menu boasts lighter fare, including such appetizers as grilled vegetable terrine with goat cheese, tomato, and ginger. The wine cellar, 40,000 bottles strong, is astonishing.

Chef/Proprietor Jean-Jacques Rachou

AWARD WINNER
SINCE 1993

Le Cirque 2000

The Maccioni family

Le Cirque 2000's award-winning cuisine, awarded four stars by *The New York Times*, is all its own. Led by the Cambodia-born, French-trained Executive Chef Sottha Khunn, Sous-Chef Pierre Schaedelin, and Executive Pastry Chef Jacques Torres, Le Cirque 2000 is unlike any other restaurant. The menu features luscious new dishes that bring the enticing flavors and fragrances of France, Italy, and even Cambodia to the table. But regulars who yearn for old and beloved favorites will still find foie gras ravioli with black truffles, sea bass wrapped in potatoes with Barolo sauce, and, for dessert, the classic chocolate stove.

The Blue Room

The bar

The entrance

AWARD WINNER
SINCE 1999

Directions

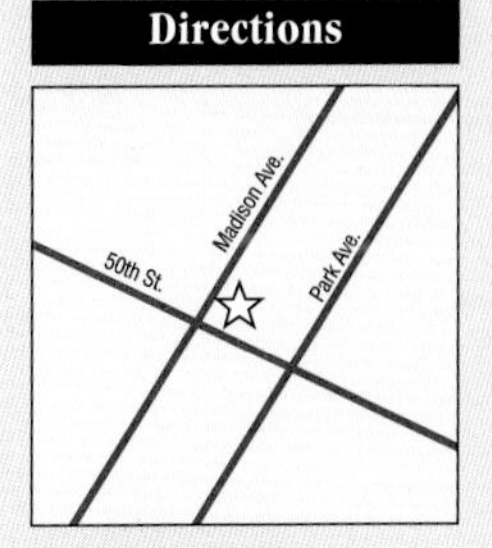

On Madison Avenue between E. 50th and 51st streets in midtown Manhattan, 40 min. from LaGuardia Airport

455 Madison Avenue
New York, NY 10022
PH: (212) 303-7788
FAX: (212) 303-7712
www.lecirque.com

Owners
Sirio Maccioni

Cuisine
Modern French/Italian

Days Open
Open Mon.-Sat. for lunch, daily for dinner

Pricing
Dinner for one, without tax, tip, or drinks: $60-$80

Dress Code
Jacket and tie required

Reservations
Required

Parking
Garage nearby

Features
Private room/parties, near theater

Credit Cards
AE, VC, MC, CB, DC

Le Perigord

Private dining room

Directions

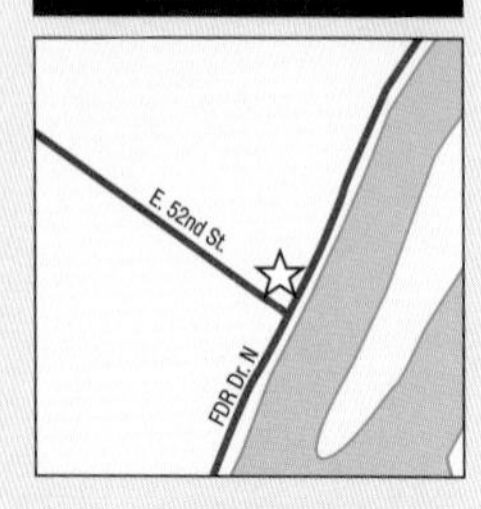

On E. 52nd Street between First Avenue and the East River, 25 min. from LaGuardia Airport

405 E. 52nd Street
New York, NY 10022
PH: (212) 755-6244
FAX: (212) 486-3906
www.leperigord.com

Owners
The Briguet family

Cuisine
Contemporary French

Days Open
Open Mon.-Fri. for lunch, daily for dinner

Pricing
Dinner for one,
without tax, tip or drinks:
$40-$60

Dress Code
Jacket and tie required

Reservations
Recommended

Parking
Garage nearby

Features
Private room/parties

Credit Cards
AE, VC, MC, CB, DC, DS

According to *The New York Times*, "Le Perigord is a survivor among an endangered species in New York: a solid French restaurant in a civilized setting that is conducive to both tranquil socializing and discreet business entertaining." The food is scintillating and the service exemplary at this luxury establishment. Chef Jacques Qualin offers traditional dishes executed with care, including sauteed veal kidneys in Armagnac and mustard.

Fresh lobster

Beef filet mignon

Georges and Marie Therese Briguet

AWARD WINNER
SINCE 1994

Maloney & Porcelli

Main dining room

This bustling, two-story restaurant reflects Executive Chef/author David Burke's creative approach to food, and its smart menu and dramatic decor draws crowds from the business and entertainment worlds. The classic American fare includes steak and lobsters, but goes beyond the traditional with such innovative dishes as crackling pork shank with firecracker applesauce and thin-crusted Robiola pizza with white truffle oil. Desserts are equally spirited and scrumptious: Try drunken doughnuts or a towering coconut layer cake.

Pork shank with firecracker applesauce

Chef Patrick Vaccariello

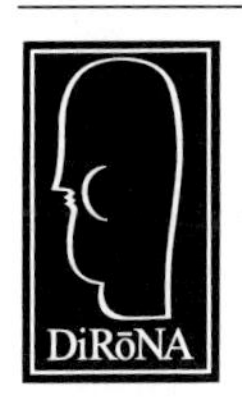

AWARD WINNER SINCE 2001

Directions

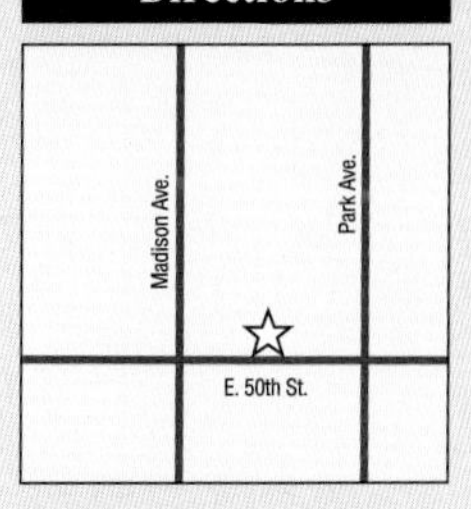

On E. 50th Street between Park and Madison avenues in midtown, 30 min. from LaGuardia Airport

37 E. 50th Street
New York, NY 10022
PH: (212) 750-2233
FAX: (212) 750-2252
www.maloneyandporcelli.com

Owners
Alan Stillman

Cuisine
Contemporary steakhouse

Days Open
Open daily for lunch and dinner

Pricing
Dinner for one, without tax, tip or drinks: $40-$60

Dress Code
Business casual

Reservations Policy
Recommended

Parking
Garage nearby

Features
Private room/parties

Credit Cards
AE, VC, MC, DC, DS

Directions

Central Park
Central Park South
Madison Ave.
Park Ave.
E. 58th St.
Ave. of the Americas
Fifth Ave.

On 58th Street between Fifth and Sixth avenues, 35 min. from LaGuardia Airport

57 West 58th Street
New York, NY 10019
PH: (212) 371-7777
FAX: (212) 371-9362
www.manhattanocean
club.com

Owners
Alan Stillman

Cuisine
Seafood

Days Open
Open daily for lunch and dinner

Pricing
Dinner for one,
without tax, tip, or drinks:
$60-$80

Dress Code
Business casual

Reservations
Recommended

Parking
Garage nearby

Features
Private room/parties

Credit Cards
AE, VC, MC, DC, DS

Manhattan Ocean Club

Picasso Room

Set in a sleek, two-tiered dining room, this classic seafood restaurant has won raves as one of Manhattan's best fish houses, with the day's fresh catch seared, sauteed, poached, or steamed to order. The menu also offers such dishes as seared tuna with grapefruit and deep-fried Leeks, and blackfish roasted with shiitake mushrooms and penne. Scrumptious desserts include the signature Belgian chocolate bags filled with white chocolate mousse with raspberry sauce.

Shellfish bouquet

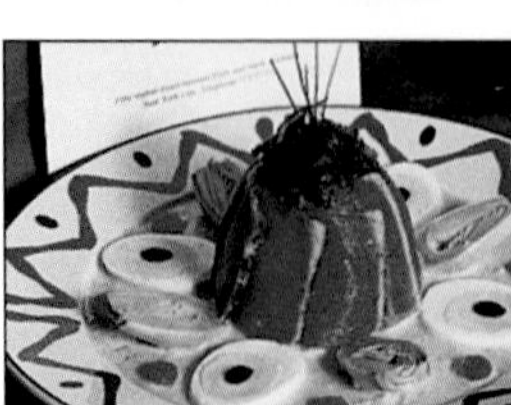

Creative entrees

Bounty from the sea

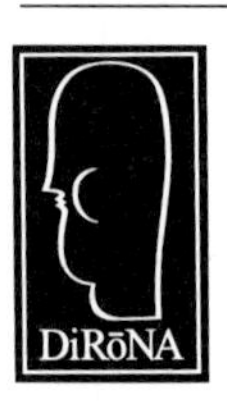

AWARD WINNER
SINCE 1998

Park Avenue Cafe

Main dining room

The acclaimed Park Avenue Cafe is a fine-dining restaurant showcasing signature dishes of Chef/Partner David Burke and Pastry Chef Richard Leach. Casual, warm, and welcoming, the cutting-edge American fare is served to diners in whimsical presentations. The eatery combines country and contemporary design elements with authentic American crafts. Don't miss such delectable items as the pastrami salmon, salmon tartare, and salmon bacon.

Owner Alan Stillman

Chef David Burke

The Flag Room

AWARD WINNER
SINCE 1997

Directions

Central Park
E. 63rd St.
Park Ave.
Lexington Ave.
Central Park South
E. 58th St.
Fifth Ave.

At Park Avenue and 63rd Street on the Upper East Side, 30 min. from LaGuardia Airport

100 East 63rd Street
New York, NY 10021
PH: (212) 644-1900
FAX: (212) 688-0373
www.parkavenuecafe.com

Owners
Alan Stillman

Cuisine
American

Days Open
Open daily for lunch and dinner

Pricing
Dinner for one, without tax, tip, or drinks: $60-$80

Dress Code
Business casual

Reservations
Recommended

Parking
Garage nearby

Features
Private room/parties

Credit Cards
AE, VC, MC, DC, DS

Peacock Alley

Directions

E. 63rd St.
Central Park
Lexington Ave.
Central Park South
Park Ave.
Fifth Ave.
E. 50th St.

In the Waldorf-Astoria Hotel, midtown, 40 min. from LaGuardia and Kennedy International Airports

Waldorf-Astoria Hotel
301 Park Avenue
New York, NY 10022
PH: (212) 872-4895
FAX: (212) 872-1266
www.waldorf.com

Owners
Hilton Hotels Corp.

Cuisine
Contemporary French

Days Open
Open Mon.-Fri. for breakfast, Tues.-Sat. for dinner, Sun. brunch

Pricing
Dinner for one,
without tax, tip, or drinks:
$60-$80

Dress Code
Jacket required

Reservations
Recommended

Parking
Valet, garage nearby

Features
Private room/parties, near theater, entertainment at brunch

Credit Cards
AE, VC, MC, CB, DC, ER, JCB, DS

Four-star dining

Peacock Alley, a Mobil four-star rated restaurant, stands out in New York's highly competitive culinary scene. Anointed with three stars from *The New York Times*, the eatery offers Chef de Cuisine Laurent Gras's elegantly innovative French cuisine-classic dishes reinterpreted for contemporary tastes, often incorporating American ingredients. The physical attractions of the luxurious dining room and lounge, overlooking the historic Waldorf-Astoria's elegant Art Deco lobby, complement Peacock Alley's exquisite gastronomic presentations.

Chef Gras and brigade

Innovative French cuisine

Chef Laurent Gras

AWARD WINNER
SINCE 1999

Picholine

Front dining room

Directions

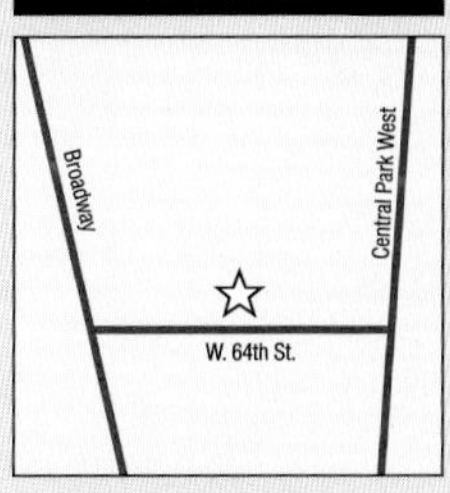

At Picholine, Chef/Proprietor Terrance Brennan showcases French Mediterranean cuisine, using the best and freshest ingredients from local organic farmers as well as from around the world. His seasonal dishes include poached halibut with cauliflower mousseline, pistachio, and black truffles; wild mushroom and duck risotto; Maine lobster with rhubarb marmalade; and organic loin of lamb with fennel-artichoke barigoule. Picholine is known for "the best cheese cart in NYC."

Back dining room

Private dining room

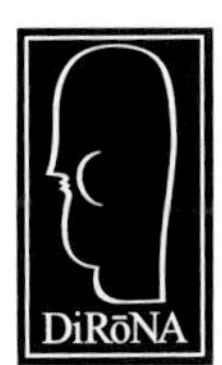

AWARD WINNER
SINCE 1999

Between Broadway and Central Park West, near Lincoln Center and 30 min. from LaGuardia Airport

35 W. 64th Street
New York, NY 10023
PH: (212) 724-8585
FAX: (212) 875-8979

Owners
Terrance Brennan

Cuisine
French Mediterranean

Days Open
Open Tues.-Sat. for lunch, daily for dinner

Pricing
Dinner for one, without tax, tip, or drinks: $40-$60

Dress Code
Business casual

Reservations
Recommended

Parking
Garage nearby

Features
Private room/parties, near theater

Credit Cards
AE, VC, MC, DC

The Post House

Directions

Central Park
E. 63rd St.
Madison Ave.
Park Ave.
Central Park South
E. 58th St.
Fifth Ave.

At E. 63rd Street between Madison and Park avenues, 30 min. from LaGuardia Airport

28 East 63rd Street
New York, NY 10021
PH: (212) 935-2888
FAX: (212) 371-9264
www.theposthouse.com

Owners
Alan Stillman

Cuisine
American

Days Open
Open daily for lunch and dinner

Pricing
Dinner for one,
without tax, tip, or drinks:
$60-$80

Dress Code
Business casual

Reservations
Recommended

Parking
Garage nearby

Credit Cards
AE, VC, MC, DC, DS

Main dining room

Distinctive and dramatic, this award-winning steak and chophouse is a prime cut above the usual, offering a variety of mouthwatering meat entrees seared to juicy perfection. Other specialties include seafood dishes, such as Maryland crab cakes and cornmeal fried oysters, and grilled chicken breast with couscous. The eatery also features a wide variety of seasonal desserts and an extensive wine list and library of rare wines from Bordeaux, Burgundy, and California.

More than just steak

AWARD WINNER
SINCE 1996

Ristorante Primavera

Main dining room

Ristorante Primavera and its owner Nicola Civetta have been delighting discriminating diners since 1978. This award-winning Italian favorite has a tasteful, stylish look, with walls and ceilings paneled in rich Italian walnut. The crispy zucchini sticks, the delicately fried portabello mushrooms, the phenominal sea bass crusted in potato with its hint of mustard and horseradish, and for dessert, the perfect raspberry and strawberry custard tart make for a memorable meal.

Chef Giorgio Bottazzi

Giorgio's favorite dish

Proprietors Peggy and Nicola Civetta

AWARD WINNER
SINCE 2001

Directions

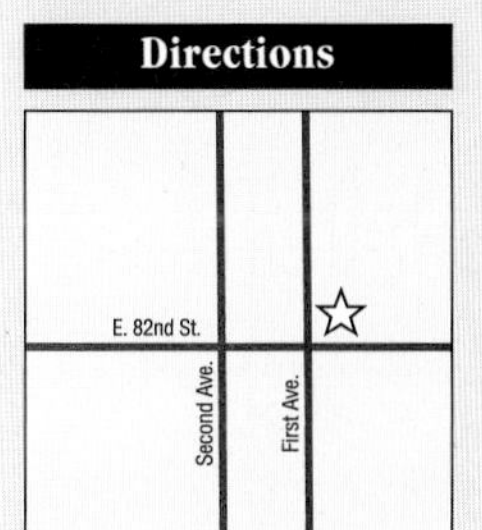

On the corner of 82nd Street and First Avenue, 25 min. from LaGuardia Airport

1578 First Avenue
New York, NY 10028
PH: (212) 861-8608
FAX: (212) 861-9620
www.nytoday.com/primavera

Owners
Mr. and Mrs. Nicola Civetta

Cuisine
Northern Italian

Days Open
Open daily for dinner

Pricing
Dinner for one,
without tax, tip or drinks:
$40-$60

Dress Code
Jacket required

Reservations Policy
Recommended

Parking
Garage nearby

Features
Private room

Credit Cards
AE, VC, MC, CB, DC

San Domenico

Directions

At Central Park South (59th Street) and Broadway, 35 min. from LaGuardia Airport, 45 min. from Kennedy International Airport

240 Central Park South
New York, NY 10019
PH: (212) 265-5959
FAX: (212) 397-0844
www.sandomenicony.com

Owners
Tony May and daughter Marisa May

Cuisine
Contemporary Italian

Days Open
Open Mon.-Fri. for lunch, daily for dinner

Pricing
Dinner for one, without tax, tip, or drinks: $40-$60

Dress Code
Jacket and tie required

Reservations
Recommended

Parking
Garage nearby

Features
Private room/parties

Credit Cards
AE, VC, MC, CB, DC, JCB

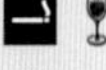

Main dining room

An extraordinary, refined restaurant that reflects the cooking of modern Italy, San Domenico has remained unparalleled in reputation, innovation, and imagination. The cooking is light, incorporating traditional tastes and flavors. Signature dishes—made with the finest and freshest products—include the uovo in raviolo, a homemade soft-egg-yoke filled raviolo with truffle butter and risotto with beef glaze and parmigiano.

Sea urchin ravioli with tomato, garlic, and peperoncino

Private dining room

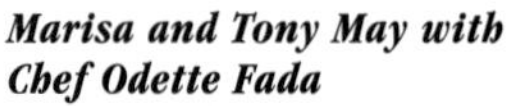

Marisa and Tony May with Chef Odette Fada

AWARD WINNER
SINCE 1992

Smith & Wollensky

Third Avenue landmark

The steaks, chops, and seafood here have been highly praised by food critics around the globe. The establishment is also noted for its outstanding wine list, service, and ambience. But steaks are the stars, including double sirloin, chateaubriand (for two), filet mignon, and sliced steak Wollensky. The meat is superbly flavorful and tender; all beef is prime grade and dry-aged in house for 28 days.

At your service

Steaks, and then some

Main dining room

AWARD WINNER
SINCE 1992

Directions

Central Park · Park Ave. · Third Ave. · Second Ave. · E. 58th St. · Fifth Ave. · 49th St.

At 49th Street and Third Avenue, 30 min. from LaGuardia Airport

797 Third Avenue
New York, NY 10022
PH: (212) 753-1530
FAX: (212) 751-5446
www.smithandwollensky.com

Owners
Alan Stillman

Cuisine
Steakhouse

Days Open
Open daily for lunch and dinner

Pricing
Dinner for one,
without tax, tip, or drinks:
$60-$80

Dress Code
Business casual

Reservations
Recommended

Parking
Garage nearby

Features
Private room/parties

Credit Cards
AE, VC, MC, DC, DS

Sparks Steak House

Directions

Central Park
Park Ave.
Third Ave.
Second Ave.
E. 58th St.
Fifth Ave.
46th St.

On E. 46th between Second and Third avenues, 30 min. from LaGuardia Airport

210 E. 46th Street
New York, NY 10017
PH: (212) 687-4855
FAX: (212) 557-7409

Owners
Michael Cetta

Cuisine
Steakhouse

Days Open
Open Mon.-Fri. for lunch, Mon.-Sat. for dinner

Pricing
Dinner for one, without tax, tip, or drinks: $60-$80

Dress Code
Jacket preferred

Reservations
Recommended

Parking
Garage nearby

Features
Private room/parties, cigar bar

Credit Cards
AE, VC, MC, CB, DC, DS

Hudson Room

This all-American, robust outpost is everything a popular steakhouse should be. The rosey dry-aged steaks with charred-edge crusts are cooked to mouthwatering perfection. Jumbo lobster, fresh fish, and veal and lamb chops, plus fresh vegetables cooked to order. The extensive wine list is a consistent *Wine Spectator* Grand Award Winner. Diners also enjoy the restaurant's close proximity to the United Nations.

Victorian Room

Main dining room

AWARD WINNER
SINCE 1993

Terrace in the Sky

City view

Atop Columbia University's Butler Hall, Terrace in the Sky is one of New York's most romantic restaurants, with full-length windows giving everyone a smashing view of the Manhattan skyline and the city's bridges and rivers. A fireplace, pristine white tablecloths, and red roses decorate the original 1930 terrace floor and the teak environs of the main dining room. Executive Chef Jason Patanovich combines traditional culinary arts with an eclectic approach. Typical of his skill is day-boat fish en Papillote, with black truffles, Provencal vegetables, and celery root truffle sauce.

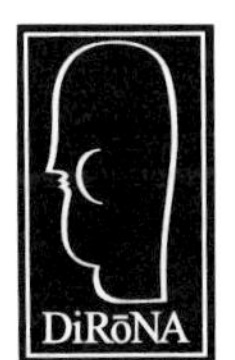

AWARD WINNER
SINCE 1992

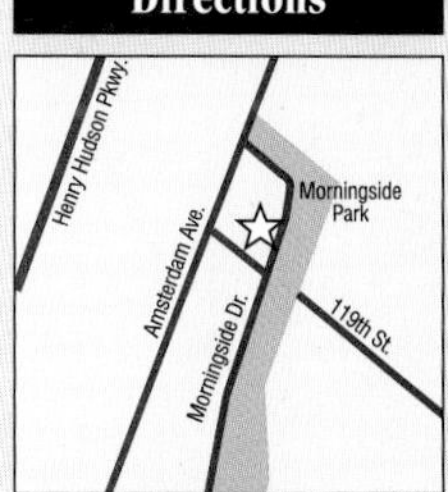

At W. 119th Street and Morningside Drive atop Columbia University's Butler Hall, 25 min. from LaGuardia Airport

400 W. 119th Street
New York, NY 10027
PH: (212) 666-9490
FAX: (212) 666-3471
www.terraceinthesky.com

Owners
Morningside Restaurant Corp.

Cuisine
French, Mediterranean

Days Open
Open Tues.-Fri. for lunch, Tues.-Sat. for dinner

Pricing
Dinner for one, without tax, tip, or drinks: $60-$80

Dress Code
Business casual

Reservations
Recommended

Parking
Free on site, valet

Features
Private room/parties, entertainment, cigar/cognac events

Credit Cards
AE, VC, MC, CB, DC

Union Square Cafe

An oasis of sophistication

Since Danny Meyer opened this smart and sophisticated restaurant in 1985, it has maintained its reputation for offering consistent excellence in fine food and service. One of Manhattan's most popular dining spots, Union Square features New American cuisine with rustic Italian flavors. Chef Michael Romano dazzles diners with dishes that celebrate both delicate and hearty flavors, such as the appetizer of porcini and gnocchi with Swiss chard and parmigiano reggiano.

Directions

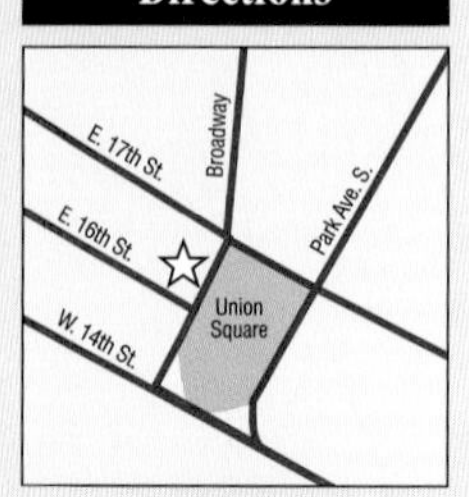

On 16h Street near Union Square, 45 min. from LaGuardia Airport

21 E. 16th Street
New York, NY 10003
PH: (212) 243-4020
FAX: (212) 627-2673

Owners
Danny Meyer, Michael Romano, Paul Bolles-Beaven

Cuisine
New American with rustic Italian accents

Days Open
Open Mon.-Sat. for lunch, daily for dinner

Pricing
Dinner for one, without tax, tip, or drinks: $40-$60

Dress Code
No dress code

Reservations
Recommended

Parking
Garage nearby

Credit Cards
AE, VC, MC, DC, DS

AWARD WINNER
SINCE 1992

Vong

Exquisite dining room

Vong is Chef Jean-Georges Vongerichten's homage to the exotic spices and flavors of the Far East. Thai-inspired French food is served amid beautiful Thai silks, red paint under gold leaf, and a Buddha altar with bowls of fragrant spices. Signature dishes include sauteed foie gras with ginger and mango, and crisp squab with egg noodle pancake and honey-ginger glazed pearl onions.

AWARD WINNER
SINCE 1996

Directions

Central Park
Park Ave.
Third Ave.
Second Ave.
E. 54th St.
Fifth Ave.
E. 53rd St.

On 54th Street just off Third Avenue, 30 min. from LaGuardia Airport

200 East 54th Street
New York, NY 10022
PH: (212) 486-9592
FAX: (212) 980-3745
www.jean-georges.com

Owners
Jean-Georges Vongerichten, Phil Suarez, Bob Giraldi

Cuisine
Thai-inspired French

Days Open
Open Mon.-Fri. for lunch, daily for dinner

Pricing
Dinner for one,
without tax, tip, or drinks:
$40-$60

Dress Code
Business casual

Reservations
Required

Parking
Garage nearby

Features
Private parties (must rent entire restaurant)

Credit Cards
AE, VC, MC, DC

Xaviars at Piermont

Directions

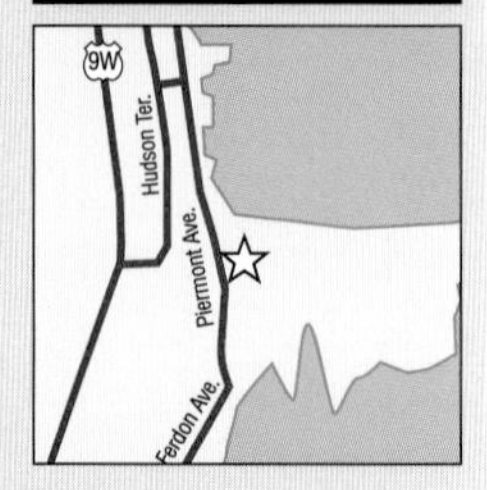

Off Route 9W in Piermont, 45 min. from New Jersey's Newark International Airport

506 Piermont Avenue
Piermont, NY 10968
PH: (914) 359-7007
FAX: (914) 359-4021
www.xaviars.com

Owners
Peter X. Kelly

Cuisine
Contemporary American

Days Open
Open Fri. for lunch, Tues.-Sun. for dinner, Sun. for brunch

Pricing
Dinner for one,
without tax, tip, or drinks:
$40-$60

Dress Code
Jacket and tie required

Reservations
Required

Parking
Free on site, valet

Credit Cards
None accepted

The Bully Boy Bar

Xaviars is located in Piermont, a picturesque community on the west bank of the Hudson River, 20 minutes north of Manhattan. It is the only restaurant north of Manhattan to have received a four-star "extraordinary" rating from *The New York Times*. Peter X.Kelly's contemporary American cuisine has been roundly applauded, and is served in an intimate, 40-seat dining room adorned with fresh flowers, candlelight, Versace china, and Riedel stemware. The comprehensive wine list has more than 750 selections.

Peter X. Kelly

Hudson Valley foie gras

Crisp crayfish tempura with cucumber jus

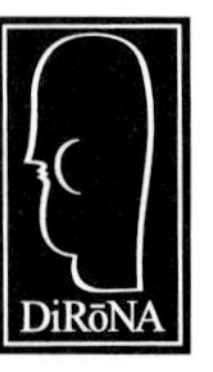

AWARD WINNER
SINCE 1994

La Panetiére

19th century grace

Jacques Loupiac followed his dreams to the United States, and in 1985 opened La Panetiére in a warm, welcoming 19th century home. The restaurant's ambience and decor invoke Provence, with the dining room on the first floor separated by hand-painted fresco arches, supported by original beams, and furnished with a working buffet, paintings, and tapestries. The contemporary French menu changes with the seasons and is reflective of the bounty provided by market gardeners, fishermen, free-range poultry farmers, and other quality purveyors.

Charming decor

The Greenhouse (Private room)

First floor dining room

AWARD WINNER SINCE 1992

Directions

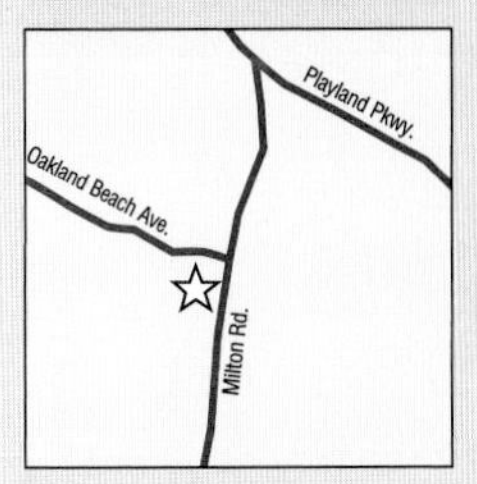

Short distance off New England Thruway's Exit 19, 15 min. from Westchester County Airport

530 Milton Road
Rye, NY 10580
PH: (914) 967-8140
FAX: (914) 921-0654
www.lapanetiere.com

Owners
Jacques Loupiac

Cuisine
French

Days Open
Open Mon.-Fri. for lunch, daily for dinner

Pricing
Dinner for one, without tax, tip, or drinks: $40-$60

Dress Code
Jacket required

Reservations
Recommended

Parking
Valet

Features
Private room/parties

Credit Cards
AE, VC, MC, CB, DC, DS

The American Hotel

Main dining room

This historic brick hotel has been serving vacationers since 1876, and has developed a worldwide reputation for its excellent food. The fruits de mer platter is a revelation — the finest lobster, Petrosian caviar, mussels, clams, oysters, and more. Other menu highlights include Kobe beef and a variety of game. Prepare to spend time perusing the wine list, all 80 pages of it. The American Hotel's eight guest rooms have been enlarged to include modern amenities, and are uniquely decorated with Victorian-era antiques.

Bar area dining room

The Drew Room

AWARD WINNER
SINCE 1992

Directions

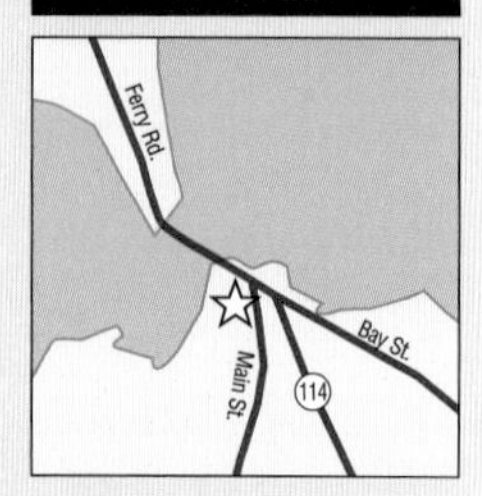

In the Hamptons, 1 hr. from McArthur (Islip) Airport and 2 hrs. from LaGuardia and Kennedy International airports

Main Street
P.O. Box 1349
Sag Harbor, N.Y. 11963
PH: (631) 725-3535
FAX: (631) 725-3573
www.theamericanhotel.com

Owners
Ted Conklin

Cuisine
French/American

Days Open
Open Sat.-Sun. for lunch, daily for dinner

Pricing
Dinner for one, without tax, tip, or drinks: $40-$60

Dress Code
Business casual

Reservations
Recommended

Parking
Free on street

Features
Private parties, outdoor dining, entertainment

Credit Cards
AE, VC, MC, DC, DS

Harralds

The main house

Harralds, located in a charming Tudor compound in countrified Dutchess County, north of New York City, exemplifies the highest standards of excellence in cuisine and service. For 28 years, Harrald Boerger and his wife, chef Ava Dürrschmidt, have done what perhaps only a dozen or so American restaurateurs have done: They've created a legend, a restaurant whose menu never reflects fads, yet never goes out of style. Come for such specialties as truite au bleu, fresh from the stocked trout tank, and let Harrald and Ava and their devoted staff remind you how joyful life can be.

Bucolic setting

AWARD WINNER
SINCE 1992

Directions

On Route 52 in Stormville, 6 miles east of Taconic Parkway, 45 min. from Westchester County Airport and 1 hr. 30 min. from LaGuardia Airport

3760 Route 52
Stormville, NY 12582
PH: (914) 878-6595

Owners
Ava Dürrschmidt and Harrald Boerger

Cuisine
Traditional and classic

Days Open
Open Wed.-Sat. for dinner

Pricing
Dinner for one, without tax, tip, or drinks: $60-$80

Dress Code
Business casual

Reservations
Required

Parking
Free on site

Features
Private room

Credit Cards
None

Tavern at Sterup Square

Van Rensselaer Room

Sterup Square exudes European atmosphere, with casual dining in the Tavern and fine dining in the Van Rensselaer Room. Chef Larry Schepici and his culinary staff prepare such house specialties as ostrich, antelope, and fresh Dover sole. Mouthwatering signature dishes include pistachio-encrusted rack of lamb and Black Angus beef. The restaurant complex also offers banquet facilities, a bakery, and a gourmet deli.

Desserts made on site

International Tavern

Lobster and Dover sole Imperial

AWARD WINNER
SINCE 1998

Directions

On Route 7, 30 min. from Albany International Airport

2113 N.Y. Route 7
Troy, NY 12180
PH: (518) 663-5800
FAX: (518) 663-9261-8006
www.sterupsquare.com

Owners
Peter N. Matzen

Cuisine
Progressive regional American and European

Days Open
Open daily for lunch and dinner

Pricing
Dinner for one, without tax, tip, or drinks: $20-$40

Dress Code
Business casual

Reservations
Recommended

Parking
Free on site

Features
Private room/parties, outdoor dining

Credit Cards
AE, VC, MC, DC, DS

The Angus Barn

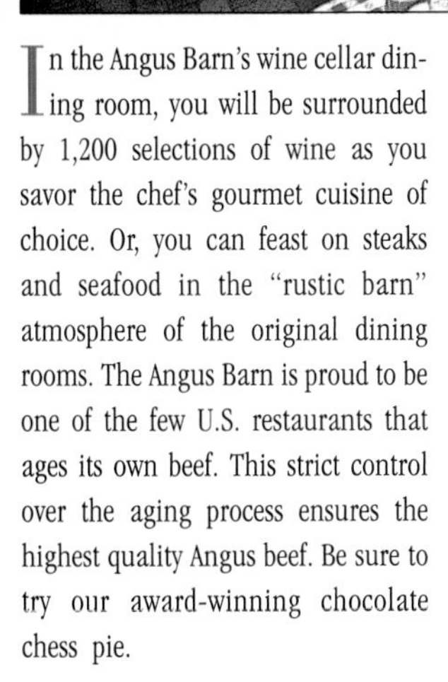
Rustic barn atmosphere

In the Angus Barn's wine cellar dining room, you will be surrounded by 1,200 selections of wine as you savor the chef's gourmet cuisine of choice. Or, you can feast on steaks and seafood in the "rustic barn" atmosphere of the original dining rooms. The Angus Barn is proud to be one of the few U.S. restaurants that ages its own beef. This strict control over the aging process ensures the highest quality Angus beef. Be sure to try our award-winning chocolate chess pie.

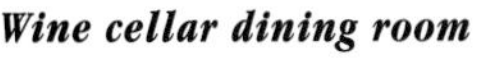
Wine cellar dining room

Quality aged beef

Owner Van Eure

AWARD WINNER
SINCE 1996

Directions

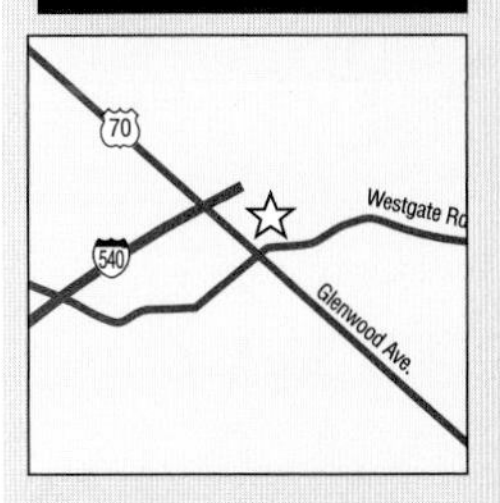

On Highway 70 between Raleigh and Durham, 7 min. from Raleigh-Durham Airport

9401 Glenwood Avenue
Raleigh, NC 27617
PH: (919) 787-3505
FAX: (919) 783-5568
www.angusbarn.com

Owners
Van Eure

Cuisine
American steakhouse

Days Open
Open daily for dinner

Pricing
Dinner for one,
without tax, tip, or drinks:
$40-$60

Dress Code
Business casual

Reservations
Recommended

Parking
Free on site, complimentary valet

Features
Private room/parties, entertainment, cigar/cognac events

Credit Cards
AE, VC, MC, DC, DS

Alberini's

Directions

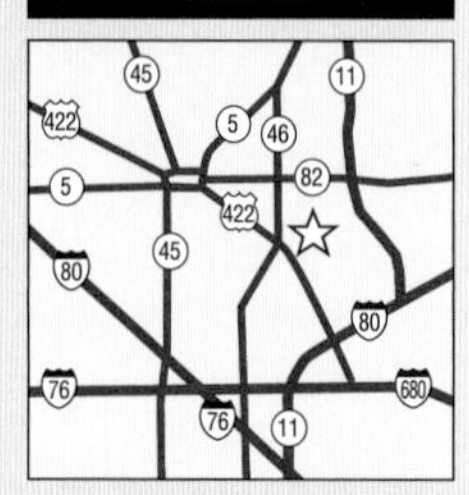

On U.S. 422 in Niles, 15 min. from Youngstown Airport, 1 hr. from Cleveland Hopkins International Airport, and 1 hr. from Pittsburgh International Airport

1201 Youngstown-Warren Road
Niles, OH 44446
PH: (330) 652-5895
and (888) 236-8294
FAX: (330) 652-7041
www.alberinis.com

Owners
Alberini family

Cuisine
Classic Italian

Days Open
Open Mon.-Sat. for lunch and dinner

Pricing
Dinner for one, without tax, tip, or drinks: $20-$40

Dress Code
Business casual

Reservations
Recommended

Parking
Free on site

Features
Private room/parties

Credit Cards
AE, VC, MC, DC, DS

The Terrace Room

The marriage of fine wines and outstanding cuisine consummate the ultimate dining experience. Alberini's atmosphere is sociable and unpretentious, yet maintains a subtle touch of sophistication. Enjoy a variety of pastas enhanced with fragrant Italian spices, succulent seafood, and choice cuts of fork-tender meats. There is a room for every mood, a menu for every occasion, and a wine for every palate. And there is always an Alberini when you need one.

Wine cellar

Ossobuco Milanese

The Arbor Room

AWARD WINNER
SINCE 1995

Ristorante Giovanni's

The Mantel Room

U.S. restaurateurs and food critics regard Giovanni's as one of the Cleveland area's finest restaurants. Carl Quagliata's innovative food techniques and his creative cuisine shine in this elegant setting. Specializing in original pastas and interesting veal, lamb, and seafood dishes, the chef and his eatery have garnered numerous commendations and earned a national reputation.

Grilled Atlantic salmon with citrus beurre blanc

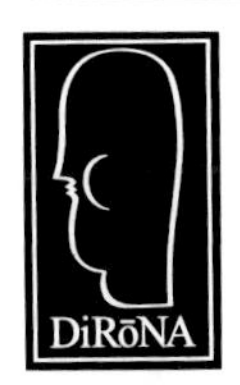

AWARD WINNER
SINCE 1992

Directions

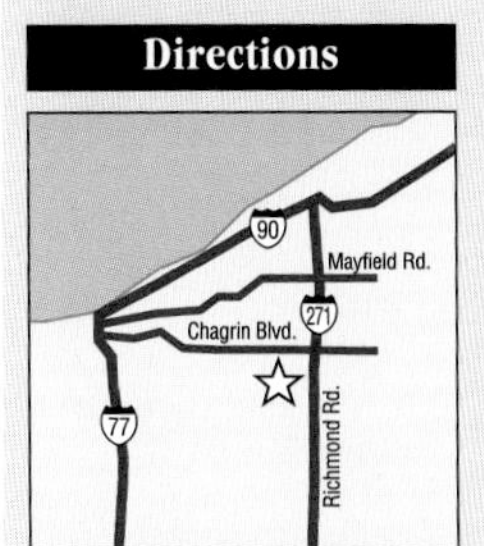

On corner of Chargin Blvd. and Richmond Road in suburban Beachwood, 20 min. from Cleveland Hopkins International Airport

25550 Chagrin Boulvard
Beachwood, OH 44122
PH: (216) 831-8625
FAX: (216) 831-4338

Owners
Carl Quagliata

Cuisine
Northern Italian, with seafood, and steaks

Days Open
Open Mon.-Fri. for lunch, Mon.-Sat. for dinner

Pricing
Dinner for one, without tax, tip, or drinks: $20-$40

Dress Code
Business casual

Reservations
Recommended

Parking
Free on site, valet

Features
Semi-private room, private parties, wine-tasting events

Credit Cards
AE, VC, MC, CB, DC, DS

Maisonette

Dining room

For over 50 years, Maisonette has been renowned for unsurpassed excellence. Under the direction of Jean-Robert de Cavel, an international staff presents exquisitely prepared cuisine, complemented by the perfect selection from an extensive wine cellar. Diners enjoy seasonal specialties created with fresh regional ingredients, all in an elegant environment. The entire experience is brought to the table with incomparable service.

Executive Chef Jean-Robert de Cavel and Nat Comisar

Owners Michael E. and Nat Comisar

The bar

AWARD WINNER
SINCE 1989

Directions

In the heart of downtown Cincinnati, 20 min. from Greater Cincinnati-Northern Kentucky International Airport

114 E. Sixth Street
Cincinnati, OH 45202
PH: (513) 721-2260
FAX: (513) 287-7785
www.maisonette.com

Owners
Michael E. and Nat Comisar

Cuisine
French

Days Open
Open Tues.-Fri. for lunch, Mon.-Sat. for dinner

Pricing
Dinner for one, without tax, tip, or drinks: $60-$80

Dress Code
Business casual

Reservations
Required

Parking
Valet, garage nearby

Features
Private room/private parties, near theater

Credit Cards
AE, VC, MC, CB, DC, DS

The Palace Restaurant

Dining room

Long the destination for the discriminating gourmet, The Palace Restaurant features Executive Chef Sean Kagy's seasonal American cuisine, made with only the freshest ingredients. Along with the menu's Epicurean delights, the gracious service staff meets all diners' expectations, and the setting's understated elegance beautifully complements each culinary creation. With an outstanding list of over 350 wines, one easily finds the perfect companion for any dish.

Splendid times

Executive Chef Sean Kagy

The Cincinnatian Hotel

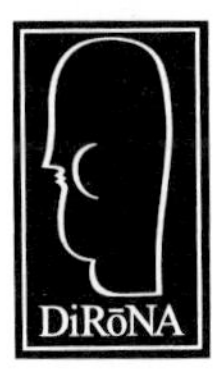

AWARD WINNER
SINCE 1992

Directions

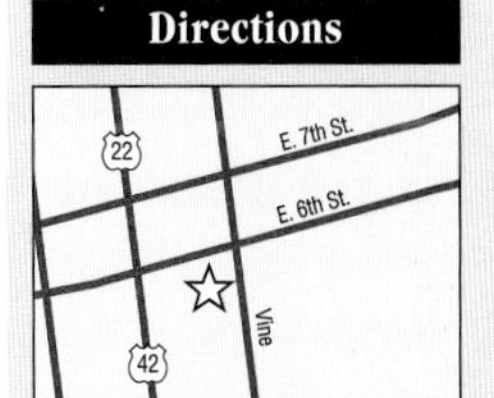

In downtown's Cincinnatian Hotel, 30 min. from Greater Cincinnati-Northern Kentucky International Airport

601 Vine Street
Cincinnati, OH 45202
PH: (513) 381-3000
FAX: (513) 381-2659
www.cincinnatianhotel.com

Owners
Brother's Property Management

Cuisine
American

Days Open
Open daily for breakfast, lunch, and dinner (no lunch on Sun.)

Pricing
Dinner for one, without tax, tip, or drinks: $40-$60

Dress Code
Jacket and tie required

Reservations
Recommended

Parking
Valet

Features
Private room, entertainment, near theater

Credit Cards
AE, VC, MC, DC, JCB, DS

The Baricelli Inn

Directions

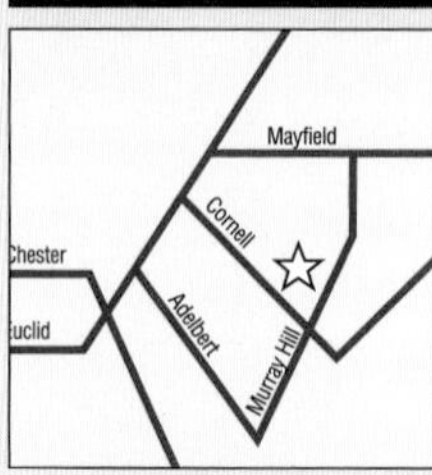

In University Circle area, 20 min. from Cleveland Hopkins International Airport

2203 Cornell Road
Cleveland, OH 44106
PH: (216) 791-6500
FAX: (216) 791-9131
www.baricelli.com

Owners
Paul Minnillo

Cuisine
Continental

Days Open
Open Mon.-Sat. for breakfast (for Inn guests) and dinner

Pricing
Dinner for one,
without tax, tip, or drinks:
$40-$60

Dress Code
None

Reservations
Recommended

Parking
Free on site, valet

Features
Private room/parties, outdoor dining, guest rooms, catering, takeout

Credit Cards
AE, VC, MC, DC

The Baricelli Inn

The Baricelli Inn is a turn-of-the-century brownstone in the heart of Cleveland's cultural center. Paul Minnillo's internationally acclaimed restaurant is dedicated to creating fine European and American cuisine. From his larder he creates a seasonal menu reflecting the freshest regional ingredients available, prepared in a style that is uniquely his. "Simplicity in cooking is a greatly underrated virtue." Minnillo states. "I love grains, beans and fresh herbs."

Typical guest room

Dining room

Chef/Owner Paul Minnillo

AWARD WINNER
SINCE 1998

The Refectory

The culinary team

The culinary creations of Chef Richard Blondin, a native of Lyon, France, are at the heart of the dining experience at The Refectory. His exceptional French cuisine, both classic and contemporary, is complemented by a world-class wine cellar with more than 700 selections. For a quarter-century, The Refectory has been dedicated to presenting each guest with gracious yet unpretentious service.

Executive Chef Richard Blondin

Elegant entrees

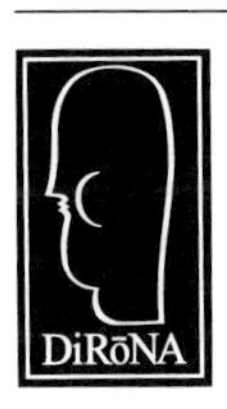

AWARD WINNER
SINCE 1992

Directions

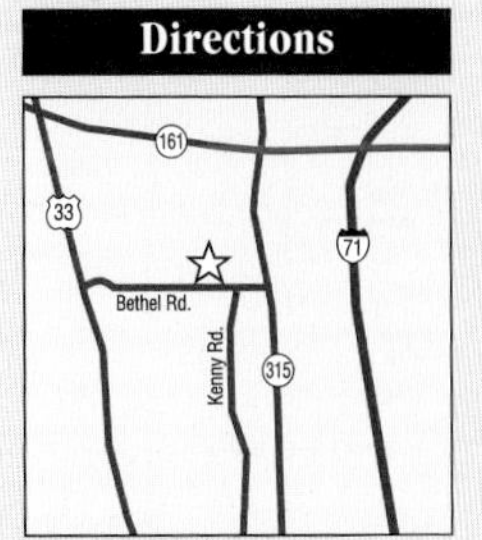

Near the corner of Bethel and Kenny roads between Routes 33 and 315, 15 min. from Port Columbus International Airport

1092 Bethel Road
Columbus, OH 43220
PH: (614) 451-9774
FAX: (614) 451-4434
www.therefectoryrestaurant.com

Owners
Kamal Boulos

Cuisine
French

Days Open
Open Mon.-Sat. for dinner

Pricing
Dinner for one,
without tax, tip, or drinks:
$20-$40

Dress Code
Business casual

Reservations
Recommended

Parking
Free on site

Features
Private room/parties, outdoor dining, business meetings, wine events

Credit Cards
AE, VC, MC, CB, DC, JCB, DS

Chanterelle

Dining room

Directions

5th Ave.
Pearl St.
6th Ave.
High St.
7th Ave.

In downtown, 20 min. from Eugene Airport

207 E. 5th Avenue
Suite 109
Eugene, OR 97401
PH: (541) 484-4065

Owners
Ralf Schmidt

Cuisine
Classical

Days Open
Open Tues.-Sat. for dinner

Pricing
Dinner for one, without tax, tip, or drinks: $20-$40

Dress Code
Business casual

Reservations
Recommended

Parking
Free on site

Features
Near theater

Credit Cards
AE, VC, MC, DC, JCB

Now in its 17th year, this intimate little hideaway — all 13 tables of it — is the loving creation of German-born Ralf Schmidt, who works alone in the kitchen, turning out such delicacies as paillard d'boeuf and dishes using pheasant, buffalo, emu, and other game. "And we are famous for our tiramisu and French silk pie," the chef-owner says, giving credit where credit is due to "the lady who does the desserts" — his wife, Gisela.

Rack of lamb

Lounge

Owner Ralf Schmidt

AWARD WINNER SINCE 1992

The Dining Room

The Westin Salishan Resort

The Dining Room at the Westin Salishan features Pacific Northwest cuisine impeccably served in an atmosphere of quiet elegance. Executive Chef Noah Bekofsky places special emphasis on seasonal seafood, game, and other regional delicacies. The Dining Room offers guests an intimate culinary experience by candlelight with magnificent views of Siletz Bay.

Guest room

Resort lobby

Fine dining

AWARD WINNER
SINCE 1992

Directions

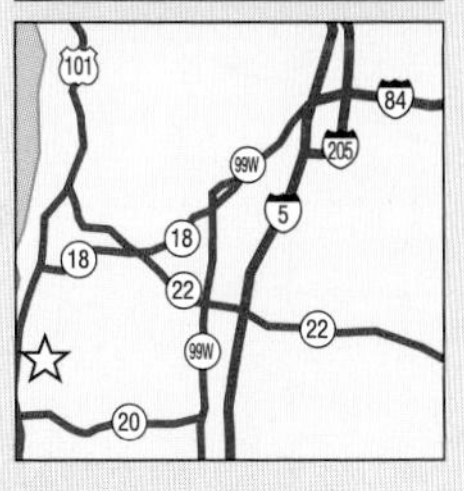

At the Westin Salishan on Highway 101, south of Lincoln City, 2 hr. from Portland International Airport

7760 Highway 101 north
Gleneden Beach, OR 77388
PH: (800) 452-2300
FAX: (541) 764-3681
www.salishan.com

Owners
The Westin Salishan

Cuisine
Pacific Northwest

Days Open
Open daily for dinner

Pricing
Dinner for one,
without tax, tip, or drinks:
$20-$40

Dress Code
Business casual

Reservations
Recommended

Parking
Free on site

Credit Cards
AE, BC, MC, DC, DS

Atwaters Restaurant & Bar

Directions

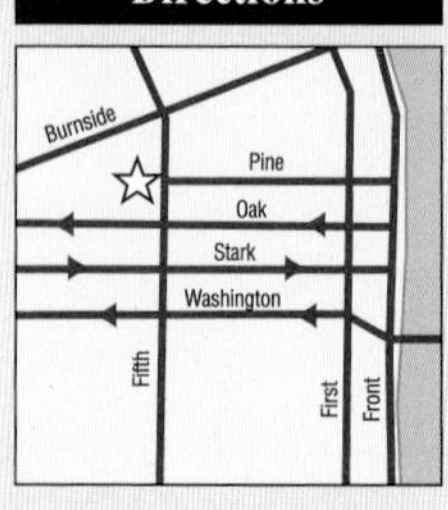

In the U.S. Bancorp Tower downtown, 25 min. from Portland International Airport

111 S.W. 5th Avenue
Portland, OR 97215
PH: (503) 205-9400
FAX: (503) 220-3659
www.atwaters.com

Owners
ARAMARK

Cuisine
Modern American

Days Open
Open daily for dinner

Pricing
Dinner for one,
without tax, tip, or drinks:
$20-$40

Dress Code
None

Reservations
Recommended

Parking
Garage nearby

Features
Private room/private parties, entertainment, near theater

Credit Cards
AE, VC, MC, DC, DS

A fresh view

With each turn, you see Portland in every direction from the 30th-floor vantage point. Atwater's cuisine comes from these views: mushrooms from the forest, wild greens hand-picked by a gardener across town, salmon from fresh Northwest waters, and pinot noir from the Willamette Valley. With these local products, Executive Chef Flynt Payne creates food experiences that fuse the energy of cultures from around the world. Cool jazz is played nightly.

Wild spring-run Chinook salmon spirals

Executive Chef Flynt Payne

AWARD WINNER
SINCE 1993

Appennino Ristorante

Front entrance

Appennino Ristorante, in the beautiful Lehigh Valley, occupies an 18th century building adorned with rustic fieldstone and exposed wood beams, the perfect setting for a romantic dinner, a special celebration, or an important business meeting. Owners Hody and Anna Jenkins, Executive Chef Blake Morgan, and their staff present Northern Italian cuisine using the finest imported ingredients and fresh local produce. The Veneto Room offers private dining for groups of 10 to 40 people.

The perfect setting

Romantic dining

The foyer

AWARD WINNER
SINCE 1999

Directions

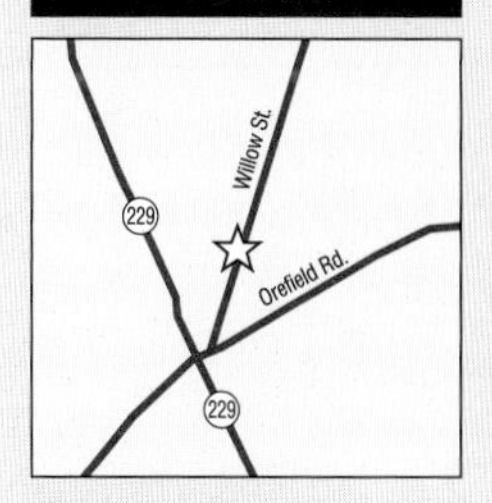

North of Allentown in Meyersville, 15 min. from Lehigh Valley International Airport

3079 Willow Street
Allentown, PA 18104
PH: (610) 799-2727
FAX: (610) 799-2741

Owners
Hody and Anna Jenkins

Cuisine
Northern Italian

Days Open
Open Tues.-Sat. for dinner

Pricing
Dinner for one,
without tax, tip, or drinks:
$20-$40

Dress Code
Business casual

Reservations
Recommended

Parking
Free on site

Features
Private room/parties

Credit Cards
AE, VC, MC, DS

Haydn Zug's

Directions

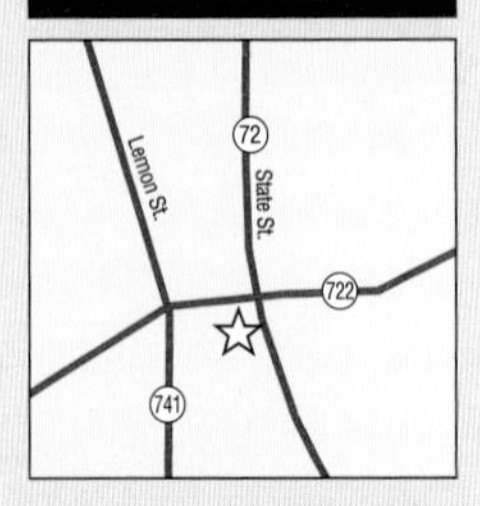

Near Lancaster on Route 72 north, 25 min. from Harrisburg International Airport

1987 State Street
East Petersburg, PA 17520
PH: (717) 569-5746
FAX: (717) 569-8450

Owners
The Lee family

Cuisine
Classic American

Days Open
Open Tues.-Sat. for dinner

Pricing
Dinner for one, without tax, tip, or drinks: $20-$40

Dress Code
Business casual

Reservations
Recommended

Parking
Free on site

Features
Private room/parties

Credit Cards
AE, VC, MC, CB

Gallery dining room

Haydn Zug's offers a taste of Williamsburg in scenic Lancaster County. The glow of candlelight enhances the tasteful restaurant's fine linen, crystal, and china in an atmosphere of warmth, hospitality, and casual elegance. Relax amid fine art and unique memorabilia while enjoying the diverse menu, which includes such house specialties as lamb tenderloin and lump crab cakes in season. Take your choice from six dining rooms. Winner of the *Wine Spectator* Award of Excellence since 1997.

Grilled lamb tenderloin Dijonnaise

Patty Lee, Terry Lee, and Chef Byron Kehr

AWARD WINNER
SINCE 1997

EverMay On-The-Delaware

The Garden Terrace

At this serene hotel, set on 25 acres of gardens and wooded paths, visitors feel like house guests at a country home. Listed in the National Register of Historic Places, EverMay serves an elegant dinner of contemporary American fare in a conservatory garden room or more formal Victorian room. Dinner is one seating beginning with an aperitif, followed by six courses with a choice of entree. The wine list is carefully selected, and there is a well-stocked bar.

The Garden Room

18th century charm

The Parlor

AWARD WINNER
SINCE 1992

Directions

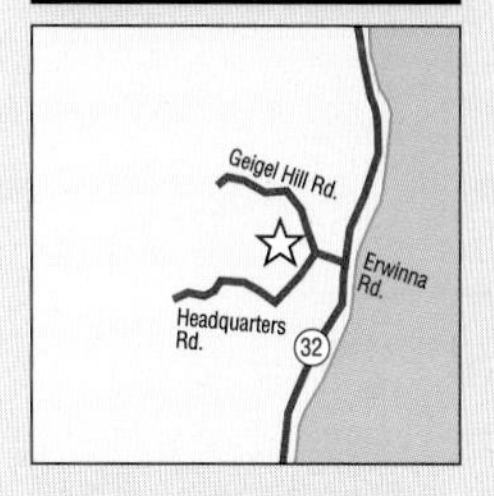

In Bucks County, 13 miles north of New Hope, 50 min. from Newark International Airport

889 River Road
Erwinna, PA 18920
PH: (610) 294-9100
FAX: (610) 294-8249
www.evermay.com

Owners
William and Danielle Moffly

Cuisine
New American

Days Open
Open Fri.-Sun. for dinner

Pricing
Dinner for one,
without tax, tip, or drinks:
$60-$80

Dress Code
Jacket required

Reservations
Required

Parking
Free on site

Features
Private parties

Credit Cards
VC, MC

Vallozzi's

Intimate dining

Vallozzi's nationally acclaimed menu combines traditional and contemporary Italian dishes ranging from market fresh seafood to thick steaks and chops. Among the house specialties are veal chop Romano, rack of lamb, Maryland crab cakes, and cappelletti and lobster. Vallozzi's is nestled in an Italian villa with an award-winning inventory of Italian, French, and American wines.

The Tent Room

Directions

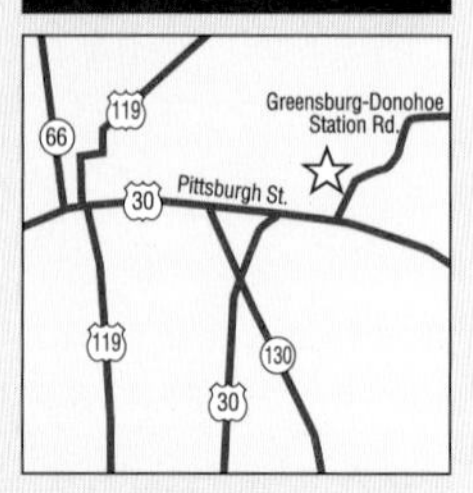

On Route 30 East, 15 min. from Arnold Palmer Airport and 1 hr. from Pittsburgh International Airport

---

Georges Station Road and Route 30 East
Greensburg, PA 15601
PH: (724) 836-7663
FAX: (724) 836-7917

Owners
Ernie Vallozzi

Cuisine
Italian and American

Days Open
Open Mon.-Fri. for lunch, Mon.-Sat. for dinner

Pricing
Dinner for one, without tax, tip, or drinks: $20-$40

Dress Code
Business casual

Reservations
Recommended

Parking
Free on site, valet in evening

Features
Private room/parties, near theater, cigar/cognac events

Credit Cards
AE, VC, MC, DC, DS

AWARD WINNER
SINCE 1997

Scatton's Restaurant

Owners Suzie and Larry Dull

A Hazelton area tradition for more than 60 years, this little restaurant it dediacted to the finest quality and consistency of food, service, and comfort. Chef-owners Larry and Suzanne Dull use only the finest quality and freshest products, specializing in veal, seafood, and homemade pasta dishes. The desserts are homemade, too! The Masters Chef Institue of America declares that "Scatton's is a major destination for gastronomes who especially appreciate Northern Italian cuisine." Each dish is prepared to order and can be varied to suit a diner's taste or special diet

Scampi Suzanne

Your hosts

AWARD WINNER
SINCE 1997

Directions

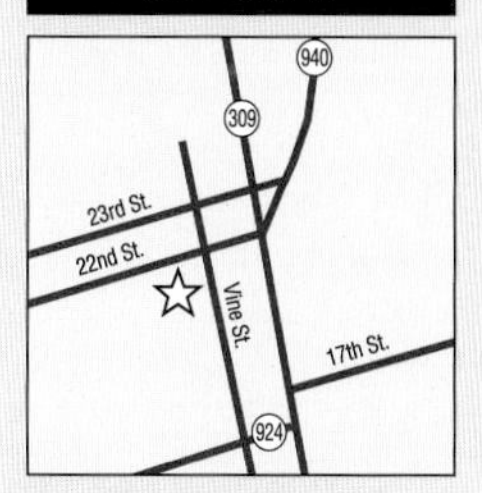

One block west of Route 309 N. at 22nd Street, 2 min. from Hazleton Municipal Airport, 50 min. from Wilkes-Barre/Scranton International Airport

1008 Vine St.
Hazleton, PA 18201
PH: (570) 455-6630
FAX: (570) 459-0724
www.epix.net/~scattons

Owners
Lawrence and Suzanne Dull

Cuisine
Classic Northern Italian

Days Open
Open for dinner Mon.-Sat.

Pricing
Dinner for one, without tax, tip, or drinks: $20-$40

Dress Code
Business casual

Reservations
Recommended

Parking
Free on site

Features
Private parties on Sundays, wine-tasting events

Credit Cards
AE, VC, MC, CB, DC, DS

La Bonne Auberge

Directions

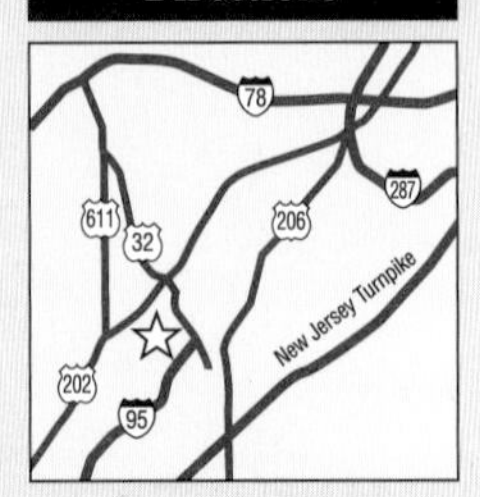

Off Mechanic Street, 1 hr. from Philadelphia International Airport

Village 2
New Hope, PA 18938
PH: (215) 862-2462
FAX: (215) 862-6350
www.bonneauberge.com

Owners
Gerard Caronello

Cuisine
Classic French

Days Open
Open Wed.-Sun. for dinner

Pricing
Dinner for one, without tax, tip, or drinks: $40-$60

Dress Code
Jacket and tie required

Reservations
Required

Parking
Free on site

Features
Outdoor terrace for drinks and hors d'oeuvres

Credit Cards
AE, VC, MC

Charming stone farm house

La Bonne Auberge is a charming, chef-owned, 200-year-old farmhouse serving exquisite food in elegant surroundings. Renowned for its gracious service and attention to detail, it is both a romantic hideaway and a superb location for special occasions. This is a place for all seasons: Cozy fireplaces in winter provide a warm welcome, and cocktails and hors d'oeuvres can be savored in beautifully landscaped gardens in the spring.

Dessert selection

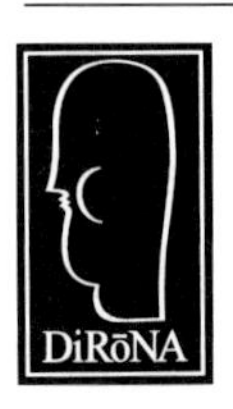

AWARD WINNER SINCE 1992

Ciboulette

Fine dining in the Bellevue Building

Located in the historic Bellevue Building on Philadelphia's Avenue of the Arts, Ciboulette has one of the city's most beautiful dining rooms. Executive Chef Bruce Lim prepares an award-winning, contemporary French cuisine. The menu changes frequently and is influenced by the freshest food on the market. Specialties include foie gras, warm lobster salad, and roasted lamb chop. The wine list is varied and the service exquisite.

Owner Ian Mark

AWARD WINNER SINCE 1994

Directions

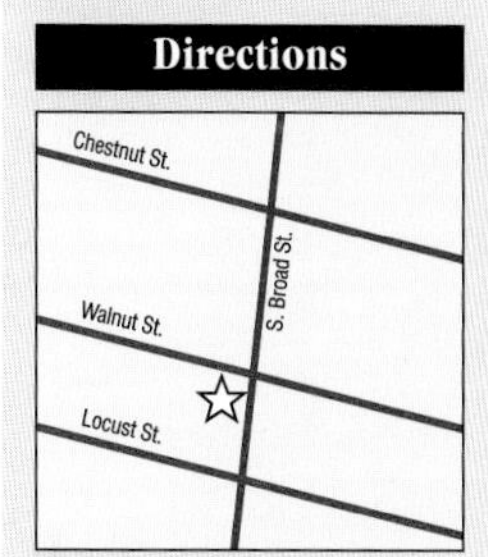

In the Bellevue Building on Broad Street, 15 min. from Philadelphia International Airport

200 South Broad Street
Philadelphia, PA 19102
PH: (215) 790-1210
FAX: (215) 790-1209
www.ciboulette.com

Owners
Ian Mark

Cuisine
French contemporary

Days Open
Open Mon.-Sat. for dinner

Pricing
Dinner for one,
without tax, tip, or drinks:
$40-$60

Dress Code
Business casual

Reservations
Recommended

Parking
Valet, garage nearby

Features
Private room/parties, near theater

Credit Cards
AE, VC, MC, DC

Founders Restaurant

Directions

Ben Franklin Pkwy.
Broad St.
Arch St.
Market St.
Independence Sq.
Walnut St.
Park Hyatt Philadelphia
Chancellor Ct.

At Park Hyatt Philadelphia at the Bellevue, four blocks from Pennsylvania Convention Center and 15 min. from Philadelphia International Airport

200 South Broad Street
Philadelphia, PA 19102
PH: (215) 790-2814
FAX: (215) 893-9865
www.hyatt.com

Owners
Priet-Rubin

Cuisine
French with Asian influences

Days Open
Open daily for breakfast, lunch, and dinner

Pricing
Dinner for one,
without tax, tip, or drinks:
$40-$60

Dress Code
Business casual

Reservations
Recommended

Parking
Garage on site

Features
Private room/parties, entertainment on weekends

Credit Cards
AE, VC, MC, CB, DC, ER, JCB, DS

The Park Hyatt

Located on the 19th floor of the Park Hyatt Philadelphia at the Bellevue, Founders Restaurant features outstanding French cuisine with an Asian flair and top-notch service. The menu is innovative, coupling classic dishes and delicacies made with only the finest and freshest ingredients. The wine list is one of the best in the region.

Intimate dining

Sommelier Eric Simonis in wine cellar

Dining with Ben Franklin

AWARD WINNER
SINCE 1996

The Garden Restaurant

The oyster bar

For over 25 years, The Garden, located within an easy walk of center city hotels and the Convention Center, has served an impressive menu. Lobsters, Dover sole, oysters, langoustines, as well as prime aged 16-oz. sirloins, Chateaubriand, filet mignon, double Colorado lamb chops, and seasonal game are among the menu items that have made this warm and friendly restaurant famous. Pasta and salads are also available; desserts are spectacular.

The shellfish plateau

The main dining room

The garden

AWARD WINNER
SINCE 1995

Directions

676
16th St.
Spruce St.

On Spruce near Rittenhouse Square downtown, 20 min. from Philadelphia International Airport

1617 Spruce Street
Philadelphia, PA 19103
PH: (215) 546-4455
FAX: (215) 546-1753
www.gopphilly.com

Owners
Kathleen Mulhern

Cuisine
Continental American

Days Open
Open Tues.-Fri. for lunch, Mon.-Sat. for dinner

Pricing
Dinner for one, without tax, tip, or drinks: $20-$40

Dress Code
Business casual

Reservations
Recommended

Parking
Valet, garage nearby

Features
Private room/parties, outdoor dining, near theater

Credit Cards
AE, VC, MC, CB, DC

The Monte Carlo Living Room

The dining room

Directions

At South and 2nd streets, 25 min. from Philadelphia International Airport

150 South Street
Philadelphia, PA 19147
PH: (215) 925-2220
FAX: (215) 925-9956

Owners
Umberto Degli Esposti

Cuisine
Italian

Days Open
Open daily for dinner

Pricing
Dinner for one,
without tax, tip, or drinks:
$20-$40

Dress Code
Business casual

Reservations
Recommended

Parking
Valet

Features
Private room/parties, entertainment, near theater, cigar/cognac events

Credit Cards
AE, VC, MC, DC

Food and Wine magazine has placed The Monte Carlo Living Room among the top 100 restaurants in the United States, and the wine list has received accolades from *Wine Spectator* Chef Nunzio Patruno's cuisine is always artful and creative yet classic in preparation. In addition to a wide variety of fresh fish, specialties include sauteed breast of duck with dried figs and port wine sauce, rabbit loin sauteed with sage and white wine, and roasted rack of lamb with fresh herbs and garlic.

AWARD WINNER
SINCE 1992

Hyeholde Restaurant

Castle-like charm

Directions

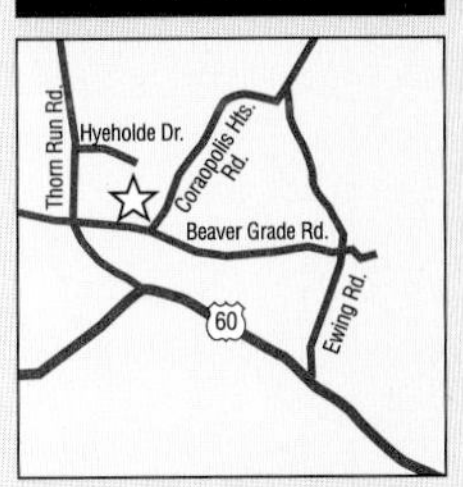

At Coraopolis Heights and Beaver Grade roads in Moon Township, 20 min. from downtown Pittsburgh and 10 minutes from Pittsburgh International Airport

Hyeholde Restaurant is the definition of romance. Located on acres of woodland gardens in a castle with slate-roofed towers, the establishment is the perfect escape. Inside, intimate dining rooms are enhanced with beautiful tapestries, fireplaces, slate floors, and bouquets of fresh flowers. A tunnel leads to a large stone and glass dining room for private functions. A chef's table in the kitchen and elegant picnics culminate in a feast for all the senses.

Artistic entrees

Banquet room

Great Hall

AWARD WINNER
SINCE 1992

Coraopolis Heights Road
Moon Township, PA 15108
PH: (412) 264-3116
FAX: (412) 264-5723

Owners
Barbara and Quentin McKenna

Cuisine
New American

Days Open
Open Mon.-Fri. for lunch, Mon.-Sat. for dinner

Pricing
Dinner for one, without tax, tip, or drinks: $40-$60

Dress Code
Business casual

Reservations
Recommended

Parking
Valet

Features
Private room/parties, outdoor dining

Credit Cards
AE, VC, MC, CB, DC, DS

Restaurant Passerelle

The management and staff of Restaurant Passerelle are truly dedicated to the art of hospitality. The eatery's contemporary American cuisine encompasses the very freshest ingredients found in the marketplace. From the elegance of the Venetian chandelier to the beautiful garden and swan-filled pond, no detail is overlooked. Come and enjoy the award-winning food and extensive wine selection. Private dining rooms and outside dining are available.

Private dining in Garden Room

Alfresco dining

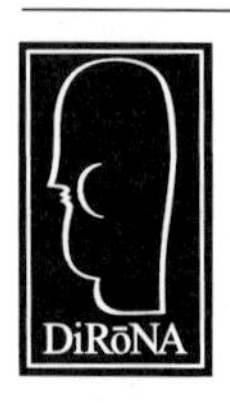

AWARD WINNER SINCE 2001

Directions

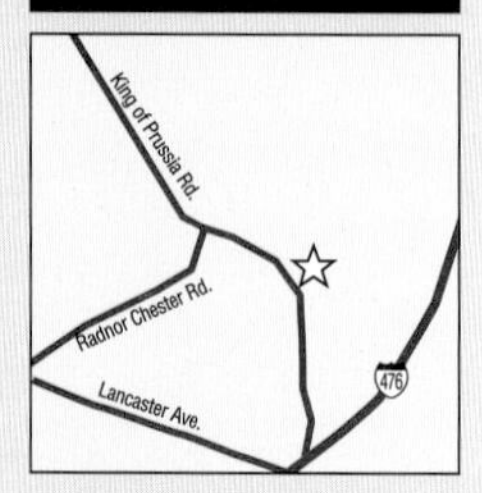

Located half block off Route 30 (Lancaster Avenue), 20 min. from Philadelphia International Airport

175 King of Prussia Road
Radnor, PA 19087
PH: (610) 293-9411
FAX: (610) 293-0161
www.passerellerestaurant.com

Owners
Martin Grims

Cuisine
Contemporary American

Days Open
Open Mon.-Fri. for lunch, daily for dinner, brunch on Sun.

Pricing
Dinner for one,
without tax, tip or drinks:
$40-$60

Dress Code
Business casual

Reservations Policy
Recommended

Parking
Free on site

Features
Private room/parties, outdoor dining

Credit Cards
AE, VC, MC, DC

Dilworthtown Inn

The Dilworthtown Inn

Since 1758, the Dilworthtown Inn has been known for its warm hospitality and wonderful food—an outstanding culinary jewel in a historic setting. Glowing fireplaces and friendly smiles make visitors feel at home as they savor the Inn's delicious gourmet cooking. Weather permitting, the stone wall remains of the original stables offer a unique outdoor dining experience.

Proprietor Jim Barnes welcomes guests

Private meeting facilities

Elegant outdoor dining

AWARD WINNER
SINCE 1998

Directions

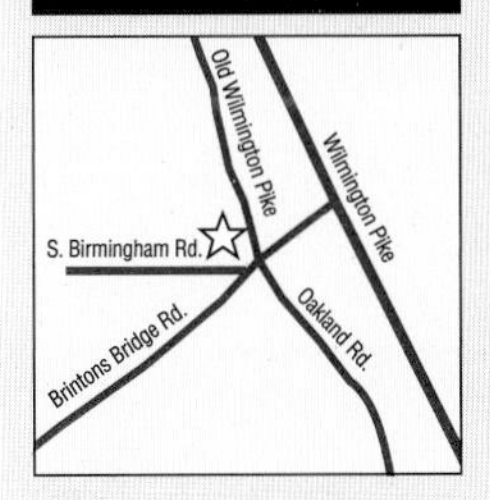

In the heart of Brandywine Valley, 20 min. from Philadelphia International Airport

1390 Old Wilmington Pike
West Chester, PA 19382
PH: (610) 399-1390
FAX: (610) 399-1504
www.dilworthtown.com

Owners
Jim Barnes and Bob Rafetto

Cuisine
Continental

Days Open
Open daily for dinner

Pricing
Dinner for one,
without tax, tip, or drinks:
$20-$40

Dress Code
Jacket required

Reservations
Required

Parking
Free on site

Features
Private room/parties, outdoor dining

Credit Cards
AE, VC, MC, CB, DC, DS

Restaurant Bouchard

Directions

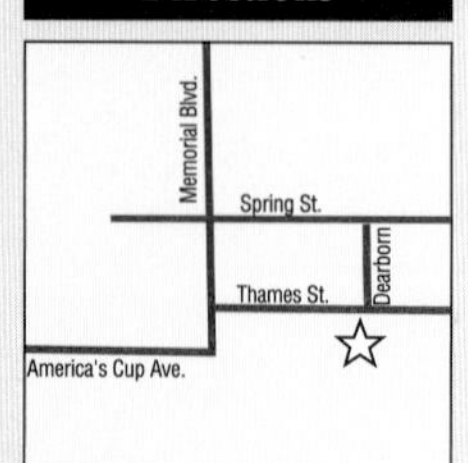

Near Waites Wharf on Thames Street, 45 min. from T.F. Green/Providence International Airport

505 Thames Street
Newport, RI 02840
PH: (401) 846-0123
FAX: (401) 841-8565
www.restaurantbouchard.com

Owners
Albert and Sarah Bouchard

Cuisine
Creative classic French

Days Open
Open Wed.-Mon. for dinner

Pricing
Dinner for one,
without tax, tip or drinks:
$20-$40

Dress Code
Business casual, jacket preferred

Reservations
Recommended

Parking
Lot nearby

Features
Private parties

Credit Cards
AE, VC, MC, DS

Intimate lounge area

Newport, known for its grand mansions and grand yachts, now has another treasure: the grand cuisine of Restaurant Bouchard. Situated in a post-and-beam home, the ambience is created by Sarah Bouchard, complemented by her husband Albert's delectable culinary creations. Whether sitting by the fireplace or in the cozy bar, or even overlooking the action of Thames Street, diners relax and enjoy the marvels of the innovative classic French menu.

Owners Albert and Sarah Bouchard

Superb cuisine

Wild boar, asparagus, with morels and fruit napoleon

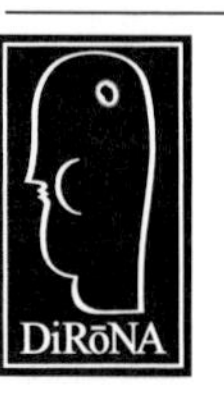

AWARD WINNER
SINCE 1999

Sea Fare Inn

The Inn, circa 1887

The Sea Fare Inn, Rhode Island's only Five-Star restaurant, is the perfect location for any special occasion. It is set on 10 acres of beautifully landscaped flower gardens and fruit orchards and housed in an elegant 1887 Victorian mansion. Master Chef George Karousos derives his culinary inspiration from Archestratus, the most famous chef in ancient Greece, and uses fresh ingredients in simple presentations.

Chef George Karousos with wife Anna, left, and daughter Kathy

Seafood symphony

The Garden Room

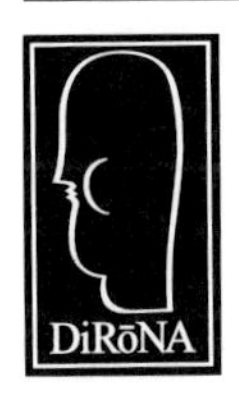

AWARD WINNER
SINCE 1993

Directions

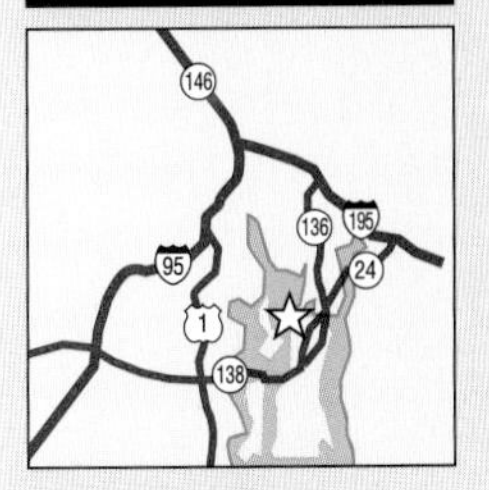

20 min. from Newport, 40 min. from T.F. Green Airport, 1 hr. from Boston's Logan International

3352 E. Main Road
Portsmouth, RI 02871
PH: (401) 683-0577
FAX: (401) 683-2910
www.seafareinn.com

Owners
The Karousos family

Cuisine
American regional

Days Open
Open Tues.-Sat. for dinner

Pricing
Dinner for one,
without tax, tip, or drinks:
$20-$40

Dress Code
Business casual

Reservations
Recommended

Parking
Free on site

Features
Private parties

Credit Cards
AE, VC, MC

1109 South Main

Directions

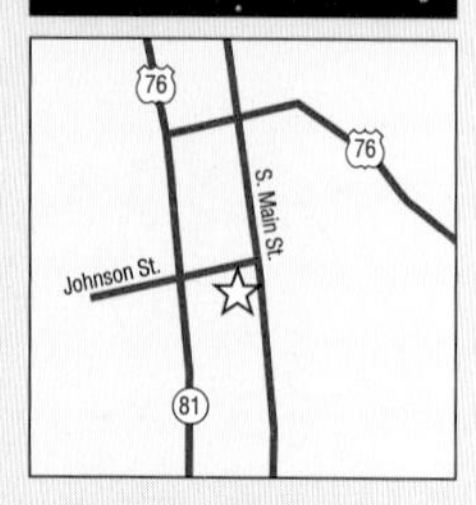

At S. Main and Hampton streets in Anderson, 1 hr. from Greenville-Spartanburg International Airport

1109 S. Main Street
Anderson, SC 29621
PH: (864) 225-1109
FAX: (864) 225-3884

Owners
Peter and Myrna Ryter

Cuisine
Continental and sushi bar

Days Open
Open Thurs.-Sat. for dinner, other days by special request for groups of 10 or more

Pricing
Dinner for one, without tax, tip, or drinks: $20-$40

Dress Code
Business casual

Reservations
Recommended

Parking
Free on site

Features
Private room/parties

Credit Cards
AE, VC, MC, CB, DC, DS

Restaurant entrance

Revisit the days of *Gone With the Wind* in Anderson, where the two exquisitely restored mansions make up 1109 South Main. One mansion houses a plush spa and the other the gourmet restaurant where Swiss-trained Chef/ Owner Peter Ryter turns out such specialties as wild mushrooms in puff pastry, duck l'orange, tuna tartare, and lump crab cake with spicy red pepper coulis. Guests can choose from three separate dining rooms and an upstairs sushi bar.

Chocolate mousse

Porchside elegance

The Palmetto Room

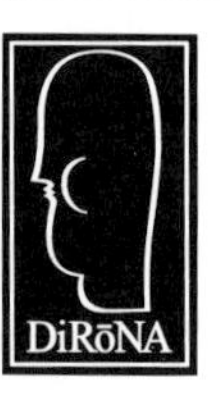

AWARD WINNER
SINCE 1993

Charleston Grill

Elegant club-like atmosphere

With its relaxed yet elegant ambience, Charleston Grill, at Charleston Place, features contemporary Lowcountry cuisine with a French accent. A local favorite is the pan-seared pheasant breast over a fresh fennel and walnut ragout, with foie gras and smoked bacon ravioli in a virgin olive oil emulsion. Visit the Grill for cocktails, live jazz, and exciting cuisine that blends Executive Chef Bob Waggoner's culinary talent with an emphasis on the freshest ingredients, unique presentations, and sophisticated textures.

Intimate dining

Seared diver scallops with herbed pink peppercorn cream

Executive Chef Bob Waggoner

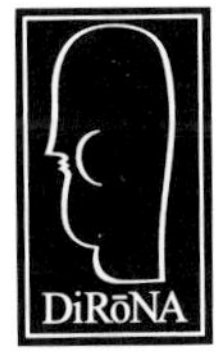

AWARD WINNER
SINCE 1993

Directions

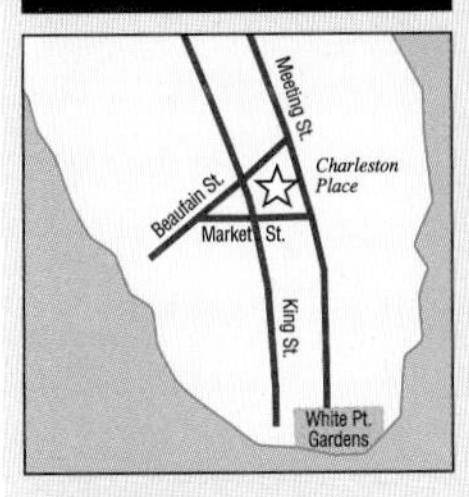

At Charleston Place, 15 min. from Charleston International Airport

224 King Street
Charleston, SC 29401
PH: (843) 577-4522
FAX: (843) 724-8405
www.charlestongrill.com

Owners
Orient Express Hotels

Cuisine
Contemporary, Lowcountry with French flair

Days Open
Open daily for dinner

Pricing
Dinner for one, without tax, tip, or drinks: $20-$40

Dress Code
Elegantly casual

Reservations
Recommended

Parking
Valet, garage nearby

Features
Private room/parties, entertainment, special events, wine tastings

Credit Cards
AE, VC, MC, CB, DC, DS

Magnolias

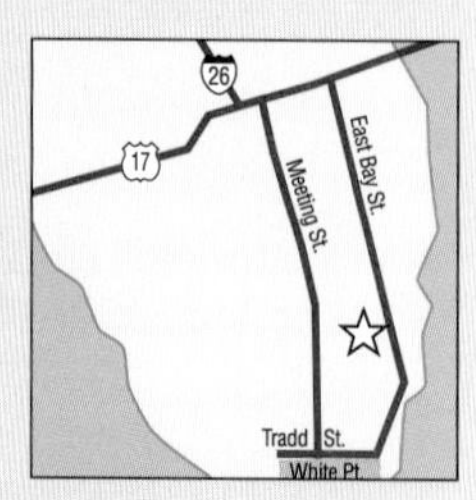

In the downtown Historic District, 25 min. from Charleston International Airport

185 E. Bay Street
Charleston, SC 29401
PH: (843) 577-7771
FAX: (843) 722-0035
www.magnolias-blossom.com

Owners
Thomas Parsell and Donald Barickman

Cuisine
New Southern/regional

Days Open
Open daily for lunch and dinner

Pricing
Dinner for one, without tax, tip, or drinks: $20-$40

Dress Code
Resort casual

Reservations
Recommended

Parking
Free on site evenings and holidays

Features
Private room/parties

Credit Cards
AE, VC, MC, DC

The Upper Level Gallery

Celebrating a decade of Uptown/Down South, Magnolias combines Old World charm with contemporary excitement. Executive Chef Donald Barickman utilizes the Lowcountry's bounty, creating specialties such as the Down South egg roll, shellfish over creamy white grits with lobster butter, and grilled filet of beef with house-made pimiento cheese. These delicious Dixie classics, an award-winning wine list, and sophisticated atmosphere have won the establishment rave reviews and drawn countless visitors.

The dining room

AWARD WINNER
SINCE 1993

Peninsula Grill

The dining room

Located in the historic Planters Inn on the corner of Meeting and North Market streets in Charleston's Historic District, Peninsula Grill is a tasteful blending of traditional Charleston style with contemporary accents. The dining room's walls are covered with rich velvet, antique Cypress woodwork, and local art. The interior combines with views of lush gardens to create an elegant yet relaxed setting for exquisitely prepared and presented local cuisine.

Benne-crusted rack of lamb

Executive Chef Robert Carter

Alfresco dining

AWARD WINNER SINCE 2001

Directions

Hayne St.
Meeting St.
N. Market St.
S. Market St.
Church St.

At Meeting and N. Market streets in the Historic District, 20 min. from Charleston International Airport

112 N. Market Street
Charleston, SC 29401
PH: (843) 723-0700
FAX: (843) 577-2125
www.plantersinn.com

Owners
Robert Carter

Cuisine
New American with Southern influence

Days Open
Open daily for dinner

Pricing
Dinner for one, without tax, tip, or drinks: $40-$60

Dress Code
Business casual

Reservations
Recommended

Parking
Garage nearby

Features
Private room/parties, outdoor dining

Credit Cards
AE, VC, MC, DC, DS

The Orangery

Old world atmosphere

At The Orangery, diners luxuriate at Knoxville's poshest and most acclaimed restaurant, the recipient of numerous awards over 30 years, including the Best of Excellence Award from *Wine Spectator*. Executive Chef David Pinckney's menu is diverse, ranging from classic French to inspired international. Specialties include Chilean sea bass with red curry sauce, buffalo with fresh foie gras, and elk chop with root vegetable purees and port wine glaze.

Sumptuous cuisine

Owners Karen Kendrick and David Pinckney

The Georgian Room

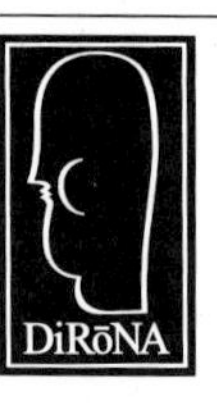

AWARD WINNER SINCE 1993

Directions

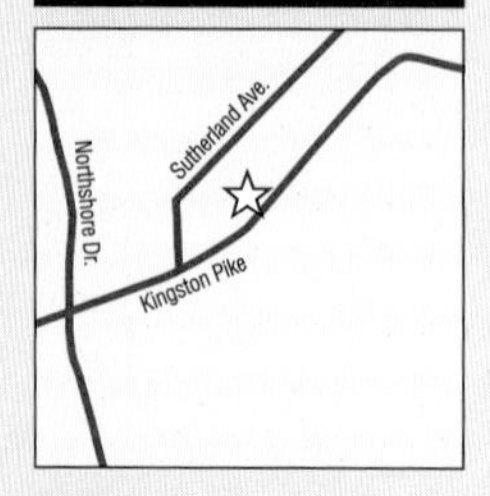

At Kingston Pike and Homberg Drive, 25 min. from McGhee-Tyson Airport

5412 Kingston Pike
Knoxville, TN 37919
PH: (865) 588-2964
FAX: (865) 588-5499

Owners
Karen and Stuart Kendrick, David Pinckney

Cuisine
Continental

Days Open
Open Mon.-Fri. for lunch, Mon.-Sat. for dinner

Pricing
Dinner for one, without tax, tip, or drinks: $20-$40

Dress Code
Business casual

Reservations
Recommended

Parking
Free on site

Features
Private room/parties, entertainment

Credit Cards
AE, VC, MC, DC

Regas Restaurant

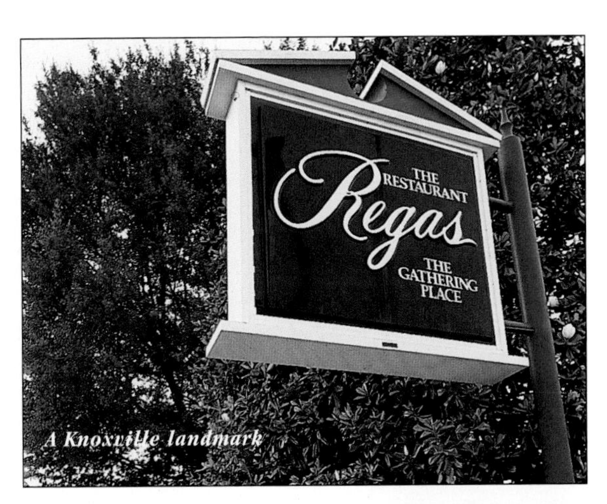

A Knoxville landmark

The Regas family has been making memories in Knoxville since 1919. The culinary team uses only hand-carved, heavy aged prime and choice beef, and the finest seafood flown in daily. Specialties include prime steak, prime rib, and New Zealand lobster. A world-class wine cellar offers the perfect complement to any meal. Breads and desserts are prepared fresh daily.

House specialty

Regas Restaurant

World-class wines

AWARD WINNER
SINCE 1995

Directions

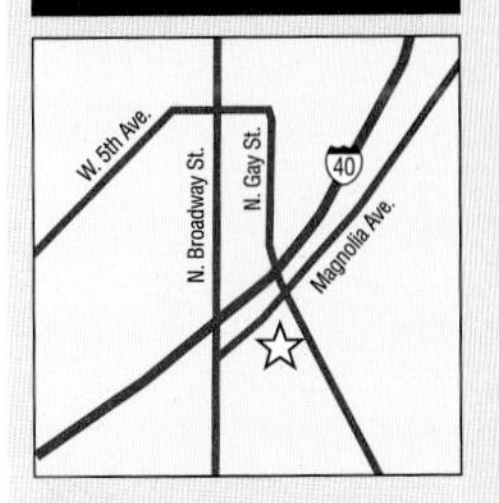

At North Gay Street and Magnolia Avenue, 10 min. from McGhee Tyson Airport

318 N. Gay Street NW
Knoxville, TN 37917
PH: (865) 637-9805
FAX: (865) 546-5031
www.regasbrothers.com

Owners
William F. Regas, Costa G. Regas, and W. Grady Regas

Cuisine
American

Days Open
Open Mon.-Fri. for lunch, Mon.-Sat. for dinner

Pricing
Dinner for one, without tax, tip, or drinks: $20-$40

Dress Code
Business casual

Reservations
Recommended

Parking
Free on site

Features
Private room/parties, entertainment

Credit Cards
AE, VC, MC, CB, DC, DS

Chez Philippe

Directions

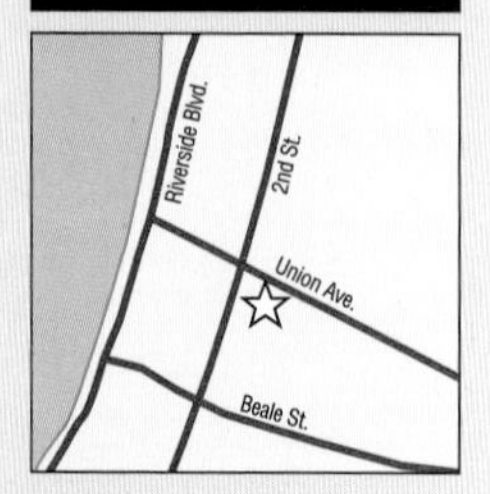

At The Peabody Hotel in downtown Memphis, 15 min. from Memphis International Airport

149 Union Avenue
Memphis, TN 38103
PH: (901) 529-4188
FAX: (901) 529-3639
www.peabodymemphis.com

Owners
Belz Enterprises

Cuisine
French

Days Open
Open Mon.-Sat. for dinner

Pricing
Dinner for one, without tax, tip, or drinks: $40-$60

Dress Code
Jacket and tie required

Reservations
Recommended

Parking
Valet

Features
Private parties, near theater

Credit Cards
AE, VC, MC, CB, DC, JCB, DS

Classic French dining

A classic French approach to combining ingredients from around the world distinguishes Chez Philippe's cuisine as the best in Memphis. Seafood, exotic spices, Southern specialties, and fine meats by award- winning Executive Chef Jose Gutierrez – one of only 50 Master Chefs of France working in the United States – are featured. The setting in the fabled Peabody Hotel is opulent and the presentation is classical French.

Executive Chef Jose Gutierrez

AWARD WINNER
SINCE 1992

Folk's Folly Prime Steak House

Folk's Folly Prime Steak House

This longtime Memphis tradition is known for the finest prime steaks and freshest seafood. The establishment is Memphis' only locally owned and operated prime steakhouse, and pairs fine dining with a cozy, comfortable atmosphere. Savor your favorite vintage from the extensive wine list, which received *Wine Spectator*'s Award of Excellence. Enjoy cocktails before dinner while listening to live grand piano music in the Cellar lounge.

Prime steaks

Freshest seafood flown in daily

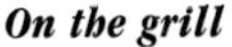

On the grill

AWARD WINNER
SINCE 2001

Directions

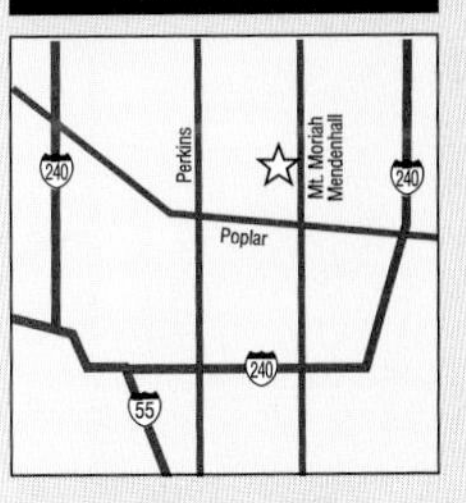

On S. Mendenhall Road, two blocks north of Poplar Avenue, 20 min. from Memphis International Airport

551 S. Mendenhall Road
Memphis, TN 38117
PH: (901) 762-8200 or
(800) 467-0245
FAX: (901) 762-8287
www.folksfolly.com

Owners
Humphrey Jr., Tripp, Michael, Chris, and Carey Folk

Cuisine
Steak and Seafood

Days Open
Open daily for dinner

Pricing
Dinner for one, without tax, tip or drinks: $40-$60

Dress Code
Business casual

Reservations
Recommended

Parking
Free on site, valet

Features
Private room/parties, entertainment

Credit Cards
AE, VC, MC, DC

La Tourelle Restaurant

Directions

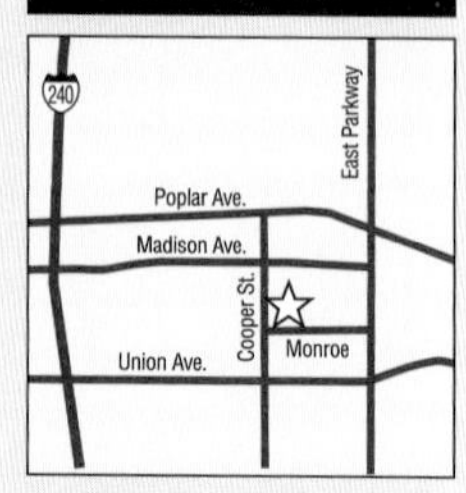

On Monroe Avenue in midtown, 15 min. from Memphis International Airport

2146 Monroe Avenue
Memphis, TN 38104
PH: (901) 726-5771
FAX: (901) 272-0492
www.latourellememphis.com

Owners
Glenn T. Hays

Cuisine
French

Days Open
Open daily for dinner, Sun. for brunch

Pricing
Dinner for one,
without tax, tip, or drinks:
$40-$60

Dress Code
Business casual

Reservations
Recommended

Parking
Free on site

Features
Private room/parties, near theater

Credit Cards
VC, MC

Experience exquisite food in a romantic and intimate setting at Memphis' oldest fine-dining restaurant. La Tourelle, set in a Queen Anne cottage, serves French cuisine under the direction of Executive Chef Ralph McCormick. The menu, which changes seasonally, features rack of lamb, foie gras, and fresh seafood among other standbys. Their list of French and American wines is impressive.

A romantic setting

Seasonal French cuisine

Intimate atmosphere

AWARD WINNER
SINCE 1993

Arthur's

Intimate dining

Arthur's 24-foot ceilings, Tiffany stained glass windows, well-spaced tables, and candlelight ensure privacy for romantic or business dinners alike. A verbal presentation of the menu is recited by the captains each evening. Executive Chef Julio Orantes prepares Continental fare, including such entrees as roast rack of Colorado lamb and wild game. Fresh fish is flown in daily. Arthur's is near all in downtown Nashville and a short walk from the convention center.

Roast rack of lamb

Captains Romano Allegranti and Dino Buonanno

Owners Sheila Thraikill and Jaime Camara with Executive Chef Julio Orantes

AWARD WINNER
SINCE 1992

Directions

Charlotte Ave.
10th Ave.
7th Ave.
5th Ave.
Broadway
Union Station

Located in the Union Station Hotel at Broadway and 10th Avenue downtown, 20 min. from Nashville International Airport

1001 Broadway
Nashville, TN
PH: (615) 255-1494
FAX: (615) 255-1496
www.arthursrestaurant.com

Owners
Sheila Thrailkill and Jaime Camara

Cuisine
Continental

Days Open
Open daily for dinner

Pricing
Dinner for one, without tax, tip, or drinks: $40-$60

Dress Code
Business casual

Reservations
Recommended

Parking
Free on site, valet

Features
Private parties, near theater

Credit Cards
AE, VC, MC, CB, DC, DS

Mario's

Directions

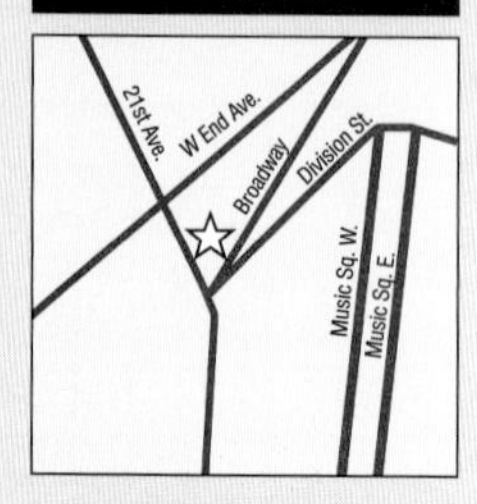

On Broadway near Vanderbilt University, 10 min. from Nashville International Airport

2005 Broadway
Nashville, TN 37203
PH: (615) 327-3232
FAX: (615) 321-2675

Owners
Mario Ferrari

Cuisine
Northern Italian

Days Open
Open Mon.-Sat. for dinner

Pricing
Dinner for one,
without tax, tip, or drinks:
$40-$60

Dress Code
Classy casual

Reservations
Recommended

Parking
Free on site

Features
Private room/parties, cigar/cognac events

Credit Cards
AE, VC, MC, CB, DC, DS

Upper dining room at Mario's

Internationally acclaimed for its overall dining experience, Mario's is celebrating its 35th year. The delicious food, elegant atmosphere, and superb service make it perfect for all occasions. Specializing in Northern Italian cuisine, owner and Executive Chef Mario Ferrari prepares such entrees as fresh Dover sole with pine nuts, breast of chicken stuffed with prosciutto and fontina cheese, and medallions of filet mignon with green peppercorn sauce. The wine list boasts more than 700 selections.

Chef/Owner Mario Ferrari

Chef Mario Ferrari preparing entrees

Banquet room LaDolce Vita

AWARD WINNER
SINCE 1992

Sunset Grill

For affordable, casually elegant dining and excellent service, the trend-setting Sunset Grill is a Nashville must. Nestled in historic Hillsboro Village, Sunset Grill's artistic bistro-style ambience and delicious modern American cuisine has earned many fans. The menu stays fresh with delectable seafood, steaks, pastas, low-fat and vegetarian dishes, and daily specials. The wine list offers over 80 top-rated wines poured by the glass, and 300 additional selections by the bottle.

Randy Rayburn and Executive Chef Brian Uhl

Chef Brian Uhl

Ahai seared tuna

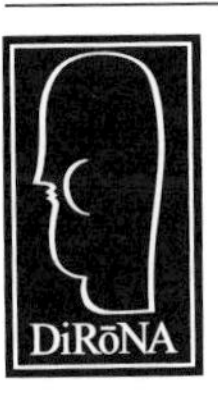

AWARD WINNER SINCE 2001

Directions

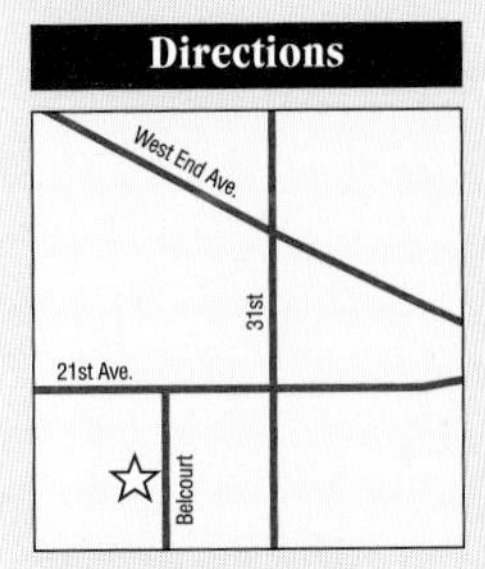

On Belcourt in Hillsboro Village, 10 min. from Nashville International Airport

2001 Belcourt Ave.
Nashville, TN 37212
PH: (615) 386-3663
FAX: (615) 386-0495
www.sunsetgrill.com

Owners
Randy Rayburn

Cuisine
Contemporary American

Days Open
Open Mon.-Fri. for lunch, daily for dinner

Pricing
Dinner for one, without tax, tip, or drinks: $20-$40

Dress Code
Casual

Reservations
Recommended

Parking
Free on site, valet

Features
Private room/parties, outdoor dining, cigar/cognac events

Credit Cards
AE, VC, MC, CB, DC, JCB, DS

The Wild Boar

Main dining room

With an exceptional wine list and the contemporary French cuisine, of Executive Chef Guillaume Burlion, the Wild Boar, which opened in 1993, has quickly established itself as a premier fine dining establishment. Specialties include potato crusted rouget barbet, filet mignon of Texas antelope, and braised Maplewood Farms quail. The 15,000-bottle wine cellar is a veritable Bordeaux lover's dream. For exceptional food and attention to detail, there's no place quite like The Wild Boar.

Roasted Maine lobster

Red wine cellar

AWARD WINNER SINCE 1994

Directions

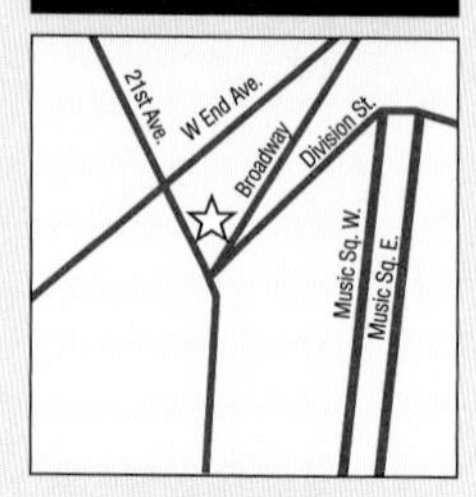

On Broadway near Vanderbilt University, 10 min. from Nashville International Airport

2014 Broadway
Nashville, TN 37203
PH: (615) 329-1313
FAX: (615) 329-4930
www.wboar.com

Owners
Brett Allen

Cuisine
Contemporary French

Days Open
Open Mon.-Sat. for dinner

Pricing
Dinner for one,
without tax, tip, or drinks:
$60-$80

Dress Code
Jacket suggested

Reservations
Recommended

Parking
Valet

Features
Private parties

Credit Cards
AE, VC, MC, CB, DC, DS

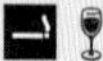

Bob's Steak & Chop House

Texas' No. 1 steakhouse gives patrons great food and plenty of it. Bob's offers three sizes each of prime filet mignon and New York strip steaks, a 16-ounce prime T-bone, and a dazzling 28-ounce prime porterhouse. The signature entree is a 20-ounce bone-in prime rib broiled like a steak. Other entrees include rack of lamb, veal chop, roasted duck with green peppercorn sauce, and succulent lobster tail. A rich atmosphere and impeccable service complete the dining experience.

28-ounce prime porterhouse

AWARD WINNER
SINCE 1999

Directions

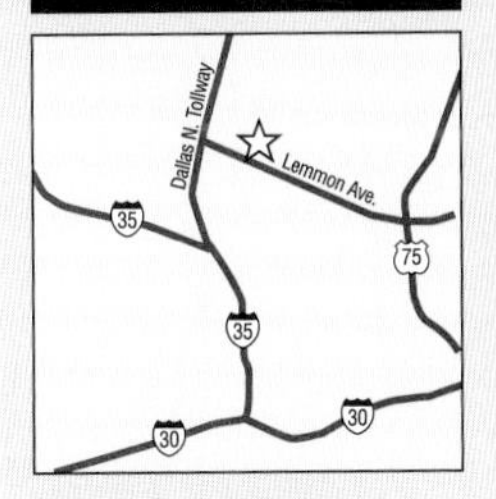

At Lemmon and Wycliff avenues, 25 min. from Dallas-Fort Worth International Airport

4300 Lemmon Avenue
Dallas, TX 75219
PH: (214) 528-9446
FAX: (214) 526-8159
www.bobs-steakand
chop.com

Owners
Bob and Judi Sambol

Type of Cuisine
Steakhouse

Days Open
Open Mon.-Sat. for dinner

Pricing
Dinner for one,
without tax, tip or drinks:
$40-$60

Dress Code
Business casual

Reservations
Recommended

Parking
Valet

Credit Cards
AE, VC, MC, DC, DS

Café Pacific

Directions

Dallas North Tollway
Preston Rd.
Highland Park Village

In Highland Park Village off Preston Road, 20 min. from Dallas-Fort Worth International Airport

24 Highland Park Village
Dallas, TX 75205
PH: (214) 526-1170
FAX: (214) 526-0332

Owners
Jack Knox

Cuisine
New American and seafood

Days Open
Open Mon.-Sat. for lunch and dinner

Pricing
Dinner for one, without tax, tip, or drinks: $20-$40

Dress Code
Business casual

Reservations
Recommended

Parking
Valet

Features
Outdoor dining

Credit Cards
AE, VC, MC, DC, DS

Highland Park Village

Starched white linens, rich dark paneling, etched glass, and gleaming brass accents create an upscale environment at Café Pacific, which caters to many of Dallas' business and social leaders. The restaurant, ranked No. 1 for seafood among Dallas restaurants in the *Zagat Survey* and recipient of a *Gourmet* "America's Top Table Award," serves classic cuisine, including the highest quality steaks and seafood, in elegant surroundings.

See and be seen among Dallas' elite

Maitre d' Jean-Pierre Albertinetti

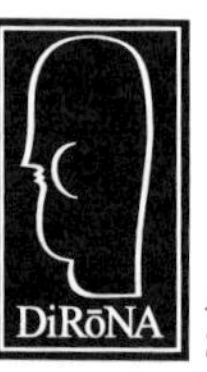

AWARD WINNER
SINCE 1994

The French Room at Hotel Adolphus

Main dining room

Executive Chef William Koval's genius for adapting classic French cooking to contemporary tastes has earned him widespread acclaim and positioned The French Room at Hotel Adolphus as one of the nation's finest dining rooms. No less an authority than *Condé Nast Traveler* has named The French Room one of America's "Top 20" restaurants. A sampling of dishes includes sake-marinated Norwegian salmon with sauteed spinach on a hot and sour red curry with a crisp potato ringlet, and Pennsylvania beef tenderloin with an onion potato tart on cracked grain mustard sauce.

At Hotel Aldolphus

Elegant entrees

Chefs Marcos Segovia and William Koval

AWARD WINNER
SINCE 1993

Directions

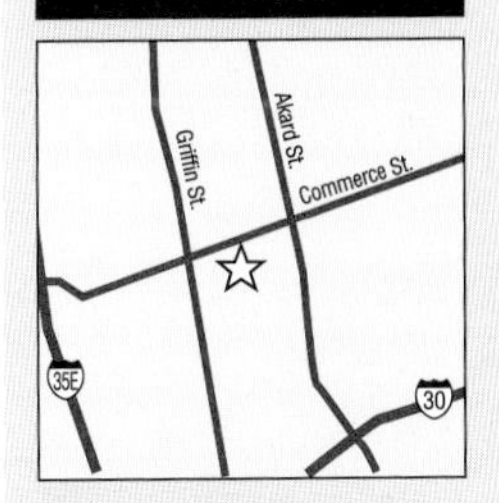

In the Hotel Adolphus in downtown Dallas, 25 min. from Dallas-Fort Worth International Airport

Hotel Adolphus
1321 Commerce Street
Dallas, TX 75202
PH: (214) 742-8200
FAX: (214) 651-3561
www.hoteladolphus.com

Owners
Noble House Hotels & Resorts

Cuisine
Upscale American

Days Open
Open Tues.-Sat. for dinner

Pricing
Dinner for one, without tax, tip, or drinks: $60-$80

Dress Code
Jacket and tie required

Reservations
Recommended

Parking
Valet

Credit Cards
AE, MC, CB, DC, DS

The Riviera

Directions

Near the intersection of Inwood Road and Lovers Lane in the Park Cities area, 10 min. from Love Field and 30 min. from Dallas/Fort Worth International Airport

7709 Inwood Road
Dallas, TX 75209
PH: (214) 351-0094
FAX: (214) 351-3344
www.riviera-dallas.com

Owners
Enter-Dine Ltd.

Type of Cuisine
Southern French

Days Open
Open Mon.-Sat. for dinner

Pricing
Dinner for one,
without tax, tip, or drinks:
$40-$60

Dress Code
Business casual

Reservations
Recommended

Parking
Valet

Credit Cards
AE, VC, MC, DC, CB

Dining room

The perfect venue for a quiet, romantic dinner, The Riviera offers a beautiful setting in a convenient location. The restaurant specializes in the cuisine of the South of France, and is known for such dishes as Provencal bouillabaisse and pan-seared filet of striped bass with citrus fennel salad and Provencal butter sauce. Founded by Franco Bertolasi, the Riviera recently celebrated its 15th anniversary.

Host and owner Franco Bertolasi

Executive Chef Tom Flemming

A quiet, romantic spot for dinner

AWARD WINNER
SINCE 1992

Brennan's of Houston

The ballroom

For more than 30 years, Brennan's has been a preferred choice for those seeking a memorable dining experience in Houston. Bringing its Crescent City flavor to every table, Brennan's exquisitely blends the best of its mixed heritage into its signature Texas Creole cuisine. Specialties include Gulf of Mexico crab cakes, shrimp remoulade, Louisiana pecan-crusted fish, the famous turtle soup, and such mouthwatering desserts as white chocolate bread pudding and bananas Foster.

Kitchen dining room

Chef's table

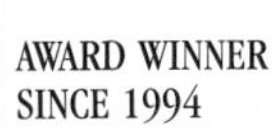

AWARD WINNER
SINCE 1994

Directions

On the southern edge of downtown, 20 min. from Hobby Airport and 35 min. from George Bush Intercontinental Airport

3300 Smith Street
Houston, TX 77006
PH: (713) 522-9711
FAX: (713) 522-9714
www.brennanshouston.com

Owners
Alex Brennan-Martin

Cuisine
Texas Creole

Days Open
Open Mon.-Fri. for lunch, Sat. and Sun. for brunch, daily for dinner

Pricing
Dinner for one, without tax, tip, or drinks: $20-$40

Dress Code
Jacket required in main dining room only

Reservations
Recommended

Parking
Valet

Features
Private room/parties, outdoor dining, near theater

Credit Cards
AE, VC, MC, CB, DC, DS

Directions

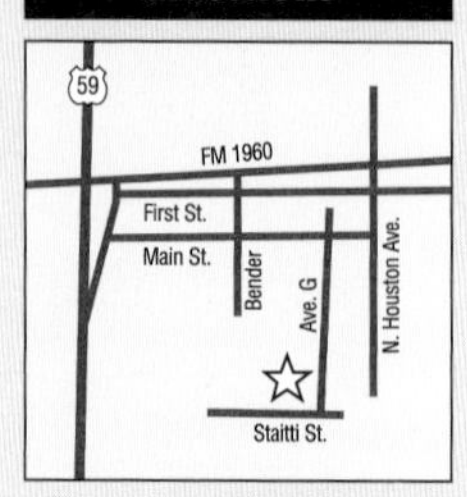

In suburban Humble, 10 min. from George Bush Intercontinental Airport

217 S. Avenue G
Humble, TX 77338
PH: (281) 446-6717
FAX: (281) 446-8612

Owners
Gerard Brach

Cuisine
French

Days Open
Open Mon.-Sat. for dinner

Pricing
Dinner for one,
without tax, tip, and drinks:
$40-$60

Dress Code
Jacket and tie suggested

Reservations
Recommended

Parking
Free on site

Features
Private room, wine tastings

Credit Cards
AE, VC, MC, DC, DS

Chez Nous

The owner is the chef, as it should be, and the chef is in the kitchen where he belongs. So it is at Gerard Brach's Chez Nous, where classic French cuisine is served in a delightful, intimate setting just 20 minutes from downtown Houston. Specialties include fresh foie gras with caramelized apple and honey vinegar, Alaskan halibut with mussels and scallops, and Grand Marnier chocolate mousse in chocolate bag. *The Houston Chronicle* has one word for it: "incomparable."

Standing, from left: Sous-Chef Barbara Farrar, Maitre d' Ruben Cuellar, and Executive Chef Stephen Gasaway. Seated: Sandra Brach, left, and Danielle Noble-Brach.

Exquisite dining

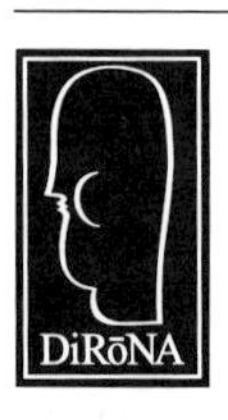

AWARD WINNER
SINCE 1994

La Reserve

Main dining room

Grandly elegant and sophisticated, La Reserve, at the AAA Five Diamond Omni Houston Hotel, appeals to the most discriminating diner. Exquisitely prepared contemporary French cuisine is served in a dramatic setting of luxurious fabrics, beveled glass, and crystal chandeliers. Executive Chef Mercer A. Mohr and his talented team use farm-raised fowl, game, and beef and the most exotic fish in concert with the freshest and finest ingredients to create a culinary experience that is second to none.

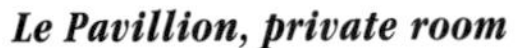
Le Pavillion, private room

Dessert delights

Le Bar

AWARD WINNER
SINCE 1996

Directions

10
610
10
Woodway
San Felipe
Riverway
River Oaks
610

Just off Highway 610 North, 40 min. from George Bush Intercontinental Airport

Omni Houston Hotel
4 Riverway
Houston, TX 77056
PH: (713) 871-8177
FAX: (713) 871-8116
www.omnihotels.com

Owners
Omni Houston Hotel

Type of Cuisine
Contemporary French

Days Open
Open Tues.-Sat. for dinner, Sun. for brunch

Pricing
Dinner for one, without tax, tip, and drinks: $40-$60

Dress Code
Business casual

Reservations
Recommended

Parking
Froo on cito, valet

Features
Private room/parties, cigar/cognac events, wine dinners

Credit Cards
AE, VC, MC, CB, DC, JCB, DS

Mark's

Owners Lisa and Mark Cox

Chef-owner Mark Cox has given Houstonians an amazing dining experience in Mark's, his innovative namesake restaurant situated in an old church. The food reflects inspirations from many countries, creating a unique melting pot menu. American regional ingredients are used to create diverse dishes, with taste sensations that echo the authentic food of many different cultures, including Asian and Italian.

Dining room

Cloisters private party room

Sample seasonal entree

AWARD WINNER
SINCE 2001

Directions

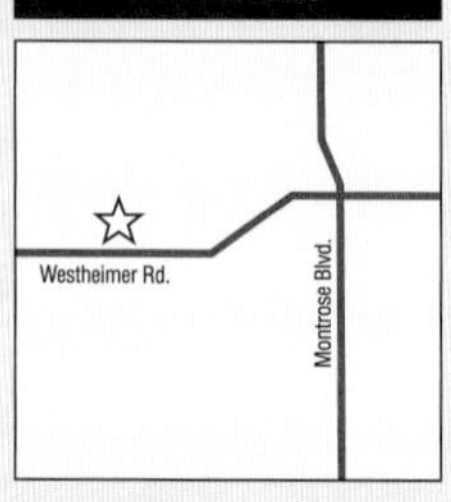

At the corner of Westheimer and Dunlavy, 30 min. from George Bush Intercontinental Airport

1658 Westheimer
Houston, TX 77006
PH: (713) 523-3800
FAX: (713) 523-9292
www.marks1658.com

Owners
Lisa and Mark Cox

Cuisine
American

Days Open
Open Mon.-Fri. for lunch, daily for dinner

Pricing
Dinner for one, without tax, tip or drinks: $40-$60

Dress Code
Casual

Reservations Policy
Recommended

Parking
Free on site, valet

Features
Private room/parties, near theater

Credit Cards
AE, VC, MC, DC, DS

Maxim's Restaurant & Piano Bar

Owner Ronnie Bermann

For more than 50 years, Maxim's—"Restaurant of the Century," according to Patricia Sharpe of *Texas Monthly*—has kept up a grand tradition while keeping up with changing times. Executive Chef Les Thorpe invites you to savor his traditional favorites, such as cream of lobster bisque, rack of lamb, and whole roasted capon, as well as newly created dishes. Save room for dessert, which includes baked Alaska, crepes Suzettes, and fresh strawberries jubilee flamed tableside. A piano bar and one of the nation's finest wine cellars add to the Maxim's experience.

Chef de Cuisine Les Thorpe

Baked Alaska

Snapper Charlie Belle

AWARD WINNER
SINCE 1995

Directions

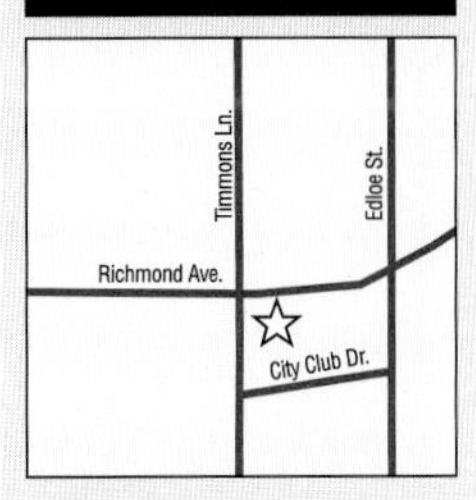

In Greenway Plaza, close to downtown and 15 min. from Hobby Airport

3755 Richmond Avenue
Houston, TX 77046
PH: (713) 877-8899
FAX: (713) 877-8855
www.maximshou.com

Owners
Ronnie Bermann

Cuisine
French Continental

Days Open
Open Mon.-Fri. for lunch, Mon.-Sat. for dinner

Pricing
Dinner for one, without tax, tip, or drinks: $20-$40

Dress Code
Business casual

Reservations
Recommended

Parking
Complimentary valet

Features
Private room/parties, entertainment, near theater

Credit Cards
AE, VC, MC, CB, DC, DS

Rotisserie for Beef and Bird

A Houston landmark since 1978

Directions

On Wilcrest just north of Westheimer, and 35 min. from George Bush Intercontinental Airport

2200 Wilcrest
Houston, TX 77042
PH: (713) 977-9524
FAX: (713) 977-9568
www.rotisserie-beef-bird.com

Owners
Joe Mannke

Type of Cuisine
Steaks, wild game, lobster

Days Open
Open Mon.-Fri. for lunch, Mon.-Sat. for dinner

Pricing
Dinner for one, without tax, tip, or drinks: $20-$40

Dress Code
Jacket suggested

Reservations
Recommended

Parking
Free on site, valet

Features
Private room/parties

Credit Cards
AE, VC, MC, CB, DC, DS

The glories of the Rotisserie for Beef and Bird are well known to Houstonians who have long enjoyed the finest in traditional American cooking, prepared under the watchful eye of proprietor Joe Mannke, who doubles as executive chef. The menu changes seasonally, using the bounties from the forest, the sea, and the rich agriculture of Texas. The wine list is one of the finest in Texas, with more than 950 selections.

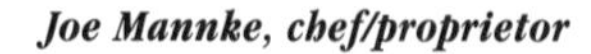

Joe Mannke, chef/proprietor

Spit-roasted duck a la orange

Sommelier Vince Baker

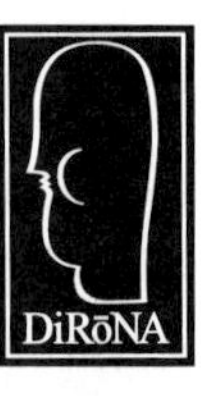

AWARD WINNER
SINCE 1996

Tony's Restaurant

Main dining room

Cool and classical meets hot creative ingenuity inside Houston's most favored—and most honored—professional kitchen. For 35 years, Tony's has been a tasteful destination for the world's smartest palates. Owner Tony Vallone and Executive Chef Bruce McMillian have created an innovative, contemporary menu steeped in classical European traditions, guaranteeing extraordinary dining. Professionalism and warm hospitality are the hallmarks of Tony's elegant service. Tony's resonates with perfection.

Owner Tony Vallone

Poached bosc pear

Executive Chef Bruce McMillian

AWARD WINNER SINCE 1996

Directions

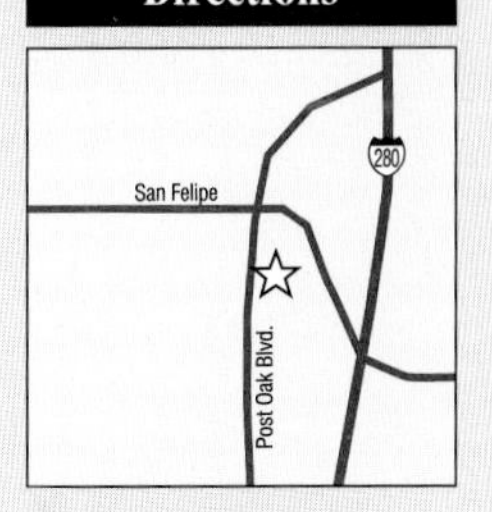

On the southern edge of downtown, 20 min. from Hobby Airport and 35 min. from George Bush Intercontinental Airport

1801 Post Oak Boulevard
Houston, TX 77056
PH: (713) 622-6778
FAX: (713) 626-1232

Owners
Tony Vallone

Type of Cuisine
European, Mediterranean

Days Open
Open Mon.-Sat. for dinner

Pricing
Dinner for one,
Without tax, tip, or drinks:
$40-$60

Dress Code
Jacket and tie required

Reservations
Recommended

Parking
Free on site,valet

Features
Private room/parties, entertainment, near theater, cigar/cognac events

Credit Cards
AE, VC, MC, CB, DC, DS

The Fig Tree

Patio dining

Directions

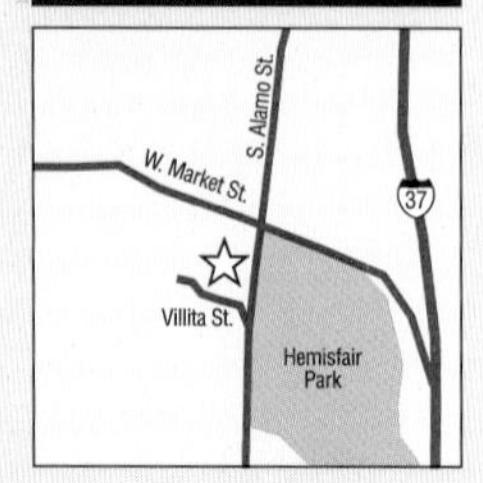

Just off the Riverwalk in downtown, 10 min. from San Antonio International Airport

515 Villita
San Antonio, TX 78205
PH: (210) 224-1976
FAX: (210) 271-9180
www.figtreerestaurant.com

Owners
Thomas E. Phelps

Cuisine
Global

Days Open
Open daily for dinner

Pricing
Dinner for one,
without tax, tip, or drinks:
$60-$80

Dress Code
Business casual

Reservations
Recommended

Parking
Garage nearby (three-hour validation)

Features
Private room/parties, outdoor dining

Credit Cards
AE, VC, MC, CB, DC, DS

The Fig Tree celebrates tradition in a gracious setting just steps from the Riverwalk and near major hotels and the convention center. Fine linen drapes tables set with elegant china, sparkling crystal, and ever-present flowers. Famous for its Continental and eclectic cuisine, The Fig Tree classically prepares chateaubriand, herb-crusted rack of lamb, and bananas Foster tableside. Comfortably elegant areas are available for social and business gatherings.

Executive Chef Tan Nguyen

Memorable entrees

The Crystal Room

AWARD WINNER
SINCE 1998

Fresco Italian Cafe

Charming outdoor dining

As close as you can get to Italy without a passport, Fresco is an intimate, romantic restaurant and a longtime Salt Lake City favorite. Tucked away in a neighborhood, the cozy cottage houses 13 tables with a roaring fireplace in the winter. In the warm-weather months, the restaurant expands onto a flowering garden patio. The menu is nothing short of exquisite — especially anything with polenta — and there are nightly specials. Attentive service and a great wine list complete the dining experience.

Romantic cottage dining

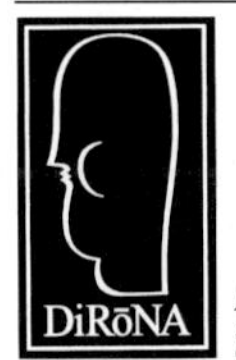

AWARD WINNER SINCE 1996

Directions

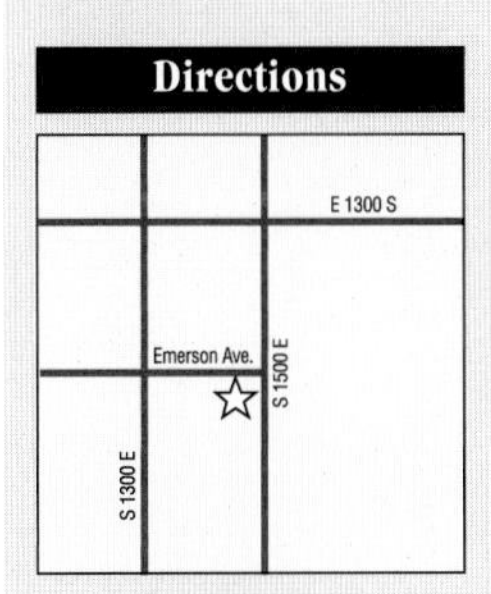

At S. 1500 East and Kensington Avenue, 20 min. from Salt Lake City International Airport

1512 S. 1500 East
Salt Lake City, UT 84103
PH: (801) 486-1300
FAX: (801) 487-5379
www.refectory.com

Owners
David Harries

Cuisine
Northern Italian

Days Open
Open daily for dinner

Pricing
Dinner for one,
without tax, tip, or drinks:
$20-$40

Dress Code
Business casual

Reservations
Recommended

Parking
Free on site

Features
Private parties, outdoor dining

Credit Cards
AE, VC, MC, CB, DC, DS

Metropolitan

Bistro and bar

One of the West's brightest new stars, Metropolitan presents exquisite, handcrafted New American cuisine amid stunning decor. Signature dishes from California-trained Executive Chef Frank Mendoza include seared Hudson Valley foie gras, wild mushroom ragout, roasted loin of caribou, and sauteed Arctic char. The attention to detail is reflected by the professionalism of the serving staff, the award-winning wine list, and the "Best Restaurant of the Year" honors from *Salt Lake Magazine*. Come and enjoy this cosmopolitan experience in the city hosting the 2002 Winter Olympics.

Bright star downtown

Wild mushroom ragout

Executive Chef Frank Mendoza and owner Karen Olsen

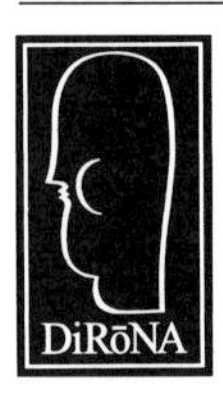

AWARD WINNER SINCE 1998

Directions

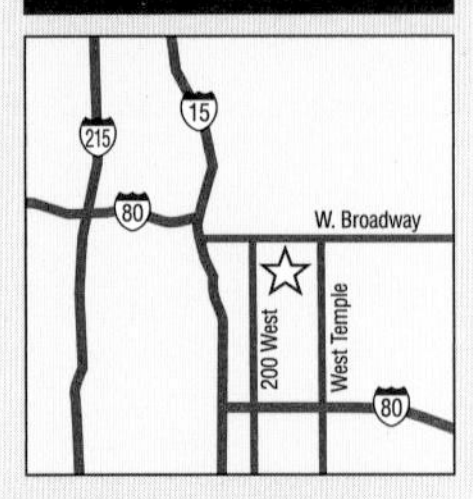

On West Broadway (300 South), 20 min. from Salt Lake International Airport

173 W. Broadway
Salt Lake City, UT 84101
PH: (801) 364-3472
FAX: (801) 364-8671
www.themetropolitan.city-search.com

Owners
Karen Olson

Cuisine
New American

Days Open
Open Tues.-Sat. for dinner

Pricing
Dinner for one, without tax, tip, or drinks: $40-$60

Dress Code
Business casual

Reservations
Recommended

Parking
Free on site, garage nearby

Features
Private room/parties, live jazz on Saturdays, near theater

Credit Cards
AE, VC, MC, DS

Hemingway's

Romantic retreat

A warm, gracious evening awaits in this beautifully restored 1860 country home, cited by *Esquire* magazine as one of the most romantic restaurants in America. The menu is filled with such handcrafted specialties as Arctic char with white beans and braised greens; hand-rolled tortellini with truffles; and roast Vermont pheasant with butternut squash pudding. For a special treat, reserve a fireside table or dine in the Old World stone wine cellar.

Fine dining

Applewood smoked salmon and salmon tartare

Linda and Ted Fondulas

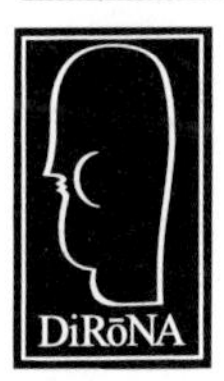

AWARD WINNER
SINCE 1992

Directions

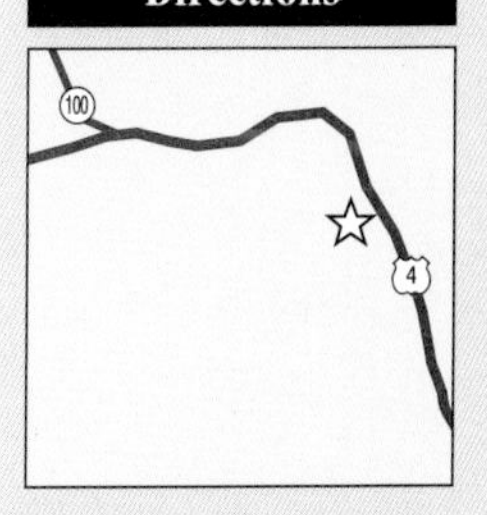

On Route 4, two-and-a-half miles east of the junction of northbound Route 100, 30 min. from Rutland Regional Airport

U.S. Route 4
Killington, VT 05751
PH: (802) 422-3886
FAX: (802) 422-3468
www.hemingwaysrestaurant.com

Owners
Ted and Linda Fondulas

Cuisine
International

Days Open
Open Wed.-Sun. for dinner (Tues. during ski season)

Pricing
Dinner for one, without tax, tip, or drinks: $40-$60

Dress Code
Dressy casual

Reservations
Recommended

Parking
Free on site

Features
Private room/parties

Credit Cards
AE, VC, MC, CB, DC

The Inn at Sawmill Farm

Directions

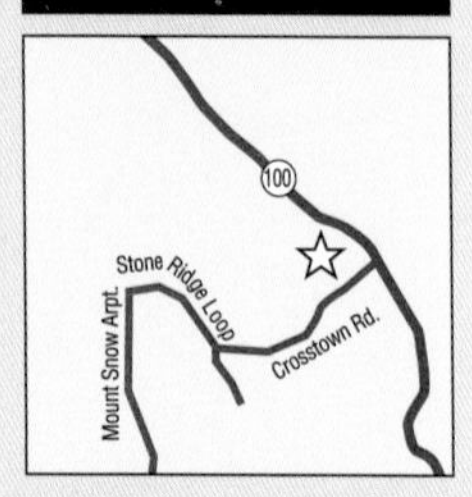

On Route 100, 1 hr. 15 min. from Connecticut's Bradley International Airport

---

Crosstown Road and Route 100
West Dover, VT 05356
PH: (802) 464-8131
FAX: (802) 464-1130
www.vermontdirect.com/sawmill

Owners
Rodney Williams Jr.

Cuisine
American, Continental

Days Open
Open daily for dinner

Pricing
Dinner for one, without tax, tip, or drinks: $40-$60

Dress Code
Business casual

Reservations
Recommended

Parking
Free on site

Features
Private parties, entertainment (weekends only)

Credit Cards
AE, VC, MC, DC

Dining room

Raves reverberate through the Vermont mountains praising the culinary feats of Chef/Owner "Brill" Williams at his Inn at Sawmill Farm. This fine member of Relais & Chateaux and Mobil Four-Star recipient delights guests with selections such as potato-crusted black sea bass on a bed of wild mushrooms, farm-raised squab with a Perigueux sauce, and the ever-demanded rack of lamb. The wine list has garnered Wine Spectator magazine's Grand Award.

Rack of lamb

Chef/Owner "Brill" William and Sous-Chef James Hadley

Wine cellar

AWARD WINNER
SINCE 1992

Elysium

Elysium, Morrison House's intimate treasure, provides "show" and "substance" with prix fixe menus that change weekly. Chef Christopher Brooks creates three-, four-, and five-course masterpieces paired with signature "Flights of Wine" for an experience that keeps audiences raving. Top-notch entrees include the lemon pepper tuna with tempura vegetable sushi, mango slaw, and Asian dressing, and the home-cured buck breast with squash and duck confit tart and a foie gras jus.

Dining room

Creative appetizers

Chef Christopher Brooks

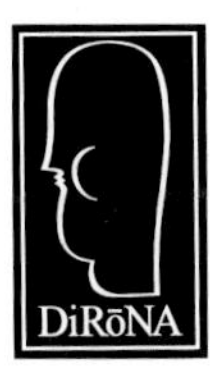

AWARD WINNER
SINCE 1999

Directions

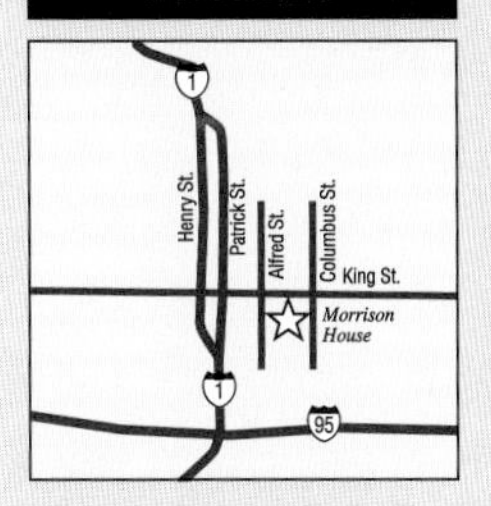

At the Morrison House in Old Town Alexandria, 10 min. from Reagan National Airport

116 South Alfred Street
Alexandria, VA 22314
PH: (703) 838-8000
FAX: (703) 684-6283
www.morrisonhouse.com

Owners
Old Town Alexandria Partners

Cuisine
Eclectic American

Days Open
Open daily for breakfast, Tues.-Sat. for dinner

Pricing
Dinner for one, without tax, tip, or drinks: $40-$60

Dress Code
Business casual

Reservations
Recommended

Parking
Complimentary valet

Features
Private room/parties

Credit Cards
AE, VC, MC, CB, DC

La Bergerie

Main dining room

Serving award-winning French and Basque cuisine since 1976, La Bergerie is renowned for its intimate, charming atmosphere and professional, friendly service. Whether it's an intimate lunch or dinner, a special occasion party, or a business affair, the Campagne brothers are always on hand to pay close attention to the smallest details and to make sure their guests enjoy a wonderful dining experience. Among the house specialties are confit of duck, parillade of fresh seafood Basque-style, and raspberry soufflé.

Party room

Seasonal specialties

AWARD WINNER
SINCE 1997

Directions

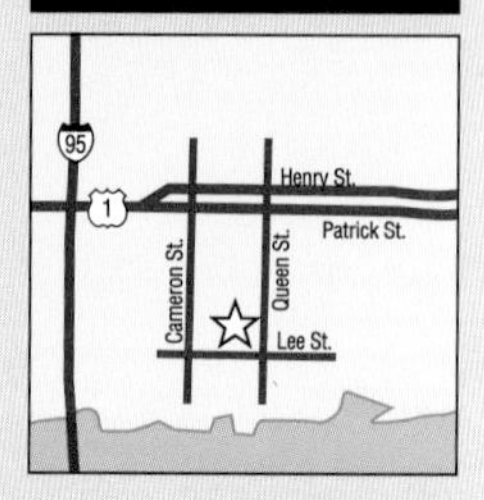

In the heart of Old Town, 10 min. from Reagan National Airport

218 North Lee Street
Alexandria, VA 22314
PH: (703) 683-1007
FAX: (703) 519-6114
www.labergerie.com

Owners
Jean and Bernard Campagne

Cuisine
French and Basque

Days Open
Open Mon.-Sat. for lunch and dinner

Pricing
Dinner for one,
without tax, tip, or drinks:
$20-$40

Dress Code
Business casual

Reservations
Recommended

Parking
Garage across the street

Features
Private room/parties

Credit Cards
AE, VC, MC, CB, DC, DS

Clifton–The Country Inn and Estate

Dining room

Clifton–The Country Inn and Estate is located on 40 acres in the heart of Virginia's rolling countryside, east of Charlottesville. Its restaurant has received wide national acclaim in its nine years of operation. Executive Chef Jeramie Garlick selects many local and regional products from the daily market to create her seasonal five- and six-course prix fixe menus. Come for a true taste of Virginia - locally raised Black Angus beef, fruits and berries from the Shenandoah Valley, and herbs and edible flowers from the inn's own estate gardens. The mahogany-paneled wine cellar has more than 5,000 bottles.

Seasonal entrees

The wine cellar

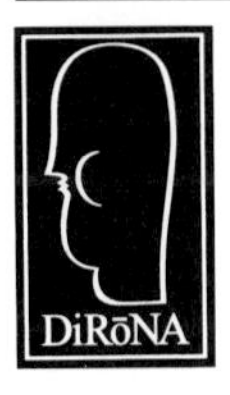

AWARD WINNER
SINCE 1999

Directions

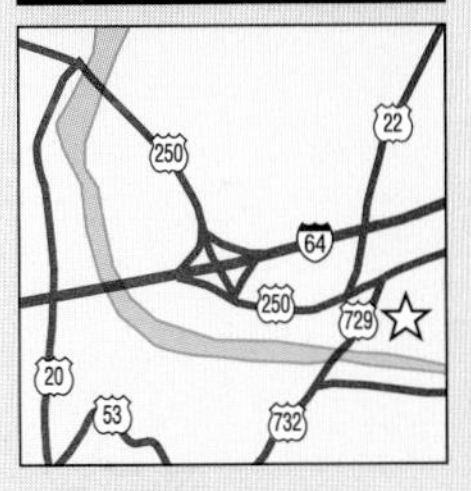

Six miles east of Charlottesville, 30 min. from Charlottesville Airport

1296 Clifton Inn Drive
Charlottesville, VA 22911
PH: (804) 971-1800
FAX: (804) 971-7098
www.cliftoninn.com

Owners
T. Mitchell Willey

Cuisine
Blend of American, European, and Asian

Days Open
Open daily for breakfast and dinner

Pricing
Dinner for one, without tax, tip, or drinks: $60-$80

Dress Code
Business casual

Reservations
Required

Parking
Free on site

Features
Private room/parties, entertainment

Credit Cards
AE, VC, MC, DC

L' Auberge Chez Francois

Patio dining

A French country inn situated in the verdant hills of northern Virginia, this gastronomic delight satisfies our secret longings to escape to a peaceful spot to be pampered and revived. The restaurant has received national acclaim for its fine French-Alsatian cuisine, and the accommodating service and homemade pastries and desserts create a harmony to be cherished.

L'entre côte

Owner François Haeringer

Dining room

AWARD WINNER
SINCE 1992

Directions

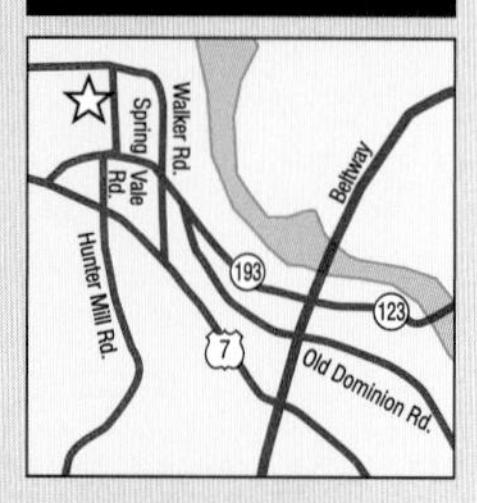

At Springvale and Walker roads, 30 min. from Washington Dulles International Airport

332 Springvale Road
Great Falls, VA 22066
PH: (703) 759-3800

Owners
François Haeringer

Cuisine
French-Alsatian

Days Open
Open Tues.-Sun. for dinner

Pricing
Dinner for one, without tax, tip, or drinks: $40-$60

Dress Code
Business casual

Reservations
Required

Parking
Free on site

Features
Private parties, outdoor dining

Credit Cards
AE, VC, MC, DC, DS

Prince Michel Restaurant

Lafayette Room

Located at Virginia's leading winery, with the dining room overlooking the vineyard, Prince Michel Restaurant is a true delight for the senses. Executive Chef Alain Lecomte's signature dishes include foie gras with Calvados sauce and stuffed filet of sole with lobster. An easy drive from both Washington, D.C., and Richmond, Prince Michel Restaurant provides a wonderful respite. For those desiring a longer escape, overnight guest suites are available.

Strawberry Bavarian

French Master Chef Alain Lecomte

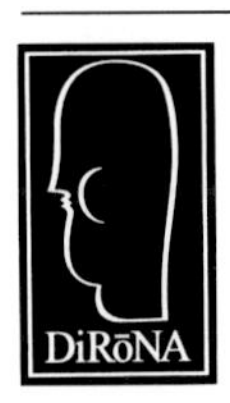

AWARD WINNER
SINCE 1997

Directions

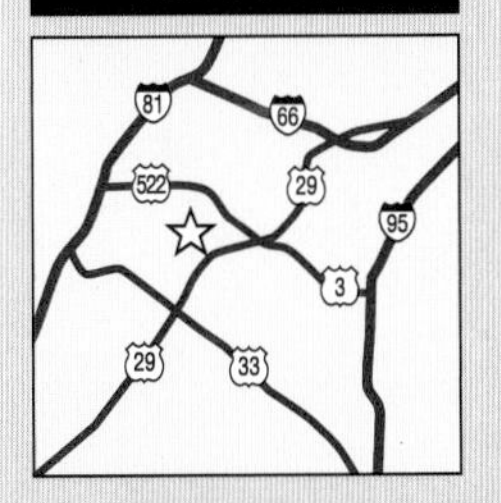

On Route 29 South, 90 min. from suburban Washington and 30 min. from Charlottesville Airport

HCR 4, Box 77 (Route 29)
Leon, VA 22725
PH: (800) 800-WINE
FAX: (540) 547-3088
www.princemichel.com

Owners
Jean Leducq

Cuisine
French

Days Open
Open Thurs.-Sun. for lunch, Thurs.-Sat for dinner

Pricing
Dinner for one, without tax, tip, or drinks: $60-$80

Dress Code
Business casual

Reservations
Required

Parking
Free on site

Features
Private room/parties

Credit Cards
AE, VC, MC, DC, DS

Lemaire

Directions

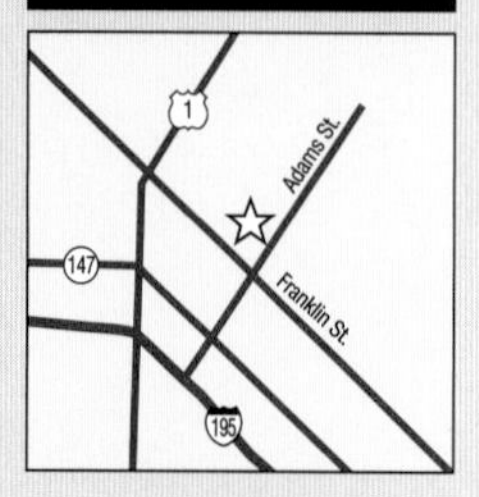

In downtown Richmond, near the Convention Center and 20 min. from Richmond International Airport

The Jefferson Hotel
101 W. Franklin Street
Richmond, VA 23220
PH: (804) 788-8000
FAX: (804) 649-4623
www.jefferson-hotel.com

Owners
The Jefferson Hotel

Cuisine
Regional

Days Open
Open daily for breakfast, Mon.-Fri. for lunch, Mon.-Sat. for dinner

Pricing
Dinner for one, without tax, tip, or drinks: $40-$60

Dress Code
Jacket and tie required

Reservations
Recommended

Parking
Valet

Features
Private room/parties, cigar/cognac events

Credit Cards
AE, VC, MC, DC, DS

The Conservatory

Lemaire, named for Etienne Lemaire, President Thomas Jefferson's maitre d'hotel, is Richmond's only AAA Five Diamond restaurant. Etienne Lemaire is widely credited with introducing the fine art of cooking with wines, and the restaurant honors its namesake, as well as Thomas Jefferson's own fondness for food prepared with light sauces and garden-fresh herbs. The menu features updated regional Southern cuisine, to which Executive Chef Jeffrey Waite adds his own classical European and contemporary American influences.

The Library

Manager John Brown and Executive Chef Jeffrey Waite

The Valentine Room

AWARD WINNER
SINCE 1997

Tivoli Restaurant

Main dining room

With award-winning wines, freshly made pastas, and daily specials of seafood and game, Tivoli Restaurant offers the finest Northern Italian dining experience in the Washington, D.C., area. The sparkling dining room and personable and attentive service make a meal at Tivoli a memorable affair. A generous pre-theater menu is available for those attending performances at the Kennedy Center, across the Potomac a mere five minutes away.

Ravioli

Chef/owner Klaus Helmin

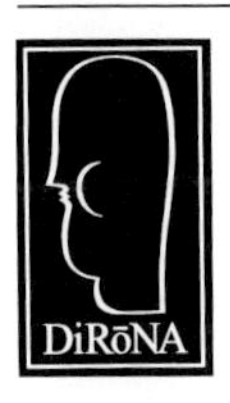

AWARD WINNER
SINCE 1992

Directions

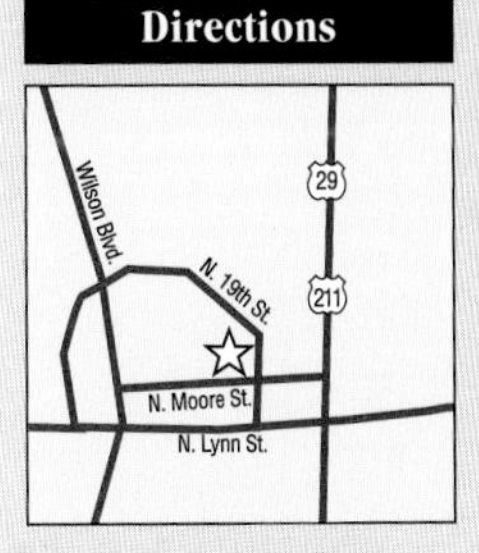

Just west of the Key Bridge, 5 min. from Reagan National Airport

1700 N. Moore Street
Rosslyn, VA 22209
PH: (703) 524-8900
FAX: (703) 524-4971
www.erols.com/tivolirestaurant

Owners
Klaus Helmin

Cuisine
Northern Italian

Days Open
Open Mon.-Fri. for lunch, Mon.-Sat. for dinner

Pricing
Dinner for one, without tax, tip, or drinks: $20-$40

Dress Code
Business casual

Reservations
Recommended

Parking
Free on site

Features
Private room/parties, near theater

Credit Cards
AE, VC, MC, CB, DC, DS

The Dining Room at Ford's Colony

Directions

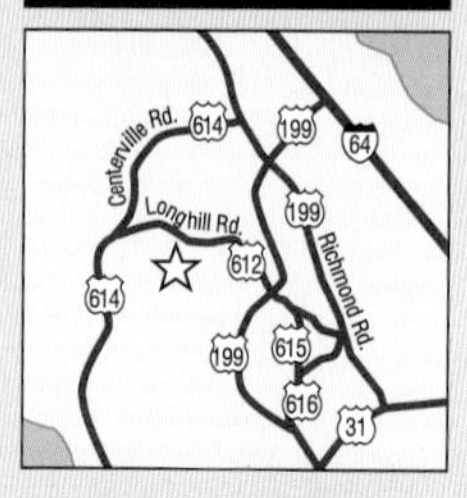

Four miles from Colonial Williamsburg, 35 min. from Newport News/Williamsburg Airport and 1 hr. from Richmond International

240 Ford's Colony Drive
Williamsburg, VA 23188
PH: (757) 258-4107
FAX: (757) 258-4168
www.fordscolony.com

Owners
Richard J. Ford

Cuisine
Regional American

Days Open
Open Tues.-Sat. for dinner

Pricing
Dinner for one,
without tax, tip, or drinks:
$40-$60

Dress Code
Jacket required, tie optional

Reservations
Recommended

Parking
Free on site

Features
Private room/parties,
cigar/cognac events

Credit Cards
AE, VC, MC

Georgian -style dining room

This highly acclaimed restaurant at the Ford's Colony Resort, four miles from Colonial Williamsburg, showcases the modern American cuisine of Executive Chef David Everett. The elegant Georgian-style dining room has intimate seating and a golf course view. Details are important here: The wine list is extensive and fresh local ingredients are mixed with the finest of imports to produce a truly world-class dining experience.

Executive Chef David Everett chooses a vintage wine

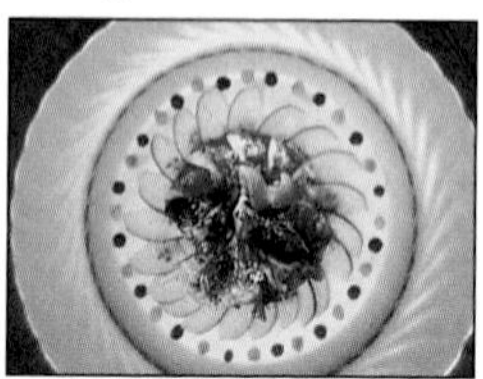

Lobster and green apple salad with sea urchin vinaigrette

David Everett in herb garden

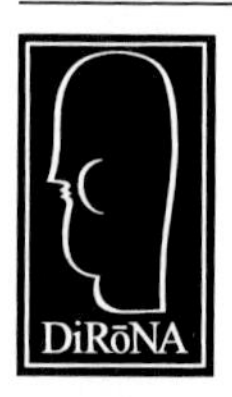

AWARD WINNER
SINCE 1993

Campagne

Located in the heart of Pike Place Market, this cozy establishment serves award-winning French country food in an elegant dining room overlooking Elliott Bay. Drawing inspiration from the sun-drenched cuisine of Southern France, the chef uses only the freshest ingredients, many from the Pacific Northwest. Signature dishes include foie gras parfait on puff pastry, and rack of lamb with tomato confit and potato galette.

Courtyard

Cafe Campagne

Lounge

AWARD WINNER
SINCE 1992

Directions

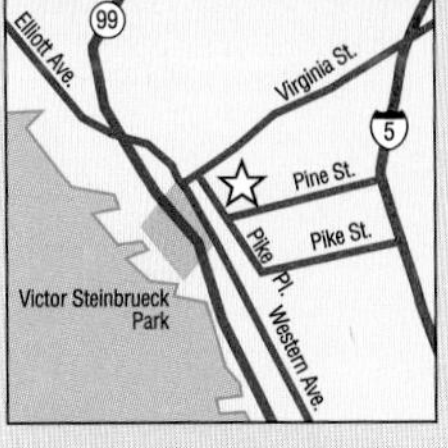

At Pike Place Market, 20 min. from Seattle-Tacoma International Airport

86 Pine Street
Seattle, WA 98101
PH: (206) 728-2800
FAX: (206) 448-7740

Owners
Peter Lewis

Cuisine
Country French

Days Open
Open daily for dinner

Pricing
Dinner for one,
without tax, tip, or drinks:
$40-$60

Dress Code
Business casual

Reservations
Required

Parking
Valet nearby

Features
Outdoor dining, near theater

Credit Cards
AE, VC, MC, CB, DC

Canlis

Dining room

For more than 50 years, the Canlis family has made their restaurant an extension of their home. The award-winning Pacific Northwest menu — Pacific king salmon and seared rare ahi are particularly popular — extensive wine list, and elegant surroundings are a Seattle tradition. Enjoy being pampered with impeccable service while enjoying the panoramic views of Lake Union and the dramatic Cascade Mountains.

Blazing hearth in foyer

Alice and Chris Canlis

Creative entrees

AWARD WINNER
SINCE 1993

Directions

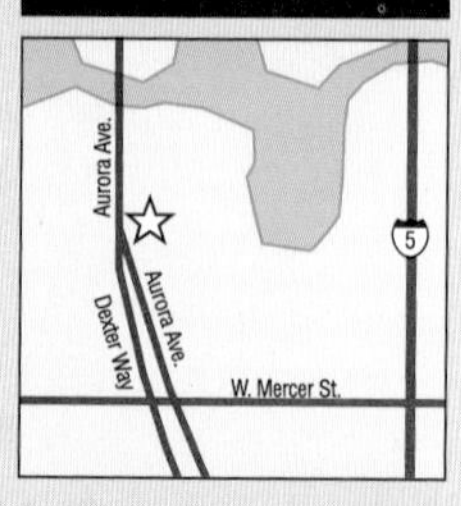

On Aurora Avenue North just before the Aurora Bridge in Queen Anne, 30 min. from Seattle-Tacoma International Airport

2576 Aurora Avenue North
Seattle, WA 98109
PH: (206) 283-3313
FAX: (206) 283-1766
www.canlis.com

Owners
Chris and Alice Canlis

Cuisine
Pacific Northwest

Days Open
Open Mon.-Sat. for dinner

Pricing
Dinner for one,
without tax, tip, or drinks:
$40-$60

Dress Code
Business casual

Reservations
Required

Parking
Valet

Features
Private room/parties, entertainment

Credit Cards
AE, VC, MC, CB, DC, JCB, DS

The Fox & Hounds

Located in the wooded rolling hills of the Kettle Moraine, The Fox & Hounds is a rambling log cabin-style restaurant where the dinner menu includes such expertly prepared specialties as goose, duck, pork chops, steaks, and seafood. The seven dining areas are adorned with European and American antiques, and seven natural-burning fireplaces add a final touch to the warmth and charm of the dining experience.

Executive Chef Lederhause and Owner Joseph Ratzsch

Early American ambience

The entrance

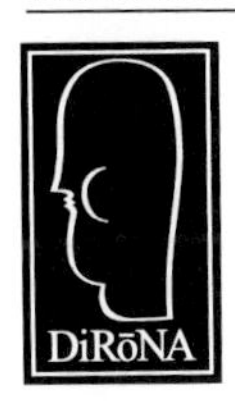

AWARD WINNER
SINCE 2001

Directions

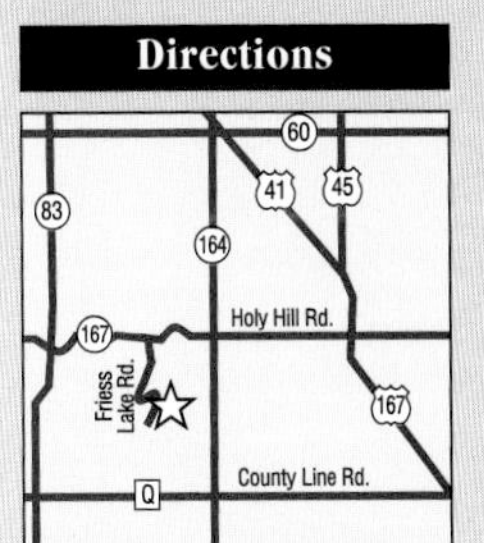

On Friess Lake Road off Hwy. 167 , 45 min. from Mitchel International Airport

1298 Friess Lake Road
Hubertus, WI 53033
PH: (262) 628-1111
FAX: (262) 628-2440
www.ratzsch.com

Owners
Josef W. Ratzsch

Cuisine
American, German

Days Open
Open Tues.-Sat. for dinner

Pricing
Dinner for one,
without tax, tip, or drinks:
$20-$40

Dress Code
Casual

Reservations
Recommended

Parking
Free on site, valet

Features
Private parties

Credit Cards
AE, VC, MC, CB, DC, DS

The Immigrant Restaurant & Winery

The American Club

The Immigrant Restaurant & Winery is located at The American Club, the Midwest's only AAA Five-Diamond resort hotel and a member of Historic Hotels of America. Contemporary cuisine, fine wines, and exceptional service are the hallmarks of this restaurant, whose six rooms are decorated to salute the European heritage of Wisconsin's early settlers. Seared St. George's Bank scallops and hazelnut-crusted rack of Midwestern lamb are among the award-winning specialties.

The Dutch Room

Fine cuisine

The French Room

AWARD WINNER SINCE 1992

Directions

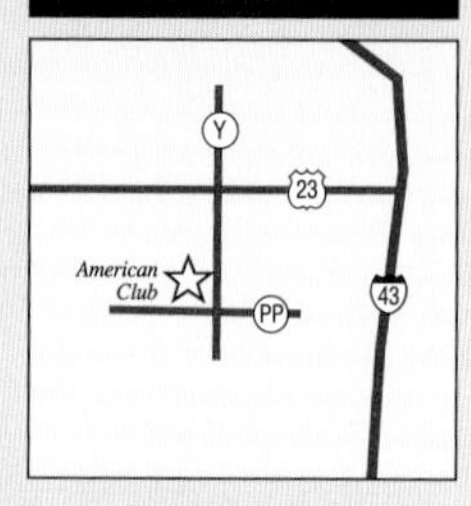

South of the junction of Highways 23 and Y, 1 hr. from Milwaukee's General Mitchell International Airport

The American Club
Highland Drive
Kohler, WI 53044
PH: (920) 457-8888 or
(800) 344-2838
FAX: (920) 457-0299
www.americanclub.com

Owners
Kohler Co.

Cuisine
Contemporary

Days Open
Open Tue.-Sat. for dinner

Pricing
Dinner for one,
without tax, tip, or drinks:
$40-$60

Dress Code
Jacket required

Reservations
Recommended

Parking
Free on site

Features
Private parties,
entertainment

Credit Cards
AE, VC, MC, CB, DC, DS

Bartolotta's Lake Park Bistro

A Milwaukee landmark

Housed in a landmark building overlooking Lake Michigan, Bartolotta's Lake Park Bistro was an instant classic upon its opening in 1995. Owner Joe Bartolotta and his brother Paul, a James Beard Award-winning chef, brought in Chef Mark Weber to oversee Milwaukee's most authentic French bistro. Specialties include foie gras, filet au poivre, and the ethereal crème brulée. The *Milwaukee Journal* named Bartolotta's Lake Park Bistro the city's Best New Restaurant of 1995 and has awarded it a four-star rating ever since.

Zinc bar

Dining room

The Bistro, by Guy Buffet

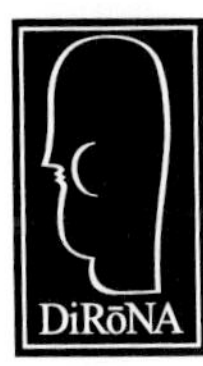

AWARD WINNER
SINCE 1999

Directions

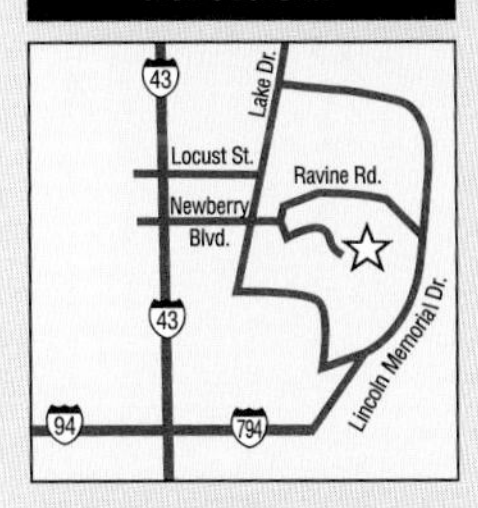

North of downtown on the lakefront, 20 min. from General Mitchell International Airport

3133 E. Newberry Boulevard
Milwaukee, WI 53211
PH: (414) 962-6300
FAX (414) 962-4248
www.bartolottas.com

Owners
Joe Bartolotta

Cuisine
French bistro

Days Open
Open Mon.-Fri., for lunch, Mon.-Sun. for dinner, Sun. for brunch

Pricing
Dinner for one, without tax, tip, or drinks: $20-$40

Dress Code
Business casual

Reservations
Recommended

Parking
Free on site

Features
Private room/parties

Credit Cards
AE, VC, MC, DC

Karl Ratzsch's

Directions

Broadway St.
Milwaukee St.
Van Buren St.
Mason St.
794

On Mason Street between Milwaukee and Broadway streets, 15 min. from General Mitchell International Airport

320 E. Mason Street
Milwaukee, WI 53202
PH: (414) 276-2720
FAX: (414) 276-3534

Owners
Josef Ratzsch

Cuisine
German Continental

Days Open
Open Mon. -Sat. for dinner

Pricing
Dinner for one,
without tax, tip, or drinks:
$20-$40

Dress Code
Business casual

Reservations
Recommended

Parking
Valet

Features
Private room/parties, entertainment, near theater

Credit Cards
AE, VC, MC, CB, DC, DS

Main dining room

Owned and operated by three generations of the Ratzsch family Karl Ratzsch's is, quite simply a Milwaukee tradition and a citadel for German cuisine. Housed within its walls is a priceless collection of German steins, porcelain, and glassware. The top-teir dishes include roast goose shank, sauerbraten, planked whitefish, and roast duck, and the selection of German wines is impressive indeed.

The finest German fare

Goose shank

A Milwaukee tradition since 1904

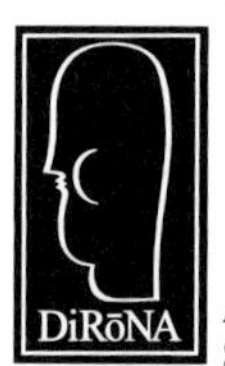

AWARD WINNER
SINCE 1992

The Granary

Spring Creek Ranch

Perched atop the Gros Ventre Butte overlooking the Teton Mountains, The Granary is, to say the very least, an unforgettable dining experience. Part of Spring Creek Ranch, Wyoming's award-winning resort, The Granary offers superb cuisine and views that elevate fine dining to unprecedented heights. Elk tenderloin with black bay sauce, lamb loin with garlic flan, and garlic and sesame encrusted rainbow trout are among the memorable specialties.

Fireside dining

Priceless Teton views

AWARD WINNER
SINCE 1997

Directions

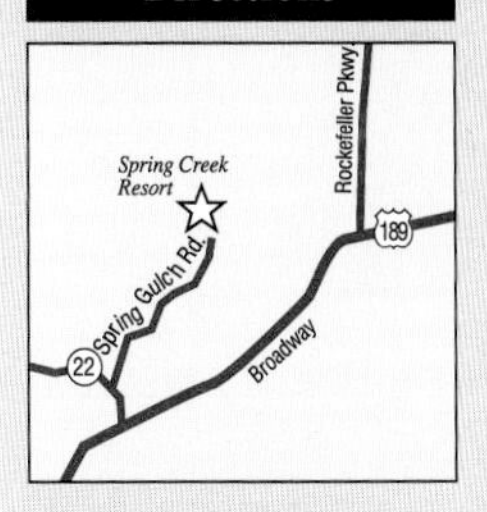

Atop East Gros Ventre Butte just outside of town and 15 min. from Jackson Hole Airport

1800 Spirit Dance Road
Jackson Hole, WY 83001
PH: (307) 733-8833
FAX: (307) 733-1524
www.springcreekranch.com

Owners
Stephen Price

Cuisine
Regional American

Days Open
Open daily for dinner

Pricing
Dinner for one, without tax, tip, or drinks: $40-$60

Dress Code
Casual

Reservations
Recommended

Parking
Free on site

Features
Outdoor dining, entertainment

Credit Cards
AE, VC, MC, CB, DC, DS

La Chaumiére Restaurant

Patio area

Directions

Fourth St.
Centre St.
1st St.
Macleod Tr.
17th Ave.

On 17th Avenue SW three blocks from Stampede Park, 15 min. from Calgary International Airport

139 17th Avenue SW
Calgary, Alberta T250A1
PH: (403) 228-5690
FAX: (403) 228-4448
www.calgarymenus.com/lachaumiere

Owners
Joseph DeAngelis

Cuisine
French Market

Days Open
Open Mon.-Fri. for lunch, Mon.-Sat. for dinner

Pricing
Dinner for one,
without tax, tip, or drinks:
$20-$40

Dress Code
Business casual

Reservations
Recommended

Parking
Free on site

Features
Private room/parties, outdoor dining, cigar/cognac events

Credit Cards
AE, VC, MC, DC, ER

La Chaumiére Restaurant serves French market cuisine in an elegant dining room or comfortable patio overlooking Rouleauville Square. Executive Chef C. Bob Matthews prepares an imaginative menu with entrees such as ahi tuna with bok choy and spinach, sesame beurre blanc with sweet chilies, and veal medallions and foie gras with Madeira sauce. The extensive wine list has 750 selections from around the world.

Main dining room

Banquet room

The wine cellar

AWARD WINNER
SINCE 1993

The Owl's Nest Dining Room

Owl's Nest

This Four Diamond Award-winning Owl's Nest Dining Room is in its 36th year of offering impeccable first-class service, an extensive top-flight wine list, and fine cuisine of international and French flavors. The lavish menu consists of poultry, game, seafood, and AAA Alberta beef. Savor the delectable sauteed prawns Marseillaise, lobster bisque, and steak tartar prepared at your table. Signature chocolate-covered cherries and sumptuous, delicate soufflés are a voluptuous finale.

Rack of lamb

Signature chocolate covered cherries

Tempting desserts

AWARD WINNER SINCE 1993

Directions

In The Westin Calgary, near entertainment/shopping districts, 30 min. from Calgary International Airport

320 4th Avenue SW
Calgary, Alberta,
Canada T2P 2S6
PH: (403) 266-1611
FAX: (403) 233-7471
www.westin.com

Owners
The Westin Calgary

Cuisine
International with French accents

Days Open
Open Mon.-Fri. for lunch, Mon.-Sat.for dinner

Pricing
Dinner for one, without tax, tip, or drinks: $20-$40

Dress Code
Business casual

Reservations
Recommended

Parking
Valet, underground garage

Features
Private parties

Credit Cards
AE, VC, MC, CB, DC, ER, JCB, DS

Post Hotel Dining Room

Post Hotel

Set amidst the natural wonders of Banff National Park in the majestic Canadian Rocky Mountains, the Post Hotel Dining Room offers a menu of fresh market cuisine complemented by an award-winning wine list. With over 1,000 selections and an inventory of 27,000 bottles, the wine list was recognized by *Wine Spectator*, winning the magazine's Best of Award of Excellence. Fine cognacs and hand-rolled cigars are also available in an adjacent smoking room.

Chef Wolfgang Vogt

Alberta rack of lamb

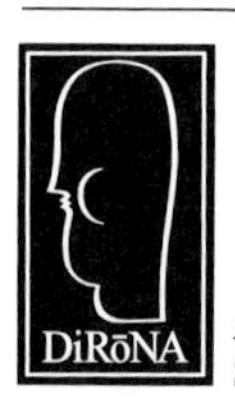

AWARD WINNER
SINCE 1993

Directions

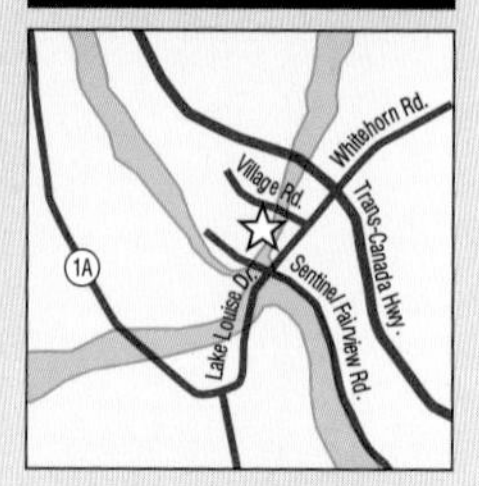

In the Canadian Rockies, 2 hrs. from Calgary Int'l Airport

Post Hotel
200 Pipestone Road
Lake Louise, Alberta,
T0L 1E0 Canada
PH: (403) 522-3989
FAX: (403) 522-3966
www.posthotel.com

Owners
André and George Schwarz

Cuisine
Fresh market cuisine

Days Open
Open daily for breakfast, lunch, and dinner; closed mid-Oct. to mid-Dec.

Pricing
Dinner for one, without tax, tip, or drinks: $40-$60

Dress Code
Smart casual

Reservations
Required

Parking
Free on site

Features
Private room/parties, entertainment, cigar/cognac lounge

Credit Cards
AE, VC, MC

Caffe de Medici

Private dining room

Caffe de Medici has gained renown for its superb service, outstanding cuisine, and extensive wine list. Executive Chef Robert Byford infuses traditional Italian taste and modern variety into all the entrees. The seafood, unique pasta dishes, and antipasto are all prepared fresh. Specialties include lobster ravioli filled with ricotta cheese and spinach in a saffron and thyme sauce, and grilled beef tenderloin on crabmeat potatoes with seared foie gras served with a pork reduction. Attention to detail makes Caffe de Medici ideal for important luncheons or candlelight dinners.

From left, Steve Punzo, Daniel Ondzik, and Dean Punzo

Roasted rack of lamb in basil jus

Front dining room

AWARD WINNER
SINCE 1993

Directions

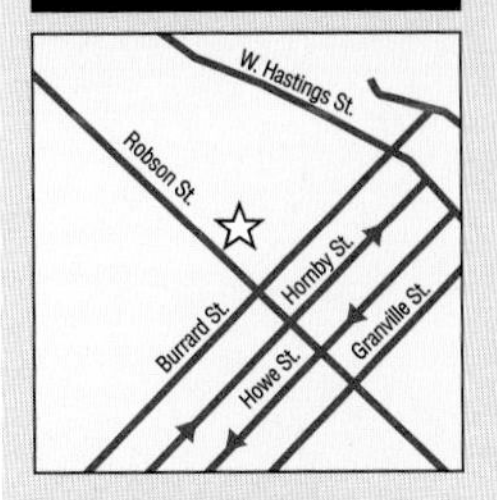

On Robson Street between Burrard and Thurlow, 30 min. from Vancouver International Airport

1025 Robson Street
Vancouver, British Columbia, Canada V6E 1A9
PH: (604) 669-9322
FAX: (604) 669-3771
www.medici.cc

Owners
Steve Punzo and Daniel Ondzik

Cuisine
Italian

Days Open
Open Mon.-Fri. for lunch, daily for dinner (brunch on Sun.)

Pricing
Dinner for one, without tax, tip, or drinks: $20-$40

Dress Code
Business casual

Reservations
Recommended

Parking
Free on site, garage nearby

Features
Private room/parties, outdoor dining, near theater, themed dinner events

Credit Cards
AE, VC, MC, DC, ER, JCB, DS

The Five Sails Restaurant

Stunning views

Directions

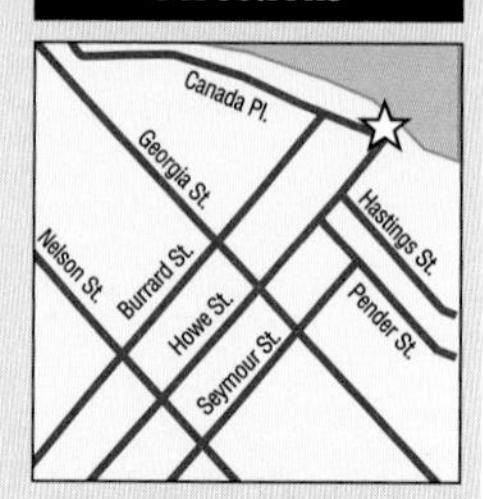

In Pan Pacific Hotel on Canada Place, 30 min. from Vancouver International Airport

999 Canada Place
Suite 300
Vancouver, British Columbia
Canada V6C 3L5
PH: (604) 662-8111
FAX: (604) 891-2864
www.panpac.com

Owners
Pan Pacific Hotel

Cuisine
Pacific Northwest/international

Days Open
Open daily for dinner

Pricing
Dinner for one,
without tax, tip, or drinks:
$40-$60

Dress Code
Business casual

Reservations
Recommended

Parking
Valet, free on site

Features
Private room/parties

Credit Cards
AE, VC, MC

The Five Sails Restaurant, specializing in exquisite Pacific Northwest and international cuisine, offers guests a bonus: stunning panoramic harbor and mountain views. The award-winning menu, created by Executive Chef Ernst Dorfler, is unique with a touch of European and Asian influence. Entrees include veal medallion, slow-roasted British Columbia salmon, and roast rack of lamb. There are three tasting menus offering the best of the season.

Exquisite cuisine

AWARD WINNER
SINCE 1993

Imperial Chinese Seafood Restaurant

Main dining room

At the award-winning Imperial Restaurant in the art deco Marine Building, Executive Chef T. Ip's superb Chinese cuisine is combined with classic French service. The dining room, with floor-to-ceiling windows, offers a magnificent view of the North Shore and its snowcapped mountains. Come for the imaginative dim sum lunch, for which the Imperial Chinese Seafood Restaurant is justly famous.

Main dining room

Variety of succulent courses

Dim Sum lunch

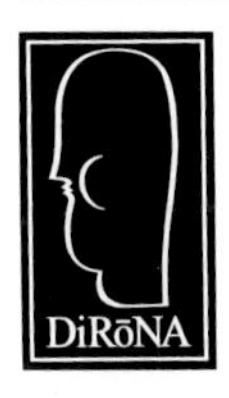

AWARD WINNER
SINCE 1993

Directions

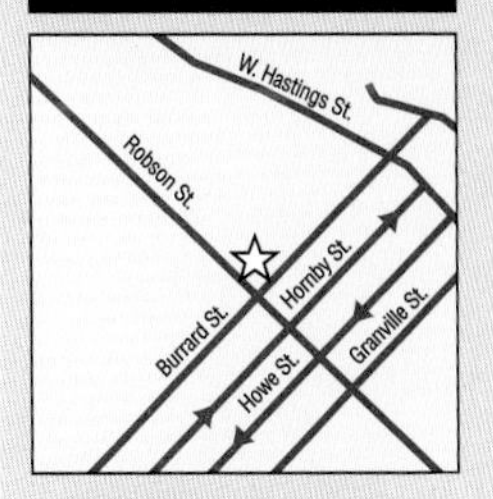

In the Marine Building on Burrard Street, 45 min. from Vancouver International Airport

355 Burrard Street
Vancouver, British Columbia, Canada V6C 2G8
PH: (604) 688-8191
FAX: (604) 688-8466
www.imperialrest.com

Owners
K.L. Wong

Cuisine
Seafood and dim sum

Days Open
Open daily for lunch and dinner

Pricing
Dinner for one, without tax, tip, or drinks: $20-$40

Dress Code
Casual

Reservations
Recommended

Parking
Valet after 5:30p.m.

Features
Private room/parties

Credit Cards
VC, MC, DC

Directions

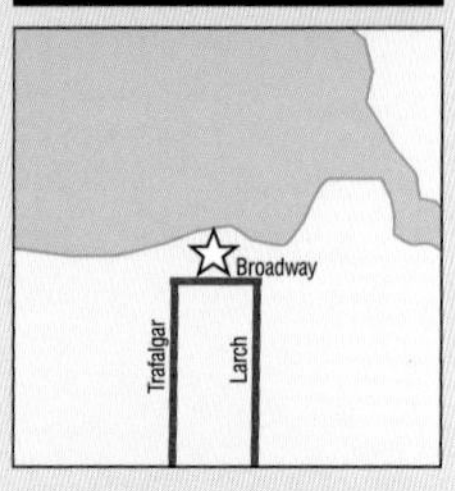

On West Broadway (9th Avenue) between Larch and Trafalgar, 30 min. from Vancouver International Airport

2551 West Broadway
Vancouver, British Columbia,
Canada V6K 2E9
PH: (604) 739-8185
FAX: (604) 739-8139

Owners
Robert Feenie

Cuisine
Contemporary Canadian, French-influenced

Days Open
Open Tues.-Sun. for dinner

Pricing
Dinner for one, without tax, tip, or drinks: $80+

Dress Code
Jacket and tie suggested

Reservations
Recommended

Parking
Free on site

Features
Outdoor dining

Credit Cards
AE, VC, MC

Lumiére

Elegant dining

Small and elegant, Lumiére is considered one of Canada's best restaurants. A master of subtle tastes, Chef-Owner Robert Feenie's contemporary Canadian cuisine uses classic, light French techniques with regional ingredients incorporatng Asian influences. The wine program offers a perfect range of both Old World and new selections, including some of the region's best British Columbian wines. Service is delightful yet formal, and the meal creates a lasting impression.

Chef Robert Feenie

Smoked Alaska black cod salad

AWARD WINNER
SINCE 2001

Restaurant Dubrovnik

Old World mansion

A part of Winnipeg's fine dining community for 25 years, Restaurant Dubrovnik is famed for its exquisite international cuisine and sophisticated elegance. Step into the mansion on the Assiniboine River and find yourself in an Old World environment that backdrops Executive Chef Gojko Bodiroga's innovative fare. Dishes include seared foie gras with sweet apple chips and port wine, and fresh salmon coated with cashew nuts in a chardonnay reduction with quince.

Owner Milan Bodiroga, Pastry Chef Borka Bodiroga and Executive Chef Gojko Bodiroga

Elegant entrees

Main dining room

AWARD WINNER
SINCE 1998

Directions

On Assiniboine Avenue near the Manitoba Legislative Building, 15 min. from Winnipeg International Airport

390 Assiniboine Avenue
Winnipeg, Manitoba
Canada R3C 0Y1
PH: (204) 944-0594
FAX: (204) 957-7750

Owners
Milan Bodiroga

Cuisine
French, Continental

Days Open
Open Mon.-Fri. for lunch, Mon.-Sat. for dinner

Pricing
Dinner for one, without tax, tip, or drinks: $40-$60

Dress Code
Business casual

Reservations
Recommended

Parking
Free on site

Features
Private room/parties, outdoor dining, entertainment, near theater

Credit Cards
AE, VC, MC

The Left Bank Restaurant

The back patio

Directions

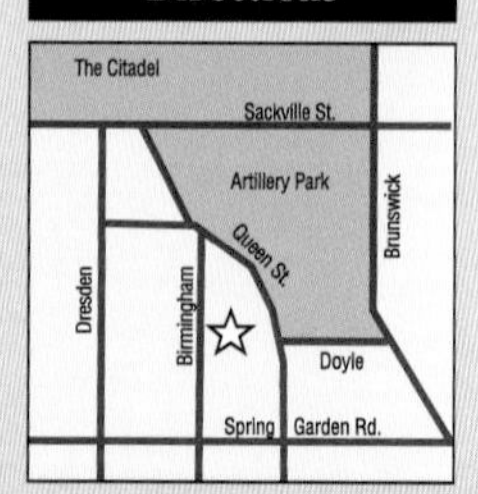

On Birmingham Street near the Citadel, 35 min. from Halifax International Airport

1541 Birmingham Street
Halifax, Nova Scotia,
Canada B3J 2J6
PH: (902) 492-3049

Owners
Ed Bleicher

Cuisine
Global/eclectic

Days Open
Open Mon.-Fri. for lunch, daily for dinner

Pricing
Dinner for one, without tax, tip, or drinks: $20-$40

Dress Code
Business casual

Reservations
Recommended

Parking
Garage nearby

Features
Private room/parties, outdoor dining, near theater

Credit Cards
AE, VC, MC, DC, ER

The Left Bank is situated in a Victorian town house with comfortable, understated decor and, in warmer weather, patio dining overlooking one of Halifax's many lovely green areas. The menu offers a delicious variety of dishes, all creatively conceived and presented artistically to provide a satisfying dining experience. Signature dishes include vodka-spiced tomato vichyssoise, and veal sweetbreads with double-smoked bacon. The service staff is friendly and knowledgeable, and the wine list is short and smart with thoughtful selections.

The front dining room

Sit and sip

The back bar

AWARD WINNER
SINCE 1992

Langdon Hall

Dining terrace

At Langdon Hall, a country house built for a descendant of the legendary financier John Jacob Astor, Executive Chef James Saunders prepares contemporary Canadian cuisine. He incorporates vegetables, fruits, and edible flowers grown on the property into every entree to create fresh, seasonal, Canadian flavors. Guests may choose to dine indoors by soft candlelight or outdoors under the arbor.

Creative entrees

Luxurious appointments

Elegant desserts

AWARD WINNER
SINCE 1993

Directions

At Blair Road and Langdon Drive in Cambridge, near Highway 401 and 40 min. from Toronto's Pearson International Airport

R.R. 33
Cambridge, Ontario
Canada N3H 4R8
PH: (519) 740-2100
FAX: (519) 740-8161
www.relaischateaux.fr/langdon

Owners
William Bennett and Mary Beaton

Cuisine
Modern country house

Days Open
Open daily for breakfast, lunch, and dinner

Pricing
Dinner for one, without tax, tip, or drinks: $40-$60

Dress Code
Casual

Reservations
Recommended

Parking
Free on site, valet

Features
Private room/parties, outdoor dining, entertainment

Credit Cards
AE, VC, MC, CB, DC, ER

Inn on the Twenty

Inn on the Twenty

Directions

In the Niagara Escarpment village of Jordan, 1 hr. from both Toronto's Pearson International Airport and Buffalo (N.Y.) International Airport

3836 Main Street
Jordan, Ontario
Canada L0R 1S0
PH: (905) 562-7313
FAX: (905) 562-3348
www.innonthetwenty.com

Owners
Helen Young

Cuisine
Regional wine country

Days Open
Open daily for breakfast, lunch, and dinner

Pricing
Dinner for one, without tax, tip, or drinks: $40-$60

Dress Code
Business casual

Reservations
Required

Parking
Free on site

Features
Private room/parties, near theater

Credit Cards
AE, VC, MC, DC

Inn on the Twenty is Ontario's premier estate winery restaurant. The culinary team, led by Executive Chef Michael Olson, are champions of regional cuisine, committed to the flavors of Niagara's bountiful harvest. Ingredients are carefully selected from the best local producers. Among the exciting regional foods that make their way to Inn on the Twenty's kitchens are fabulous tree fruits and berries, quail, trout, and organically grown vegetables, greens, and herbs. A panoramic view of Twenty Mile Creek enhances the dining experience.

Pan-fried salmon

Main dining room

Elegant guest accommodations

AWARD WINNER
SINCE 1997

Hogan's Inn at Four Corners

Historic inn circa 1851

Just minutes north of Toronto, Hogan's Inn has been part of the local landscape since 1851. Executive Chef Robert Steele prepares a unique menu that reflects his commitment to using only the freshest ingredients. Specialties include sea scallops, lobster ragout, mosaic of game and foie gras, and Sterling Silver beef. The award-winning wine list, featuring over 250 labels, is one of the finest in the province.

Award-winning cuisine

The main dining room

Private room

AWARD WINNER
SINCE 1995

Directions

King Rd.
Major Mackenzie
400
Keele
Dufferin
Bathurst
7

At Keele Street and King Road, 20 min. from Toronto's Pearson International Airport

P.O. Box 40
12998 Keele Street
King City, Ontario
Canada L7B 1A4
PH: (905) 833-5311
FAX: (905) 833-2912

Owners
Craig Rose

Cuisine
Continental

Days Open
Open Mon.-Fri. for lunch, Mon.-Sat. for dinner

Pricing
Dinner for one, without tax, tip, or drinks: $40-$60

Dress Code
Smart casual

Reservations
Recommended

Parking
Free on site, garage nearby

Features
Private room/parties, outdoor dining, entertainment, wine and guest chef events

Credit Cards
AE, VC, MC, CB, DC, ER

Biagio Ristorante

Dining room

Directions

Lombard St.
Adelaide St.
Church St.
Jarvis St.
King St.
Wellington
Front St.

On King Street East at Jarvis, 40 min. from Pearson International Airport

155 King Street East
Toronto, Ontario, Canada
M5C 1G9
PH: (416) 366-4040
FAX: (416) 366-4765
www.biagio.tordine.net

Owners
Biagio Vinci

Cuisine
Authentic Italian

Days Open
Open Mon.-Fri. for lunch, Mon.-Sat. for dinner

Pricing
Dinner for one, without tax, tip, or drinks: $60-$80

Dress Code
Casual

Reservations
Recommended

Parking
Garage nearby

Features
Private room/parties, outdoor dining

Credit Cards
AE, VC, MC, DC

Historic St. Lawrence Hall forms the backdrop of this classically elegant restaurant with an authentic Italian pedigree. The long menu, expertly executed by Chef Gianpiero Tondina, draws mainly from Northern Italy with risotti and fresh pastas as its specialties. Don't skip dessert — the lineup is delectable and memorable. Choose a selection from Biagio's extensive wine list. The vintages are varied with a predominance of great Italian wines.

Biagio's private wine cellar

Biagio Vinci

Executive Chef Gianpiero Tondina

AWARD WINNER
SINCE 1995

Chiaro's

Main dining room

Chiaro's is the definition of superb dining. Executive Chef John Higgins' inventive cuisine reflects his classical European training and influences gleaned from his global travels with Culinary Team Canada. Higgins, who also worked for Britain's Royal Family at Buckingham Palace, uses only the freshest and very best ingredients in all his menus. Exquisite service and more than 400 exciting wines complete this unique dining experience.

Executive Chef John Higgins

King Edward Lobby

AWARD WINNER SINCE 1993

Directions

Yonge St.
Church St.
Richmond St.
Adelaide St.
King St.
Wellington St.

At the Le Royal Meridien King Edward Hotel on King Street E. between Yonge and Church streets, 20 min. from Pearson International Airport

37 King Street E.
Toronto, Ontario
Canada M5C 1E9
PH: (416) 863-3131
FAX: (416) 367-5515

Owners
Forte Hotels

Cuisine
International

Days Open
Open Mon.-Sat. for dinner

Pricing
Dinner for one,
without tax, tip, or drinks:
$80+

Dress Code
Business casual

Reservations
Recommended

Parking
Complimentary valet

Features
Private parties, near theater, chef's tables

Credit Cards
AE, VC, MC, CB, DC, ER

Far Niente

The bar

Directions

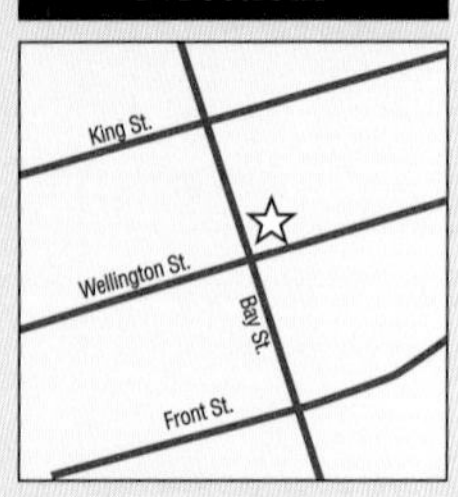

In financial district two blocks from the Air Canada Centre, 40 min. from Lester B. Pearson International Airport

187 Bay St., Commerce Court Station, P.O. Box 517
Toronto, Ontario
Canada M5L 1G5
PH: (416) 214-9922
FAX: (416) 214-1895
www.toronto.com/farniente

Owners
Hieu Nguyen

Cuisine
California grilled

Days Open
Open Mon.-Fri. for lunch, daily for dinner

Pricing
Dinner for one, without tax, tip, or drinks: $20-$40

Dress Code
Business casual

Reservations
Recommended

Parking
Validated on site after 5:30

Features
Private parties, outdoor dining, near theater, cigar/cognac events

Credit Cards
AE, VC, MC, DC, ER

In the heart of Toronto's financial district lies Far Niente, an exceptional steak and seafood house. Executive Chef Hugh Kerr offers distinctive California grilled cuisine, award-winning "Living Well" entrees, and decadent desserts created daily from the bakery. Select a wine from the 10,000-bottle cellar to complement the meal. Specialties include grilled ahi tuna steak, served with charred California zucchini, yellow squash, Bermuda onions, sweet peppers, Kalamata olives, and basil-infused olive oil.

The dining room

From the 10,000-bottle wine cellar

AWARD WINNER
SINCE 1999

La Fenice

Main dining room

La Fenice offers traditional Italian cuisine with regional and seasonal highlights, beautifully enhanced by the simplicity and purity of the ingredients. Fresh grilled fish, wonderful pastas and risottos, game, and truffles in season are among the specialties. La Fenice is a must for theatergoers, a destination for tourists, and a mecca for gourmets. Adrianó will be pleased to share a special wine bin selection.

AWARD WINNER
SINCE 1997

Directions

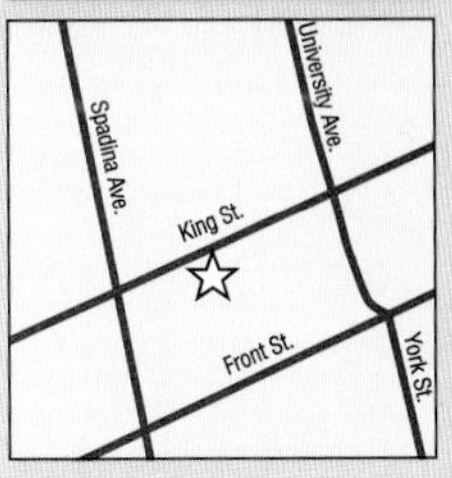

At King and John streets downtown, 30 min. from Pearson International Airport

319 King Street West
Toronto, Ontario M5V 1J5
PH: (416) 585-2377
FAX: (416) 585-2709

Owners
Luigi Orgera

Cuisine
Italian

Days Open
Open Mon.-Fri. for lunch, Mon.-Sat. for dinner

Pricing
Dinner for one, without tax, tip, or drinks: $40-$60

Dress Code
Business casual

Reservations
Recommended

Parking
Garage nearby

Features
Private room/parties, near theater

Credit Cards
AE, VC, MC, DC, ER

Prego della Piazza

The Enoteca Room

Sophisticated, confident, and glamorous, Prego della Piazza looks onto a tented piazza nestled against the Church of the Redeemer. Owner Michael Carlevale has gathered a team of seasoned professionals providing first-rate service and a kitchen founded on the ingredients, style, and techniques of Italian cooking. Located in Toronto's upscale shopping district, the outstanding eatery is enjoying its 14th year.

Owner Michael Carlevale

Directions

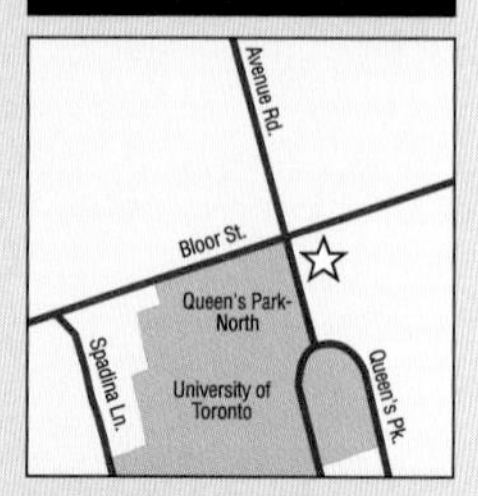

On Bloor Street West between Yonge Street and Avenue Road, 30 min. from Pearson International Airport

150 Bloor Street W.
Toronto, Ontario
Canada M5S 2X9
PH: (416) 920-9900
FAX: (416) 920-9949

Owners
Michael E. Carlevale

Cuisine
Continental Italian

Days Open
Open Mon.-Sat. for lunch, daily for dinner

Pricing
Dinner for one, without tax, tip, or drinks: $20-$40

Dress Code
Business casual

Reservations
Recommended

Parking
Garage nearby (2 hours free at lunch with validation, free at dinner)

Features
Private room/parties, outdoor dining, entertainment, near theater, cigar/cognac events

Credit Cards
AE, VC, MC, DC, ER

AWARD WINNER
SINCE 1995

360 Restaurant at the CN Tower

The dining room

This outstanding restaurant offers fine cuisine, impeccable service, and an internationally recognized wine cellar of nearly 500 choice labels. Feast on traditional items, such as Canadian AAA prime rib of beef and braised lamb shank, or savor a selection of seafood like fresh crab, mussels, lobster, or smoked fish. Add the spectacular view, and you have an eatery like no other. Dining at 360 is an absolute must when visiting Toronto.

Stuffed saddle of rabbit

Dark chocolate tower

Intimate dining

AWARD WINNER SINCE 1997

Directions

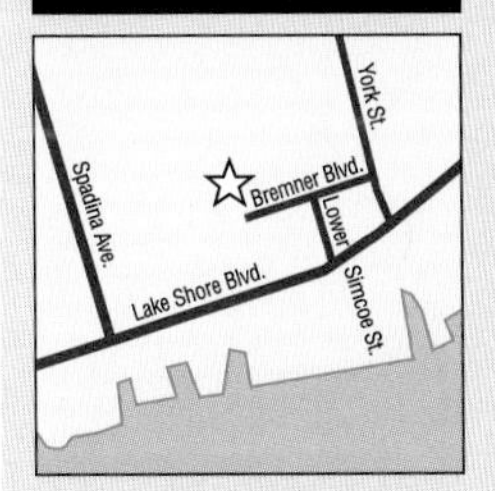

On Front Street West downtown, just north of Bremner Boulevard, 30 min. from Pearson International Airport

301 Front Street West
Toronto, Ontario
Canada M5V 2T6
PH: (416) 362-5411
FAX: (416) 601-4722
www.cntower.ca

Owners
CN Tower

Cuisine
International

Days Open
Open daily for dinner (brunch and lunch in summer only)

Pricing
Dinner for one, without tax, tip, or drinks: $40-$60

Dress Code
Business casual

Reservations
Recommended

Parking
Garage nearby

Features
Private parties

Credit Cards
AE, VC, MC, DC, ER, JCB

Café Henry Burger

Directions

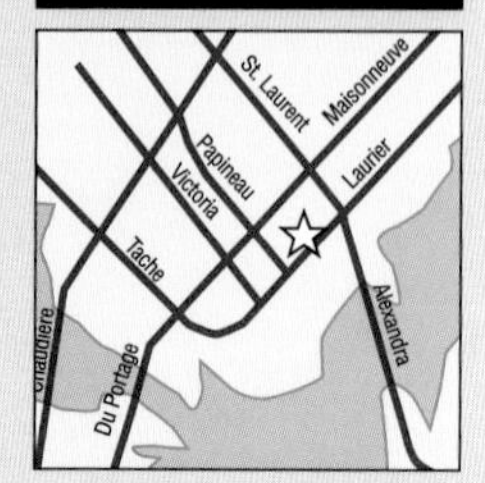

Adjacent to the Canadian Museum of Civilization, 25 min. from Ottawa (Macdonald-Cartier) International Airport

69 Rue Laurier
Hull, Quebec
Canada J8X 3V7
PH: (819) 777-5646
FAX: (819) 777-0832
www.cafehenryburger.com

Owners
Robert C. Bourassa

Cuisine
French seasonal

Days Open
Open Mon.-Fri. for lunch, daily for dinner

Pricing
Dinner for one, without tax, tip, or drinks: $20-$40

Dress Code
Business casual

Reservations
Recommended

Parking
Free on site

Features
Private room/parties, outdoor dining

Credit Cards
AE, VC, MC, DC, ER, JCB

Turn-of-the-century charm

In the oldest restaurant in the National Capital Region and one of the oldest in Canada, a tradition of excellence set by Marie and Henry Burger continues. Refined cuisine, impeccable service, and elegant surroundings... it's easy to see why Café Henry Burger is still the preferred rendezvous of diplomats, politicians, artists, and connoisseurs. The spring/summer menu offers the scents and flavors of Provence; the autumn menu features a variety of game and foods of the harvest; and wintertime brings light and hearty fare from Quebec and France. The establishment is near the Parliament buildings and Hull Casino.

Elegant four-course dinner

Chef-proprietor Robert C. Bourassa

At your service

AWARD WINNER
SINCE 1992

Restaurant Le Mitoyen

Owner Richard Bastien and his staff

For more than 20 years, this award-winning restaurant, ensconced in the owner's ancestral home, has offered its guests quality service and a generous, varied menu. Owner and Executive Chef Richard Bastien prepares such specialties as roast rack of Quebec lamb with fennel puree, and medallions of caribou with raspberries and cranberries. The charm of Restaurant Le Mitoyen will enhance both an intimate dinner or a business gathering.

Award-winning French cuisine

Owner Richard Bastien is also the executive chef

Front entrance

AWARD WINNER SINCE 1992

Directions

Vers 148 Ouest
Boul. St.-Martin Ouest
Place publique
Autoroute 13
Autoroute Des Laurentide 15

In Laval on Place Publique, 20 min. from Montreal's Dorval International Airport

652 Place Publique
Ste-Dorothée, Laval,
Quebec, Canada H7X 1G1
PH: (450) 689-2977
FAX: (450) 689-0385

Owners
Richard Bastien

Cuisine
French

Days Open
Open Tues.-Sun. for dinner

Pricing
Dinner for one,
without tax, tip, or drinks:
$20-$40

Dress Code
Casual

Reservations
Recommended

Parking
Free on site

Features
Private room/parties,
outdoor dining

Credit Cards
AE, VC, MC, DC, ER

The Beaver Club

Elegant surroundings

Recognized as one of Canada's very best tables, the legendary Beaver Club offers a culinary adventure you won't soon forget. Taste a legend and experience the unique and innovative gourmet cuisine promoting the best of local Canadian ingredients which for four consecutive years has earned this storied establishment the Five Star Mobil Travel Guide rating.

Executive Chef Alain Pignard

Directions

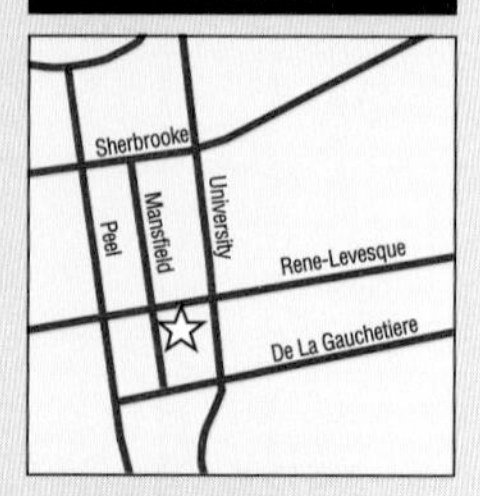

In The Queen Elizabeth Hotel, 30 min. from Dorval International Airport

900 René-Levesque Boulevard West
Montreal, Quebec, Canada
H3B 4A5
PH: (514) 861-3511
FAX: (514) 954-2873
www.cphotels.ca
www.fairnmont.com

Owners
The Queen Elizabeth Hotel

Cuisine
Haute cuisine using Canadian products

Days Open
Open Mon.-Fri. for lunch, Tues.-Sat, for dinner

Pricing
Dinner for one, without tax, tip, or drinks: $40-$60

Dress Code
Jacket and tie required

Reservations
Recommended

Parking
Garage nearby

Features
Private parties, entertainment on Sat.

Credit Cards
AE, VC, MC, CB, DC, ER, DS

AWARD WINNER SINCE 1993

Chez La Mère Michel

Wine cellar dining room

Since 1965, Montreal denizens and visitors have enjoyed the best in classic French cooking at Chez La Mère Michel. The exceptional quality of its cuisine and service has won rave reviews from restaurant critics everywhere, and garnered the Mobil Four Star rating, one of the highest gastronomic awards. For special dining events, a private room is available, and the wine cellar can be reserved for receptions and wine tasting.

Les crêpes Suzette flambée

The spring is back

Decanting good wine

AWARD WINNER
SINCE 1993

Directions

On Rue Guy between Ste. Catherine and René-Levesque, 15 min. from Dorval International Airport

1209 Rue Guy
Montreal, Quebec
Canada H3H 2K5
PH: (514) 934-0473
FAX: (514) 939-0709

Owners
Micheline and
René Delbuguet

Cuisine
Classical French

Days Open
Open Mon.-Sat. for lunch and dinner

Pricing
Dinner for one,
without tax, tip, or drinks:
$60-$80

Dress Code
Business casual

Reservations
Recommended

Parking
Lot nearby

Features
Private room/parties, near theater

Credit Cards
AE, VC, MC, DC, ER, JCB

Le Passe-Partout Restaurant

An authentic taste of Quebec

Le Passe-Partout, minutes from downtown Montreal, serves French market cuisine in intimate, elegant surroundings. The dining room is decorated with contemporary prints and sculptures. Co-owner and Executive Chef James J. MacGuire prepares everything fresh, from the breads to desserts, and is careful that every item retains the authentic taste of the region. Specialties include smoked salmon and homemade paté. The wine list is carefully chosen.

Elegant atmosphere

Intimate dining

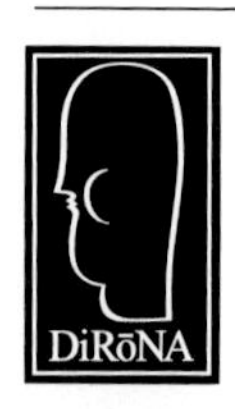

AWARD WINNER
SINCE 1993

Directions

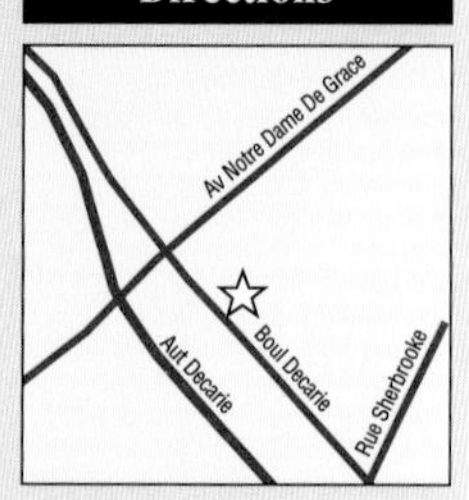

Two blocks north of Sherbrooke Street, 10 min. from Dorval International Airport

3857 Boulevard Décarie
Montreal, Quebec H4A 3J6
PH: (514) 487-7750
FAX: (514) 487-5673

Owner
James J. MacGuire and Suzanne Baron-Lafreniére

Cuisine
French market

Days Open
Open Tues.-Fri. for lunch, Thurs.-Sat. for dinner

Pricing
Dinner for one, without tax, tip, or drinks: $40-$60

Dress Code
Business casual

Reservations
Recommended

Parking
Free on site

Features
Private room/parties, art gallery

Credit Cards
AE, VC, MC, DC, ER, JCB

Le Piment Rouge

Main dining room

Don't be fooled by the French name—the cuisine at Le Piment Rouge is haute Chinese, with a focus on Szechuan specialties. Owners Hazel and Chuck Mah are the recipients of numerous international awards, and their restaurant, located in the historic Windsor Building in the heart of downtown Montreal with panoramic views of Dominion Square, has been called "the most elegant Chinese restaurant in the whole of Canada" by the *Montreal Gazette*. The atmosphere is elegant and relaxing, the service is courteous and efficient, and the wine collection is stunning.

The wine cellar

The bar

Reception area

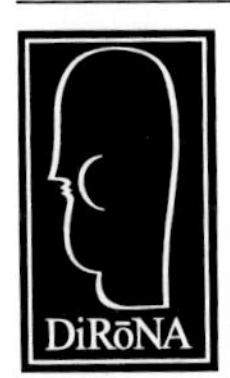

AWARD WINNER SINCE 1996

Directions

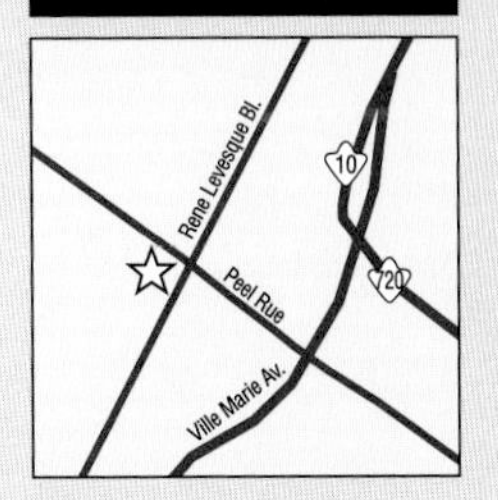

In the Windsor Building downtown, 20 min. from Dorval International Airport

1170 Peel Street
Montreal, Quebec, Canada
H3B 4P2
PH: (514) 866-7816
FAX: (514) 866-1575

Owners
Hazel and Chuck Mah

Cuisine
Haute Chinese

Days Open
Open daily for lunch and dinner

Pricing
Dinner for one, without tax, tip, or drinks: $40-$60

Dress Code
Business casual

Reservations
Recommended

Parking
Garage nearby

Features
Private room/parties, entertainment

Credit Cards
AE, VC, MC, DC, ER, JCB

Restaurant Les Halles

Directions

Rue de la Montagne
Rue Sherbrooke
Boul. Maisonneuve
Rue Ste-Catherine
Rue Crescent
Rue Bishop

In the center of Montreal, 30 min. from Dorval International Airport

1450 Rue Crescent
Montreal, Quebec
Canada H3G 2BG
PH: (514) 844-2328
FAX: (514) 849-1294
www.restaurantleshalles.com

Owners
Ita and Jacques Landurie

Cuisine
French

Days Open
Open Mon.-Sat. for dinner

Pricing
Dinner for one,
without tax, tip, or drinks:
$40-$60

Dress Code
Business casual

Reservations
Recommended

Parking
Lot nearby

Features
Private rooms

Credit Cards
AE, VC, MC, CB, DC, ER, JCB, DS

Downstairs dining area

Les Halles is a seamless, sensuous must for aficionados of the art of fine dining. During its history in the century-old greystone, honors have been heaped upon this establishment, including the coveted Le Trophé Ulysse, crowning it the people's choice as Montreal's finest gourmet restaurant. Themed after the Old Market in Paris, Les Halles has undergone a joyful rejuvenation. A formidable wine cellar complements the seasonal cuisine with 400 different wines.

French cuisine

Executive Chef Dominique Crevoisier

Owners Jacques and Ita Landurie

AWARD WINNER
SINCE 1994

Auberge Hatley

A charming country house with magnificent views of Lake Massawippi, Auberge Hatley, a member of Relais & Chateaux, is the 2000 Gold Table Award winner as the best restaurant in Quebec. The French menu features seasonal entrees using fresh produce from the greenhouses on the premises. A popular specialty is the tournedos of duck with sauteed escalope of fresh foie gras and wild berry sauce. The award-winning wine list carries more than 1,000 labels.

Warm surroundings

Scallops with watercress and lemongrass sauce

Patio dining

AWARD WINNER
SINCE 1993

Directions

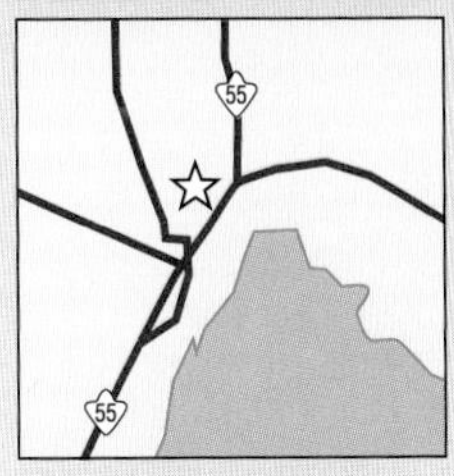

On Virgin Hill in North Hatley, 20 miles north of the Vermont border and 2 hrs. from Montreal's Dorval International Airport

325 Virgin Hill
P.O. Box 330
North Hatley, Quebec,
Canada JOB 2C0
PH: (819) 842-2451
FAX: (819) 842-2907
www.relaischateaux.fr/hatley

Owners
Robert and Liliane Gagnon

Cuisine
French

Days Open
Open daily for breakfast and dinner

Pricing
Dinner for one,
without tax, tip, or drinks:
$40-$60

Dress Code
Business casual

Reservations
Required

Parking
Free on site

Features
Private room/parties

Credit Cards
AE, VC, MC

Le Champlain

Directions

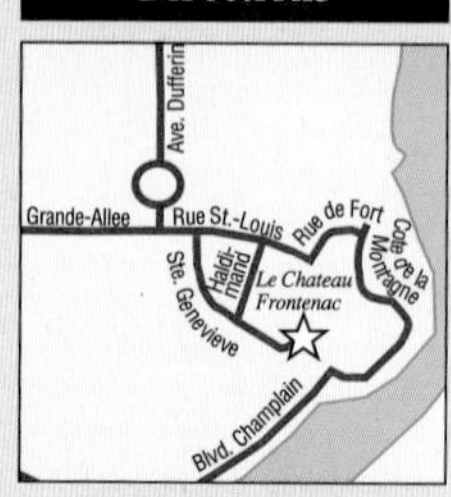

In the Chateau Frontenac, 20 min. from International Airport Jean-Lesage

Chateau Frontenac
1 Rue des Carrieres
Quebec City, Quebec,
Canada G1R 4P5
PH: (418) 692-3861
FAX: (418) 692-4353
www.fairmont.ca

Owners
Canadian Pacific Hotels

Cuisine
Classic French

Days Open
Open daily for dinner (Tues.-Sat. in winter), Sun. brunch year-round

Pricing
Dinner for one, without tax, tip, or drinks: $40-$60

Dress Code
Jacket/tie requested

Reservations
Recommended

Parking
Valet

Features
Private room/parties, near theater

Credit Cards
AE, VC, MC, CB, DC, ER, JCB, DS

Attentive wait staff

Inside the renowned Chateau Frontenac, this stately dining room overlooking the St. Lawrence River is steeped in Canada's illustrious French heritage. Under the enlightened direction of world-renowned Master Chef Jean Soulard, the freshest of local ingredients marry the flavors of the past with the sophistication of the present. Wait staff, dressed in delightful period costumes, take guests a step back in time and offer gracious service. On weekends the soft tones of harp music enhance the atmosphere. Chef Soulard, who has his own TV show, has just published his third cookbook.

Master Chef Jean Soulard

The historic Chateau Frontenac

AWARD WINNER
SINCE 1993

L' Eau a la Bouche

Hotel L' Eau a la Bouche

At L' Eau a la Bouche, nestled in the Laurentian Mountains, co-owner and Executive Chef Anne Desjardins prepares delicious regional French cuisine in a beautiful setting. Tuna, quail, pork, rack of lamb, beef fillet, and venison loin are among the freshly made entrees. The wine selection is outstanding.

Chef/Owner Anne Desjardins

The dining room

A superior room at the inn

AWARD WINNER
SINCE 1993

Directions

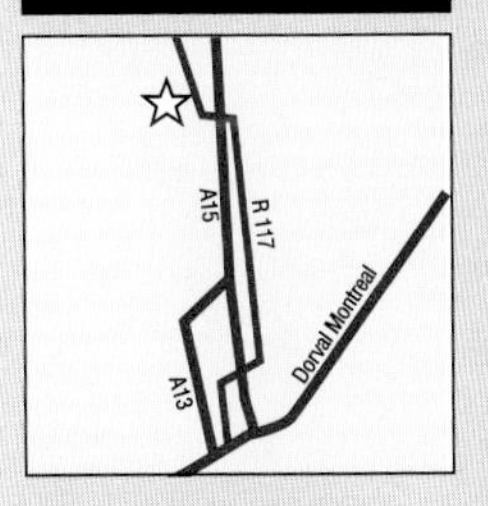

In the village of Sainte-Adèle, 60 min. from Montreal's Dorval International Airport

3003 BD Ste.-Adèle
Sainte-Adèle, Quebec
Canada J8B 2N6
PH: (450) 229-2991
FAX: (450) 229-7573
www.
relaischateaux.fr/eaubouche

Owners
Anne Desjardins and Pierre Audette

Cuisine
French

Days Open
Open daily for breakfast and dinner

Pricing
Dinner for one, without tax, tip, or drinks: $60-$80

Dress Code
Business casual

Reservations
Required

Parking
Free

Features
Private room/parties, entertainment, near theater

Credit Cards
AE, VC, MC, DC, ER

Ristorante Michelangelo

Directions

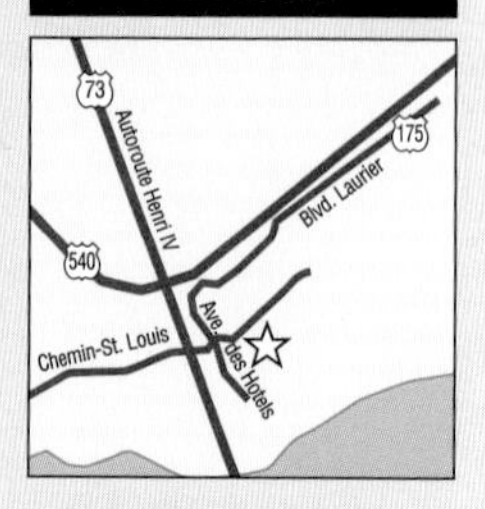

Located near city access bridges, 10 min. from International Airport Jean-Lesage

3111 Chemin Saint-Louis
Sainte Foy, Quebec
Canada G1W 1R6
PH: (418) 651-6262
FAX: (418) 651-6771
www.ristomichelangelo.com

Owners
Nicola Cortina

Cuisine
Italian

Days Open
Open Mon.-Fri. for lunch, Mon.-Sun. for dinner

Pricing
Dinner for one, without tax, tip, or drinks: $60-$80

Dress Code
Business casual

Reservations
Recommended

Parking
Valet

Features
Private room/parties, outdoor dining, complimentary limo service

Credit Cards
AE, VC, MC, DC, ER

Exquisite gardens

Located near the bridges that access the city, the Michelangelo's first-class dining room charms guests with its intimate, elegant atmosphere and Art Deco style. The extensive wine list (1,000 selections), high-quality food, and excellent service are a must for visitors. It has won *Wine Spectator's* Award of Excellence in 1997 and 1998 and has been named one of the few genuine Italian restaurants outside the country by the Italian government.

Main dining room

Lounge

Lobby

AWARD WINNER SINCE 1999

Las Mañanitas

Garden surroundings

Directions

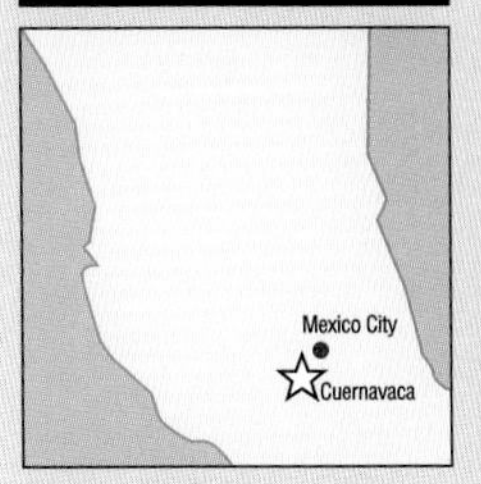

In Cuernavaca, 1 1/2 hr. from Mexico City International Airport

Ricardo Linares 107
Col. Centro
Cuernavaca, Morelos,
Mexico 62000
PH: 011-52-73-14-14-66
FAX: 011-52-73-18-36-72
www.lasmananitas.com.mx

Owners
Margot Krause and Ruben Cerda

Cuisine
International

Days Open
Open daily for lunch and dinner

Pricing
Dinner for one, without tax, tip, or drinks: $20-$40

Dress Code
Business casual

Reservations
Required

Parking
Valet

Features
Private room/parties, outdoor dining, entertainment

Credit Cards
AE

Exquisite gardens populated with exotic birds set the scene for this beloved restaurant in Cuernavaca, called "the city of eternal spring" by the Aztecs. For more than four decades, Las Mañanitas–a member of the Relais & Chateaux collection of luxury hostelries–has been the worthy recipient of various awards. The menu, featuring Mexican and international cuisine, offers a wide selection of culinary delights, and the staff of over 150 are trained to satisfy the customer's every whim.

Red snapper cappy

Ruben Cerda

AWARD WINNER
SINCE 1993

La Embotelladora Vieja

Directions

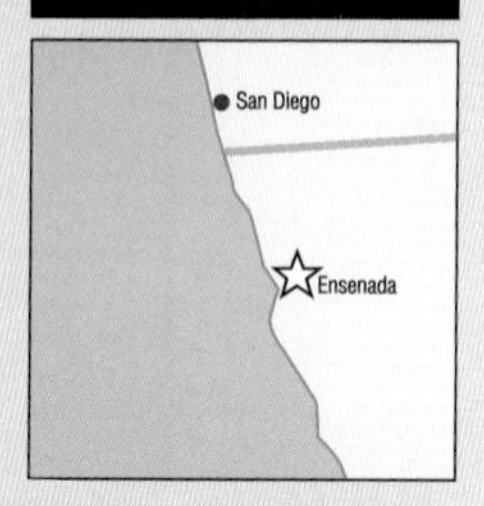

At Miramar and 7th streets in Ensenada, 1 hr. 30 min. from San Diego International Airport

666 Miramar Zona Centro
Ensenada, Baja California,
Mexico 22800
PH: (011) 52-61-74-08-07
FAX: (011) 52-61-78-16-60
www.santotomas.com.mx

Owners
Bodegas Santo Tomas

Cuisine
Mediterranean/Mexican

Days Open
Open daily (except Tues.) for lunch and dinner

Pricing
Dinner for one, without tax, tip, or drinks: $20-$40

Dress Code
Casual

Reservations
Recommended

Parking
Free on site

Features
Private parties, cigar/cognac events

Credit Cards
AE, VC, MC

Main dining room

La Embotelladora Vieja is in the heart of Ensenada, where the Santo Tomas winery was once located. The enormous wooden casks dating to the 1880's create an old-style ambience. The chef has created a menu inspired by local and Mediterranean flavors. The award-winning wine list includes the entire spectrum of Mexican wines.

Fine Mexican wines

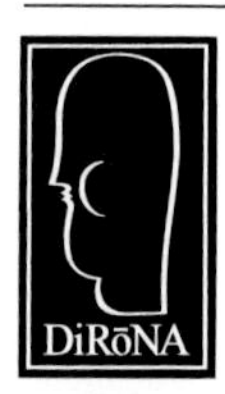

AWARD WINNER
SINCE 1999

Antiguo San Angel Inn

Ancient hacienda

Guests at Antiguo San Angel Inn, housed in an old Carmelite monastery, dine on delicious Mexican gourmet food and international cuisine amid beautiful gardens set with flowers and fountains. Specialties include sea bass Veracruz style, chicken with mole poblano, and roast duckling in blackberry sauce. Often a favorite of celebrities, the establishment is an ideal choice for special occasions.

Dining by fountain

Jumbo shrimp with Pernot

Relaxing patio

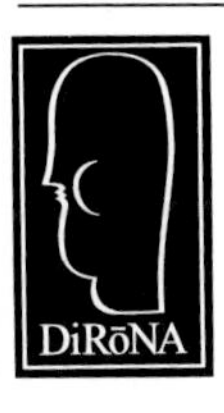

AWARD WINNER
SINCE 1994

Directions

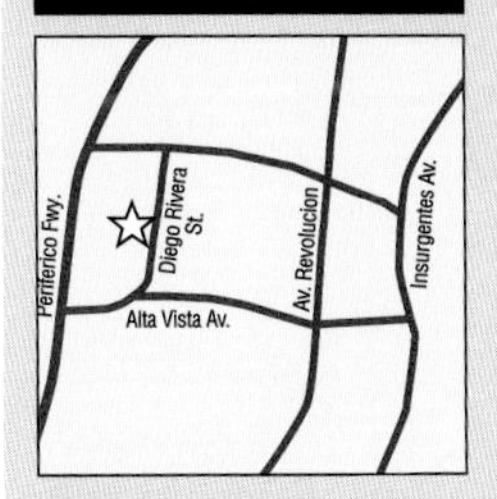

45 min. from Benito Juarez International Airport

Diego Rivera No. 50
Mexico D.F. 01060
PH: 011-52–56-16-14-02
FAX: 011-52-56-16-09-77
www.sanangelinn.com

Owners
Partnership

Cuisine
International

Days Open
Open daily for lunch and dinner

Pricing
Dinner for one, without tax, tip, or drinks: $20-$40

Dress Code
Jacket and tie required

Reservations
Recommended

Parking
Free on site, valet

Features
Private room/parties, outdoor dining, entertainment

Credit Cards
AE, VC, MC, DC, JCB

Estoril

Directions

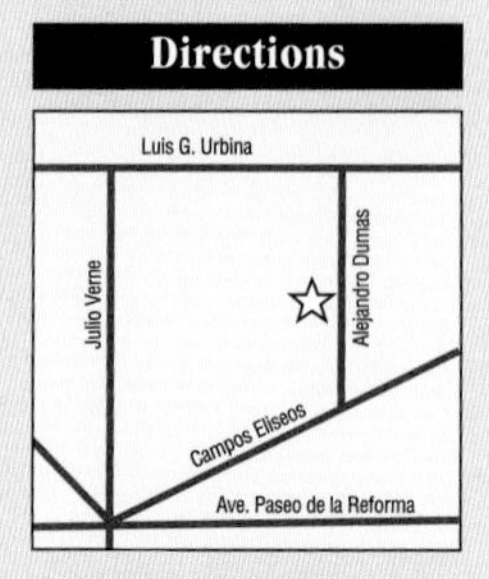

30 min. from Benito Juarez International Airport

Alejandro Dumas No. 24
Polanco
11560 Mexico, DF
PH: 011-52-52-80-34-14
011-52-52-80-98-28
FAX: 011-52-52-80-93-11
www.estorilmex.com

Owners
Rosa Martin and Guillaume Martin de Giau

Cuisine
Fusion

Days Open
Open Mon.-Sat. for lunch and dinner

Pricing
Dinner for one,
without tax, tip, or drinks:
$40-$60

Dress Code
Jacket and tie preferred

Reservations
Recommended

Parking
Free on site, valet

Features
Private room/parties, cigar/cognac events

Credit Cards
AE, VC, MC, DC

Since its establishment in 1971, Estoril has been the chosen meeting place for the most interesting personalities of modern Mexico. Upscale cuisine, prepared by Chef Pedro Ortega, a blend of gastronomic cultures, and the creative talent of the restaurant's founder, supply the ideal frame for an impeccable business meal or an intimate dinner among friends in a refined environment.

Scrumptious dining

Elegant surroundings

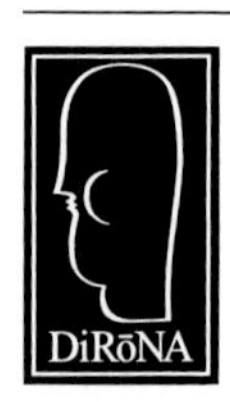

AWARD WINNER
SINCE 1993

La Cava

A dining tradition since 1954

La Cava is a palatial yet inviting restaurant with breathtaking vistas and exciting international fare. Some of the most famous Mexican cuisine is impeccably created and served here. Tantalizing Spanish, French, Italian, and Mediterranean cuisine are also offered. Specialties of the house include, flaming skewered quails and roast duckling in aged wine sauce. The wait staff is personable, knowledgeable, and willing to assist in any way to make your visit a memorable one.

Elegant surroundings

AWARD WINNER
SINCE 1993

Directions

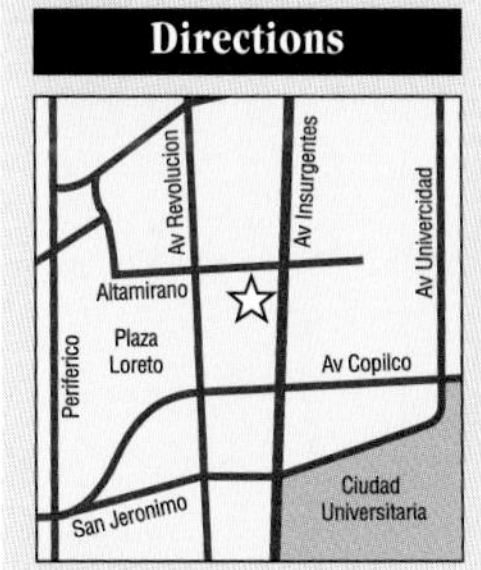

Cross streets: Altamirano and Avenida Insurgentes Sur, 40 min from Aeropuerto Benito Juarez

Avenida Insurgentes Sur, 2465
Mexico, D.F. 01000
PH: 011-52-55-50-08-52
or, 011-52-55-50-11-06
FAX: 011-52-55-50-38-01

Owner
Jordi Escofet

Cuisine
Mexican and Continental

Days Open
Open daily for lunch, Mon.- Sat. for dinner

Pricing
Dinner for one, without tax, tip, or drinks $20-$40

Dress Code
Business casual

Reservations
Recommended

Features
Private room/parties, entertainment, cigar/ cognac events

Credit Cards
AE, VC, MC, DC

Villa Jacaranda

Directions

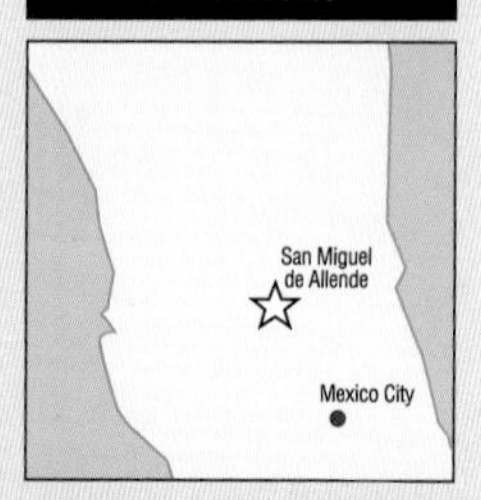

In the town of San Miguel de Allende in central Mexico, 90 min. from Leon International Airport and 3 hr. from Mexico City

Aldama 53
San Miguel de Allende,
Guanajuato, Mexico 37700
PH: 011-52-41-52-10-15
FAX: 011-52-41-52-08-83
www.villajacaranda.com

Owners
Donald Fenton

Cuisine
International

Days Open
Open daily for breakfast, lunch, and dinner

Pricing
Dinner for one, without tax, tip, or drinks: $20-$40

Dress Code
Casual

Reservations
Recommended

Parking
Free on site

Features
Private room/parties, outdoor dining, entertainment, near theater

Credit Cards
AE, VC, MC, JCB

Colonial charm

On the high plateau of central Mexico, Villa Jacaranda is a converted Colonial mansion on a quiet cobblestone street, where the discerning traveler will find serenity and impeccable dining reminiscent of a fine European inn. For more than 25 years, Villa Jacaranda's chefs have created international gourmet fare and authentic Mexican specialties from fresh, organically grown ingredients and the finest meats and seafoods available. Poblano chilies stuffed with meats, pecans, and raisins and covered with pecan sauce is one unforgettable dish.

International cuisine

Serene surroundings

Intimate dining

AWARD WINNER
SINCE 1993

Index of Recipients

103 West (Atlanta, GA) 124
208 Talbot (St. Michaels, MD) 162
360 Restaurant at the CN Tower (Toronto, Ontario) 341
701 Restaurant (Washington, DC) 75
1109 South Main (Anderson, SC) 280
1789 (Washington, DC) 76
The 1848 House (Atlanta, GA) 120

A

The Abbey (Atlanta, GA) 116
Alberini's (Niles, OH) 256
Alison on Dominick Street (New York, NY) 222
Al's (St. Louis, MO) 190
Ambria (Chicago, IL) 133
The American Hotel (Sag Harbor, NY) 252
Anaheim White House (Anaheim, CA) 28
Andrea's Restaurant (Metairie, LA) 147
Andre's French Restaurant (Las Vegas, NV) 198
The Angus Barn (Raleigh, NC) 255
Anthony's in the Catalinas (Tucson, AZ) 6
Anthony's Pier 4 (Boston, MA) 164
Anthony's Star of the Sea (San Diego, CA) 48
Antiguo San Angel Inn (Mexico City, Mexico) 355
Antrim 1844 (Taneytown MD) 163
The Anuenue Room (Maui, HI) 130
Appennino Ristorante (Allentown, PA) 265
Aquavit (New York, NY) 223
Armani's (Tampa, FL) 111
Arnaud's Restaurant (New Orleans, LA) 148
Arthur's (Nashville, TN) 289
Arturo's Ristorante Italiano (Boca Raton, FL) 81
Arun's (Chicago, IL) 134
Atlantis (Orlando, FL) 98
Atwaters Restaurant & Bar (Portland, OR) 264
Auberge Hatley (North Hatley, Quebec) 349
Aureole (New York, NY) 224

B

Bali by-the-Sea (Honolulu, HI) 128
Barbetta (New York, NY) 225
The Baricelli Inn (Cleveland, OH) 260
Bartolotta's Lake Park Bistro (Milwaukee, WI) 321
Bayona (New Orleans, LA) 149
Beano's Cabin (Beaver Creek, CO) 54
Beau Rivage (Medford, NJ) 210
The Beaver Club (Montreal, Quebec) 344
Bedford Village Inn (Bedford, NH) 206
Benedetto's Ristorante (St. Louis, MO) 191
The Bernards Inn (Bernardsville, NJ) 209
Bern's Steak House (Tampa, FL) 112
Beverly's Restaurant (Coeur d'Alene, ID) 131
Biagio Ristorante (Toronto, Ontario) 336
Biba (Sacramento, CA) 16
Bistro at Maison de Ville (New Orleans, LA) 150
The Black Pearl (Dunedin, FL) 86
Bob's Steak & Chop House (Dallas, TX) 293
Bombay Club (Washington, DC) 68
Bone's Restaurant (Atlanta, GA) 117
Brennan's of Houston (Houston, TX) 297
Briarhurst Manor (Manitou Springs, CO) 60
Brooks Restaurant (Deerfield Beach, FL) 85
Broussard's Restaurant (New Orleans, LA) 151
Burt & Jack's (Fort Lauderdale, FL) 87

C

Cafe Allegro (Kansas City, MO) 189
The Café Budapest (Boston, MA) 165
Cafe Del Rey (Marina del Rey, CA) 39
Café du Soir (Vero Beach, FL) 114
Café Henry Burger (Hull, Quebec) 342
Cafe L'Europe (Palm Beach, FL) 103
Café L'Europe (Sarasota, FL) 109
Café Pacific (Dallas, TX) 294
Café Portofino (Lihue, HI) 129
Café 36 (LaGrange, IL) 139
Caffe de Medici (Vancouver, British Columbia) 327
Campagne (Seattle, WA) 317
Canlis (Seattle, WA) 318
Capriccio Ristorante (Pembroke Pines, FL) 106
Carlos' Restaurant (Highland Park, IL) 138

Index of Recipients

Cavey's Restaurant (Manchester, CT) 66
The Cellar (Fullerton, CA) 35
The Chancellor Grille Room (Palm Beach, FL) 104
Chanterelle (Eugene, OR) 262
The Chanticleer (Siasconset, MA) 175
The Chaparral (Scottsdale, AZ) 3
Charles Court (Colorado Springs, CO) 56
Charleston Grill (Charleston, SC) 281
Chef Allen's (Aventura, FL) 80
Chez La Mère Michel (Montreal, Quebec) 345
Chez Nous (Houston, TX) 298
Chez Philippe (Memphis, TN) 286
Chiaro's (Toronto, Ontario) 337
Chillingsworth (Brewster, MA) 172
Chops (Atlanta, GA) 118
Christian's Restaurant (New Orleans, LA) 152
Ciao Europa (New York, NY) 226
Ciboulette (Philadelphia, PA) 271
Cité (New York, NY) 227
Clay Hill Farm (York, ME) 157
Clifton – The Country Inn and Estate (Charlottesville, VA) 311
Coco Pazzo (Chicago, IL) 135
The Colony Dining Room (Longboat Key, FL) 92
Columbus Inn (Wilmington, DE) 67
The Covey (Carmel, CA) 8
Coyote Cafe (Santa Fe, NM) 218
The Crow's Nest (Anchorage, AK) 1

D

Dal Baffo (Menlo Park, CA) 13
D'Amico Cucina (Minneapolis, MN) 184
Da Mimmo Finest Italian Cuisine (Baltimore, MD) 159
Daniel (New York, NY) 228
The Dan'l Webster Inn (Sandwich, MA) 174
Darrel & Oliver's Café Maxx (Pompano Beach, FL) 107
Diamond's (Trenton, NJ) 213
Dilworthtown Inn (West Chester, PA) 277
The Dining Room at Ford's Colony (Williamsburg, VA) 316
The Dining Room, Hilton at Short Hills (Short Hills, NJ) 212
The Dining Room, Ritz-Carlton, Boston (Boston, MA) 166
The Dining Room, Ritz-Carlton, Buckhead ((Atlanta, GA) 119
The Dining Room, Westin Salishan (Gleneden Beach, OR) 263
Dominic's (St. Louis, MO) 192
Donatello (Tampa, FL) 113
Downey's (Santa Barbara, CA) 52
DUX (Orlando, FL) 99

E

El Bizcocho (San Diego, CA) 49
Elysium (Alexandria, VA) 309
The English Room at the Deer Path Inn (Lake Forest, IL) 140
Estoril (Mexico City, Mexico) 356
Euphemia Haye (Longboat Key, FL) 93
EverMay on the Delaware (Erwinna, PA) 267

F

Fairbanks Steakhouse (Robinsonville, MS) 188
Far Niente (Toronto, Ontario) 338
Ferraro's Restaurant (Las Vegas, NV) 199
The Fig Tree (San Antonio, TX) 304
Fior d'Italia (San Francisco, CA) 18
Five Crowns (Corona del Mar, CA) 34
The Five Sails Restaurant (Vancouver, British Columbia) 328
The Florentine (Palm Beach, FL) 105
Folk's Folly Prime Steak House (Memphis, TN) 287
Founders Restaurant (Philadelphia, PA) 272
The Four Seasons (New York, NY) 229
Fournou's Ovens (San Francisco, CA) 19
The Fox & Hounds (Hubertus, WI) 319
The French Room at Hotel Adolphus (Dallas, TX) 295
Fresco Italian Cafe (Salt Lake City, UT) 305
Fresh Cream Restaurant (Monterey, CA) 14
Friends Lake Inn (Chesterton, NY) 221

G

Galatoire's Restaurant (New Orleans, LA) 153
Galileo (Washington, DC) 69
The Garden Restaurant (Philadelphia, PA) 273
Gennaro's Ristorante (Glendale, CA) 36
George's at the Cove (La Jolla, CA) 37
Geronimo (Santa Fe, NM) 219
Giovanni's (St. Louis, MO) 193

Index of Recipients

Giovanni's Ristorante (Detroit, MI) 177
The Glass Chimney Restaurant (Carmel, IN) 142
The Golden Mushroom (Southfield, MI) 182
Goodfellow's (Minneapolis, MN) 185
G.P. Agostino's (St. Louis, MO) 194
Gramercy Tavern (New York, NY) 230
The Granary (Jackson, WY) 323
Grant Grill (San Diego, CA) 50
The Grill on the Alley (Beverly Hills, CA) 32

H

Haifeng (Orlando, FL) 100
Halcyon (New York, NY) 231
Hampton's (Baltimore, MD) 160
Harrah's Steak House (Reno, NV) 203
Harralds (Stormville, NY) 253
Harris' Restaurant (San Francisco, CA) 20
Hasting's Grill (Anaheim, CA) 30
Haydn Zug's (East Petersburg, PA) 266
Hemingway's (Killington, VT) 307
Highlawn Pavilion (West Orange, NJ) 214
The Hobbit (Orange, CA) 43
Hogan's Inn at Four Corners (King City, Ontario) 335
Hyeholde Restaurant (Pittsburgh, PA) 275

I

Icarus (Boston, MA) 167
Il Tartufo on Las Olas (Fort Lauderdale, FL) 88
The Immigrant Restaurant and Winery (Kohler, WI) 320
Imperial Chinese Seafood Restaurant (Vancouver, British Columbia) 329
The Inn at Sawmill Farm (West Dover, VT) 308
Inn on the Twenty (Jordan, Ontario) 334

J

John Mineo's Italian Restaurant (St. Louis, MO) 195
JoJo (New York, NY) 232
JW's Steakhouse (Anaheim, CA) 29

K

Karl Ratzsch's (Milwaukee, WI) 322
Kinkead's, an American Brasserie (Washington, DC) 71

L

La Bergerie (Alexandria, VA) 310
La Bonne Auberge (New Hope, PA) 270
La Caravelle (New York, NY) 233
La Cava (Mexico City, Mexico) 357
La Chaumière (Calgary, Alberta) 324
La Coquina (Orlando, FL) 101
La Cote Basque (New York, NY) 234
La Embotelladora Vieja (Ensenada, Mexico) 354
La Fenice (Toronto, Ontario) 339
La Finestra Restaurant (Boca Raton, FL) 82
Lafite (Naples, FL) 95
Lafitte's Landing Restaurant at Bittersweet Plantation (Donaldsonville, LA) 146
La Folie (San Francisco, CA) 21
La Grotta Ristorante Italiano (Atlanta, GA) 121
Langdon Hall (Cambridge, Ontario) 333
La Panetiere (Rye, NY) 251
La Parisienne (St. Augustine, FL) 108
La Reserve (Houston, TX) 299
The Lark (West Bloomfield, MI) 183
The Lark Creek Inn (Larkspur, CA) 11
Las Mañanitas (Cuernavaca, Mexico) 353
La Tourelle (Memphis, TN) 288
L'Auberge Chez Francois (Great Falls, VA) 312
L'Auberge de Sedona (Sedona, AZ) 5
La Vie en Rose (Brea, CA) 33
L'Eau a la Bouche (Sainte-Adèle, Quebec) 351
Le Central Bistro (San Francisco, CA) 22
Le Champlain (Quebec City, Quebec) 350
Le Cirque 2000 (New York, NY) 235
Left Bank Restaurant (Vail, CO) 61
The Left Bank Restaurant (Halifax, Nova Scotia) 332
Lemaire (Richmond, VA) 314
Le Mouton Noir (Saratoga, CA) 26
Le Passe-Partout Restaurant (Montreal, Quebec) 346
Le Perigord (New York, NY) 236
Le Petit Chateau (North Hollywood, CA) 42

Index of Recipients

Le Piment Rouge (Montreal, Quebec) 347
L'Espalier (Boston, MA) 168
Le Titi de Paris (Arlington Heights, IL) 132
Le Vichyssois (Lakemoor, IL) 141
LG's Prime Steakhouse (Palm Desert, CA) 44
Llewellyn's (Stateline, NV) 205
Locke-Ober (Boston, MA) 169
Lord Fletcher's on Lake Minnetonka (Spring Park, MN) 187
Ludwig's (Vail, CO) 62
Lumière (Vancouver, British Columbia) 330

M

Magnolias (Charleston, SC) 282
Maison & Jardin (Altamonte Springs, FL) 79
Maison Robert (Boston, MA) 170
Maisonette (Cincinnati, OH) 258
Maloney & Porcelli (New York, NY) 237
Manhattan Ocean Club (New York, NY) 238
The Manor (West Orange, NJ) 215
Manuel's on the 28th (Orlando, FL) 102
The Marine Room (La Jolla, CA) 38
Mario's (Nashville, TN) 290
Mark's (Houston, TX) 300
Marker 88 Restaurant (Islamorada, FL) 89
Marquesa (Scottsdale, AZ) 4
Maxim's Restaurant & Piano Bar (Houston, TX) 301
Melvyn's Restaurant (Palm Springs, CA) 45
Metropolitan (Salt Lake City, UT) 306
Michael's (Las Vegas, NV) 200
Michael's on East (Sarasota, FL) 110
Mille Fleurs (Rancho Santa Fe, CA) 47
Mirabelle Restaurant at Beaver Creek (Avon, CO) 55
Mr. Stox (Anaheim, CA) 31
Monte Carlo (Las Vegas, NV) 201
The Monte Carlo Living Room (Philadelphia, PA) 274
Morrison-Clark Inn (Washington, DC) 72

N

Nava (Atlanta, GA) 122
Nikolai's Roof (Atlanta, GA) 123
Northwoods (Annapolis, MD) 158

O

The Oakroom at the Seelbach Hilton (Louisville, KY) 144
Opus One (Detroit, MI) 178
The Orangery (Knoxville, TN) 284
The Oval Room (Washington, DC) 73
The Owl's Nest Dining Room (Calgary, Alberta) 325

P

The Palace Restaurant (Cincinnati, OH) 259
Panico's (New Brunswick, NJ) 211
Pano's & Paul's (Atlanta, GA) 125
Paolo's Restaurant (San Jose, CA) 25
Park Avenue Cafe (New York, NY) 239
Pavilion (Newport Beach, CA) 40
Peacock Alley (New York, NY) 240
Peninsula Grill (Charleston, SC) 283
Peppermill's White Orchid (Reno, NV) 204
Peregrines' (Atlantic City, NJ) 208
Peter Scott's (Longwood, FL) 94
Picholine (New York, NY) 241
Piero's (Las Vegas, NV) 202
The Plumed Horse (Saratoga, CA) 27
Post Hotel Dining Room (Lake Louise, Alberta) 326
The Post House (New York, NY) 242
Prego della Piazza (Toronto, Ontario) 340
Pricci (Atlanta, GA) 126
Primitivo Wine Bar (Colorado Springs, CO) 57
Prince Michel Restaurant (Leon, VA) 313
The Pump House (Fairbanks, AK) 2
The Pump Room (Chicago, IL) 136

R

Raffaello (Carmel, CA) 9
Rainwater's on Kettner (San Diego, CA) 51
Ram's Head Inn (Absecon, NJ) 207
Ranchers Club of New Mexico (Albuquerque, NM) 217
The Rattlesnake Club (Detroit, MI) 179
The Refectory (Columbus, OH) 261
Regas Restaurant (Knoxville, TN) 285
Renaissance (Aspen, CO) 53
Restaurant on the Bay by Marie-Michelle (Naples, FL) 96

Index of Recipients

Restaurant Bouchard (Newport, RI) 278
Restaurant at the Canterbury (Indianapolis, IN) 143
Restaurant Dubrovnik (Winnipeg, Manitoba) 331
Restaurant Le Mitoyen (Laval, Quebec) 343
Restaurant Les Halles (Montreal, Quebec) 348
The Restaurant at Meadowood (St. Helena, CA) 17
Restaurant Passerelle (Radnor, PA) 276
Restaurant Picasso (Edwards, CO) 59
Restaurant St. Michel (Coral Gables, FL) 83
Ristorante Café Cortina (Farmington Hills, MI) 180
Ristorante Giovanni's (Beachwood, OH) 257
Ristorante i Ricchi (Washington, DC) 70
Ristorante La Bussola (Coral Gables, FL) 84
Ristorante Michelangelo (Sainte Foy, Quebec) 352
Ristorante Primavera (New York, NY) 243
The Ritz Restaurant and Garden (Newport Beach, CA) 41
The Riviera (Dallas, TX) 296
Rotisserie for Beef and Bird (Houston, TX) 302
Ruth's Chris Steak House (New Orleans, LA) 154
Ruth's Chris Steak House (North Palm Beach, FL) 97
Ruth's Chris Steak House (Winter Park, FL) 115
The Ryland Inn (Whitehouse, NJ) 216

S

The St. Paul Grill (St. Paul, MN) 186
Sam & Harry's (Washington, DC) 74
San Domenico (New York, NY) 244
The Sardine Factory (Monterey, CA) 15
Scatton's Restaurant (Hazleton, PA) 269
Sea Fare Inn (Portsmouth, RI) 279
The Seventh Inn (St. Louis, MO) 196
Silks (San Francisco, CA) 23
Silks at Stonehedge Inn (Tyngsboro, MA) 176
Smith & Wollensky (New York, NY) 245
Smith's Louis XVI Restaurant Francais (New Orleans, LA) 155
Sparks Steak House (New York, NY) 246
Square One Restaurant (Key West, FL) 90
Stone Manor (Middletown, MD) 161
Strings (Denver, CO) 58
Sunset Grill (Nashville, TN) 291

T

Taberna Del Alabardero (Washington, DC) 77
Tavern at Sterup Square (Troy, NY) 254
Terra Bistro (Vail, CO) 63
Terrace in the Sky (New York, NY) 247
Tivoli Restaurant (Rosslyn, VA) 315
Tommy Toy's Cuisine Chinoise (San Francisco, CA) 24
Tony's Restaurant (Houston, TX) 303
Tony's (St. Louis, MO) 197
Top of the Hub (Boston, MA) 171
Trader Vic's (Emeryville, CA) 10
Tribute (Farmington Hills, MI) 181
The Tyrolean (Vail, CO) 64

U

Union Square Cafe (New York, NY) 248

V

Vallozzi's (Greensburg, PA) 268
Veni Vidi Vici (Atlanta, GA) 127
Ventana Room (Tucson, AZ) 7
Victoria & Albert's (Orlando, FL) 91
Vidalia (Washington, DC) 78
Villa Fontana (Taos, NM) 220
Villa Jacaranda (San Miguel de Allende, Mexico) 358
Vincenzo's (Louisville, KY) 145
Vivere (Chicago, IL) 137
Vong (New York, NY) 249

W

Wally's Desert Turtle (Rancho Mirage, CA) 46
Wente Vineyards (Livermore, CA) 12
Wheatleigh (Lenox, MA) 173
White Barn Inn (Kennebunkport, ME) 156
The Wild Boar (Nashville, TN) 292
Wildflower (Vail, CO) 65

X

Xaviars at Piermont (Piermont, NY) 250

Index of Cuisine

American

208 Talbot (St. Michaels, MD) 162
701 Restaurant (Washington, DC) 75
1789 Restaurant (Washington, DC) 76
The American Hotel (Sag Harbor, NY) 252
Anthony's Pier 4 (Boston, MA) 164
Antrim 1844 (Taneytown, MD) 163
Atwaters Restaurant & Bar (Portland, OR) 264
Aureole (New York, NY) 224
Beano's Cabin (Beaver Creek, CO) 54
Bedford Village Inn (Bedford, NH) 206
The Bernards Inn (Bernardsville, NJ) 209
The Black Pearl (Dunedin, FL) 86
Brooks Restaurant (Deerfield Beach, FL) 85
Briarhurst Manor (Manitou Springs, CO) 60
Burt & Jack's (Ft. Lauderdale, FL) 87
Cafe Allegro (Kansas City, MO) 189
Cafe Del Rey (Marina del Rey, CA) 39
Cafe L'Europe (Palm Beach, FL) 103
Café Pacific (Dallas, TX) 294
Canlis (Seattle, WA) 318
The Chaparral (Scottsdale, AZ) 3
Charles Court (Colorado Springs, CO) 56
Cité (New York, NY) 227
Clay Hill Farm (York, ME) 157
Clifton – The Country Inn and Estate (Charlottesville, VA) 311
Columbus Inn (Wilmington, DE) 67
The Covey (Carmel, CA) 8
Coyote Cafe (Santa Fe, NM) 218
The Crow's Nest (Anchorage, AK) 1
The Dan'l Webster Inn (Sandwich, MA) 174
Darrel & Oliver's Café Maxx (Pompano Beach, FL) 107
The Dining Room at Ford's Colony (Williamsburg, VA) 316
The Dining Room, Hilton at Short Hills (Short Hills, NJ) 212
The Dining Room, Westin Salishan (Gleneden Beach, OR) 263
Downey's (Santa Barbara, CA) 52
DUX (Orlando, FL) 99
Elysium (Alexandria, VA) 309
EverMay on the Delaware (Erwinna, PA) 267
Far Niente (Toronto, Ontario) 338
The Five Sails Restaurant (Vancouver, British Columbia) 328
The Four Seasons (New York, NY) 229
Fournou's Ovens (San Francisco, CA) 19
The Fox & Hounds (Hubertus, WI) 319
The French Room at Hotel Adolphus (Dallas, TX) 295
Friends Lake Inn (Chesterton, NY) 221
The Garden Restaurant (Philadelphia, PA) 273
Geronimo (Santa Fe, NM) 219
Goodfellow's (Minneapolis, MN) 185
Gramercy Tavern (New York, NY) 230
The Granary (Jackson, WY) 323
The Grill on the Alley (Beverly Hills, CA) 32
Halcyon (New York, NY) 231
Hampton's (Baltimore, MD) 160
Harralds (Stormville, NY) 253
Hasting's Grill (Anaheim, CA) 30
Haydn Zug's (East Petersburg, PA) 266
Highlawn Pavilion (West Orange, NJ) 214
Hyeholde Restaurant (Pittsburgh, PA) 275
Icarus (Boston, MA) 167
The Immigrant Restaurant and Winery (Kohler, WI) 320
The Inn at Sawmill Farm (West Dover, VT) 308
Kinkead's, an American Brasserie (Washington, DC) 71
Lafite (Naples, FL) 95
The Lark Creek Inn (Larkspur, CA) 11
Le Mouton Noir (Saratoga, CA) 26
Locke-Ober (Boston, MA) 169
Magnolias (Charleston, SC) 282
Mark's (Houston, TX) 300
Metropolitan (Salt Lake City, UT) 306
Michael's on East (Sarasota, FL) 110
Morrison-Clark Inn (Washington, DC) 72
Nava (Atlanta, GA) 122

Index of Cuisine

The Oakroom at the Seelbach Hilton (Louisville, KY) 144
Opus One (Detroit, MI) 178
The Oval Room (Washington, DC) 73
The Palace Restaurant (Cincinnati, OH) 259
Pano's & Paul's (Atlanta, GA) 125
Park Avenue Cafe (New York, NY) 239
Pavilion (Newport Beach, CA) 40
Peninsula Grill (Charleston, SC) 283
The Post House (New York, NY) 242
Primitivo Wine Bar (Colorado Springs, CO) 57
The Pump House (Fairbanks, AK) 2
Rainwater's on Kettner (San Diego, CA) 51
Ram's Head Inn (Absecon, NJ) 207
Ranchers Club of New Mexico (Albuquerque, NM) 217
The Rattlesnake Club (Detriot, MI) 179
Regas Restaurant (Knoxville, TN) 285
Restaurant at the Canterbury (Indianapolis, IN) 143
The Restaurant at Meadowood (St. Helena, CA) 17
Restaurant Passerelle (Radnor, PA) 276
Restaurant St. Michel (Coral Gables, FL) 83
The Ritz Restaurant and Garden (Newport Beach, CA) 41
The Ryland Inn (Whitehouse, NJ) 216
The St. Paul Grill (St. Paul, MN) 186
Sea Fare Inn (Portsmouth, RI) 279
Silks (San Francisco, CA) 23
Square One Restaurant (Key West, FL) 90
Stone Manor (Middletown, MD) 161
Strings (Denver, CO) 58
Sunset Grill (Nashville, TN) 291
Tavern at Sterup Square (Troy, NY) 254
Terra Bistro (Vail, CO) 63
Top of the Hub (Boston, MA) 171
The Tyrolean (Vail, CO) 64
Union Square Cafe (New York, NY) 248
Vallozzi's (Greensburg, PA) 268
Ventana Room (Tucson, AZ) 7
Victoria & Albert's (Orlando, FL) 91
Vidalia (Washington, DC) 78
Wente Vineyards (Livermore, CA) 12
Wheatleigh (Lenox, MA) 173
White Barn Inn (Kennebunkport, ME) 156
Wildflower (Vail, CO) 65
Xaviars at Piermont (Piermont, NY) 250

Asian

Bombay Club (Washington, DC) 68
Clifton – The Country Inn and Estate (Charlottesville, VA) 311
Haifeng (Orlando, FL) 100
Silks (San Francisco, CA) 23
Tommy Toy's Cuisine Chinoise (San Francisco, CA) 24
Tribute (Farmington Hills, MI) 181

Continental

103 West (Atlanta, GA) 124
701 Restaurant (Washington, DC) 75
1109 South Main (Anderson, SC) 280
Anthony's in the Catalinas (Tucson, AZ) 6
Antrim 1844 (Taneytown MD) 163
Arthur's (Nashville, TN) 289
The Baricelli Inn (Cleveland, OH) 260
Briarhurst Manor (Manitou Springs, CO) 60
Brooks Restaurant (Deerfield Beach, FL) 85
The Café Budapest (Boston, MA) 165
Café L'Europe (Sarasota, FL) 109
The Chancellor Grille Room (Palm Beach, FL) 104
Clifton – The Country Inn and Estate (Charlottesville, VA) 311
The Colony Dining Room (Longboat Key, FL) 92
Dilworthtown Inn (Westchester, PA) 277
The English Room at The Deer Path Inn (Lake Forest, IL) 140
Five Crowns (Corona del Mar, CA) 34
The Garden Restaurant (Philadelphia, PA) 273
The Glass Chimney Restaurant (Carmel, IN) 142

Index of Cuisine

The Golden Mushroom (Southfield, MI) 182
Grant Grill (San Diego, CA) 50
Harrah's Steak House (Reno, NV) 203
Harralds (Stormville, NY) 253
Highlawn Pavilion (West Orange, NJ) 214
The Hobbit (Orange, CA) 43
Hogan's Inn at Four Corners (King City, Ontario) 335
The Inn at Sawmill Farm (West Dover, VT) 308
La Cava (Mexico City, Mexico) 357
Lafite (Naples, FL) 95
The Lark (West Bloomfield, MI) 183
Llewellyn's (Stateline, NV) 205
Ludwig's (Vail, CO) 62
Maison & Jardin (Altamonte Springs, FL) 79
The Marine Room (La Jolla, CA) 38
Marker 88 Restaurant (Islamorada, FL) 89
Maxim's Restaurant & Piano Bar (Houston, TX) 301
Melvyn's Restaurant (Palm Springs, CA) 45
Michael's (Las Vegas, NV) 200
Michael's on East (Sarasota, FL) 110
Mirabelle Restuarant at Beaver Creek (Avon, CO) 55
Mr. Stox (Anaheim, CA) 31
Northwoods (Annapolis, MD) 158
Opus One (Detroit, MI) 178
The Orangery (Knoxville, TN) 284
Pano's & Paul's (Atlanta, GA) 125
Peppermill's White Orchid (Reno, NV) 204
Peregrines' (Atlantic City, NJ) 208
Peter Scott's (Longwood, FL) 94
Restaurant at the Canterbury (Indianapolis, IN) 143
Restaurant Dubrovnik (Winnipeg, Manitoba) 331
Restaurant Picasso (Edwards, CO) 59
Ristorante i Ricchi (Washington, DC) 70
The Ritz Restaurant and Garden (Newport Beach, CA) 41
The Seventh Inn (St. Louis, MO) 196
Tavern at Sterup Square (Troy, NY) 254
The Tyrolean (Vail, CO) 64
Vincenzo's (Louisville, KY) 145
Vivere (Chicago, IL) 137
Wally's Desert Turtle (Rancho Mirage, CA) 46

Creole/Cajun/Island

Arnaud's Restaurant (New Orleans, LA) 148
Bistro at Maison de Ville (New Orleans, LA) 150
Brennan's of Houston (Houston, TX) 297
Broussard's Restaurant (New Orleans, LA) 151
Christian's Restaurant (New Orleans, LA) 152
Galatoire's Restaurant (New Orleans LA) 153
Lafitte's Landing Restaurant at Bittersweet Plantation (Donaldsonville, LA) 146
Trader Vic's (Emeryville, CA) 10

Eclectic

Chef Allen's (Aventura, FL) 80
Elysium (Alexandria, VA) 309
Euphemia Haye (Longboat Key, FL) 93
The Fig Tree (San Antonio, TX) 304
George's at the Cove (La Jolla, CA) 37
The Left Bank Restaurant (Halifax, Nova Scotia) 332
The Manor (West Orange, NJ) 215
Rotisserie for Beef and Bird (Houston, TX) 302
Wheatleigh (Lenox, MA) 173

French

Alison on Dominick Street (New York, NY) 222
Ambria (Chicago, IL) 133
The American Hotel (Sag Harbor, NY) 252
Andre's French Restaurant (Las Vegas, NV) 198
Arnaud's Restaurant (New Orleans, LA) 148
Auberge Hatley (North Hatley, Quebec) 349
Bartolotta's Lake Park Bistro (Milwaukee, WI) 321
Bayona (New Orleans, LA) 149
Beau Rivage (Medford, NJ) 210
Broussard's Restaurant (New Orleans, LA) 151
Café 36 (LaGrange, IL) 139
Café Del Rey (Marina del Rey, CA) 39
Café du Soir (Vero Beach, FL) 114
Café Henry Burger (Hull, Quebec) 342

Index of Cuisine

Café L'Europe (Palm Beach, FL) 103
Carlos' Restaurant (Highland Park, IL) 138
Campagne (Seattle, WA) 317
Cavey's Restaurant (Manchester, CT) 66
The Cellar (Fullerton, CA) 35
The Chanticleer (Siasconset, MA) 175
Chez Nous (Houston, TX) 298
Chez Philippe (Memphis, TN) 286
Chillingsworth (Brewster, MA) 172
Christian's Restaurant (New Orleans, LA) 152
Ciboulette (Philadelphia, PA) 271
The Crow's Nest (Anchorage, AK) 1
Daniel (New York, NY) 228
The Dining Room, Hilton at Short Hills (Short Hills, NJ) 212
The Dining Room, Ritz-Carlton, Boston (Boston, MA) 166
The Dining Room, Ritz-Carlton, Buckhead (Atlanta, GA) 119
Downey's (Santa Barbara, CA) 52
El Bizcocho (San Diego, CA) 49
The Florentine (Palm Beach, FL) 105
Founders Restaurant (Philadelphia, PA) 272
Fresh Cream Restaurant (Monterey, CA) 14
Galatoire's Restaurant (New Orleans, LA) 153
Grant Grill (San Diego, CA) 50
JoJo (New York, NY) 232
La Bergerie (Alexandria, VA) 310
La Bonne Auberge (New Hope, PA) 270
La Caravelle (New York, NY) 233
La Chaumière (Calgary, Alberta) 324
La Cote Basque (New York, NY) 234
La Folie (San Francisco, CA) 21
La Panetiere (Rye, NY) 251
La Parisienne (St. Augustine, FL) 108
La Reserve (Houston, TX) 299
La Tourelle (Memphis, TN) 288
L'Auberge Chez Francois (Great Falls, VA) 312
L'Auberge de Sedona (Sedona, AZ) 5
La Vie en Rose (Brea, CA) 33
L'Eau a la Bouche (Sainte-Adèle, Quebec) 351
Le Central Bistro (San Francisco, CA) 22
Le Champlain (Quebec City, Quebec) 350
Le Cirque 2000 (New York, NY) 235
The Left Bank Restaurant (Halifax, Nova Scotia) 332
Le Mouton Noir (Saratoga, CA) 26
Le Passe-Partout Restaurant (Montreal, Quebec) 346
Le Perigord (New York, NY) 236
Le Petit Chateau (North Hollywood, CA) 42
L'Espalier (Boston, MA) 168
Le Titi de Paris (Arlington Heights, IL) 132
Le Vichyssois (Lakemoor, IL) 141
Lumière (Vancouver, British Columbia) 330
Maison Robert (Boston, MA) 170
Maisonette (Cincinnati, OH) 258
The Marine Room (La Jolla, CA) 38
Maxim's Restaurant & Piano Bar (Houston, TX) 301
Mille Fleurs (Rancho Santa Fe, CA) 47
The Monte Carlo Living Room (Philadelphia, PA) 201
Nikolai's Roof (Atlanta, GA) 123
Peacock Alley (New York, NY) 240
Picholine (New York, NY) 241
The Plumed Horse (Saratoga, CA) 27
Prince Michel Restaurant (Leon, VA) 313
The Pump Room (Chicago, IL) 136
The Refectory (Columbus, OH) 261
Renaissance (Aspen, CO) 53
Restaurant Bouchard (Newport, RI) 278
Restaurant Le Mitoyen (Laval, Quebec) 343
Restaurant Les Halles (Montreal, Quebec) 348
Restaurant St. Michel (Coral Gables, FL) 83
The Riviera (Dallas, TX) 296
The Ryland Inn (Whitehouse, NJ) 216
Silks at Stonehedge Inn (Tyngsboro, MA) 176
Smith's Louis XVI Restaurant Francais (New Orleans, LA) 155
Terrace in the Sky (New York, NY) 247
Tommy Toy's Cuisine Chinoise (San Francisco, CA) 24
Tribute (Farmington Hills, MI) 181

Index of Cuisine

Vong (New York, NY) 249
Wally's Desert Turtle (Rancho Mirage, CA) 46
The Wild Boar (Nashville, TN) 292

German

The Fox & Hounds (Hubertus, WI) 319
Karl Ratzsch's (Milwaukee, WI) 322

Hawaiian

The Anuenue Room (Maui, HI) 130

Italian

Alberini's (Niles, OH) 256
Al's (St. Louis, MO) 190
Anaheim White House (Anaheim, CA) 28
Andrea's Restaurant (Metairie, LA) 147
Appennino Ristorante (Allentown, PA) 265
Armani's (Tampa, FL) 111
Arturo's Ristorante Italiano (Boca Raton, FL) 81
Barbetta (New York, NY) 225
Benedetto's Ristorante (St. Louis, MO) 191
Biagio Ristorante (Toronto, Ontario) 336
Biba (Sacramento, CA) 16
Cafe Del Rey (Marina del Rey, CA) 39
Café Portofino (Lihue, HI) 129
Caffe de Medici (Vancouver, British Columbia) 327
Capriccio Ristorante (Pembroke Pines, FL) 106
Cavey's Restaurant (Manchester, CT) 66
Ciao Europa (New York, NY) 226
Coco Pazzo (Chicago, IL) 135
D'Amico Cucina (Minneapolis, MN) 184
Da Mimmo Finest Italian Cuisine (Baltimore, MD) 159
Diamond's (Trenton, NJ) 213
Dominic's (St. Louis, MO) 192
Donatello (Tampa, FL) 113
Ferraro's Restaurant (Las Vegas, NV) 199
Fresco Italian Cafe (Salt Lake City, UT) 305
Fior d'Italia (San Francisco, CA) 18
Galileo (Washington, DC) 69
Gennaro's Ristorante (Glendale, CA) 36
Giovanni's (St. Louis MO) 193
Giovanni's Ristorante (Detroit, MI) 177
G.P. Agostino's (St. Louis, MO) 194
Hemingway's (Killington, VT) 307
Il Tartufo on Las Olas (Fort Lauderdale, FL) 88
John Mineo's Italian Restaurant (St. Louis, MO) 195
La Fenice (Toronto, Ontario) 339
La Finestra Restaurant (Boca Raton, FL) 82
La Grotta Ristorante Italiano (Atlanta, GA) 121
Le Cirque 2000 (New York, NY) 235
Mario's (Nashville, TN) 290
The Monte Carlo Living Room (Philadelphia, PA) 274
The Owl's Nest Dining Room (Calgary, Alberta) 325
Panico's (New Brunswick, NJ) 211
Paolo's Restaurant (San Jose, CA) 25
Piero's (Las Vegas, NV) 202
Prego della Piazza (Toronto, Ontario) 340
Pricci (Atlanta, GA) 126
Raffaello (Carmel, CA) 9
Ristorante Café Cortina (Farmington Hills, MI) 180
Ristorante Giovanni's (Beachwood, OH) 257
Ristorante i Ricchi (Washington, DC) 70
Ristorante La Bussola (Coral Gables, FL) 84
Ristorante Michelangelo (Sainte Foy, Quebec) 352
Ristorante Primavera (New York, NY) 243
San Domenico (New York, NY) 244
Scatton's Restaurant (Hazleton, PA) 269
Tivoli Restaurant (Rosslyn, VA) 315
Tony's (St. Louis, MO) 197
Vallozzi's (Greensburg, PA) 268
Veni Vidi Vici (Atlanta, GA) 127
Villa Fontana (Taos, NM) 220
Vincenzo's (Louisville, KY) 145
Vivere (Chicago, IL) 137

Mediterranean

Fournou's Ovens (San Francisco, CA) 19
La Embotelladora Vieja (Ensenada, Mexico) 354
Marquesa (Scottsdale, AZ) 4
Pavilion (Newport Beach, CA) 40
Picholine (New York, NY) 241

Index of Cuisine

Primitivo Wine Bar (Colorado Springs, CO) 57
Restaurant on the Bay by Marie-Michelle (Naples, FL) 96
Terrace in the Sky (New York, NY) 247
Tony's Restaurant (Houston, TX) 303

Mexican

La Cava (Mexico City, Mexico) 357
La Embotelladora Vieja (Ensenada, Mexico) 354

Scandinavian

Aquavit (New York, NY) 223

Seafood

Andrea's Restaurant (Metairie, LA) 147
Anthony's Pier 4 (Boston, MA) 164
Anthony's Star of the Sea (San Diego, CA) 48
Atlantis (Orlando, FL) 98
Beverly's Restaurant (Coeur d'Alene, ID) 131
Café Pacific (Dallas, TX) 294
The Chanticleer (Siasconset, MA) 175
Chops (Atlanta, GA) 118
Harris' Restaurant (San Francisco, CA) 20
Imperial Chinese Seafood Restaurant (Vancouver, British Columbia) 329
Manhattan Ocean Club (New York, NY) 238
Marker 88 Restaurant (Islamorada, FL) 89
The Pump House (Fairbanks, AK) 2
Rotisserie for Beef and Bird (Houston, TX) 302
Ruth's Chris Steak House (New Orleans, LA) 154
Ruth's Chris Steak House (North Palm Beach, FL) 97
Ruth's Chris Steak House (Winter Park, FL) 115
The Sardine Factory (Monterey, CA) 15

Spanish

Taberna Del Alabardero (Washington, DC) 77

Steakhouse

The Angus Barn (Raleigh, NC) 255
Bern's Steak House (Tampa, FL) 112
Bob's Steak & Chop House (Dallas, TX) 293
Bone's Restaurant (Atlanta, GA) 117
Chops (Atlanta, GA) 118
Fairbanks Steakhouse (Robinsonville, MS) 188
Folk's Folly Prime Steak House (Memphis, TN) 287
Harrah's Steak House (Reno, NV) 203
Harris' Restaurant (San Francisco, CA) 20
JW's Steakhouse (Anaheim, CA) 29
LG's Prime Steakhouse (Palm Desert, CA) 44
Maloney & Porcelli (New York, NY) 237
Rotisserie for Beef and Bird (Houston, TX) 302
Ruth's Chris Steak House (New Orleans, LA) 154
Ruth's Chris Steak House (North Palm Beach, FL) 97
Ruth's Chris Steak House (Winter Park, FL) 115
Sam & Harry's (Washington, DC) 74
Smith & Wollensky (New York, NY) 245
Sparks Steak House (New York, NY) 246

Other

360 Restaurant at the CN Tower (Toronto, Ontario) 341
The 1848 House (Atlanta, GA) 120
The Abbey (Atlanta, GA) 116
Antiguo San Angel Inn (Mexico City, Mexico) 355
Arun's (Chicago, IL) 134
Bali by-the-Sea (Honolulu, HI) 128
The Beaver Club (Montreal, Quebec) 344
Cafe Allegro (Kansas City, MO) 189
The Café Budapest (Boston, MA) 165
Chanterelle (Eugene, OR) 262
Charleston Grill (Charleston, SC) 281
Chez La Mère Michel (Montreal, Quebec) 345
Chiaro's (Toronto, Ontario) 337
Estoril (Mexico City, Mexico) 356
The Five Sails Restaurant (Vancouver, British Columbia) 328

Index of Cuisine

Harralds (Stormville, NY) 253
Imperial Chinese Seafood Restaurant (Vancouver, British Columbia) 329
Inn On the Twenty (Jordan, Ontario) 334
La Bergerie (Alexandria, VA) 310
La Coquina (Orlando, FL) 101
Langdon Hall (Cambridge, Ontario) 333
Las Mañanitas (Cuernavaca, Mexico) 353
The Left Bank Restaurant (Halifax, Nova Scotia) 332
Lemaire (Richmond, VA) 314
Le Piment Rouge (Montreal, Quebec) 347
Lumière (Vancouver, British Columbia) 330
Manuel's on the 28th (Orlando, FL) 102
Mirabelle Restaurant at Beaver Creek (Avon, CO) 55
Peppermill's White Orchid (Reno, NV) 204
Post Hotel Dining Room (Lake Louise, Alberta) 326
Ristorante i Ricchi (Washington, DC) 70
The Sardine Factory (Monterey, CA) 15
Strings (Denver, CO) 58
Taberna Del Alabardero (Washington, DC) 77
Tony's Restaurant (Houston, TX) 303
Villa Jacaranda (San Miguel de Allende, Mexico) 358
Wente Vineyards (Livermore, CA) 12